Cooking in Other Women's Kitchens

Cooking

The John Hope Franklin Series in African American History and Culture

Waldo E. Martin Jr. and Patricia Sullivan, editors

in Other Women's Kitchens

DOMESTIC WORKERS IN THE SOUTH, 1865–1960

Rebecca Sharpless

THE UNIVERSITY OF NORTH CAROLINA PRESS   CHAPEL HILL

All rights reserved. Manufactured in the United States of America. Designed by Kimberly Bryant and set in Miller by Tseng Information Systems, Inc. The paper in this book meets the guidelines for permanence and durability of the Committee on Production Guidelines for Book Longevity of the Council on Library Resources. The University of North Carolina Press has been a member of the Green Press Initiative since 2003.

Library of Congress Cataloging-in-Publication Data
Sharpless, Rebecca.
Cooking in other women's kitchens : domestic workers in the South, 1865–1960 /
Rebecca Sharpless.
p. cm. — (The John Hope Franklin series in African American history and culture)
Includes bibliographical references and index.
ISBN 978-0-8078-3432-9 (cloth : alk. paper)
ISBN 978-1-4696-0686-6 (pbk. : alk. paper)
1. African American women household employees—Southern States—History. 2. Women cooks—Southern States—Social conditions 3. African American women—Southern States—Social conditions 4. Southern States—Race relations—History. I. Title.
HD6072.2.U52S574 2010
331.4′816415—dc22

2010015805

cloth   14 13 12 11 10   5 4 3 2 1
paper   17 16 15 14 13   5 4 3 2 1
THIS BOOK WAS DIGITALLY PRINTED.

for Tom

Siempre juntos

Contents

Illustrations

Preface

Twenty-two-year-old Cleora Thomas was not happy. Smart, pretty, energetic, with first-rate culinary training, she had more in mind for herself than being the second-floor custodian at Central High School in Muskogee, Oklahoma. When opportunity came to her, she jumped at it. Sixty-two years later, she wrote: "Early in the summer of 1923, my Aunt Minnie came home for a weekend visit with the news that her employer's neighbor needed someone to take over their kitchen. My heart leapt to hear that she had recommended me; and it leapt again when Dad finally gave his consent for me to go."[1] Thomas (later Butler) was on her way to a distinguished career as a cook in the wealthiest homes in Tulsa. To Butler, cooking for rich white people in the big city was better than sweeping floors at a school, the best job she could find in Muskogee.

For centuries, women like Cleora Butler have used domestic work as a means of leaving their old lives and starting new ones. In eighteenth- and nineteenth-century Europe, domestic work frequently served as a method for women to move from the countryside to the city. In the twenty-first century, it is a way for women to move from developing countries to wealthier nations.[2] For African American women in the United States, the process of going from where they were to where they wanted to be took several generations, as domestic work served as a middle ground between slavery and an open economy.[3] Between emancipation in 1865 and the civil rights movement in the 1950s and 1960s, African American women did domestic work, including cooking, to earn wages and support their families, biding their time until better opportunities opened. When those chances came, most of them took other types of jobs as quickly as possible.

The first purpose of this book is to look at the way that African American women such as Cleora Thomas Butler used domestic work, particularly cooking, to bridge the old ways and the new, from slavery to employment of their own choosing. Just as Butler moved from Muskogee to Tulsa and from custodial work to cooking, between the Civil War and the 1960s, hundreds of thousands of African American women went, first, from being slaves to becoming free women. They next migrated from farms, plantations, and small towns to cities, and they shifted their paid labor from field work to domestic work (including cooking), and then from domestic work to manufacturing, clerical, and professional positions. Until better employment opportunities became available, African American women cooked in other people's homes to make "a way out of no way."[4]

I concentrate specifically on cooks rather than domestic workers in general for several reasons. This study began as a part of a larger work on southern women who used cooking to push the boundaries of women's so-called spheres. While I remain interested in boardinghouse keepers, tearoom proprietors, caterers, and cookbook writers, the situations of African American domestic cooks differed substantially from those of the white women who worked in food services. And so this study took on a life of its own, defined by race and place. Like domestic workers in general in the American South, the women in this study were African American, hired almost exclusively by white housewives, and race shaped their labors significantly. They worked, not in the public, but in the private homes of their employers, largely isolated from their peers and nurturing work cultures.

Cooking differs from cleaning, laundry, and child care, the other types of domestic labor that African American women did, and it provides an excellent medium for telling the intertwined stories of African American women and the American South. Food preparation carries a great deal of weight in human society at large, in the postbellum South as in the present. Food is a significant cultural symbol, and women's involvement in its production indicates a great deal about the way a society functions. Historian Donna Gabaccia observed, "Psychologists tell us that food and language are the cultural traits humans learn first and the ones that they change with the greatest reluctance. Humans cannot easily lose their accents after the age of about twelve; similarly, the food they ate as children forever defines familiarity and comfort."[5] As individuals become imprinted with their food preferences, so too do entire societies. Food delineates a culture, demonstrating who is and is not a part of that culture and expressing status and prestige.[6] What humans eat at home and what they offer guests are general markers for their society.[7] As cooks, African American women profoundly shaped the foodways of the South and, hence, its overall culture.[8]

Defining who was and was not a cook proved to be difficult, for job descriptions were notoriously unpredictable and ill-defined. The U.S. Census Bureau struggled with the classification of domestic work for decades in the late nineteenth and early twentieth centuries and eventually gave up.[9] I have basically taken nomenclature at face value: if a woman called herself a cook, if someone else called her a cook, or if she cooked as a significant part of her daily chores, I included her in this study. Sometimes I refer to domestic workers with the assumption that cooks are included in this group. Not all domestic workers were cooks, but all cooks in this study were domestic workers.[10]

THE LABOR OF DOMESTIC COOKS remained in some ways unaltered between the Civil War and the 1960s, and in other ways it changed significantly, in large part because of active contestation by the cooks themselves. Cooking was never easy, however, and women found themselves fighting powerful odds to create satisfactory work situations. Hence, the second purpose of the book is to discover how African American cooks successfully functioned within a world of extremely hard work, low wages, and omnipresent racial strife. They made homes for their families with enormous effort, and they comprised the largest group of African American women who left their own homes to go to white people's houses every day. As a group, they gained the most benefit and suffered most keenly from being sequestered in white homes on a daily basis. While many African Americans dealt with the indignities of Jim Crow by avoiding contact with white people as much as possible, cooks lacked that option. Rather, by being in close contact with white people all day, every day, these women had to come up with coping mechanisms of their own.[11] Cooks, therefore, created a vanguard of resistance to the iniquities of segregation, as they found myriad ways to maintain their dignity and sense of self-worth.[12]

A THIRD, ORIGINALLY UNINTENDED purpose of this book is to refute the widespread popular stereotypes about African American cooks. I did not begin this project with that outcome in mind, but racist clichés surfaced at every turn and had to be dealt with. Other scholars have expertly parsed the Mammy and Aunt Jemima tropes,[13] and I am chiefly interested in seeing through those images to the real lives beneath them. The stereotypes have been so pervasive, however, that I have constantly found myself working in opposition to them. And so they warrant brief discussion here.

Since the middle of the nineteenth century, the figure of the African American woman as a cook has been a mainstay in white American popular culture. In books, movies, cookbooks, and advertising, a rotund, head-ragged figure has been made to grin broadly, speak in crude dialect, comfort white children, and always put the needs of other people before her own.[14] These so-called Mammy cooks were the creations of white people's imaginations, awash in longing for a golden age that never existed.[15] Doris Witt, in her brilliant study *Black Hunger*, remarks that such nostalgia vividly expressed "individual and collective fears about threats to white patriarchal power in a volatile social order."[16] The memories hark back to slavery, when a cook almost always lived on the premises of her owner's home, was on call twenty-four hours a day, 365 days a year, and could not quit.

After emancipation, the economic relationships were laid bare, as much of the old paternalism began to die. Cooks no longer automatically prepared meals for their "white families" day in and day out; rather, they expected to receive money to use for their own families in exchange for their labors. African American women strove to rationalize their tasks, to limit the number of hours that they would be expected to work, and to receive compensation commensurate with their considerable exertions. Although many white women chose to believe that the relationships between them and their employees remained affective, African American women knew that the arrangements were in fact material. To be sure, many worked out of love. But the love was not for their employers but for their own families.[17]

Historians have documented well the reactions of southern whites after emancipation to African Americans' desires for "what they had seen whites enjoy—the vote, schools, churches, legal marriages, judicial equity, and the chance . . . to retain the rewards of their labor."[18] After 1865, white southerners created dramatic systems of segregation and racial violence to command "black lives and black labor by any means necessary."[19] African Americans, male and female, knew what it was to live in constant fear—for one's dignity, for one's livelihood, for one's very life. Stereotypes were among the means that white southerners developed and expanded in the hope of controlling African Americans. Powerful white people created images of African American women as subservient and jolly, images designed to persuade both whites and Africans Americans of the truth of such a description.[20]

Ascribing the role of cook to African American women well suited the purposes of white southern racists. To many white southerners, "cook" meant African American, and in fact African Americans represented an ever-growing percentage of domestic workers in the post–Civil War South as white women found other employment opportunities. Social commentator Orra Langhorne, writing in 1901, observed that "Negroes and servants" were "synonymous terms in the average [white] Southerner's vocabulary."[21] Sentimental writers, longing for the lost fantasy of closeness between African Americans and whites, remarked on the use of wet nurses during slavery, in which African American women suckled white infants with the breast milk that they produced for their own babies.[22] Associating African American women with food, furthermore, branded them as being closer to nature, wilder, less refined than their white employers.

Into the mix of racism and power also came corporate capitalism, powerfully shaping the conceptions of white Americans, North and South, about African American female cooks. The mythical figure of the African American cook became entrenched in the white American imagination in 1893, when Missouri businessman R. T. Davis hired former slave Nancy Green to cook pancakes from his company's mix at the 1893 World's Columbian Exposition. Green proved hugely popular, and with sharp marketing by the Davis Milling Company, her portrayal of a fictitious former slave named Aunt Jemima became a nationally recognized icon.[23] Throughout the twentieth century the figure of Aunt Jemima appeared on an array of goods, from cookie jars to flour scoops, rag dolls, mixing bowls, pancake spatulas, toy stoves, and of course, the boxes of the pancake mix itself.[24] The image of Aunt Jemima rooted itself deeply into the white American consciousness, representing a reassuring tie with the Old South in which cooks worked happily for whatever reward came their way.

Although African American women strove to control their own lives, not merely to exist in reaction to white people's imaginations, the "continuing effects of both racial slavery and popular historical memory" shaped twentieth-century domestic work.[25] Art historian Michael Harris argues that the stereotype of Mammy "terribly" affected African Americans.[26] Certainly the images had real consequences for real people's lives. When Cleora Butler took that first cooking job in 1923, she was young and slender. Working for the Robertson family of Tulsa, she replaced an older cook, "a large woman" named Hattie, "who was moving north," likely as part of the Great Migration of African Americans from the southern United States to the urban North. Butler's initial wage was fourteen dollars a week, considered very good money even in oil-rich Tulsa. After a year, Mrs. Robertson raised Butler's pay to $17.50 a week, the level that Hattie had been receiving when she departed. Robertson explained that, when she hired Butler, "she couldn't conceive that one so young and tiny, (especially compared to Hattie), could be as qualified." In Robertson's mind, a competent cook had to be middle-aged and fat—to look like Aunt Jemima. From the very beginning of her lengthy career, Butler found herself struggling against an imaginary nemesis: the widespread, popular stereotype of the African American cook held by white southerners.[27]

Realizing that the exterior experiences did not match what they felt on the inside, African Americans knew full well that Mammy "did not represent what African Americans thought, felt, or believed black women to be."[28] Like Cleora Butler, most of the African American women who worked as cooks in white people's homes were not fat. They did not all wear bandannas. They did not smile all the time, and they did not automatically adore white children. Some were skillful cooks, and others were merely adequate. None of them was born simply knowing how to cook. Across the South through the early twentieth century, hundreds of thousands of African American women strove to maintain their personhood in the face of pervasive fantastic expectations by their employers and the public at large.[29]

From the time of its appearance, the figures of Aunt Jemima and the Mammy cook provoked sharp reaction by African Americans. In the early 1920s, the National Association of Colored Women fought against a proposed Black Mammy Memorial Monument. Hallie Q. Brown, president of the NACW in 1923, criticized the proposed monument as "a STONE to a class of dead saints for faithfulness."[30] Scholar Carter G. Woodson, writing in 1930, remarked, "The Negroes of this country keenly resent any such thing as the mention of the Plantation Black Mammy, so dear to the hearts of those who believe in the traditions of the Old South. Such a reminder of that low status of the race in the social order of the slave régime is considered a gross insult."[31] The recoil against the image of the black Mammy has continued unabated, which is unmistakable evidence of its negative power. In the 1980s, author Alice Walker declared that Al Jolson's singing about "Mammy" was "as if he's murdered our true grandmothers . . . before our very eyes."[32]

Late-twentieth-century poet Kate Rushin uses a teasing children's insult from the game known as "the dozens" to express the historic tensions in the lives of African American cooks:

Aunt Jemima
Aunt Jemima on the Pancake Box
Aunt Jemima on the Pancake Box?
AuntJemimaonthepancakebox?
Auntjemimaonthepancakebox?
Ainchamamaonthepancakebox?
Ain't chure Mama on the pancake box?

Mama Mama
Get off that box
And come home to me[33]

Through her recasting of Aunt Jemima, "the ultimate symbol and personification of the black cook, servant, and mammy,"[34] Rushin shows that African American domestic workers were more than an image. Each was someone's mother—someone's daughter, sister, wife—and, somewhere, people were waiting on her to finish her daily work, leave the employer's space, and come home. Despite American society's attempts to commodify the African American cook and her work, the women themselves resisted stereotyping and lived their lives according to their own dictates to the greatest extent that they could.

RATHER THAN WORKING WITHIN the filters of the media and white people's sentiments and prejudices, I have strived to use the women's own words and ideas throughout this study—as historian Psyche Williams-Forson's says, "to read African American lives from the perspective of the people and not from the imagery that tried to define them."[35] To render this task faithfully, one must listen to the voices of the African American women themselves, and not only to those of the white people who would represent them to their own ends.

As historian Mia Bay has noted, for most of America's history, most African Americans were neither literate nor "in any position to be at all candid in expressing their views of white character."[36] But while few African American women wrote or published before 1900, after emancipation their voices were never completely silent. The remarkable nineteenth-century women who did put their words into print, such as Anna Julia Cooper and Frances Ellen Watkins Harper, numbered among the elite who earned their livings by teaching, writing, and speaking, not by cooking or scrubbing. But they did evince concern about the plight of working women in publications such as Cooper's "Colored Women as Wage-Earners" (1899). In 1912, a woman with the pen name "Negro Nurse" wrote eloquently and forcefully about her life in an article titled "More Slavery at the South" in the progressive periodical *The Independent*, which featured life stories of ordinary Americans.

After World War I, ordinary women began expressing themselves in writing through their letters. Dozens of women wrote to the *Chicago Defender*, requesting positions as cooks in the North. While the letters are generally quite short, they reveal women's poor living and working conditions, passionate desires to leave the South and improve their lives, and wishes to use their culinary skills to do so. Written as they were by people living on farms owned by white people, working in white people's houses, these letters were bold cries for social change.[37] Equally daring were the letters written during the 1930s to New Deal agencies. As they thought about the New Deal, domestic workers came to believe that President Franklin Roosevelt, First Lady Eleanor Roosevelt, and Secretary of Labor Frances Perkins cared personally about them. Hundreds of African American women poured out their woes in letters that eventually found their way to the Women's Bureau of the U.S. Department of Labor. The letters provide rare glimpses into the lives of women who hoped that the people who brought about the New Deal would bring benefits to them. The women discuss wages, working conditions, and their wishes and dreams in their correspondence.

Beginning in the 1930s, African American women spoke with interviewers, articulating their ideas, hopes, and fears. The first substantial body of interviews came through the Federal Writers' Project during the New Deal, included in both the Former Slave Narratives project and the Folklore project. While the FWP interviews are far from perfect as historical evidence, they remain among the richest sources of information on African American lives between 1850 and 1930.[38] In 1958, Elizabeth Kytle, who was white, wrote a "first-person biography" of Atlanta cook Willie Mae Wright,[39] published by Alfred A. Knopf. Although Kytle concealed Wright's name during the initial publication, the idiomatic speech and the apparent lack of interposition by Kytle render *Willie Mae* a plausible and useful study of one woman's life.[40] During the last third of the twentieth century, the explosion of interest in social history, African American history, and women's history led to a number of significant, extremely valuable oral history projects. In 1979–80, public radio station WRFG in Atlanta created the "Living Atlanta" oral history project, documenting the lives of working people in the city, and some of the interviews were published in 1990 in a book with the same name. *Telling Memories among Southern Women*, Susan Tucker's foundational study of domestic workers in New Orleans and Mobile, appeared in 1988 as the product of an oral history project at Tulane University's Newcomb College Center for Research on Women. And in the late 1980s, Duke University began its project titled "Behind the Veil: Documenting African American Life in the Jim Crow South." The resulting book, *Remembering Jim Crow: African Americans Tell about Life in the Segregated South*, appeared in 2001. Dozens of interviews with African American women in smaller projects across the South augmented these large projects.

In the last decades of the twentieth century, at least two autobiographies by African American cooks appeared. Cleora Butler published her memoir, *Cleora's Kitchens: The Memoir of a Cook and Eight Decades of Great American Food*, in 1985.[41] Idella Parker brought out her story in two volumes, *Idella: Marjorie Rawlings' "Perfect Maid"* and *Idella Parker: From Reddick to Cross Creek*, in 1992 and 1999, respectively. Butler's and Parker's books contrast strongly in style and tone. Butler's upbeat book focuses on her mostly positive experiences and features a wealth of recipes. Parker's two volumes concentrate on her relationship with her employer, Pulitzer Prize–winning novelist Marjorie Kinnan Rawlings, and the circumstances of her life in Florida, and there are no recipes. Along with Willie Mae Wright's "first-person biography," Butler's and Parker's accounts clearly express African American cooks' thoughts and feelings in their own words.[42] Although Butler and Parker both wrote with the help of others, they plainly are the authors, and the books depict as no others the experiences of two intelligent, thoughtful, reflective African American women who worked in other women's kitchens.

[Cookbooks] are documents of the time and place in which they are produced, and they can be useful, if sometimes maddening, sources for researching the lives and work of African American women.[43] Cookbooks written by African American women remained rare until the 1960s. Of the twenty-five cookbooks that Doris Witt has identified as written by African Americans between 1800 and 1960, it appears that none was written by a cook in a private home. Two were written by women formerly from the South who had left the region and crafted celebrated careers by cooking for the public. The earliest cookbook attributed to an African American woman is *What Mrs. Fisher Knows about Old Southern Cooking, Soups, Pickles, Preserves, Etc.*, published in San Francisco in 1881. Abby Fisher moved from Mobile to California by the 1870s and, although illiterate, became a caterer of high regard. In her book, Fisher reveals little about herself or her past. She refers only once in a recipe to her own life experience; in "Pap for Infant Diet," Fisher comments, "I have given birth to eleven children and raised them all, and nursed them with this diet. It is a Southern plantation preparation."[44] About "Blackberry syrup—For dysentery in children" she notes, "This recipe is an old Southern plantation remedy among colored people."[45] Many of the recipes are unmistakably southern: fried chicken, oyster gumbo soup, "ochra" gumbo, sweet potato pie, chowchow and Creole chowchow, sweet pickle recipes for peaches, pears, prunes, and watermelon rind, "Jumberlie—a Creole Dish" (resembling present-day jambalaya), and peach cobbler, to cite only a few. Abby Fisher left Alabama, headed west, and proceeded to win acclaim and awards for the cookery that she had learned in the South. Her recipes represent the work of African Americans in their diaspora across the United States.

In 1959, New York restaurateur Lessie Bowers published *Plantation Recipes*. Like Abby Fisher seventy years earlier, she moved from her native South and found commercial success. The granddaughter of a South Carolina slave noted for her cooking ability, Bowers grew up on her family's land and learned to cook as a child, taking over the Sunday cooking duties for the family at age twelve. She attended Claflin College, then moved to New York in 1932, where she completed a degree in dietetics. After working at a New York restaurant, Bowers opened her own restaurant, The Virginian, in Bronxville, New York, during World War II.[46] Bowers gives no autobiographical narrative, speaking only through her recipes, and a slight handful of them relate overtly to her life: "Grandmother Mary's Spicy Pear Pie," "My Grandmother's Jelly Pie," and a recipe for corned beef in which she notes, "This is a recipe long treasured in the family."[47] The recipes in *Plantation Recipes* really have nothing to do directly with the plantation and cannot be traced to the kitchens in private homes. Bowers and her handlers may have been attempting to connect with the continuing sentimental evocation of the Old South that was so widespread in the United States at the beginning of the civil rights movement.

TO AUGMENT THE WORDS of African American women, I have also used—cautiously—cookbooks written by white authors. Cookbooks published about and in the South since the Civil War number in the hundreds, possibly thousands. Many of these cookbooks and the recipes contained in them can give important insights into the lives of African American women, but because many of these recipes were written down and reported by white women with particular cultural attitudes and tones, each one must be evaluated carefully. While the authors sometimes write with a type of affection, they often "perpetuate a hierarchical and marginalizing relationship" between themselves and African American culture.[48]

To a large extent, I have ignored the prose that white women wrote to frame the recipes, instead looking mostly at the recipes that are clearly attributed to African American women, usually designated as "Aunt" or "Mammy." Much superb work continually appears on southern and African American foodways, but because this is designed to be a book about the women and not the food per se, I have used recipes only when they demonstrate something pertinent about the cook—her tastes, her preferences, her skills.

Examining recipes codified by white women can be problematic. African Americans have long been wary about the expropriation of their cooking knowledge. Throughout her distinguished career, food historian Karen Hess pointed out the theft of African American women's creations by their employers. In her afterword to the reprint of *What Mrs. Fisher Knows about Old Southern Cooking*, Hess declares: "I should note that most of the recipes in *all* Southern cookbooks are, in fact, largely recipes gleaned by the writers from African American cooks, their own and others."[49] Author Alice Walker commented on such hijacking: "I believe that the worst part of being in an oppressed culture is that the oppressive culture—primarily because it controls the production and dispersal of images in the media—can so easily make us feel ashamed of ourselves, of our saying, our doings, and our ways. And it doesn't matter whether these sayings, doings, or ways are good or bad. What is bad about them, and therefore, worthy of shame, is that they belong to us. Even our folklore has been ridiculed and tampered with."[50]

White women mishandled African American women's recipes in several ways. First, African American women may not have wanted to share their culinary knowledge and may have been pressed to do so. Critic Doris Smith points to Ntozake Shange's novel *Sassafras, Cypress & Indigo*, which embeds recipes in the text as gifts of love handed down from mother to daughter.[51] Smith contends, "Knowledge of a recipe, and the power to withhold that knowledge, perhaps has been one of the ways in which African-American slaves and servants have exerted control (albeit limited) over mistresses and employers. And this knowledge was not to be given away."[52] Cooks who did not wish to give away their recipes might give incorrect proportions or directions to people who pushed them. White cookbook writer Marion Flexner told of a family cook named Molly, whom Flexner's aunt tried to beg for the recipe for her "famous Shredded Apple Pie." Molly gave her a recipe with ingredients left out and incorrect proportions. Flexner asked Molly why she didn't give away the recipe and reported Molly's response in dialect: "'Lissen chile,' she said seriously, shaking her finger at me, 'dat pie is ma specialty—see? Effen Ah gives my receipts to everybody what axes for 'em, what Ah gwine ter hafe lef' ter surprise 'em wid?' She put her hand kindly on my arm. 'Ah'll give you a piece of advice from an ol' woman—always keep sumpin' in reserve what you kin do better'n ennybody else, and don' share dat secret wid no one.'"[53] Molly realized that she had created a very special dish, and she wanted to continue to use that creation for her own advantage.

Cleora Butler, longtime cook for the elite white families of Tulsa, confirmed the power to give or withhold as she recalled the pleasure she felt in sharing a recipe with a wealthy white woman who had benefited the city's African American community: "Following dinner, Mrs. Phillips came into the kitchen, not only to congratulate the staff on the boned squab stuffed with wild rice, but also to secure my recipe for the torte (with her promise never to pass it on to anyone). I told her she was most welcome to pass it on to anyone she wished, explaining I felt it was little enough in return for the many wonderful things the Phillips family had done for the citizens of North Tulsa."[54] Butler firmly believed that a recipe could be a suitable gift to a generous benefactor. African American women freely shared advice and skills with one another. Their understandable reticence seems to have been mainly toward white women.

Like Butler, African American women, either willingly or through coercion, did give their recipes to their employers and others. The white appropriation of the African American voice and her work through recipes appears throughout cookbooks beginning about 1900, and it continues today.[55] As critic Sylvia Wynter has pointed out, whites marginalized and contained African American creative cultural activity as "black culture . . . became an original source of raw material to be exploited."[56]

Much is made in white-authored cookery books of African American women's either unwillingness or inability to write down recipes. With a long legacy of illiteracy, African American women did cook by feel much of the time rather than by the codified recipes of domestic science writers.[57] "Negro Nurse," writing in 1912, coolly appraised the matter of cooking by instinct: "We do not cook according to scientific principles because we do not know anything about scientific principles. Most of our cooking is done by guesswork or by memory. We cook well when our 'hand' is in, as we say, and when anything about the dinner goes wrong, we simply say, 'I lost my hand today!'"[58] Idella Parker recalled the beginning of the cookbook titled *Cross Creek Cookery*, which Marjorie Kinnan Rawlings assembled in the early 1940s: "As I have said before, my recipes were in my hands and head. I never wrote them down until Mrs. Rawlings started on that cookbook. When I cooked, I put in a pinch of this and pinch of that, but I couldn't say just how much of anything I used. I tasted and added like all good cooks."[59] Parker claimed for herself the right of an experienced cook to make adjustments rather than being dominated or intimidated by a printed recipe.

Parker's style of cooking and the written culture of the cookbook clashed in Rawlings's kitchen. Parker wrote that Rawlings "would have none of that. . . . We were months and months together in that tiny kitchen, because she was determined that every recipe would have just the right ingredients, in just the right amounts."[60] Rawlings and Parker set up a common trope, in which the supposedly exotic, "other" African American woman cooked by innate ability and the supposedly more intelligent, rational white woman empiricized her work. The contrast between the primitive, natural state of African American cookery and the relatively more ordered white world appears over and over in white-authored cookbooks as African American women thus became mediators between nature and culture.[61]

White cookbook writers congratulated themselves for capturing their booty. In recording the recipe for Cleo's Chopped Oysters, cookbook author Betty Patterson used the editorial "we," writing, "The evolution of this recipe is a story in itself. With rare tact we obtained rather definite proportions, though Cleo spurned measuring anything." For Mam Jude's Battercakes, she remarked, "We claim credit for evolving a definite measure for this recipe."[62]

Such situations establish the African American cook as exotic and other. In the world of the southern cookbook, African American women's cooking skill is magical and innate.[63] The cooks' work may be depicted, if not as magic, then as haphazard. As Doris Smith observed, "White people have denigrated the intelligence of black cooks by calling their work improvisatory."[64] Doris Witt finds ample evidence of cookbook writers' contrasting attitudes in Mary Stuart Smith's 1885 *Virginia Cookery*. Mary Stuart Smith contradicts herself in her discussion of intelligence versus intuition in bread making. Witt writes, "When African American cooks succeed in bread-making, they are 'stupid people' who have 'magic in the touch'; when white cooks want to 'learn' bread-making, they need have only a 'willing mind.'"[65]

Frequently, white authors printed recipes of African American cooks with absolutely no credit or attribution. In the 1940s, white cookbook writer Marion Brown asked Mrs. William H. Clinkscales of Pawleys Island, South Carolina, for her clam chowder recipe. Brown observed, "Mrs. Clinkscales promised that she would let me have it, if she could persuade her Negro cook to give exact proportions. After a long period of waiting, the recipe arrived with the notation, 'This is as near it as possible.'" Yet, apparently without irony, Brown titled the recipe "Mrs. Clinkscales' Clam Chowder."[66] In Brown's mind, the question of ownership seemed to come down on the side of the person who paid the creator, and the creator received no acknowledgment.

Clinkscales's cook was never able to claim her creation, but Idella Parker, longtime cook for Marjorie Kinnan Rawlings, commented almost fifty years later on recipes for which she received no credit in *Cross Creek Cookery*: "Many of the recipes in the book were mine, but she only gave me credit for three of them, including 'Idella's Biscuits.' There were several others that were mine, too, such as the chocolate pie, and of course it was me who did most of the cooking when we were trying all the recipes out. All I ever got from the cookbook was an autographed copy, but in those days I was grateful for any little crumb that white people let fall, so I kept my thoughts about the cookbook strictly to myself."[67]

IN THINKING ABOUT white people telling the stories of African Americans, critic Lorne Fienberg notes that "the white narrator's frame creates the illusion of distance for the comfortable reader, a kind of *cordon sanitaire* which makes it safe to contemplate the words and deeds of social and racial inferiors." In the hands of a white interlocutor, "the black narrator tells precisely the tale the white Southern listener would wish to hear." Fienberg concludes that such work is characterized by a "radical lack of racial tension," indicating the values of the white writer, who wants to believe that all is harmonious.[68] White-authored cookbooks featuring the recipes and sometimes the voices of African American women do not tell the same story that they would if the African American woman herself were speaking. The voices in the recipes are, in Catherine Clinton's words, "black voices produced by white ventriloquism."[69]

Most cookbooks that use African American recipes and voices identify the cooks only by first name, mirroring daily face-to-face practice in the Jim Crow South. By giving African American women's recipes without any discussion except their first names, white authors erase the women's identities and, in fact, conflate them with their work. In a Texas cookbook published in 1888, "Clara" and "Manerva" are in the list of contributors, but they appear in the list alphabetized under their first names and with "Cook" following their first names as though it were their family name. The latter appears in the body of the text as "'Manerva'" (in quotation marks), "Manerva Cook," and "Minerva Cook." The recipes reveal that Manerva/Minerva lived in Missouri and that she made potato stuffing, fried chicken, and smothered chicken of high quality. "Clara Cook," from St. Louis, prepared a custard cake with a sweet cream filling.[70] The sender(s) of the recipes thought enough of the cooks to include their recipes and to attribute them to their creators (as opposed to taking credit for the recipes themselves). They could not bring themselves, however, to give these women family names, and someone—perhaps the recipe contributor, perhaps the editor—grafted the women's occupation onto their first names as if it adequately identified them.

At the end of the nineteenth century there began a torrent of cookbooks by white people expropriating African American cooks' work and words. At first, white cookbook writers began to include recipes attributed to African American cooks, then to put recipes into African American dialect, and finally, by the 1920s, to write cookbooks almost entirely in dialect. Scattered recipes attributed to "aunt" appeared between 1890 and 1910. Around the turn of the twentieth century, a genre sometimes called Mammy cookbooks began, with recipes attributed to figures such as "Mammy," "Maum Peggy," "Maum Sarah," and "Maum Maria."[71] Martha McCulloch-Williams, with the 1913 publication of *Dishes and Beverages of the Old South*, epitomized the Mammy craze in cooking. It is entirely unclear how McCulloch-Williams had access to recipes made by a slave woman fifty years earlier, but eight recipes appear attributed to "Mammy." Further, McCulloch-Williams quotes Mammy on numerous topics, putting her conversations into dialect and direct quotations. McCulloch-Williams's Mammy figure is judgmental and class-conscious. About corn-bread she says, according to McCulloch-Williams, "'Salt in corn-bread hit does taste so po' white-folks'y.' She had little patience with those neighbors of ours who perforce had no butter to their bread."[72] McCulloch-Williams writes without irony of the Old South, and she does not hesitate to employ Mammy's voice to demonstrate the glory of the past.

In 1922, Emma and William McKinney published *Aunt Caroline's Dixieland Recipes* with the Chicago firm of Land & Lee. According to the frontispiece, the dishes in the cookbook were "drawn from the treasured memories of Aunt Caroline Pickett, a famous old Virginia cook." Although the book is dedicated to "Aunt Caroline," it contains only four recipes attributed to "Aunt Caroline" and seven to "Mammy," otherwise unidentified. The McKinneys give very little context to the recipes, and the reader learns little about Caroline Pickett or Mammy. The McKinneys appear to be using the Dixieland theme to gain an audience for their cookbook, and one wonders how many of the recipes actually came from Caroline Pickett and for which she wasn't given credit.

Two cookbooks published two years apart not only use African American women's work but also persistently attempt to use their voices, or someone's version of their voices. Natalie Scott published *Mirations and Miracles of Mandy: Some Favorite Louisiana Recipes* in 1929, and Betty Benton Patterson followed with *Mammy Lou's Cook Book* in 1931. Both authors cast much of their books in the voices of hypothetical African American cooks, writing in stereotypical dialect and putting their commentary into direct quotations that make it appear that the cooks themselves are speaking. Such a blurring of women renders them and their work invisible, as only the author's labor is visible in the text.[73]

Both Patterson and Scott use the supposed voices of African American women to discuss proper cookery techniques, ingredients, and, not infrequently, life in general. By the 1920s, folklorists such as Zora Neale Hurston were earnestly beginning to collect dialect and folk tales from African Americans. But the two white women writing in dialect as late as the 1920s say more about the writers' attitudes than about the documented speech patterns of African American cooks. As critic Michele Birnbaum points out, writing in African American dialect relates to "the agitated reaction of some Southern whites to radical shifts in the social order resulting from Emancipation."[74]

Historian Stephanie Yuhl writes convincingly of the antimodernism in cultural productions such as the preservation of spirituals and, by inference, cookbooks written in dialect. Cultural arbiters like Patterson and Scott, says Yuhl, "turned to the past as a means of responding to the present."[75] White fascination with African American culture was widespread in the 1920s, a time when very few southerners, white or African American, had experienced antebellum plantation life firsthand.[76] The cookbooks written in dialect reveal more about the white authors' fascination with African American culture than they do about the real women who cooked the recipes.

Patterson's and Scott's works, furthermore, are not simply transcriptions of what they heard. Rather, the authors created composite figures through which they spoke. Scott drew her character from the women who were in the employ of white New Orleans residents in the 1920s. She observed, "Mandy, of course is a composite. . . . My own Mandy's name is Pearl. . . . There are the Mandys of all my friends,—Mammy Lou, and Phrosine, and Tante Celeste, Venida, Mande, Titine, Elvy, Mona, Relie." Scott, however, attributed only a handful of recipes to their actual creators: three to Celeste and one each to Aunt Melissa, Melanie, and Bertha.[77]

Patterson likewise idealized African American cooks, but her view was more nostalgic, more attuned to the rhythms of the past. She commented, "Mammy Lou's cook book had to be written, for Mammy Lou is a composite characterization of all the negro mammies we have known, loved, and lost awhile."[78] She quickly brought in the affective aspects of white employers' love for their cooks and the wistfulness at having "lost" them. By creating a composite, Patterson was able to pick and choose among aspects of the various cooks' personalities, leaving off the rough edges and conveying only the cheeriest aspects.

Despite her concoction of the composite "Mammy Lou," Patterson bestowed more recognition on African American cooks than any other cookbook writer of the period. By attaching to recipes names such as "Cleo's Chopped

Oysters" and "Mam Jude's Battercakes," Patterson at least gave limited credit where credit was due. Cleo and Mam Jude appear to have been real women, although of course absent their surnames. Attaching the women's names to the recipes was at least some acknowledgment of their labor and creativity. But we learn nothing about each woman except her cooking skill. For writers such as Patterson, the African American women and their cooking were one and the same.

Two cookbooks from the 1930s, written by white people, appear to employ the actual words of real African American women with some plausibility and a modicum of respect. In the mid-1930s, writer Robert J. Breckinridge asked "Aunt Liza" to write down her formulas for "Kentucky hog jowl and greens" and for "Kentucky soda biscuits." Breckinridge poked fun at "Aunt Liza's" phonetic spellings, such as "dandeline" for dandelion and "bord" for board, with comments such as "Aunt Liza sure could cook even if she couldn't spell." Breckenridge inadvertently pointed out the lack of formal education for women such as "Aunt Liza" and the availability of cooking jobs for women with little schooling. He also played into the derisive image of the primitive African American woman who could cook even without education. But if these recipes are indeed "Aunt Liza's" transcriptions of her own recipes, they may be among the first instances in which an African American woman recorded for publication her own methods for cooking these time-honored regional dishes.[79]

The purported voice of Emma Jane Christian, a Williamsburg, Virginia, cook, pervades the cookbook that bears her name, *Emma Jane's Souvenir Cook Book*, privately published in Williamsburg in 1937. Christian worked for the family of the book's author, Blanche Elbert Moncure, for more than half a century. It would be easy to dismiss the cookbook as a flight of sentimentality on Moncure's part, and yet the cookbook may in fact have been a collaboration. Since Christian could not read or write, she needed a transcriber for her recipes.[80] A full-page portrait of Christian appears opposite the frontispiece. She is seated in a straight chair, hands crossed in her lap. A white cap on her head visually designates her as a servant. But she is nicely dressed, wearing a flowered blouse with a bar pin and either a light-colored skirt or an apron, and she has a round ring on her left hand. The expression on Christian's face is pleasant, not quite a smile, and her gaze is direct. The image of Christian gives an overall impression of serenity, intelligence, and dignity. Under the photograph appears Christian's full name, Emma Jane Jackson Beauregard Jefferson Davis Lincoln Christian, given to her by the Union soldiers who visited shortly after her birth during the Civil War, and a quotation: "Gumshun is a seasonin' you is got to put in ev'y dish you cook. An' *no* mistake!" In constructing the page in this way, Moncure gives Christian a striking physical representation, her entire name, and a voice by attributing to her, albeit in dialect and concerning cooking, a quotation of some boldness.

A second clue that the book might be collaborative comes from a handwritten note in the copy now in the University of Denver Penrose Library. This particular book was inscribed as a gift from "Smitty" to "Betty." Above Christian's photo, "Smitty" wrote: "Betty: Emma sits out on porch Main St. here and peddles these books. Get a kick out of Emma we are pals. Smitty." Christian's sales of the book might indicate some level of satisfaction or pride at having been featured in it.

A strong personality shines through *Emma Jane's Souvenir Cook Book*. Compiled by Christian's boss, the cookbook uses outrageous dialect to present her recipes. But it shows Christian/Emma Jane as a person with definite tastes in food, who observes, "It's de onion-puddin' an' next to de fresh cawn-puddin', I likes it bes' of all I makes." Christian consumed as well as produced these tasty dishes. Christian's talents even extended to wine-making, as she included a recipe for wild cherry wine. No teetotaler, she praised Franklin Roosevelt for repealing Prohibition as she discussed the use of strong liquor in making desserts and eggnog.[81] *Emma Jane's Souvenir Cook Book* does not betray any tensions, racial or otherwise. But it does depict a woman of distinct opinions and excellent culinary skills.

Two cookbooks from the 1950s, both published in small numbers, egregiously caricature African American female cooks. Neither of them seems to actually have had input from African American cooks, but rather they trade on cartoonish images to establish linkage with cookbooks of the plantation tradition. New York import company Mitteldorfer Strauss published *Aunt Jemimy's Southern Recipes*, perhaps to accompany its tableware. The slender publication features recipes for green gooseberry tart, mint julep, charlotte russe, pineapple ice, beaten biscuits, fruit cake, Sally Lunn, waffles, ash-cake, fried chicken, and egg "nogg." The recipes are in dialect and rhyme, accompanied by drawings of African American women with their heads in rags and exaggeratedly large lips. The last page, which features the eggnog recipe, has a drawing of a woman prone on the floor with a large spilled dish in front of her. The book, with its broad negative caricature, trades on stereotypes for its supposed commercial effect.

The Norris, Tennessee, Women's Fellowship published its *Norris Economy Cook Book* in 1951 to raise money for its charitable efforts. The book is a modest, homemade affair, bound in blue checked oilcloth. The title page features a line drawing of the head of a "Mammy" with a head rag and unattributed lines from Howard Weeden's *Bandanna Ballads*, sentimental verses published fifty years earlier. The actual recipes are fairly straightforward. Most remarkable are the frontispiece and conclusion, both featuring line drawings of a Mammy and typewritten words in dialect. To open the book, the African American woman declares, "Howdy Ever'body! I'se so proud to be waitin' here right out front. I'se been ast to say, 'Thank you, to all who helped with this cook book,'" and she goes on to thank sponsors. On the back page, the drawing of the African American figure says, "Here I is yet, a waitin' at the back door 'cause dey wants you to know 'fore you leaves dat a large percentage of the proceeds from the sale of these books will be used for food and clothing for those in such dire need, both here and far away. We know this will add to the 'Happy Days' wished for You as you came in the front door, and with Tiny Tim we fervently say, 'God Bless us Every One.'" The white women of Norris mix Mammy with Dickens in an attempt to give their charitable project legitimacy. The Mammy figure seems to represent hospitality and gratitude as well as subservience, just waiting patiently for the reader to come along.

With the civil rights movement, such broad stereotypes faded from wide-scale public view. In her 1999 book *Black Hunger*, Doris Witt furnishes a bibliography of cookbooks by African Americans. As African Americans have gained access to publication, the list has grown significantly. An updated bibliography would doubtless demonstrate the continuing richness of the African American culinary heritage.[82]

COOKS PROVIDE A WINDOW into the daily world of work and family that proved typical for many African American female urban workers. In their own voices, they tell stories of skill, hard work, and human interactions, both good and ill. They were not saints, but many of them exhibited perseverance and stubbornness that allowed their children to seek other paths. Their saga begins with their arrival as slaves in the Virginia colony in the seventeenth century.

Introduction

AFRICAN AMERICAN WOMEN, FOOD, AND COOKING

For more than three hundred years, from the first importation of slaves into Jamestown until the 1960s, African American women served as cooks for privileged white families in the American South.[1] Through their labor and their talents, they fed fifteen generations of white southerners. After emancipation, the work of these women also fed their own families, in the form of wages and food left over from their employers' tables. How did African American women become the iconic—and actual—cooks of the South?

Cooking is one of the most basic human activities: the transformation of raw ingredients into something else, more tasty or digestible than in its uncooked form, a process that turns natural elements into something usable by people. The strategic application of heat or fire to raw foods is as old as humanity itself.[2] The process has changed over the centuries, with developments in techniques of baking, braising, frying, and so on. Ingredients and products continue to evolve as well.[3] Cooking is also ephemeral, as a meal over which the cook has labored for many hours is often consumed within a matter of minutes.[4] The result of a successful meal—sated diners who have received good nutrition—is basically invisible, and its effect lasts only a few hours, as the eater's body turns the food to fuel and soon needs to fill up again. Because of the fleeting nature of its product, food preparation is repetitive, for people typically like to have at least two meals a day and frequently more. A cook can never point to something permanent as the product of her labor. But cooking is easier to document than other types of domestic work. Although transitory, it creates at least a temporary physical product, more tangible than those of some other types of labor. We can, therefore, think about the meals that cooks prepared as the products of women's hands. The meals no longer exist, but some records of some of them do, in recollections and in recipes.

The physical act of cooking—bringing a meal to the table—requires, as Australian writer Michael Symons says, "a thousand things done well."[5] A successful cook will be in touch with "the raw materials, the suppliers . . . the religious dictates . . . the clock, and so many other elements, not the least being the diners."[6] Food preparation can be unforgiving; while a roast beef might tolerate some flexibility, ingredients for a cake must be measured precisely or disaster will occur, and complicated products such as yeast bread challenge the most experienced cooks.[7] The skills of a cook include not just the physical ability to chop and fry but also, in the words of British cook and writer Frances Short, "understanding and judging," "timing, planning and organizing," "creating and designing," and "knowing and discerning." The cook, in other words, has to know her ingredients and understand many minute processes required to bring them satisfactorily to table.[8] Cooking done well requires the use of all of the senses, says philosopher Lisa Heldke, "a knowledge in the eyes and in the hands. You have to be able to 'finger' a ball of pie dough to tell if it needs a bit more ice water. You must be able to smell when the garlic is just about to burn as it sautés in the oil."[9] Food historian Damon Lee Fowler refers to this indelible stamp of the cook on the dish as "wok presence," the ineffable skill and knowledge that each cook possesses in different measure from any other.[10]

Despite its complexity and importance, cooking in the home traditionally has been an occupation of low status. Lisa Heldke points out that in most societies, domestic work is assigned the least value of all occupations and given to members of society who are most oppressed and paid the worst: "Many of the daily chores of a domestic worker—shopping for food, cooking food, serving food, cleaning the kitchen after cooking—are virtually invisible to those who benefit from them, or are regarded by beneficiaries as beneath attention or comment."[11]

One reason that food preparation is typically held in low esteem is because of its direct relationship to things found in nature. As Michael Symons observes, cooking is "messy, dirty work," involving "bare hands, sticky fingers, licks of this and that, whacks on fleshy lumps, hissing lids and miscellaneous smells." It is also dangerous, "the basic tools being either very sharp or very hot."[12] Cooking requires intimate contact with things that have once been alive, as a plant or an animal. Thus, it becomes a job in which the elite remain pure and above the mess, delegating the work to those under them. According to British historian Leonore Davidoff, "Those who deal with potentially polluting activities, such as transforming the raw into the cooked, and dealing with the detritus of personal life, are very often those at the bottom of the hierarchy, indeed sometimes even outside it, i.e. 'outcasts.'"[13] Societies with servants (or slaves) often relegate cooking to them. By delegating to servants handling dead animals, dirt from the garden, and fire, an employer can then stay clean and "more ladylike," keeping her hands "free from dirt, burns[,] or callouses."[14] The social logic of the American South dictated that African American women, arguably in the lowest position, would be the cooks.

FOR THE FIRST 250 YEARS of their lives in America, almost all of the African American female cooks were slaves. It is not possible to know exactly how many female slaves worked as cooks for people in the "big house." Certainly most women labored in the fields rather than in the master's home, and some did double duty. But from the seventeenth century until the mid-1860s, African American slave women cooked for their owners. At first, everyone in the Virginia colony, slave and free, barely scraped by. Gradually, however, the skills of slave cooks increased as life in the British colonies became a little less desperate for all concerned.[15] In her pioneering work on early southern women, Julia Cherry Spruill documented the work of slave cooks chiefly through the elaborate menus that they prepared, "rich, highly seasoned, and often complicated," and through slave owners' complaints about their cooks.[16] Although Spruill failed to make the connection between the elaborate dishes served at houses like Nomini, the home of the Carter family in Virginia, and George Washington's Mount Vernon and the women who actually cooked them, the record plainly shows that some enslaved women attained high levels of culinary competence. By the late eighteenth century, the excellent staff of Eliza Pinckney in Charleston, South Carolina, had their culinary labors divided by task: Mary-Ann was the cook and "understands roasting poultry in the greatest perfection you ever saw." Daphne baked "very nice bread." Old Ebba fattened the poultry "to a nicety." Young Ebba fetched wood and water, "scoured," and was to learn "as much as she is capable of Cooking and Washing." All stayed busy. Pinckney wrote, "No one eats the bread of idleness when I am here."[17]

During the antebellum period, African American women cooked for many of their owners. Slave-owning yeomen often used their sole slaves to help in the house, and those slaves' tasks would almost undoubtedly have included food preparation.[18] More prosperous households often had at least one slave, and frequently more, committed to cooking.[19] Susan Dabney Smedes of the slave-owning family at Burleigh plantation in Mississippi recalled multiple kitchen servants: "The cook at Burleigh had always a scullion or two to help her, besides a man to cut her wood and put it on the huge andirons. The scullions brought the water and prepared the vegetables, and made themselves generally useful. The vegetables were gathered and brought from the garden by the gardener, or by one of the half-dozen women whom he frequently had to help him. A second cook made the desserts, sweetmeats, etc."[20] In the big houses across the South, the cooks provided sumptuous breakfasts and midday meals, with lighter evening meals.[21] The white Dabney family ate a diet so fancy that its preparation required the work of numerous African Americans.

In describing the work of her family's slave Mammy, sentimental cookbook writer Martha McCulloch-Williams inadvertently outlined physically taxing, difficult labor. Mammy prepared food on an open hearth with very heavy cookware, pots ranging in size from two to ten gallons and including "ovens, deep and shallow, spiders, skillets, a couple of teakettles, a stew kettle, a broiler with a long spider-legged trivet to rest on, a hoe-baker, a biscuit-baker, and waffle-irons with legs like tongs." Managing the bulky cookware, likely made of iron, took considerable effort; a wrought iron shovel to spread coals was "so big and heavy nobody but Mammy herself could wield it properly."[22] Mammy's assistant, Phoebe, served as a "sort of scullion, fetching in wood and water, gathering vegetables, picking chickens, scouring all things from the big pot to the floor."[23] Mammy possessed both great physical strength and the ability to handle a cooking repertoire that required a sizeable *batterie de cuisine*.

Nineteenth-century slave cooks attained high levels of proficiency, honed through many years, even decades, of cooking for the same families and their guests. Letitia Burwell, eager to justify slavery, lavished praise on the cooking of enslaved women in Mecklenburg County, Virginia, particularly their bread making—"loaf bread," "incomparable rice waffles, and beat biscuit, and muffins, and laplands, and marguerites, and flannel cakes, and French rolls, and velvet rolls, and lady's fingers"—but also fricasseed chicken, wine-sauces, and plum puddings.[24] It is difficult for present-day readers, unlike Burwell, to celebrate the achievements of these enslaved women without considering their conditions of employment. But the fact remains that at least some slave women were outstanding cooks.[25]

Enslaved cooks sometimes had high monetary value, indicating their importance to their owners. In 1849, for example, Virginian E. N. Noland wrote to her sister, Ella Mackenzie, about a slave woman whom the family kept while an estate was being settled: "She is a fine cook and there were a great many wealthy gentlemen wanting her, said they wouldn't stop at any price.

If she had been put up to the highest bidder, such bidding never would have been known in this part of the world."[26] This particular family valued the work of their exceptional slave cook, who made their lives easier and more pleasant. A family such as this, however, might well discover after the Civil War that the cook herself did not hold them in similar regard. Fannie Berry recalled the rejoicing near Pamplin, Virginia, after the surrender of the Confederate forces at nearby Appomattox. The slaves broke into song, and their verses included the liberation of the cook: "Mammy don't yo' cook no mo' / Yo' ar' free, yo' ar' free![27] Despite—or perhaps because of—their culinary accomplishments, freed slave cooks did not hesitate to leave their former owners following the Civil War. Georgia plantation mistress Gertrude Thomas's diaries in the late spring of 1865 showed cooks peeling off from their former places of work with alacrity. On May 29, Thomas wrote of her mother's household: "Aunt Vilet the cook a very excellent one at that left Sunday night. She was a plantation servant during her young days and another favorite of Ma's." In Thomas's own household, the cook named Tamah was "active and cheerful" just before she disappeared.[28] The cooks' superior abilities and their favored status did not deter them from seeking new lives away from their previous owners. When they remembered this period, some freedwomen ridiculed their former owners. Telling of her ex-mistress's tearful plea to Ulysses Grant in a refugee camp, one freedwoman recalled (in a dialect recorded by a white worker from the North), "My ole missus . . . hel' out her han's and say, 'General, dese han's never was in dough—I never made a cake o' bread in my life; please let me have my cook.'" To the freedwoman's delight, "all her cryin' didn't help her," as the Union general told the former owner that her cook was free and "can do as she likes about it." The white woman went off in tears and the cook stayed in the Union camp.[29]

In the immediate aftermath of the war, female domestic servants, like their field hand counterparts, attempted to stop working for their former owners.[30] An unnamed South Carolina white woman remarked about her cook: "[S]ays she is weary of cooking—been at it all her life—I do not blame her—but I know I never can replace her."[31] Necessity, however, soon drove them into work outside their homes, as they realized that no subsistence would come without employment. South Carolinian Emma Holmes commented about her brother's family: "Hannah, Maria's nurse, is cooking for them, made humble by starvation."[32]

Freedwomen actively sought to leave their owners' households and strike out on their own, preferring "to find new employers rather than fight with former owners over what they would and would not continue to do as free

Cook at Refuge plantation, Camden County, Georgia, date unknown.
Historic American Buildings Survey, HABS GA,20-WOBI.V,1-3, Library of Congress.

laborers."[33] Not long after emancipation, Leah, "an elderly mulatto woman," appeared at Gertrude Thomas's door in Burke County, Georgia, seeking a cook's position. Leah had been the cook for a Dr. Denning nearby and said that her mistress had sent her out to find a place. Leah proved to be a superior cook, baking exceptional biscuits and "one of the best plum pies I ever tasted," according to Thomas. When Thomas's husband returned home, however, he decreed that Leah must be sent back to her former master to bring a note of permission, and not until then could she work for his family. Leah did not return. Perhaps she had not in fact come to the Thomas household at her former mistress's bidding, or perhaps she declined to work for a person who would not acknowledge that she no longer belonged to anyone.[34]

Many freedwomen who left their former owners took jobs as domestics. Historian Psyche Williams-Forson declares, "Paramount in the minds of black people was progress—familial, social, economic, and political. To this end, black women sought employment wherever it could be found, and this often thrust them into the homes of white people in domestic capacities."[35] With no support from their former masters, even the aged looked for employment as domestic workers. In the uplands of South Carolina in 1870, for example, many former slaves in their sixties, seventies, and eighties worked as cooks or servants.[36]

Skilled cooks found themselves in demand. White women might be willing to clean their houses or care for their own children, but they eagerly sought workers to take on the tasks of food preparation.[37] Women who had cooked as slaves continued their labors, and other women who had worked in the fields also became cooks, despite their lack of experience in preparing food for white people. In Raleigh, North Carolina, for example, the percentage of African Americans employed in "domestic and personal service" rose from 56.6 percent in 1876 to 68.9 percent in 1888.[38]

Cooks usually followed a rural-to-urban migration pattern. From the time of emancipation, African Americans left the plantations and headed to town in a steady stream. Before World War I, when African Americans decided to move from the countryside to the city, they almost always stayed in the South, and the cities in the region grew apace.[39] Between 1860 and 1910, the number of African Americans in Norfolk, for example, grew fivefold, from 4,330 to 25,039, at a faster rate than the white population.[40] African American women were more likely to come to town than white men or women or African American men, and African American female-headed households were disproportionately likely to migrate from country to city.[41]

African Americans who moved to southern cities often merely replaced field labor with other unrewarding work at low wages. But life in the city afforded them more personal freedom, more opportunities, and chances to be part of communities, as new schools, churches, and benevolent societies abounded in urban areas.[42] Town life gave young people fresh ideas and values, different from the standards of the rural South.[43] Many young people eagerly took the chance to go to town, and a large number of young women took jobs as cooks.

Some young women who migrated from the country to the city did so at the behest of their relatives. In other instances, a member of the extended family found a position for a young kinswoman. At times parents, desperately needing some cash income, made the decision and arrangements to send their daughter to town without consulting her.[44] In other cases, the young woman herself determined to go and had to persuade her parents to allow her to leave the farm or the small town. Women such as Cleora Butler remembered their relief and joy at getting to move from the family home to the city.[45]

Many women who went to town regarded their migration as fleeing the drudgery of southern farm life. Mary Belle Jordan, born in 1907, moved from Talbot County, Georgia, to Atlanta, in the 1920s. Without extensive formal education, Jordan capitalized on her "natural intelligence and an almost superhuman drive—and the fact that she was a very good cook." Her son, civil rights attorney Vernon Jordan, wrote that his mother "escaped the share-cropper's life to try to do better in the world. She used every scrap of what she had to try to do that."[46] Vernon Jordan referred to Sister Fannie Green as "another refugee from rural Georgia who had come to the city."[47] Mary Belle Jordan and Fannie Green evidently viewed Atlanta as a place where they could breathe more easily than on the farm.[48]

Once women arrived in the city, however, they found their employment prospects highly constrained. From Reconstruction through World War II, domestic work remained by far the most common occupation of African American women in the cities of the South. Anna Mae Dickson recalled the limited opportunities for a young woman in Navasota, Texas, in the 1930s: "If you lived where I did, you did domestic work or farming, even if you finished high school. . . . For a black girl, there wasn't anything like working at the stores. They weren't open to us at that time, in the late '30s. And I don't remember any registered nurses that was colored working in the hospital then. The only nursing that you did was taking care of people's children. It was easy to find a job baby-sitting, or somebody to cook for and houseclean. So that's what I did."[49] The perpetually low wages for domestic workers allowed many white southerners, often people of small means, to exalt their social position and have African American women wait on them. Race and class formed a vicious cycle: racism kept African American women from taking other employment, and their availability to work for even the poorest whites reinforced their position as people who could do only low-paid labor.

And yet African American women held their heads up and went to work, day after day, taking pride in their actions and their products. Frances Walker, who cooked for an extremely wealthy family outside of Richmond in the first quarter of the twentieth century, told her granddaughter, Frances Jones, and other young people, "It is no disgrace to serve. It is an art." Jones observed, "It was hard but honest work. No one felt belittled by what they did. They did it well."[50] In 1923, Elizabeth Haynes spoke with one "elderly cook who had been at the business for 50 years. . . . She had never been to school a day in her life. . . . However, she felt confident that she could cook anything that was put before her to cook."[51] An anonymous cook writing to Eleanor Roosevelt in 1941 described herself as an "A-1 cook," with references from the "best of Americans,"[52] and Ida Trail of Nashville similarly wrote, "I can manage and plan around the house nicely myself and I find it very difficult to work around people that don't know or don't care. We have a lot of that here in the

Athens of the South."[53] Women such as these brought their great talents to the kitchens of their employers.

The labor of cooks mattered deeply to African American society. Most African American women simply had to work for wages, because few African Americans, male or female, earned enough to support their families single-handedly. Cooking was one avenue that was open to them. The work was hard, the hours long, and the pay meager. It was better than slavery or sharecropping, however, and women willingly made the transition, first, from agricultural labor, then from the kitchen into other types of employment. The evolution took almost a hundred years. Like Moses in the Hebrew Bible, many of the women in this study did not live to see the promised land of equal opportunity. But they walked and worked anyway, laying the pathways for their children and their children's children.

- intersection of race & class
- history of slavery

I Done Decided I'd Get Me a Cook Job

BECOMING A COOK

Cooks were made, not born, contrary to white southern stereotype, and they arrived in their profession through a variety of means. A woman or a girl sometimes decided for herself to cook rather than do field work or other types of domestic labor; at other times, her family made the choice for her, or circumstances dictated her entry into the kitchen. The types of training that women had varied widely. Some learned at their mothers' knees, others were thrown before the stove with absolutely no prior knowledge, and a few received formal training from home economists. Regardless of how they got there, generations of African American freedwomen produced meals as part of their daily work.

A COOK'S EMPLOYMENT BEGAN, of course, with identifying a position and being engaged for it. The process of hiring was an elaborate dance in which both sides negotiated for what they wanted. Relationships between employers and employees were often highly personalized, and an employer usually hired a cook for her personal qualities and not for specific job skills.[1] Word of mouth served as a powerful tool for employers and employees alike. Velma Davis, who worked in Washington, D.C., remembered, "Reference? Nobody checked that if you'd been sent by somebody they knew. That's how I always got jobs, through people."[2] Sociologist T. J. Woofter commented on such casual engagements in his 1913 study of Athens, Georgia, remarking that women hired employees "without a shred of reference." A few "housekeepers," he noted, called a recent employer on the telephone and asked "a few questions as to honesty and regularity, and usually hire the servant without reference to her knowledge of cooking and trust to chance for the rest."[3] Lack of references increased the haphazard manner of hiring.

With such disorder, some white women engaged their cooks purely on whims. "The Lil' Black Girl," interviewed as part of the Federal Writers' Project, recalled moving to Birmingham without a plan. She recalled, "While I walked about the station, a white lady and her husband came by. I will never know what attracted them to me, except that God was guiding my destiny. She stopped as she passed and asked if I wanted work." The young woman worked for that family for a year before returning to Atlanta.[4]

Alice Adams and her aunt enacted a scenario common across the South, with a trusted relative acting as middleman in finding a kinswoman a position with a white family that she or he thought trustworthy. Adams came to Atlanta about 1929 at the age of fourteen, after her aunt suggested that she leave the family farm and move to the city to earn money for her ailing parents. Adams recalled, "My father's health had began [sic] to fail. He couldn't do anything on the farm. My aunt asked him to let me come to Atlanta to work. . . . My aunt sent me to these people."[5] Word of mouth and family connections could serve whites and African Americans alike; African American women could help one another find suitable positions, and Anglo women could assist their kinswomen in locating proper workers.[6] White housewife Jane Stafford recalled that when she married in 1938, "my mother hired Nellie for me."[7] Such practices solidified family ties on both sides and may have also created friction when hirings didn't work out.

A number of African American women took the initiative to find positions for themselves. Just as former slave Leah simply showed up at the Thomas home shortly after emancipation,[8] African American women continued to seek out employment. In Washington County, Texas, white housewife Mary Hunt Affleck lived in a home reputed to be haunted. The "hant," she said, made it difficult for her to keep a cook in the days after the slaves were freed. Affleck recalled a momentous morning shortly after the Civil War when she was laboring to clear the breakfast dishes without a hired cook: "There was a light tap on the door. I opened it to find a real old-time negro woman, a veritable picture from the past, standing on the step. Her short dress of blue and white checked cotton, snowy apron and brilliant turban, proclaimed her identity with ante-bellum days. 'Good morning,' mistis',' she said, with a low courtesy [sic], while a broad smile wrinkled her black face. 'Does you want a cook?'"[9] Affleck does not indicate where the woman came from or even what her name was, but she remained with Affleck's family for forty years. Beatrice Walters seized opportunity when she saw it in 1923. Jane Stafford recalled,

"She saw them [Stafford's parrents] unloading a lot of new furniture in front of the house, and she just walked up and knocked and asked Mother if she needed help. That's how she was hired—just like that!" Walters remained with the family for forty-six years.[10] Cooks' initiative sometimes resulted in their finding jobs that lasted for decades.

Elizabeth S. Collins, a middle-aged white woman in Dalton, Georgia, maintained a remarkable correspondence with African American friends in Cherokee County, Georgia, about fifty miles away. In 1877, she wrote to Dahlia Wood, a freedwoman who was about twenty-seven years of age, trying to persuade her to come and work. First she offered to pay Wood's transportation. She wheedled, "I shall want you to cook, iron, and assist me in cleaning up; if you wash, I will pay you extra for that, and you can do as you choose about it; as I already have a washer-woman. Please write and let me know when you would be willing to come, what you are willing to work for per month, and how long you would be satisfied to stay; and then, if we can agree about these things, we will make arrangements to get you here. I had rather have you or Georgia [Grisham, Wood's neighbor,] than any body I know of."[11] Nine years later, Wood had moved to Chattanooga and Collins was trying to persuade her to work for a Mr. Holtzclaw: "He would be good pay and his wife is very pleasant and I think you would like her."[12] From Collins's constantly cajoling tone, it appears that Dahlia Wood carefully picked and chose when and for whom she would work. Cherokee County, away from urban areas, may have been a difficult place to attract domestic workers.

Migrants to Washington, D.C., after World War I looked for high-status or prestigious employers. Wealthy employers could pay salaries promptly and provide fringe benefits such as paid vacations or holiday bonuses. They would, furthermore, have more experience managing household help and likely would be fairer to their employees than less-cultured employers. Historian Elizabeth Clark-Lewis observed, "Experienced, self-confident employers were not usually inclined to browbeat and belittle servants, whereas lower-status employers sometimes resorted to bolstering their egos or reassuring their social positions by mistreating their servants."[13]

While African American women sought the highest available wages, the best conditions, and fairest treatment, most could not afford to be choosy.[14] Anna Mae Dickson, who was born about 1912 in Grimes County, Texas, said, "Actually people chose us most of the time rather than we choosing them. You'd get jobs by somebody recommending you. So I've had to work for people that treated you like they didn't have any feelings for you. Some people, I don't care what you did, it was never right."[15]

Annie Mae Hunt recalled the competition for employment in Dallas in the 1930s: "You'd see an ad in the paper, somebody'd want a maid, you go out there, there'd be 40 or 50 people already there. The employer really had their choice. The *pickaninny* didn't know who was gonna be picked."[16] With a constant supply of cheap labor, white people who could barely afford to feed themselves wanted to have hired help, as even textile mill workers employed domestic workers in their homes. Historian Walter Fleming observed in 1905, "There are some women who keep servants when they are not financially able and when they have no real need for them. They hire a poor class of African Americans and pay them even lower wages, from $2.00 to $3.00 a month."[17] This trend continued through the 1930s, when sociologist Arthur Raper commented, "The cotton mill wage scale, though generally low, is high enough to enable many white mothers to hire Negro domestic help, while they themselves work in the mills. In reality this is a comment on the small amount for which a Negro domestic can be had, and upon the Negro's consequent plane of living."[18]

THE ECONOMIC STATUS of her employer often deeply affected a cook's work. Privileged families, with large houses and elaborate lifestyles, deployed an astonishing array of household workers.[19] The McCall family, for example, employed as many as twenty domestic workers at Evan Hall near Donaldsonville, Louisiana, in the late nineteenth century. In a photograph taken between 1885 and 1890, a young woman named Lucy carries a milk pail on one arm and a water pail in the other. Historian Susan Tucker surmises that Lucy was "a cook's assistant, one who spent her time going between the garden, the barn, and the dining room," tasks that slaves who worked as scullions would have done.[20] Martha Plant Ross remembered the household of her Ross grandparents on College Street in Macon, Georgia. At the turn of the twentieth century, the Ross household employed at least seventeen servants: two stablemen, three nurses for the children, three men "in the dining room," a full-time seamstress, two maids upstairs, two maids downstairs, two laundresses, and "'Fat Anne' and her stolid daughter in the kitchen, and they lived in the back yard."[21] "Fat Anne" and her daughter may have been the only employees who lived on the premises, indicating that they were expected to be available for most hours of the day and night. While "Fat Anne" and the woman at Evan Hall whom Lucy assisted could concentrate on their kitchen duties alone, such focus may also have raised the employers' expectations for the women's performances. Cooks who devoted their days entirely to food preparation would be required to turn out elaborate meals of near-perfect quality.

Immediately following the Civil War, freedwomen preferred to do only one kind of work, and one Low Country employer searched in vain for a freedwoman who would agree to do washing as well as cooking.[22] Cooking requires different, and often greater, skill than cleaning or child care, and women who cooked often commanded higher wages than maids or nurses. Cooking remained, therefore, among the more desirable domestic tasks.[23] In the 1930s, Sarah Howard bragged on her teenage daughter, Florence Howard. After several years of working as a nursemaid, Florence had advanced to the position of cook in her employers' household, and she was making three dollars a week, her highest earnings ever. The Howards regarded cooking as a significant improvement over tending children, and Florence's mother was proud of her daughter's promotion.[24]

Sometimes women made deliberate decisions to become cooks, while, at other times, those choices were thrust upon them by life circumstances or by employers' preferences. U.S. Department of Labor researcher Mary Robinson's survey of African American women in Baltimore in 1924 revealed definite preferences. Women over the age of thirty preferred cooking and laundry to maids' and nurses' work, and they eschewed leaving Baltimore to work for families in the rural areas.[25] While washerwomen had the most autonomy and sometimes were paid the most, cooking paid more than cleaning and nursing and so was the best position outside of one's home.[26] The cook, furthermore, sometimes had access to leftover food.[27] Atlanta resident Willie Mae Wright recalled her decision to switch to cooking: "If you had a job nursing or something like that, the cooks never would give you nothing to eat fit to mention; so I had done decided I'd tell stories and get me a cook job."[28]

DESPITE THE WOMEN'S PREFERENCES, job descriptions were often extremely vague, and many women who were called "cooks" did a variety of household chores. Most southern households had only one domestic worker at a time, and that one worker usually had her hands full. Perhaps cooking dominated the list of work because of its necessity and its regularity. Employers got hungry, and it was the cook's duty to make sure their hungers were filled, at regular intervals. Dusting might go undone until another day, but meals needed to be fixed. Also, cooking was time-consuming, and other tasks could often be fitted in around the food preparation schedule. Finally, cooking required a specific skill set and knowledge base that other tasks did not. Undoubtedly, many of the women whom the federal census designated as "cook in private home" performed a variety of jobs. Food preparation remained a major part of each woman's day, however.

Want ads placed in Louisville newspapers in the 1880s indicate that almost 90 percent of employers expected their domestic workers to do some combination of tasks, including cooking, washing, and cleaning.[29] For most women, being "cooks" meant balancing their kitchen tasks with a constellation of other work, all of which their employers wanted them to perform with skill, speed, proficiency, and a cheerful attitude. Home economist Ava L. Johnson observed in 1932 that employers wanted a good cook with good manners, good English, and good table service, who was a good cleaner, and "who has a good disposition eighteen hours a day."[30] In 1939, Catherine L. Wood of Atlanta wrote bitterly to U.S. secretary of labor Frances Perkins: "In Georgia people in the country and little towns can't afford to hire *any* one, so like shoe polish 'three in one,' only its *4* people's work they get out of *one* person 1. Laundry 2. Nurse 3. Maid 4. Cook and offer you 1.25 some 1.50 per week and 2.00. Once in a great while some one offers *3.00*."[31] And an anonymous worker in Pine Bluff, Arkansas, writing in 1941, clearly referred to herself as "a negro cook" but nonetheless detailed her numerous duties, including ironing for a family of ten: "I start to work at 7 oclock and work untill 8 oclock at night[;] I have three meals to cook: 12 rooms house to clean up." She concluded, "It is very hard."[32]

Such patterns of work began shortly after emancipation. Pollie Phillips came to East Texas with her owner in the antebellum period and remained in Tyler after the Civil War, "nurs[ing] hundreds of infants and . . . cook[ing] for their weddings."[33] Mollie Holt Hall's unnamed cook lived "in a new house in the yard" built in Tyler in 1869. When Hall's skirts caught fire, the cook tried unsuccessfully to extinguish the conflagration, and Hall died. Her widower, Thomas Hunt Hall, repaired to his parents' home, and "the cook was left to take care of the house."[34] In 1871, a "cook" named Caroline came to work for Jennie Akehurst Lines in Macon, Georgia. Over the next week, Lines detailed Caroline's tasks: on the second day, Caroline ironed all day, and Lines had already determined that she was "a very good washer and cook." On the third day, "house cleaning day," "our rooms were all swept and dusted, windows, oil cloths and lamps washed by [seven?] o'clock." At the end of the first week, the cycle of laundry commenced again, stretching over two days.[35]

The multiple tasks continued into the twentieth century. Alice Adams, who began domestic work at age fourteen in the late 1920s and stayed with the same family for forty years, recalled her workday: "I would go in, fix breakfast, fix the midday dinner for the children, cook, at six o'clock serve dinner, wash the dishes. Every day I would have to go in and do the light cleaning, like dust and make the beds, change the beds, and keep the closets straight.

Next morning, back in the same routine." Additionally, she bathed the children, set out laundry for the "wash lady," and kept track of the laundry coming in and out of the house.[36] Maggie Billings started working in Louisville in the late 1930s, and she remembered the difficulty of balancing employers' expectations and her own desire to do excellent work: "Cooking, cleaning, washing, ironing, and taking care of children require a lot of time. If you're going to do your best, you're supposed to just do one thing. I like to do things thoroughly. And then when you take care of children, that requires your whole time. If you cook, that requires time; if you clean, that requires time; and if you do laundry work, that certainly requires time. But they have it in their head that cooking and children and laundry all go together; but they don't."[37]

Even the most skilled cooks performed heavy household labor. Florence Dymond described Mary Howard, who lived and worked on the Belair plantation in Plaquemines Parish, Louisiana, in the late nineteenth and early twentieth centuries, as "a generally handy woman, a splendid cook, a natural born nurse, excellent at housework, a good seamstress, [who] could make over mattresses and could turn her hand to anything."[38] In 1941, an unnamed woman in Washington, D.C., observed, "I have had years of experiences plenty references from the best of Americans A-1-cook. Also learned cooking from school and private families (the best). . . . Then you are expected to stay in on so many positions. Wax floors, wash windows take care of 4 or 5 children."[39] And Floridian Idella Parker sharply recalled her work in the 1940s: "When I wasn't cooking I was cleaning. . . . The bare, unpainted wood floors had to be scrubbed daily, especially those in the kitchen and bathrooms. This was done on my hands and knees with a bucket of water with lye soap and a scrub brush. They didn't use mops in those days."[40]

A few African American women even served as drivers for their employers. For some women, like Idella Parker and the fictional Narciss in Eudora Welty's novel *The Ponder Heart*, driving may have demonstrated a degree of freedom from some social constraints. But for others, chauffeuring may have been a time-consuming task that only took them away from the jobs that had to be done at the house.[41] Cooks' obligations could also extend into traveling with their employers. Some women considered such duties to be a boon. Chloe, according to her South Carolina employer, enjoyed a trip to New York and Washington, D.C., with visits to the White House, the U.S. Capitol, and a Buffalo Bill show.[42] Musing on why she chose to tolerate Marjorie Kinnan Rawlings's abuse for a decade, Idella Parker speculated, "It may have been because . . . I got to travel to places I never would have otherwise visited."[43] Washingtonian Nellie Willoughby, conversely, hated traveling with her employers, observing that they took her along only to "show people that they had enough money to bring a black person with them."[44] Some cooks declined to travel away from home and quit or were fired as a result of their refusal. Despite a previously happy relationship, Willie Mae Wright's employer let her go when Wright refused to go to the mountains with the white family.[45]

Some women resisted the multiple roles, believing that they had more than enough to do with their cooking responsibilities. In some instances, they used passive aggression, simply not doing what they were asked; at other times, they spoke up for themselves directly. In 1912, according to writer Harris Dickson, an elderly African American woman known only as "Aunt Mandy" responded to her employer's request to "sweep the gallery" by saying that she "couldn't sweep and cook—too hard on her." When the employer told her that she herself had been sweeping, cooking, and doing the housework, "Aunt Mandy" replied (with Dickson supplying the dialect), "Lawdee, Miss Julia, how I wishes I had yo' constitution!"[46] "Aunt Mandy" not so subtly pointed out the strength of the younger white woman and perhaps the absurdity of an older woman doing the work of which the younger woman was perfectly capable. In the 1930s, home economist Ava Johnson quoted a "colored maid" who had been "rebuffed for carelessness in cleaning." The domestic worker in question, in Johnson's version, pointed out the unlikelihood of perfection in all spheres of household work: "Lawsy, ma'am, you can't get elegant biscuits and clean corners outen the same cullud puhson!"[47] Also in the 1930s, a young woman in Mississippi responded firmly to her employer's request that she cut and fetch kindling. According to sociologist Hortense Powdermaker, who recorded the incident, she "said nothing but did not do it." When passivity failed to work, the young woman resorted to words: "Later in the day," Powdermaker wrote, "the woman asked angrily why she had not brought in the wood. Replying that she wasn't a janitor and wasn't going to do janitor's work, she put on her coat and started to walk out of the house. Thereupon her mistress asked her to stay and said they would forget about the wood."[48] Most women, however, performed multiple duties, willingly or not. Mary Robinson, writing for the Women's Bureau in 1924, reported that in Baltimore, women applying for various jobs were willing to take on other types of work: "nurses also willing to cook; cooks willing to do chamber work, waiting, first-floor cleaning or nursing children."[49]

BUT IT WAS COOKING that remained the constant in these women's shifting job descriptions. Preparing food was a task that required a variety of types of knowledge. Acclaimed cooks built up their repertoires of skills and recipes over a lifetime, and novices often suffered from their ignorance. In stark contrast to the stereotype of the innately talented African American cook, poor women migrating from the country or adolescents without prior education frequently came into their employers' kitchens with little knowledge or ability. Reformers decried the absence of culinary skill among rural African American women. Journalist Oswald Garrison Villard, dismayed at his travels in the South in 1905, reported, "Poor whites and Colored people need cooking teachers to keep them from living only on hog meat and potatoes when they have the fullness of the earth to draw upon if they but knew how."[50] Dorothy Dickins, a home economist in Mississippi, commented acidly: "The ordinary country negro woman is a poor cook and only years of careful training from some white woman can justify her reputation for good cooking. As a rule she cares for a houseful of children and works in the fields. Often the cooking is turned over to one of the children and the family is reared on fried hoecakes and soggy biscuits, yellow with soda."[51] Having had no exposure to good food or high-quality cookery, these women could not simply intuit what to do in an urban kitchen, and they often had rough transitions to employment in affluent city homes.

A woman who did know how to cook often transmitted her knowledge to her daughters and granddaughters. Numerous generations of women worked as cooks in the decades after emancipation, and older women gladly shared their wisdom with younger relatives and friends. Some young women learned by casual observation and others by direct communication of information. Sometimes a cook's training began early in life as she learned from her mother. Idella Parker credited her mother for the basic instruction she received at home: "Ethel Riley Thompson was without doubt the finest cook I have ever known and she taught me all she knew. . . . Simple dishes like beans and rice, biscuits, and gingerbread tasted like nobody else's, and the house was full of warm, wonderful smells when Mama was cooking."[52] Georgian Willie Mae Wright started serving with her mother in a white family's kitchen when she was not yet nine years old. Wright's mother worked for a family named Gruber, "and she was really a first-class cook." Wright recalled the routine: "Mrs. Gruber—we called her Miss Nell—told me to come up to the big house every day about twelve-thirty or one o'clock and get my dinner. Everybody in the country and little towns then eat exactly at twelve o'clock. After Momma and I had dinner I'd take the ashes out of the stove, sweep off the back porch, bring in the churning-cloths off the line, and help Momma get through."[53] While Wright was observing, not cooking, she nonetheless absorbed many culinary lessons from her mother that later stood her in good stead. If Wright's mother preferred that her young daughter pursue other avenues and remain out of the Grubers' kitchen, Nell Gruber saw to it that those hopes were dashed.

Other young women learned to cook in their mothers' absences, taught either by other family members or by trial and error. Sarah Hill, who was orphaned at three, learned from her sister-in-law, "a mighty good trainer," how to clean, cook, iron, and wash clothes.[54] Ironically, mothers working for white families often could not take the time to teach their daughters themselves. Thus, some girls learned cooking on their own when they were left with the responsibility of caring for their homes while their mothers labored in other locations. Katie Geneva Cannon, who grew up in Kannapolis, North Carolina, in the 1950s, remembered the frustration of being expected to know skills without being taught them:

> Part of the training for black kids to become a domestic was to learn to do that kind of work at home. Cause while your mother's taking care of white kids and cleaning up white houses, you got to do that for yourself. . . . In some kind of way, almost as if by osmosis, black girls were supposed to know how to do all these things and who was supposed to be teaching us? Mama would leave before sunup and when she got home it would be sundown, and we were not only supposed to know how to keep house but also how to cook perfect meals and not burn food up, and not to tear up all the food because it had to stretch. The wisdom was supposed to be inside of each of us, I mean, we were disciplined if we didn't know it. So that was very frustrating. That's how I learned to be a domestic, by taking care of house at home. My older sister, who was two years older than me, was responsible for teaching me how to do it.[55]

Cannon's mother expected her daughters to know the skills so familiar to her and not to waste the food that she had worked so very hard to provide for them.

Mildred Council, who eventually owned a celebrated restaurant in Chapel Hill, North Carolina, observed her older siblings' cooking and learned to cook by feel rather than by formal measurements: "It was on my trips in and out of the kitchen with water that I first learned to cook, watching how Roland or my older sisters made things with their 'dump cooking' methods and making mental notes about how ingredients went together. . . . I learned to pinch the salt or pour it in the palm of my hand. Then I would taste the juice from the pot like Roland did."[56]

EVEN WITH NO INNATE knowledge of how to cook and often no learned knowledge, African American girls sometimes began working in other people's kitchens at early ages.[57] In Mississippi in 1900, Mary Tuck was sent out to work at the age of seven to supplement the family income. She remembered, "I . . . had to get up on a chair to get to the stove."[58] Augusta Swanson, from lower Louisiana, was eight when she went to live with "Miz May," who taught her to "read and write, crochet, knit, cook, and how to housekeep." The tutelage that Swanson received from May was her only education, for she cooked from the age of eight and never attended formal school.[59]

Young African American women—girls, really—who took their first cooking jobs without the benefit of prior teaching often reacted, appropriately, with fear. Perhaps the employers' practice of immediately putting the young women in the kitchen to solo, as it were, served as a mechanism of control. It certainly created terror. Anna Mae Dickson remembered her initiation, about 1925. She was thirteen, working summers between school in her "first steady job." The event was seared into Dickson's memory: "The lady was having fifteen people for Sunday dinner. She was having these little birds they call quail. I had never seen them before. Well, she showed me the recipe book, explained it to me, and said to have it ready when they came back from church. I was so scared I must have cried the whole time I cooked those birds! But I served them. And that lady didn't let anyone say anything bad about the food or the way I was serving it. I'll never forget that day, and she wouldn't even let Mama come and be with me."[60] There would be no apprenticeship in that household. The pressure on the child was increased because of the size and difficulty of the meal and the expectation that everything be right for company. Dickson prevailed, but the likelihood of disaster had been strong, with a young, untrained girl preparing a complicated, unknown dish for a large audience.

For some cooks, even those with experience, family wisdom could prove invaluable. Maggie Billings used modern technology to tap into that wisdom, telephoning her older sister when she was stumped by a strange new ingredient. On one occasion, her employer told her to fix chestnuts and gave no further instructions. Billings said, "And you know I had never fixed a chestnut before in my life. So I got me a hammer and hit this chestnut and boop. . . . I looked at that thing and I said where on earth did it go? Well, when I found it, I hit it harder; I thought Lord have mercy, how am I going to get these chestnuts fixed? Every time I hit it, it went up to the ceiling and back and all around the floor." Fortunately, help was close at hand. Billings called in her best assistance, her sister Frances: "So my sister and I would always call one another and talk about things. So I went to the telephone and I called her, I said, 'Frances, tell me how do you fix chestnuts?' She said put them in some hot water. . . . I finally learned how." Rather than giving up or confessing her lack of knowledge to her employer, Billings was able to use know-how already in her family to handle one of the toughest foods known to humanity.[61]

Some new cooks relied on other workers to teach them. At the age of thirteen, Idella Parker worked a summer washing dishes in the Reddick, Florida, boardinghouse kitchen under the supervision of Maggie Lewis. Parker recalled, "Mrs. Maggie Lewis, a gentle, well-respected black lady, was the housekeeper and cook. Mrs. Maggie would get others to help out with the work in the summer when travelers were many. One year, when I was thirteen years old, she asked Mama if I could come and help in the kitchen. I did, and my job was to help wash dishes every day, Monday through Friday. It was my first paying job, and I earned fifty cents a week. From Mrs. Maggie I learned a lot about kitchen work."[62]

In wealthy households with large staffs, the training involved an almost formal succession from one generation of cooks to the next. Employer Louise Webster, from the New Orleans area, remembered a maid named Inez who learned in the 1930s to cook from the family cook named Juliette: "[Inez] was this good-looking young, young girl when she came to us, and she learned to press like a French laundress and learned to cook from Juliette. And later when my aunt was without help and Juliette had gotten old and couldn't manage that much cooking and doing like she had done in that big house, my mother gave Juliette to my aunt. And then Inez moved up as the cook; she had learned so many things from Juliette."[63] As bizarre as Webster's offhand comment about her mother "giving" Juliette to her aunt seems, she nonetheless made clear that Inez had learned enough from Juliette to satisfy Webster's mother.[64]

At other times, seasoned employees helped the new, young cook get started to protect her from the employer. Even on estates like Maymont in Richmond, many staff members learned through on-the-job experience. The staff was so large that individuals could find proper teachers and might be shielded from their employer's scrutiny while they learned their new skills.[65] About 1920, Ethel Beulah Woodson Bolden went to work as a cook on the Trible plantation in central Virginia. As historian Dianne Swann-Wright observes, "Ethel was barely ten years old when she went to work at the Trible plantation house as a cook. She was so young and unskilled that she had to depend on one of the farmhands to help her bake bread for the white family's meals. One of Lizzie Wade's boys had to show how much 'soda and salt' to put in the flour to make up the bread."[66] Again, the employer expected a child to function in the kitchen without proper instruction. Fortunately for Bolden, older employees shared the knowledge that she needed to succeed.

Although employers griped incessantly about having to train their cooks, some gave careful attention to the task—in historian Susan Porter Benson's words, "remodeling the people whom they hired."[67] Some employers instructed their cooks by getting in the kitchen themselves. While some white women did not know how to cook, a number of them did and apparently were quite capable. Virginian Maria Dupuy Anderson wrote in 1878: "I am getting my little cook into the traces now and am not nearly so closely confined as at first. She can now get a right good plain meal without any assistance and is learning her place a little better than at first."[68] Her comparison of her diminutive servant to a draft animal indicates that Anderson carefully taught the young woman her designated "place" as well as simple cooking skills. Augusta Swanson recalled that "Miz May . . . learned me how to house-keep and how to cook."[69] Regina Manning remembered her mother as an active instructor of a young woman named Bette: "Mother taught her how to do gourmet things as time went along."[70]

Willie Mae Wright benefited enormously from an employer who was a good cook. As a young woman, Wright decided to present herself to a potential employer as a cook despite her lack of experience: "It was an ad job, and when I got there the lady asked me did I know anything about cooking. I told her yes'm, but I didn't."[71] Wright's lack of experience soon became clear:

> She hired me, and I went to messing up the food. I called myself cooking, but I didn't a bit more know how to cook than I knew how to jump over Stone Mountain. I was trying to learn, but I really was ruining food. Every meat loaf or lemon pie or anything I'd mess up, I'd say: "Well, that's the way Mrs. So-and-So made it." Finally this lady said: "Well, Mrs. So-and-So didn't know how to cook. Do you want me to teach you the way I cook?" She let me watch her make a chicken pie, and then she showed me how she wanted snap beans fixed, and we just went on from there. Before long it come so easy to me that I just got along fine. I liked her very well, and she ever more than taught me how to be a good cook."[72]

Wright's employer either bought or overlooked her little white lie and knew enough to cultivate Wright's talent in the kitchen.

Other cooks emphasized not what their employers taught them but rather what they learned on their own. Maggie Billings recalled that one never confessed ignorance to an employer: "When I first started cooking, there was a whole lot of things I didn't know how to cook. But I sure didn't tell them I didn't know. And they would say do you know how to cook so and so and I'd say I sure do." No one, according to Billings, could have perfect knowledge, and any good cook needed to continue adding to her repertoire: "You learn as you go along. Because even though you know how to fix a whole lot of things . . . there is a whole lot of other things that you don't know how to fix."[73]

Similarly, "Lil Black Girl" remembered her early days in Atlanta: "I was very inexperienced and didn't know how to do the many things required of me. . . . I didn't know how to cook the fine foods that white people ate, having not seen them before I came here, to say nothing of having learned how to prepare them. My employer was very patient with me and she was one of the best white women I've ever known, before or after."[74] She does not indicate, however, how she learned to cook, only that her employer gave her time to learn to prepare the unfamiliar new dishes.

In 1934, seventeen-year-old Idella Parker went to work for the Bowen family in West Palm Beach, Florida. She recalled, "Mrs. Bowen was fond of having her lady friends in for fancy luncheons and teas, and soon I knew how to cook and serve all kinds of fancy dishes. Dainty sandwiches and fancy hors d'oeuvres, cheese soufflés and rich desserts, I could do it all." She concluded, "In the Bowens' home I learned correct table setting, and how to cook all types of fancy foods. Mama was a good country cook, but here I learned how to prepare and serve luncheons and big dinner parties."[75] Parker does not indicate that Bowen actually taught her, but rather that while in Bowen's employ she somehow acquired the knowledge that she needed to be successful. While Bowen might have indeed taught Parker, the African American woman does not credit the white woman with influencing her, rather making it appear that she learned by other means.

For the African American women whose employers taught them to cook, the days of learning sometimes approximated a type of culinary apprenticeship. Such apprenticeships were typically informal, and they transmitted social values as well as hands-on skills. By teaching their African American workers to cook a certain way, culinary historian Charles Camp argues, white female employers also inculcated ways of thinking in them: "a mix of information, skill, judgment, and meaning that recapitulates family, ethnic, religious, and social values."[76] While African American women may have resisted such indoctrination, certainly they received schooling on the different foods of the more affluent white citizens; both "Lil Black Girl" and Anna Mae Dickson refer to white people's food as though it were something completely foreign to them before their employment, but they learned quickly about soufflés and other fancy dishes.

Each time she joined a new employer, a cook had to figure out what would please that family and what would not, often by trial and error rather than direct instruction. A white Atlanta writer in 1897 evinced some sympathy for the cook while excoriating the housewives for their own lack of preparation: "The new cook naturally prepares the food just as she did for the family whom she previously served, and sends it to the table cooked, as she thinks, 'well enough for anybody.' Families in their taste are quite as individual as the members making them up, and what suited 'Mrs. Jones' may not suit 'Mrs. Smith.'"[77]

Learning an employer's family's tastes was a challenge for many cooks but one that had a potentially high payoff. A family that had their eggs just the way they wanted them, for instance, was likely to be happy with a cook and to provide a stable workplace.[78] A given family's culinary peculiarities might be personal, ethnic, regional, or religious. Sometimes the differences were in technique. Famed New Orleans restaurateur Leah Chase's first cooking job was at a boardinghouse in Madisonville, Louisiana. Chase remembered accommodating the proprietor's unusual ideas about roux, the flour-and-fat mixture used as the basis for Cajun and Creole soups and gumbos—but usually not for vegetables: "There was another black girl working there and we used to laugh together because this woman cooked so different. She used to cook string beans and tell us that we needed to cook a roux for these string beans. We would laugh and laugh."[79] But Chase did cook the beans in a roux, just as her employer requested.

In new situations, cooks often had to work with unfamiliar ingredients. When Ethel Woodson Bolden went to work for the Trible family in the 1920s, she learned the tastes of her employer, Gladys Trible, an Irish immigrant: "Ethel considered the foods that Gladys taught her how to make to be 'funny foods' because they were so different from the foods prepared in her mother's kitchen."[80] Henrietta Elizabeth Sellers moved from Atlanta to Jacksonville, Florida, with her employer about 1924. She remarked to a Federal Writers' Project interviewer, "I can't remember when I learned to cook—seem lak I always knowed—but I did have to learn how to cook seafood, fish, shrimp, crabs and such, after I came to Florida."[81] At times, women learned to cook without familiar seasonings to avoid religious taboos. Cleora Butler, for example, remembered making adjustments in recipes for a family that eschewed all alcohol in their food.[82] Across the South, African American women learned to cook kosher for their Jewish employers, often mastering intricate rules of kashruth. They prepared meals consisting of both traditional Jewish foods and traditional southern foods (imaginatively seasoned without pork), and they also created such hybrid dishes as lox and grits and sweet potato kugel. In Charleston, for example, during the 1930s and 1940s, Agnes Jenkins fed the Krawcheck family by alternating between meals featuring items such as fried chicken and potato latkes. In the Mississippi Delta in the mid-twentieth century, Evalina Smith prepared two batches of vegetables—one with pork, one without—at every meal for the Klumok family, which had divided ideas about dietary laws.[83]

EMPLOYERS COMPLAINED VOCIFEROUSLY about their inept and untrained employees,[84] but sympathetic observers also commented on the lack of training for domestic workers. Elizabeth Haynes, writing in 1923, reported one cook cutting a fine sirloin steak into bits and frying it, a "young girl" who said that she knew how to make Jell-O but not other desserts, and the "rank and file" who "looked upon making salad dressing and salads as an art belonging to fine cooks" and had never tried to make bread. Haynes also identified illiteracy as a problem: "The older type cook, who cannot read and write," she reported, "finds it difficult, if not impossible, to carry all the different modern salad and dessert combinations in her memory and cannot supplement her instructions by the use of literature on domestic science."[85] In commenting on old cooks' inability to cope with modernity, Haynes identified an opposite problem from many cookbook writers of the period, who complained that their cooks were too young to remember the good old ways of slavery. Too old or too young, cooks never seemed to suit their employers just right.

Inadequate preparation of cooks greatly concerned reformers, who believed that the obvious answer to the problem was formal instruction at educational institutions. Such training fell into two categories: regular curricular offerings for young people and continuing education for women already employed as cooks. When Claflin University opened in 1869, for example, it included cooking as one of the twenty trades and industries that its students could choose. By the second decade of the twentieth century, domestic science appeared in the curriculum of leading African American schools, including Spelman Seminary.[86] Even the most elite southern institutions felt compelled to come to grips with a difficult job market for its graduates.

Booker T. Washington and his colleagues at Tuskegee Institute deemed cookery training so important that every young woman enrolled there took cooking lessons, irrespective of her other academic endeavors. The "Lady Principal" and director of the Department of Domestic Service for the young women, hired in 1890, was Margaret Murray Washington, a graduate of Fisk University, who became the founder's third wife.[87] Mary L. Dotson, who first appeared at Tuskegee as a student but stayed to teach cooking, recalled with great enthusiasm the expansion of the cooking curriculum from one to four years.[88] Tuskegee graduates such as Cornelia Bowen then went forth and spread the instruction to places such as Mount Meigs, Alabama, where the curriculum for young women included cooking, laundering, housekeeping, and sewing.[89]

Female African American school leaders, including Mary McLeod Bethune, also incorporated domestic science into their curriculum.[90] In 1909, the Woman's Convention, Auxiliary to the National Baptist Convention, opened the National Training School for Women and Girls. The president, celebrated African American educator Nannie Helen Burroughs, insisted that "the Negro girl must be taught the art of home-making as a profession."[91] In this case, of course, the homes that African American women would be making would be those belonging to white people as well as their own. Unlike many of her peers in the field of education, Burroughs fervently believed in the dignity of menial work, and she sought to "re-define and re-present black women's work identities as skilled workers rather than incompetent menials."[92] In so doing, Burroughs promulgated a respectability based on her Christian duty and her belief in the gospel of "Bible, bath, and broom."[93] Accepting the fact that most African American women would be employed as domestics, Burroughs sought to improve their employment opportunities, their wages, and their images. The school's motto, "Work. Support thyself. To thine own powers appeal," emphasized the goal of improving the work skills of the young women, a goal that, Burroughs believed, would result in good things for the entire African American community.[94] In 1921, the redoubtable Burroughs established the Washington-based National Association of Wage-Earners, whose membership included some domestic workers, in support of better training for its constituents. The association, which apparently lasted until no later than 1926, aspired to establish a training house and to award annual prizes for design of the most practical housedresses and aprons, for simplifying household management, and for inventing or improving household equipment.[95]

Discussions about domestic training fell squarely into the ongoing intellectual conflicts over education of the time concerning whether young African Americans should be trained as laborers or given classical educations. Some

African American parents, inspired by the example of educators such as Anna Julia Cooper, had higher sights for their children's futures. Even in rural Mississippi they were suspicious of industrial training. William Henry Holtzclaw, principal of the Utica Normal and Industrial Institute in Mississippi, recalled that when he first opened his school in 1903, the parents objected, saying they "don't want their children taught to work for white folks."[96]

The debate showcased differing ideas on race and racism, often moving beyond pedagogy into ideology.[97] Most prominent of the disagreements was the proposal in 1910 to found a "Black Mammy Memorial Institute" in Athens, Georgia, to train African Americans as domestic servants. Samuel F. Harris, principal of Athens Colored High School, introduced extension courses in cooking, sewing, and agriculture for employed people at his school in the early twentieth century. In 1909, Harris and four African American skilled artisans began an independent evening school to teach mechanical arts and domestic service, a particular interest of Harris's, to employed adults. At the same time, a movement to memorialize Mammy figures was spreading across the South. The chancellor of the University of Georgia, D. C. Barrow, suggested that a "Black Mammy Memorial Association" be formed rather than erecting a statue. The association then chartered the Black Mammy Memorial Institute, with S. F. Harris as principal. The institute was governed by a white board of trustees, including Isma Dooley, who wrote on domestic matters for the *Atlanta Constitution* and was quite outspoken in her conservative racial views, and a "board of colored directors."[98] A fund-raising pamphlet published by the association observed that the institute would be devoted "to the education of the nine hundred and ninety of every one thousand who are not to be leaders but the INDUSTRIAL WORKERS of the negro race" (apparently believing not in W. E. B. DuBois's Talented Tenth but a Talented One Percent). It would be, the pamphlet declared, "a memorial where men and women learn to work, how to work and to love their work; where the mantle of the 'Old Black Mammy' may fall on those who go forth to serve."[99]

When T. J. Woofter wrote about Athens three years later, he made no mention of the Black Mammy Memorial Institute, so presumably its life was short. Rather, he wrote of the efforts of the West Broad Street School. A philanthropist gave kitchen equipment to the school, and regular pupils took classes in cooking on a daily basis. Attempting to reach on a continuing basis women who were already cooks, the institution held an extension cooking school once a year. "An afternoon is selected for this work so that the cooks of the town can come, and post cards are sent to the house keepers asking their coöperation in this work for the betterment of domestic service," Woofter wrote.[100]

Schools bragged on their graduates' successes. William Henry Holtzclaw of Utica crowed, "Many girls from this institution have gone into the homes of some of the best white people in this section of the country as well as in the Northern states. They have served as maids, cooks, and general house girls, and in every case but one that I have investigated they have given satisfaction."[101] Graduates of the domestic science program at Negro High School in Muskogee, Oklahoma, also made their educators proud. One year after graduation, the three members of the class of 1912 were each receiving salaries of seven to ten dollars a week, plus board and housing. The nine members of the class of 1913 each had more than twenty-five applications for her services.[102] Fifteen-year-old Cleora Butler enrolled in the Muskogee Manual Training High School in 1916. She found a curriculum that fit perfectly with her aspirations: "It was a matter of course that I would take cooking, which I had decided years before was to be my profession. The freshman class in home economics was composed of about fifteen girls—five of whom were slightly older and helped cook in private homes after school and on weekends." The teacher, Lucy Elliott, was a member of the African American elite of Muskogee, the sister of an African American clothing store proprietor who was president of the Oklahoma State Business League.

Butler recalled with great pride Elliott's selection of her class to prepare dinner for members of the Muskogee Board of Education in September 1916. Barely into the new school year, Elliott had only a week to get ready, including training her new class in the use of gas stoves, which few of them knew how to use. More than six decades later, Butler still remembered the menu: baked ham with horseradish sauce, green beans, candied sweet potatoes, Waldorf salad, dinner rolls, crabapple jelly, Lady Baltimore cake, homemade ice cream, coffee, and tea. Butler recalled that the dinner went well and the members of the class felt very proud of their efforts: "I guess we strutted around that school for weeks." Butler seemed to feel no rancor at either the short notice given or the white authorities requiring Elliott's pupils to perform on command.[103]

As the school in Athens illustrates, domestic training also extended outside of the full-time curriculum. Tuskegee Institute and Spelman Seminary held special classes in town for workers who couldn't attend school.[104] After the founding of the Cooperative Extension Service of the U.S. Department of Agriculture in 1914, home demonstration agents trained young African American women in domestic skills. Idella Parker recalled that in Marion County, Florida, "my aunt Idella, Papa's sister, was the first black homemaking teacher working for the Extension Service. I took cooking and sewing classes held at our school on Friday evenings, and would enter sewing or cook-ing projects in the [Marion County] fair."[105] While the home demonstration work was designed primarily for farm women, not urban domestic workers, for Parker, it served as a conduit into a career as a professional cook and later, vocational homemaking teacher.

In the larger cities of the South, noted white cooks occasionally instructed African Americans already working in domestic service. In 1916, for example, Henrieta Stanley Dull, who would soon write *Southern Cooking*, one of the South's most beloved cookbooks, gave a series of cooking lessons to a crowd of eight hundred African American women in Atlanta. The lessons were co-sponsored by the Atlanta Woman's Club, whose members would benefit from cooks' training, and the Atlanta Gas Light Company, which almost surely hoped to turn the cooks (and, more to the point, their employers) away from their woodstoves and into consumers for their gas-fueled products.[106] In Dallas a year later, Kate Brew Vaughn, the author of *Culinary Echoes from Dixie*, offered a single special lesson "for negro cooks only" before embark-ing on her week-long cooking school for white women.[107] Sponsors of these events doubtless recognized the desire on the parts of employers to have more formally schooled workers and obliged with short, race-segregated lessons.

The Domestic Efficiency Association of Baltimore offered a one-month training school for domestic workers in 1921 and 1922. In return for five dol-lars a week in tuition, a worker could receive instruction for her work as well as board. The tuition equaled at least three weeks' wages, and few African American women would have been able to pay the fees out-of-pocket. A stu-dent could agree to work through the association and then repay her tuition at a rate of at least $2.50 per week. The program kept domestic workers tied to association members through their indebtedness.[108]

Despite their best efforts, schools such as Claflin, Hampton Institute, and Tuskegee Institute reached only a fraction of the population. In 1895, Virginia educator I. Garland Penn estimated that thirty thousand individuals had re-ceived instruction at industrial schools since the Civil War, and in 1903–4, Tuskegee Institute enrolled 520 young women.[109] Through the first third of the twentieth century, schools built by the Rosenwald Fund included domes-tic science in their curriculum. More than five thousand schools, funded by the president of Sears, Roebuck and Company for rural African Americans between 1917 and 1932, served perhaps 20 percent of the African Ameri-can population. Despite the strenuous efforts of the Rosenwald teachers and others, formal school instruction touched only a handful of the women who could benefit from it.[110] Yet the curriculum continued: as late as 1947,

Tuskegee Institute received a grant of more than $10,000 from the General Education Board, an agency founded by John D. Rockefeller in New York, to conduct a two-year training program to prepare African American youth of Mobile, Alabama, for domestic work.[111]

AFRICAN AMERICAN WOMEN gained their cooking knowledge and skills from a variety of sources: family, peers, employers, on-the-job training, and formal culinary instruction. As literacy rates increased, some read and modified recipes from cookbooks, while others continued to cook by memory and feel. By the middle of the twentieth century, a few used technology such as the telephone to gain necessary information. Formal opportunities for training increased, but even at midcentury the vast majority of domestic workers entered the workforce with little education on how to cook effectively. With or without training, African American women entered into the world of cooking and the homes of white people. With varying amounts of care and creativity, in unpredictable circumstances, they used their knowledge and skills to shape the foodways of a region.

From Collards to Puff Pastry

THE FOOD

In 1868, white businessman Sylvanus Lines wrote to his wife, Jennie Akehurst Lines, about the abundance of food at his Macon, Georgia, boardinghouse:

> Now I suppose you would like to know what I have to eat—well for breakfast we have very good coffee, hot rolls, *warm biscuit* of course, beef steak, cold ham, hash, batter cakes, &cs at noon, not less than three kinds of meat & fowl, Irish & sweet potatoes, rice and hominy, light bread & biscuit, turnips & greens, and nearly every day dessert of pudding or pie with a glass of sweet milk or butter milk, and for supper we have the usual variety of meat & fowl with preserves and jellies and tea & coffee. On the whole I have concluded that I shall not starve.

Even in the harsh economy of the Reconstruction-era South, the unnamed proprietor of the boardinghouse where Lines was living put plentiful, tasty food on the table for her boarders. The coffee was good, the biscuit hot, and the meats varied. This particular boardinghouse had four servants. There is virtually no doubt that the bounty of plain, high-quality food that Sylvanus Lines enjoyed was the product of an African American cook.[1]

To understand fully the experiences of African American cooks, one must consider the raw ingredients with which they worked and the finished products that they turned out. Across the South, hundreds of thousands of African American women spent much of their days cooking for other women's families. From fruits, vegetables, meats, and staples, they prepared meals for their employers—meals that they would never be allowed to share at the same table with their employers but might be permitted to take home to their families as leftovers. The products varied in quality according to the ingredients and to the cook's care and skill. Like all people who prepared food, some women slapped barely edible meals on the table, while others provided elaborate, delectable feasts. In between those two extremes were legions of competent cooks who made simple, sturdy fare that kept their employers fed and in turn provided sustenance for their own loved ones through leftovers as well as the cash wages the women earned with their labor. In so doing, they contributed to one of the most noteworthy parts of southern American culture.[2]

EVERY MEAL IS THE SUM of numerous decisions, made in varying order: whom to feed, when to have the meal, what to serve, how to prepare the raw ingredients, how to serve it. For African American cooks and their employers, the decision-making process behind each choice sometimes became an extended struggle for power and authority. Some employers wanted to make each of these choices themselves, while others wanted no part in the deliberations, preferring to turn the entire procedure over to the employee. The cook had to interpret the signals from the employer and either try to follow the employer's wishes or make decisions based on the best information that she had. Every task of cooking, from planning to food acquisition to cleanup, had the potential for miscommunication and rancor. Regardless of who made the decisions regarding the content of the meals, the actual labor came from African American women. As southern food writer John T. Edge observed about the boardinghouse run by Selma Wilkes in Savannah, "The tasks of frying chicken, punching out biscuit dough, stripping collard leaves, and peeling potatoes have long been assigned to black women."[3]

SCHEDULES FOR MEALS VARIED from family to family, and cooks had to negotiate the peculiarities of each employer's schedule, from morning until night. One of L. G. Huff's numerous complaints about her employer in Fort Worth was "no system to when the meals will be served."[4] At times, employers surprised cooks with extra people who had to be accommodated at a given meal. In such situations, cooks spent their days being buffeted by other people's decisions or lack thereof.

Once the cook knew when the meal was expected and approximately how many diners to prepare for, the next step was deciding what to cook. The foods available to a given family depended upon the seasons and upon the family's financial resources. In households with formal meal planning, the housewife often decided on menus.[5] If a cook remained with a family for a period of time, learning members' tastes and earning trust, the employer might increasingly delegate this responsibility to her. Hylah Gardner Wright, who cooked for the Anderson family of Richmond for many years, determined the daily menus. Except for parties and other special occasions, "Mrs. Anderson turned it all to me," Wright recalled. "She didn't have nothing to do with cooking."[6] As Idella Parker gained the confidence of her employer, Marjorie Rawlings increasingly came to the kitchen to discuss menus, supplies, and recipes. Eventually, Parker remembered, "I was given the freedom to experiment with ingredients, without fear of wasting anything. If something didn't come out just right, Mrs. Rawlings would go to the store for more supplies until we got it right."[7] In Rawlings, Parker found an employer who loved good food, liked to cook herself, and encouraged her cook to try new dishes.

After the housewife or cook decided what the family would eat, one of them procured the food for the meals — or the process might be reversed, the meals planned around available food. Sociologists use the term "gatekeeper" to describe control of the flow of goods, specifically food, into the household.[8] In performing gatekeeper tasks, women made critical choices about expenditures of money and the family's nutrition and overall well-being. They also dictated the materials with which the family cook would do her work. A cook's day could be complicated or simplified according to the decisions and purchases made by her employer. City people sometimes grew some of their own food, particularly in the nineteenth century, but increasingly they purchased most of their groceries. While men did much of the shopping during the nineteenth century, by the twentieth century, town women in the South did the bulk of their families' food purchasing.[9] Women decided what to buy, based on the financial resources the family breadwinner provided, bought it, arranged to have it brought to the house, and coordinated its storage.

At the Jones and Willaford store in Macon, Georgia, in the 1890s, housewives, not the cooks, did almost all of the shopping. On one lone occasion the bookkeeper noted in the account of Mrs. N. M. Block the purchase of butter "by Emma."[10] The distinctive record of Emma's purchase reveals it to be an unusual circumstance at that particular store. With their constant dread of theft, most housewives preferred to control purchasing themselves. An employee with charging privileges might, housewives feared, illicitly gain access to goods or even money. Stories such as that of Bettie Ford and Elizabeth Ware in Atlanta in 1885 surely fired housewives' suspicions. Ford routinely purchased groceries for her employer Ware, taking a passbook in which to record the purchases. According to an Atlanta newspaper, one day Ford, passbook, and fourteen dollars' worth of groceries went missing. We do not learn of the story's resolution, but Ware took the matter seriously enough to report it to police, presumably ending Ford's employment in the Ware house.[11]

Like Ware, some housewives allowed their cooks, even ones of relatively new employ, to buy groceries. Georgian Gertrude Thomas, worried sick about money in 1888, wrote, "I sent Malinda my cook to buy a 10 cts beef steak. (I never give more for one.)"[12] Thomas, whose employees came and went frequently, delineated the type of food to be bought and the frugal amount to be spent, but Malinda bought the meat, brought it safely to the Thomas house, and presumably cooked it. The Thomases' financial woes constricted both women: Malinda in the limits on her work materials and, hence, the quality of her finished product, and Thomas in her family's overall food supply.

Anne Robertson, who grew up in the lower South, remembered a woman named Mae who worked in her family's home from the late 1940s until the 1970s. Mae did everything at the house except yard work: "Cooked a hot meal every day. Went to the store, got the groceries, came back and cooked." Robertson's mother never learned to drive, and perhaps she ceded the authority of shopping to Mae in return for not having to assume any responsibility or to venture outside the house.[13] Whether Mae regarded her ventures to the store as a privilege or a chore is unknown. Shopping certainly became yet another responsibility in a day likely already brimming with activity.

Cooks of long standing might exercise considerable latitude in selecting food for their employers. Emma Jane Christian worked for the same family for more than fifty years in Williamsburg, and she expressed definite preferences for acquiring food, an indication that her employer gave her significant say-so in purchases. In the 1930s, Christian admonished the readers of her cookbook with regard to purchasing turkeys (as transcribed by her employer): "To begin wid, don't you go to no *sto'* to buy yo' tucky no time! Thanksgivin', Christmus, buffdays, or *no* time! Fur *dey* isn't fitten to et!" Rather, Christian preferred to buy turkeys live and have them dressed locally.[14] She revealed similar strength of opinion in discussing Smithfield ham, the much-prized Virginia product: "But when I wants somethin' good an' tasty, jes somethin' dat fair melts in yo' mouth when it's cooked right, I goes to de store and I won't have nothin' else—de 'Boss' Ham, I calls 'em."[15]

Some white women, entering the paid workforce in the 1940s, depended on their cooks to have dinner on the table when they got home. In Mobile in the 1940s, a cook named Rosa took the initiative to prepare dinner for the Campbell family. Leigh Campbell, a young mother, was out of the house and gave no thought to the family's evening meal. "I probably had no idea what I was going to have for supper when we got home," she recalled. "We'd come in that house, and Rosa in that kitchen had made . . . [ellipses in original]. She'd gone to the store, walked up there, gotten turnip greens and maybe fixed turnip greens and cornbread, black-eyed peas, or sweet potatoes. She would pay for it out of her money. She knew I had to feed the family. She knew when we came back, she'd get her money."[16] Rosa walked to the store and bought common, stout southern food for her employers. During World War II, Willie Mae Wright worked for a couple employed at a bomber plant outside of Atlanta. She remembered: "I'd go out and cook supper for them, and sometimes I'd go to Buckhead in a cab and buy all the groceries. Sometimes I'd buy two fryers and I'd make rolls."[17]

In the segregated South, trips to the store could be fraught with tension. First, the store itself could be the site of much conflict. Maya Angelou recalled going to the butcher shop in Stamps, Arkansas, in the 1930s. White people were served first, even if the butcher were in the middle of an order for an African American customer. Next came the domestic workers buying for their employers: "In fact, a black maid or cook would be served before us, because her order was intended for white people." And last came the African Americans buying for themselves. While some domestic employees might have enjoyed the privilege of stepping to the head of the line, for others it must have felt awkward to be rude to one's peers on behalf of one's employer.[18] The self-service grocery store, pioneered by Piggly Wiggly in Memphis in 1916, often proved more comfortable for domestic workers. One entered through a turnstile, picked up a basket, selected one's own merchandise without assistance or interference from a grocery store employee, and queued up to pay. A 1925 ad touted the egalitarian nature of Piggly Wiggly: "Just one kind of a store for every kind of people, where the high and the low, the rich and the poor, all meet and are accorded the same kind, courteous treatment. Here you see with your own eyes and select with your own hands the food you buy without interruption from anyone."[19] By the 1940s, self-service grocery stores treated their customers with courtesy and equality, for the most part, but at the meat counter, sociologist Charles S. Johnson observed, "personal contacts are unavoidable" and caused African Americans "most embarrassment."[20] And the chance always existed that the employer might disapprove of the employee's selections of food.

COOKS AND EMPLOYERS CONTESTED the control of the work space. The space, however, was in the employer's home, and the employer arranged for its furnishings. Employers provided their cooks with work facilities of varying degrees of adequacy. Although the detached kitchen had mostly disappeared in the urban South, an unnamed Atlanta University sociologist wrote in 1908, its replacement "has gradually fastened itself to the house again, but with an unobtrusive, apologetic air. It sticks to an out-of-the-way corner, and is usually altogether too small for its purpose. I have seen kitchens, in the homes of well-to-do people, as small as eight or ten feet square, or about the size of my grandmother's pantry."[21] Employers had no vested interest in creating nice work space for hired workers.

Employers also provided the tools with which the cooks did their work, and the technology to which a cook had access shifted dramatically from location to location. The layout of the kitchen, the quality of the cooking utensils, the presence or lack of running water (hot or cold), and the availability of appliances such as refrigeration units and stoves all made huge differences in the relative ease or difficulty of a workday. Most cooks had to make do with what they found with each new employment, in particular learning a new stove every time they began with a different employer, and not infrequently creating conflict between employer and employee. In the 1870s, Jennie Akehurst Lines remained vexed with her cook Caroline, who "either can not or will not manage the stove so that the oven will bake." Lines believed that Caroline's inability to operate the oven resulted either from lack of intelligence ("can not") or from sheer willfulness ("will not").[22] One white woman in Reconstruction Mississippi had a stove that she would not permit her cook to use, rather consigning her to continue open-hearth cooking. She feared that the cook would break the stove and then leave, and she would end up with neither stove nor cook.[23]

By the end of the nineteenth century, most urban homes had stoves rather than open hearths for cooking. As historian Tera Hunter has pointed out, cast-iron stoves lacked thermostats and "forced cooks to gauge the level of heat through trial and error—arranging dampers and drafts or placing food in strategic spots according to estimates of the time and degree of heat required."[24] Many families used woodstoves well into the twentieth century, but gasoline or kerosene might also be the fuel of choice. While the shift to kerosene or gas did away with the need to keep the stove stoked with wood, cooking with different fuels required much relearning. A *Dallas Morning News* article in 1911, intended to be humorous, satirized "Aunt Emmy's" indignation at being presented with an oil stove. The white writer parodied the cook's indignation: "Disheah stove, hit ain' no good. No'm. How's I gwine git hit up t' fryin' heat? Cyan fry nuffin' on er stove lak dat."[25] The newspaper writer may have found the cook's lack of progressivism amusing, but a cook's concern would be real, for her employer's decision to change her tools without consulting her threatened her very livelihood. On the other hand, some employers refused to update cooking technology, forcing their employees to use outdated or even unsafe appliances and utensils. Stoves could be extremely dangerous; numerous newspaper accounts told of "negresses" badly burned by fires in their employers' kitchens. A 1906 article, for example, described a fire in the Dallas home of the Townsend family in which a can of coal oil exploded, drenching Olive Smith, the cook. The writer was mostly concerned about the burns to Mr. Townsend and a family friend, who quenched the flames with rugs and blankets. Smith, the writer mentioned casually, was in the City Hospital in critical condition.[26]

Commercially made ice became available throughout the South in the 1880s, but the distribution of ice boxes and, after the 1920s, refrigerators, varied widely from employer to employer. A cook whose employer had regular ice delivery had less trouble keeping perishable items, and refrigeration meant that grocery purchases could be spaced further apart.[27] Dishes that benefited from chilling, such as whipped cream, would be accomplished much more readily with refrigeration. Running water, electricity, and municipal waste disposal also spread unevenly throughout urban homes. A number of Texas cities installed electric plants in the 1880s, but it is virtually impossible to tell when individual private homes hooked into the delivery systems.[28] If the employer's home did not have running water, the cook could spend much time and energy bringing in water from the pump or well.

RAW INGREDIENTS AND THE cooking process join to form the finished product of a meal. A chicken, for example, may be young or old, tender or tough, and it may be baked simply or dressed with an elaborate cream sauce requiring many ingredients and much time and expertise. African American cooks in the South employed a wide variety of ingredients and an impressive range of techniques to do their work. Many of the meals that they cooked were workaday affairs, rarely noted in any cookbook. But cook they did: baked goods, meats, vegetables, and sweets, two or three meals a day, six or seven days a week.

The discovery of what cooks actually prepared is something of a detective story. Cookbooks tend to present idealized meals, prescriptive rather than descriptive of how ordinary people eat on an ordinary day, and must only be used as historical evidence with caution. Dozens of cookbooks published in or about the South since the Civil War, however, include recipes attributed to "Mammy," "Maum," or "Aunt," and one may infer that the recipes attributed to these women are things that they actually cooked regularly. Grocers' records from Macon, Georgia, include a large number from families who definitely were sufficiently wealthy to employ domestic workers. The following analysis comes largely from those two types of sources—cookbooks and merchants' records—as well as from newspaper ads from Tyler, a prosperous midsized town in East Texas.[29]

African influence on American cooking appeared early in such foods as black-eyed peas, okra, peanuts, sweet potatoes, sesame seeds, millet, sorghum, and watermelon.[30] By the nineteenth century, the African influence was firmly established in southern cookery. But cooks in the most well-to-do households learned other traditions as well: eastern and central European if they were working for a Jewish family, French if their employers expected haute cuisine.[31] Whether by choice or necessity, many cooks expanded their repertoires far beyond their ancestral roots.

Almost all Americans and Europeans classify foods into a handful of categories. Each type of food has its special characteristics, and a successful cook in a southern household had to be familiar with a broad range of foods. Looking at the specific foods that southern cooks worked with, and the meals that they produced, explains a great deal about how they spent their days in the kitchen.

Grain, often baked into loaves of some type, forms the basis of most human diets.[32] In the American South of the late nineteenth and early twentieth centuries, corn was the most common grain, followed by wheat. Quick breads, made without yeast and requiring no kneading or rising time, comprised a significant part of the domestic cook's repertoire. A plethora of recipes for quick breads made with cornmeal, as well as the quantity of cornmeal purchased by Macon housewives, attest to cornbread's ongoing popularity across the South and across time.[33] The plainest cornbreads consisted merely of cornmeal mixed with water and baked on a flat surface. As other ingredients were available, cooks refined their recipes to include eggs, whole milk (also known as sweet milk) or buttermilk, salt, sugar, and butter or bacon grease, according to taste and regional practice. Through the late nineteenth and early twentieth centuries, cookbook writers lauded "Mammy" from Texas, "Aunt Anne" from Baltimore, "Aunt Clarissy" from Maryland, "Aunt Dilsey" from Richmond, and "Mam Jude" from New Orleans for their cornmeal flatbreads, variously called ash cakes, hoecakes, corn dodgers, or corn slappers.[34] As late as 1937, Emma Jane Christian was cooking cornmeal pone and ash cake in Williamsburg, Virginia.[35]

Salt-rising bread, an early variation of cornbread, predated the use of chemical leavens, beginning with a starter of cornmeal, yeast or potato leaven, salt, and sugar. The starter could be used repeatedly, added to a batter containing some variation of cornmeal, flour, and lard or, later, shortening. In the late nineteenth and early twentieth centuries, "Mammy," from Clarksville, Tennessee, "Aunt Martha," and "Carrie" from New Orleans all excelled at this tricky product, which required careful, continued attention to the starter as well as to the bread.[36]

More typically, cornbread was leavened with baking soda and sour milk or, beginning around 1880, with commercial baking powder. Cornbread changed by region and by taste, with variables such as the use of white or yellow cornmeal, the proportion of wheat flour to cornmeal, and the amount of sugar making notably different products. "Aunt Anne" of Baltimore had recipes for at least two versions of leavened cornbread in addition to unleavened flatbread. For her "Delicious Corn-Bread" "Aunt Anne" used white cornmeal and added boiled hominy.[37] In Virginia, Caroline Pickett used a cornucopia of ingredients to make her cornbread: cornmeal, flour, baking powder, sugar, salt, egg, milk, water, and bacon fat.[38] These cooks made creative use of common ingredients at hand to develop cornbread recipes that their employers found noteworthy. Even leftover cornbread could be made useful. In New Orleans, "Mammy" made "cush": cornbread made without egg, scrambled and seasoned with butter and a generous amount of black pepper, and eaten with a spoon.[39]

Among the most highly prized southern quick breads were biscuits (sometimes referred to in the singular), made common by the increasing availability of wheat flour and the growing reliability of baking powder in the second half of the nineteenth century. Baking powder, a combination of baking soda and cream of tartar, became widespread only after the Civil War. The quality of the unstable compounds varied greatly, and several brands battled fiercely for customer loyalty. An 1888 cookbook published by an Episcopalian church in Texas featured ads for three brands of baking powder, along with baking soda, from large national companies such as Arm and Hammer.[40] While some merchants made their own compounds locally, by far the most popular brand was Royal Baking Powder, made in New York and available nationwide by the 1890s.[41]

Across the South, from Maryland to Mississippi, Florida to Kentucky, southerners recorded biscuit recipes attributed to "Aunt Sophie," "Aunt Liza," "Aunt Betsey," "Aunt Martha," and Idella Parker.[42] Each of these recipes was a variation on a theme: refined white wheat flour, fat (lard or butter), buttermilk, and baking soda, mixed, rolled, and cut. The beaten biscuit, which relied on repeated manipulation of the dough to introduce air into the layers, was a labor-intensive curiosity by the end of the nineteenth century, much extolled but little seen. Freedwomen, in fact, actively protested at making

The Food {41}

beaten biscuits. Cookbook writer Mary Stuart Harrison Smith complained in 1885, "Most servants object nowadays to the trouble of preparing this bread."[43] In the right hands, biscuits could become delicacies. Dori Sanders's aunt Vestula, for example, made sconelike lemon biscuits, lively with fresh lemon juice, lemon rind, and heavy cream.[44]

Wheat flour formed the basis of very popular cakes cooked on a griddle, known variously as battercakes, flannel cakes, or pancakes. These were the specialties of "Mam Jude" of New Orleans, "Aunt Kitty" of Petersburg, Virginia, "Aunt Tresa" of an unknown location, and "Aunt Sue" from South Carolina.[45] In Tennessee and Louisiana, "Mammy" and "Aunt Ellen" made prized waffles.[46] Most of these breads were produced and consumed at breakfast. Without yeast, they rose quickly; being thin, they cooked almost instantly and provided a fast start to the day.

By far the greatest test, and the greatest headache, of any cook and any employer was bread made with wheat flour and leavened with yeast. No topic occasioned greater discussion by cookbook writers in the last quarter of the nineteenth century. Cookbook writer Mrs. M. E. Porter, of Prince George Court-House, Virginia, in 1871 lectured her readers about the importance of bread: "As there is no one article of food that enters so largely into our daily fare as bread, so no degree of skill in preparing other articles can compensate for lack of knowledge in the art of making good, palatable and nutritious bread."[47]

Producing good bread can be an extremely difficult process. It requires high-quality flour, dependable yeast (which is a delicate living microorganism) to make it rise, a complex cycle of kneading and rising that takes several hours, and accurate baking. Making yeast bread challenged even accomplished cooks. Longtime cook Emma Jane Christian observed in the 1930s, "Some folks may think 'taint nothin' much to de makin' of bread. Dey says it's easy—but to my mine sometimes de shortes' road is de steepes' road too, to clime."[48]

As an unnamed writer from Anniston, Alabama, noted, successful bread making depended upon "good flour, good yeast, and watchful care."[49] Like baking powder, yeast production stabilized after the Civil War, and the Fleischmann's company of Cincinnati began selling standardized yeast cakes in 1868. In the 1880s, Fleischmann's marketed its product to housewives by using the figure of a stout female African American cook expressing a strong preference for its yeast.[50] The Fleischmann's company expected to find a market for its product in the South.

Until the 1880s, a cook had to check and recheck the condition of her wheat flour. Cookbook writer Marion Cabell Tyree announced in 1877 that all flour should be sunned and aired before use. If a cook tried a barrel of flour twice and the results were wet and sticky, "you had better then return it to your grocer."[51] By the 1880s, the quality of wheat flour also had become more dependable, with keen competition and endless possibilities for locally milled and nationally distributed products. Nationally marketed brands included Obelisk from Louisville, Patapsco from Baltimore, Lea's from Wilmington, and Arbitrator from Missouri.[52] Local mills stood fast amid the national competition, with products like "Belle of Bonham" flour from North Texas. The H. Y. McCord Company in Atlanta shamelessly marketed snob appeal in its humble product: "You get good, nutritious bread and pastry that you will not be ashamed to offer to the most fastidious. Our patrons are the Best People in Atlanta. We refer to them."[53] By the 1930s, Minnesota-based milling giant Pillsbury had penetrated the market in the South, particularly in chain groceries such as A&P. Yet regional mills like Burrus in Fort Worth continued marketing their products on popular radio shows well into the 1940s.[54]

African American cooks proved adept at modifying recipes to suit the local climate, available ingredients, and other circumstances. The unnamed Anniston, Alabama, housekeeper in 1893 determined to have successful bread making in her home. She studied the instructions given by novelist and domestic maven Mary Virginia Terhune (writing as Marion Harland) in her 1873 *Common Sense in the Household: A Manual of Practical Housewifery* and explained the process to her cook, "Aunt Elsie." "Aunt Elsie" then improved upon Terhune's instructions: "'Aunt Elsie,' however, flours the jar well and puts a generous coat of flour on top of dough, to keep it warm. . . . My same model housekeeper taught me to draw up a quantity of the dough with my hand, and when a very light honey-comb it is ready to mold for the pans." The housewife had the book, but it was the African American "model housekeeper" who modified and translated the instructions into hot, fragrant loaves, then instructed her employer on proper technique.[55] Nancy White, who cooked in Tennessee, had a similar experience about the time of World War I. After going by her employer's new book and producing several failures, White decided to try the recipe on her own. She took the recipe to her own house, away from her employer's anxious supervision:

> Now, I went home and made this dern bread and it came out right. The book was wrong! To make that bread with what we had, you just had to do other things and you had to know something about bread. Now, the Frenchman might be right in France — maybe they have different kinds of

flour—but it didn't make any sense to just keep on making this bread just like the book said if the bread didn't come out right. Now, I knew I did what that Frenchman said I should do and if I did that right and it came out wrong, then the Frenchman and not me had to be wrong. Now, am I right or wrong?[56]

White demonstrated knowledge of technique and ingredients, considerable culinary skill, and the ability to transfer that skill from one recipe to another. She used her own time and space, not her employer's, however, to conduct her successful experiment. Her refinement of the written recipe was not done on her employer's nickel.

Bread baking became one of the first household cooking processes to be outsourced. In the South, commercial bakeries began advertising their product as early as 1880, when the City Bakery in Tyler, Texas, offered "Nice fresh light rolls and bread . . . every evening and morning."[57] Realizing that a product made by women might retain some of its homemade appeal, women's exchanges began selling bread to beleaguered housewives by 1895, and in 1901 the Knoxville Women's Exchange presented "fresh bread" among its wares, observing, "This is the place for Housekeepers to get what they need and save trouble."[58] Picky housewives were willing to pay for a premium product. Cleora Butler, who helped deliver her mother's bread in a five-block area around their house in Muskogee, Oklahoma, around 1910, recalled that her mother's bread sold for twenty-five cents a loaf when store-bought bread cost a nickel a loaf.[59] Advertisers for commercial bakeries also played on familiar ties in naming their products. The Walter C. Michael & Co. of Roanoke, Virginia, in 1907 advertised "Our Mother's Bread 5 Cents everywhere."[60] In the middle of the Great Depression, the A&P in Tyler, Texas, touted "Grandmother's Sliced Bread, 7c/loaf."[61]

At least some Georgia families continued to eat homemade yeast bread at the turn of the twentieth century. In 1893, Jeannette Wachtel no longer had a live-in cook, but she bought yeast nonetheless, meaning that someone at the Wachtel house—most likely an African American cook—was going to make yeast bread.[62] When Sally Thomas worked for Claudia Ross in 1900, her tasks may well have included baking bread, for Ross's grocery store purchases also included yeast.[63]

A cook had to leave her bed early if she worked in a household that expected fresh homemade yeast bread for breakfast or midday dinner. In the 1880s, Mary Harrison Stuart Smith referred to the cook's "light bread dough" being in production "first thing in the morning."[64] In the sophisticated kitchen of Maymont, around the turn of the twentieth century, the cooks baked bread on Mondays, Wednesdays, and Saturdays, despite the presence of numerous commercial bakeries in Richmond. The cooks arose around four A.M. to have hot yeast rolls and bread ready for the midday meal.[65]

Cooks continued to make yeast rolls well into the 1940s, when cookbook author Marion Flexner jettisoned all of her other roll recipes in favor of those made by "Ollie, our substitute cook," and Ethel Farmer Hunter published the recipe for "Sara's Rolls (My Atlanta maid)." "Ollie's Ice Box Super Rolls" used modern technology to its best effect, resulting in a dough that would keep in "the electric refrigerator" for several weeks.[66] Ollie knew how to make an old-fashioned product with atomic age tools.

The largest space in any general cookbook is filled with recipes for sweets. Rather than revealing an exceptionally active regional sweet tooth, the recipes often explain complicated formulas that will tolerate little room for error. As with breads, the proportions of ingredients in most baked goods have to be precise so that intricate chemical reactions can occur. Cooks who were expected to prepare desserts had to pay close attention to mixing as well as baking.

Like bread bakers, dessert makers benefited from standardization of ingredients in the late nineteenth century. Sugar, which came in various forms, was available as fine granules, but the quality of its refinement could be undependable.[67] The same unnamed cookbook writer from Anniston who called in the authority of Virginia Terhune/Marion Harland for bread also used Terhune to buttress her stipulation for good sugar: "In making cake, use the best materials. Says Marion Harland, 'If you cannot afford to get good flour, dry white sugar, and the best family butter, make up your mind to go without cake, and eat bread and butter with a clear conscience.'"[68] Harland made her caveat a matter of economic status, but inferior sugar was obviously a threat to the integrity of baked goods, and a cook with lumpy or coarse sugar would have difficulty making elegant sweets.

Southern households obtained flavorings for baking from a variety of sources. Local drugstores made lemon, vanilla, orange, and bitter almond extracts. At the national level, C. F. Sauer, of Richmond, actively competed with Burnett's, a Boston Company begun in 1847, which marketed its products across the South by the 1890s.[69] The chocolate juggernaut Walter Baker and Company, founded in the 1760s in Massachusetts, advertised its products widely throughout the South by the 1890s.[70] By the 1880s, Texas housewives could easily find "pure spices" and "cocoa extract" in their local stores.[71] In the 1890s, Macon housewives bought salt, pepper, cloves, nutmeg, mace, cinnamon, and citron. A cook whose employer had the financial wherewithal to purchase high-quality and imaginative ingredients had literally a world of goods at her command.

Among the simplest sweets were puddings, which were often a way of using leftover foods. "Maum Maria" in South Carolina used raw rice for her rice pudding and "Mam Jude" in Louisiana used cooked grains, but both women enhanced the rice with butter, milk, sugar, and cinnamon, vanilla, or nutmeg.[72] In New Orleans, cooks concocted the city's signature dish of bread pudding from leftover bread; "Mam Jude" created a sauce for it by slowly beating a mixture of butter, flour, boiling water, brown sugar, vanilla, and salt.[73] In Virginia, Caroline Pickett made puddings of grated sweet potatoes.[74]

While cookies were also relatively easy to make, cooks enlivened plain recipes with imported ingredients. "Aunt Fanny" scorned cookies that were dropped rather than rolled, according to Marion Flexner, observing that "[d]ey don' tek no skill a-tall effen you got a good receipt."[75] She spiced her simple cookies with lemon juice and chopped pecans or walnuts. "Aunt Fanny" also used cinnamon and pecans or almonds in her brown sugar cookies, which she declared to be "a real old time receipt from 'way back,'" made for the white children on the plantation.[76] In Augusta, Georgia, "Aunt Betsey" flavored rolled cookies with nutmeg.[77] And "Aunt Sug" of Virginia made a nut cookie with a base of English walnuts or almonds, augmented with cinnamon, raisins, and currants.[78]

"Black Katherine," who cooked for photographer Antoinette Hervey in 1912, demonstrated her outstanding baking ability in her "marvelously crispy, melty, luscious cookies." Hervey coaxed from her an imprecise recipe, calling for indefinite amounts of butter, sugar, and seasonings. Katherine's greatest talent showed in making the recipe flexible enough to be usable in flush times or lean. She described part of the process to Hervey, who transcribed the result in dialect: "Then comes aigs. Ef they's cheap, I takes four. Ef I feels a leetle close, I takes three. Ef they's dear, I takes two. One'll do rat well. An ef they's very dear, I discharge aigs and don't use no aigs at all." Katherine knew her product well enough to adapt the recipe for the presence or absence of eggs without affecting the quality of the finished cookie.[79]

African American cooks baked pies of all sorts, and their fillings are documented better than their crusts. The most popular pie attributed to African American cooks is lemon, indicating widespread availability of the tart tropical fruit. Katie Leverett, who cooked for the E. W. Heist family in South Jacksonville, Florida, in the 1940s made a lemon pie dubbed "Divine." New Orleans cook "Cally's" recipe required both lemon juice and rind; grating rind without a special tool would have been both time-consuming and tedious.[80] Other pie makers used ingredients from closer to home, such as peaches or sweet potatoes.[81] A creative cook could fancy up humble pumpkin or the southern squash known as cushaw. Missy of New Orleans made her "punkin" pie with cinnamon, nutmeg, ginger, lemon extract, lemon juice, and lemon rind, and the result, according to cookbook writer Betty Benton Patterson, "was always a prize winner in any contest."[82] Patterson also documented the considerable culinary skill of Ozite, whose nut pies (a crust of pecans or walnuts, covered with sweetened whipped cream flavored with sherry) and petite tarts (whole strawberries boiled with sugar, mounded in tart shells, and served with "very thick cream") would do any table proud.[83]

The New Orleans woman known as "Mam Jude" mastered the extremely difficult art of puff pastry, a tricky combination of flour, butter, and air, chilled, turned, and folded numerous times to create a series of flaky layers. She kept the pastry chilled in the "icebox," and on short notice she could produce the dishes that she called "Volleys," a shortened version of the French term "vol-au-vent." Vols-au-vent, a classic French dish, could be sweet or savory. "Mam Jude" filled hers with jams or jellied custards for quick desserts made possible by painstaking preparation ahead of time.[84]

Dense, dark fruitcakes remained a seasonal specialty. Originally popular because they preserved well, fruitcakes were extremely time-consuming to prepare, with extensive chopping of numerous ingredients, and difficult to mix, with a thick, heavy batter. Emma Jane Christian warned that a fruit-cake maker would have "some powful [sic] arm beatin' to do" in the absence of an electric mixer.[85] Nonetheless, each fall, cooks like Eliza Lee of Charleston gathered a store of dried fruits such as currants, raisins, and figs; nuts, including Brazil nuts; and flavorings such as citron, mace, cloves, nutmeg, allspice, cinnamon, rose water, and lemon and orange peel. They chopped the sticky dried fruits and nuts, then bound the ingredients with a batter and baked the cake for a long while. The cook preserved the cake by pouring liquor (often brandy) over it, ensuring that it would keep for weeks or months.[86] A New Orleans cook portrayed as "Mammy Lou" used similar ingredients in her steamed suet pudding, a recipe reminiscent of traditional English puddings with raisins, currants, suet, brown sugar, bread crumbs, citron, blanched almonds, nutmeg, cinnamon, allspice, cloves, cayenne pepper, salt, flour, sherry and brandy, vinegar, soda, eggs, and thick sweet cream, all steamed for six to eight hours.[87]

Like pies, cakes ranged from simple to elaborate. In the late nineteenth century, an unnamed African American woman took great pride in producing "light, rich" loaf cakes and declared her scorn for modern layer cakes, which she called "batty cakes." Her employer, Mary Hunt Affleck of Texas, recorded the alleged instructions by the skilled cook: "Any fool niggah can make dem!'" This particular cook expected her employer to supply her with high-quality ingredients, saying, "You gimme plenty aigs, cream, flour, butter an' sugar," but she then asserted her authority, requesting, "'An' den go 'way fum here twel I calls you.'"[88] In the 1920s, "Chloe" of New Orleans made "Skillet Cake," similar to today's pineapple upside-down cake, with canned pineapple rings and batter cooked in an iron skillet.[89] While "Lucy," also from the Crescent City, spread her jam cake with blackberry jam rather than icing, the cake itself contained four spices as well as pecans.[90] Several cooks, however, acknowledged the difficulty of making fancy cakes, particularly before the use of mechanical egg beaters or electric mixers. Possibly the most difficult was angel food, consisting mostly of egg whites and air. Betty Benton Patterson remembered that "little Mammy" made "a grand angel cake" using twelve egg whites, whipped with "peeled and scrubbed peach switches" without the benefit of a wire whisk, egg beater, or electric mixer.[91] Emma Jane Christian downplayed her baking ability, nicknaming the common one-two-three-four cake (one cup butter, two cups sugar, three cups flour, one cup milk, and four eggs) the "Fool-Nigger-Proof Cake." Despite the recipe's touted simplicity, Christian emphasized the need to beat the egg whites and yolks separately, and when mixing the batter, "not bein' sparin' wid de el-bow grease, none whatsomeever."[92] Cooks also turned out extravagant creations, such as a three-layer velvet sponge cake or "Aunt Judy's Favorite" from Abingdon, Virginia, a concoction of "rich white cake" baked in four layers, with white icing, filled first with a layer of walnuts, raisins, and chocolate, then one of citron and chopped almonds, and finally a layer of coconut and orange.[93]

ONE ELEMENT OF URBAN Americans' diets that underwent significant alteration in the late nineteenth century was meat. Prior to that time, the majority of southerners ate mostly preserved pork and, occasionally, chicken. Technological change, particularly refrigeration, made it possible for consumers across the South to have increased access to beef, fish, and even shellfish. As with other products, southern buyers faced the choice of locally butchered and preserved meats and an ever-increasing supply of national brands.[94]

Pork, particularly of the cured variety, still played an important role in the southern diet in the late nineteenth and early twentieth centuries even as local producers faced escalating competition from national meatpacking companies. While hog-killing remained common in the rural South until World War II, most urban families bought their pork in serving portions rather than attempting to butcher it at home. In the 1890s, almost all of the well-to-do matrons who patronized Catherine King's Meat Market in Macon bought some pork. Their purchases included prepared pork in the form of sausage, a gelled loaf called souse (also known as headcheese), numerous hams, and large amounts of lard, which could be used for everything from frying to making piecrust.[95] Often the grocers simply wrote on the tally, "pork," which might have been fresh pork, or "meat," which may have been the ubiquitous fat pork that composed part of the diet of "meat and meal" for rural southerners.

Advertisements, too, indicated the continuing significance of pork in the southern diet and the ferocious competition for customers' loyalty. In 1880, the *Tyler National Index* touted the virtues of locally made "'star' sugar cured hams of this winters cure."[96] National meatpackers had other ideas, however. At the end of the decade, the Indianapolis-based Kingan and Company advertised its wares in Texas as the makers of "Circle K brand sugar cured meats: hams, breakfast bacon, cottage hams, California hams, spiced rolled shoulders," and three different grades of lard.[97] In 1894, Kingan announced in Richmond its "Virginia Hams" in addition to "Breakfast Bacon" and lard.[98] Chicago-based Armour and Company extolled its ham and other pork products in Maryland and Alabama.[99] Locally cured meats remained popular through the 1920s, however, when an Abingdon, Virginia, produce company publicized "country cured meats." And in Tyler, Texas, the City Meat Market advertised its wares as "both native and Fort Worth," likely referring to the presence of national giants Swift and Armour in the larger city,[100] even as Jacob E. Decker and Sons, based in Mason City, Iowa, advertised "Iowa's finest corn-fed porkers" in the same newspaper.[101]

Pork was such a commonplace in southern cooking that few cookbooks needed to explain its uses. Only a rare cookbook compiler recorded such savory dishes as "Aunt Delia's" ham and eggs, which consisted only of fried ham, fried eggs, and gravy.[102] Kentuckian Robert J. Breckinridge recorded a number of "Aunt Liza's" recipes, including her formula for Kentucky hog jowl and dandelion greens.[103] An "old Creole cook on Bayou La Fourche" cooked *cochon de lait rienza*, or suckling pig, "in a manner worthy of high-days and feast-days," according to Betty Benton Patterson. The cook rubbed a whole pig with pepper, thyme, celery leaves, bay leaf, salt, garlic, and butter, roasted it, and glazed it with brown sugar.[104] Idella Parker indicated the importance of a well-cooked ham, talking about ham fixed "the Cross Creek way": boiled in water, wine, and brown sugar and glazed with honey and more brown sugar and wine.[105] There was always a ham in the icebox at Cross Creek, said Parker, and "toward the end of the ham" she made ham croquettes, served with tiny okra and Hollandaise sauce.[106]

In her aptly titled 2006 study *Building Houses Out of Chicken Legs: Black Women, Food, and Power*, Psyche Williams-Forson details the complicated relationships of African American women and chicken. The cover illustration, a Snowdrift shortening ad from the mid-1920s, depicts a half-smiling African American woman wielding a large butcher knife in her right hand and grasping two chicken legs in her left. The message to observers, clearly unintended by the advertisers, is one of barely concealed violence. One false move, the cook seems to be saying, and it will be you and not the chicken.[107]

Poultry played a large role in the southern diet, and African American women were well acquainted with chickens, from egg to carcass. Indeed, poultry was so commonplace in the southern urban home that it frequently went unremarked. A substantial number of southern urban families kept chickens at their homes. In Macon, for example, affluent matrons bought large quantities of live chicks from their grocers. As the chicks matured, they would provide, first, eggs and, later, meat. Many women also supplemented their hens' production by buying eggs.[108]

Keeping poultry on the home property required knowledge and labor that extended well past the frying pan. The birds had to be fed, their nesting areas cleaned, and eggs collected once or twice a day. In South Carolina, "Chloe" helped her employer, Elizabeth Pringle, hatch dozens and dozens of chicks in an incubator, then cared fastidiously for the chicks until the days that each of them became dinner.[109] Living on a remote rice plantation, Pringle lacked easy access to food markets, and having her own chickens provided ready sources of meat and eggs.

Knowing how to slaughter and dress a chicken would have been a basic part of any cook's skill set through the first quarter of the twentieth century. Killing a bird could mean wringing its neck or chopping its head off, neither a pleasant prospect. In Florida, Martha Mickens worked alongside her employer, Marjorie Kinnan Rawlings, to kill chickens. Rawlings wrote that she and Mickens "ran chickens until we dropped from exhaustion, and never touched a feather" and ended up shooting the birds with a .22 rifle.[110] Mickens expended a great deal of energy for her employer's mealtime poultry.[111]

It was not unusual for a chicken that was alive at daybreak to be killed, decapitated, eviscerated, defeathered, cut into serving portions, cooked, and served at the noontime meal. Requiring the use of sharp knives and other cutting instruments, chicken preparation was not a job for the timid or squeamish. Tellingly, a cousin of Williams-Forson "explicitly refused to cook chicken in her capacity as a domestic worker because she said it was 'too much handling.'"[112] Most domestic cooks, however, could not escape working with dead poultry, for their employers plainly expected it. Employer Magnolia Le Guin wrote in 1902: "Yesterday I had Edna (a negro woman, who lived with Papa this year and one whom Ghu has hired for the coming year) to cook dinner for me. . . . Edna dressed a rooster for me and today we put on a company cloth and a vase of lovely roses and had a little Thanksgiving dinner."[113] Le Guin's image of the nice tablecloth and flowers betrays little of the work that Edna did in plucking and gutting a lifeless rooster. Idella Parker recalled that her employer, Marjorie Rawlings, killed ducks, and coworker Martha Mickens had to teach Parker to pick them. It took Parker hours to pick the first one, pulling the big feathers and singeing the tiny pin feathers, and Rawlings had to have sandwiches and milk for dinner. Parker recalled, "Mrs. Rawlings was outdone. 'Idella, I thought all you people knew how to pick ducks and chickens.'"[114] While Rawlings could have logically expected a cook to know how to prepare a chicken, her equation of "you people" with the task of picking fowl clearly indicates the racialization of poultry preparation that Williams-Forson so skillfully points out.

During the early twentieth century, commercial poultry supply varied. In 1898, prosperous Atlantans could buy "dressed poultry" and leave the mess of killing and plucking and gutting to people outside the home.[115] By the 1930s, consumers had grown sufficiently suspicious of commercial poultry that Texas grocers were buying chickens from local farms and advertising "home killed and fully dressed" hens.[116] In some areas of the South, however, the chicken yard near the house remained a fixture until at least the 1960s, and the skills of preparing a live chicken remained necessary. A chicken on the dinner table could come from one's own property or from a packinghouse far away.

The sine qua non of southern cooking has long been fried chicken.[117] Properly prepared fried chicken requires skill from the preparation of the raw meat, through the battering, through the frying to bring about the right type of crust—which varies with a family's taste, crispy or soft, spicy or not—on meat that is cooked through but not dry. Willie Mae Wright proudly remembered the meal she fixed in Washington, D.C., for the Woodson family and their guests in the spring of 1945: fifteen or sixteen fried chickens, hot light rolls, tomato aspic, pineapple salad in ring molds, and sweet lady peas.

The diners included Eleanor and Franklin Roosevelt, both of whom greeted Wright warmly.[118] To Wright's great credit, humble fried chicken was a suitable meal for a dying president and the First Lady.

While frying chicken might be as simple as battering the pieces of meat with some mixture of flour and liquid and placing them in a pan of hot grease, many cooks made the dish a production with multiple steps.[119] Women were noted more often for their fried chicken than perhaps for any other dish. Hattie Crumwell, longtime cook for the family of John J. McKay, in Macon, gave highly specific instructions for frying chicken. Chickens were to be killed and dressed the day before, salted, peppered, and left in the "ice box" overnight, then fried in shortening or lard in an iron skillet. In 1948, cookbook compilers placed a photo of Crumwell, a smiling African American woman with hair pulled back, wearing round wire-frame glasses, and a dark dress with a white collar and a pin at her throat, adjacent to the recipe and had Crumwell sign her recipe. It is a shaky signature with all lower-case letters. But it says, unmistakably, "hattie crumwell," as she laid claim to the recipe for which she was best known.[120]

A number of chicken dishes attributed to African American cooks were quite intricate, indicating advanced levels of culinary skill. An unnamed cook from Raleigh, North Carolina, a former employee of Mrs. J. Crawford Biggs, developed a "rich old recipe" that cookbook writer Marion Brown dubbed "Hardimont 'Creem' Chicken." The recipe, rich indeed, called for cooked chicken, cream, mushrooms, celery, green pepper, salt, and two sticks of butter.[121] The unnamed cook kept her original "receipts" in a little copy book, which she abandoned when she left the Biggses' employ. There are at least two troublesome aspects about this scenario: first, the question of why the cook developed a recipe book, only to leave it behind when she departed. Perhaps a rapid departure occurred. Perhaps the housewife demanded the recipe book. Perhaps the cook did not want to take a reminder with her, or she wanted the Biggs family to have the recipes. In any case, the cook did not take her intellectual property with her. Second, Brown chooses to retain the phonetic spelling of the recipe, making the cook appear primitive and possibly ignorant. Despite the mysterious circumstances of the recipe, the unnamed cook created a delicious chicken dish with heavy use of fine dairy products.[122]

Smothered chicken could be as simple as chicken in gravy, or a more elaborate recipe developed by a cook named Ellen White, with Jerusalem artichokes simmered with the chicken and fried mush served on the side.[123] One of Dori Sanders's aunt Vestula's favorite recipes was "bourbon-laced tipsy chicken with peaches": chicken leg quarters basted with orange juice and bourbon and topped with fresh peaches.[124] In Aunt Vestula's practiced hands, a common bird became flavorful with lively citrus juice, daring alcohol, and local seasonal produce.

Other poultry, both domestic and wild, also appeared on southern tables. Turkey was particularly popular at holiday times, but turkey husbandry and butchering seem to have been beyond the means of most city dwellers. Macon women occasionally bought turkeys, probably as live birds ready for slaughter, rather than trying to raise them in town. Emma Jane Christian recommended taking live turkey hens to Martha Webb, the wife of an African American grocer in Williamsburg, Virginia, for butchering: "[G]it a 'pendable pusson laike Sis Marty Webb (what knows her bizness) to kill, an' pick, an' plump dat lady, an' half yo' troubles is over!"[125] Webb made dealing with the large, fractious birds her specialty and spared the cooks and their employers big problems at holiday time.

Domestic fowl such as goose and duck materialized on southern tables mainly on special occasions. In Macon, the wives of Eastern European immigrants were the primary purchasers of geese and ducks, buying poultry familiar to them in their distant old homes, and the local grocers readily procured the birds for them.[126] Elsewhere, the recipes for their preparation reflected a sophistication commensurate with a fine holiday meal. The Louisiana cook known only as "Chloe" developed a delectable formula for "goose piquante" in the 1920s, marinating the goose in vinegar, peppercorns, bay leaf, cayenne pepper, and garlic, then adding onion and roasting it.[127] Katie Seabrook, cook to U.S. president William McKinley, created a refined recipe for roasting duck on a bed of bacon, carrots, leeks, bay leaves, and celery.[128]

Wild game, too, showed up mainly on special occasions. Peddlers brought quail to the houses of the wealthiest Maconites, whose cooks were expected to know how to prepare them as delicacies, often frying or braising them.[129] Frightened teenager Anna Mae Dickson faced a covey of raw quail, a food she had never encountered, for Sunday dinner for her employer's guests.[130] "Chloe," cooking for Elizabeth Pringle in South Carolina, prepared "English duck," partridge, snipe, wild turkey, and deer.[131] In the 1950s, Tulsan Cleora Butler prepared a game dinner for the family of Gifford C. Parker, including twelve pheasants, "a bevy" of quail, two wild ducks, and ten pigeonlike birds called chukars, all caught on the Parkers' game preserve.[132] No matter how unfamiliar the birds, cooks found ways to make meals from them.

By 1890, prosperous Georgians were eating significant amounts of beef, often purchasing steak, shanks, spareribs, brains, and roasts. In addition, Macon housewives bought preserved canned beef and corned beef.[133] African

American cooks' recipes for beef dishes tended to be plain. Caroline Pickett made ground beef or veal loaf.[134] Celeste Smith of New Orleans prepared calf's liver with veal, onion, bouillon, parsley, and macaroni, judging it as "a very vulgar dish, but a delicious one."[135] Ellen White, who was "brought up in James Madison's family," cooked the homely boiled French dish known as pot-au-feu, consisting of beef, carrots, leeks or onion, cabbage, garlic, celery, parsley, pepper, tomatoes, rice, and noodles.[136]

Southerners also depended on cows for fresh milk, cream, and butter. The quality of dairy products varied according to the season, the diet of the cow, and the skill of the person skimming the milk. A cook had to recognize the characteristics of the milk available to her and adjust her recipes accordingly. In 1885, cookbook author Mary Stuart Harrison Smith gave instructions for compensating for inferior milk in a recipe for a rich egg bread that called for unskimmed milk: "If your milk is thin and poor, add a dessert-spoonful of butter."[137]

Southern urban families kept cows in town well into the 1930s.[138] The daily responsibilities for milking the cows sometimes fell to the cooks, and they also churned butter.[139] Dori Sanders hated to milk because of the odor that lingered on her hands: "Lord knows, we had nothing in our house that could take that smell off your hands. You could use a little lilac dusting powder, or a drop of cheap perfume, but that was just a 'covering over' smell."[140] Many city housewives chose not to keep cows on their lots and purchased their dairy products. Store-bought butter became widely available as early as the 1880s.[141] Milk soon followed; by 1891, a dairyman in East Tyler, Texas, advertised that he would "deliver Pure Fresh Milk at your door every morning and evening."[142] By World War I, commercial dairies supplied many households.[143] Southern production of hard cheese was never large, but cheese consumption grew over time, becoming noticeable in the 1890s. During that decade, Macon housewives bought significant quantities of unspecified cheese, most likely a basic cheddar, while wealthy Richmond residents could buy imported cheeses (as well as olive oil and "queen olives").[144] By the 1920s, Chicago-based Kraft packaged cheeses were making their way into southern stores and onto southern tables.[145]

Southerners living in or near seaports or waterways had ready access to fresh fish, and oysters also appeared in abundance. "Chloe," Elizabeth Pringle's cook, baked or made soup from "cooter," as locals called freshwater turtles, and she also prepared the much-prized seasonal delicacy known as planked shad, in which fresh shad was baked on a wooden board.[146] Fresh saltwater fish and oysters also made their way inland, as early as 1888, which was made possible, almost surely, by refrigerated railroad cars.[147] In 1898, the L. J. Jones Market in Atlanta, 150 miles inland, advertised "Fish dressed and delivered to any portion of the city or orders amounting to 25 cents and upwards."[148]

In its most pedestrian forms, preserved fish appeared on everyday tables. Macon housewives frequently bought canned mackerel, salmon, and sardines, and codfish, probably dried and salted. At other times, even as early as the 1880s, fish and seafood became the rarest of delicacies. Agnes Hoge, the wife of a Macon pharmacist, once bought lobster. Hoge and other Macon housewives occasionally purchased shrimp, mostly likely brought in on ice on the railroad from Savannah.[149] Wealthy Tulsan Paul J. McIntyre frequently ordered delicacies from around the world for his family. In 1944, he had trout shipped overnight by train from a fishery in Denver, a feat that impressed cook Cleora Butler, who was used to preparing fine foods.[150]

Coastal cooks made elaborate feasts from the nearby salt waters. Recipes included fin fish, such as that from a Louisiana cook named Monica, who fried tautog, a saltwater fish found in the Atlantic, with butter and then stewed it in wine, salt, and pepper.[151] New Orleanian "Chloe" broiled flounder or redfish with a savory sauce of butter, garlic, lemon juice, horseradish, black pepper, salt, and commercially made Worcestershire and Tabasco sauces, both widely available by the late nineteenth century.[152] "Mam Jude" cooked fish en papillote—a refined technique made cozy by her using "pages torn from the children's composition books" in which to bake the fish rather than the traditional parchment.[153] She augmented the fish with a sauce made of sweet milk, fish jelly (a gelatinous substance made by boiling fish), butter, flour, minced parsley, onion juice, nutmeg, salt, egg yolk, lemon juice, sugar, pepper, paprika, and cayenne pepper.[154]

Oysters were among the most widely available seafood, and cooks made good with them. In Roanoke, Virginia, "Old Mammy" fixed oyster soup with mace, celery, white pepper, cayenne, salt, butter, flour, cream, and milk, recommending that the server "pour [it] into a hot tureen and give thanks."[155] In the 1930s, "Bridget, a famous Savannah cook," developed oyster and chicken croquettes with butter, parsley, mace, onion juice, salt, pepper, and bread crumbs, fried in hot fat.[156] And in New Orleans, Cleo's chopped oysters consisted of oysters, butter, mushrooms, flour, celery salt, nutmeg, cayenne, parsley, egg yolks, and cream, served in pastry shells or over hot, crisp toast.[157]

Coastal cooks also excelled at preparing shellfish. Idella Parker commented on the challenge that went into these dishes: "I would cook, clean, and pick them all. . . . If you have ever boiled crabs you know how they are, and you can imagine me in the kitchen at Cross Creek, with crabs jumping out of the big pot and crawling all over the floor. Me with a big prong catching them and putting them back in that boiling water. When the battle was over, the poor crabs had to give up."[158] "Mam Jude" took pride in the seasoning for her boiled crab creole, made with sweet basil, thyme, marjoram, whole cloves, hot red peppers, black pepper, bay leaves, and coarse salt.[159] Cleo developed her own version of the classic recipe shrimp Newburg, consisting of shrimp in a complex sauce of butter, cream, Worcestershire sauce, salt, cayenne pepper, Tabasco sauce, soda, sherry, egg yolks, and lemon juice.[160] She apparently did not hesitate to integrate into her recipe commercially made ingredients such as highly flavored Worcestershire and Tabasco sauces.

Cooks also made stuffing, or dressing, beloved to southerners, to accompany meat dishes. "Mam Jude" made a typical bread dressing of cornbread, cold biscuit, bread crumbs, baking powder, raw eggs, minced green onion top, onion juice, celery juice, butter, parsley, salt, and plentiful amounts of black pepper.[161] But it was "Lucy's Stuffing with Nuts"—stale bread crumbs, pecans, boiled egg yolks, chicken or turkey stock, parsley, celery leaves, thyme, bay leaf, cooked mushrooms, onion juice, sherry, salt, pepper, and cayenne that won the comment, "This has always been judged a perfect dressing."[162]

Cooks made soups from every conceivable ingredient. "Lucy's Vegetable Soup" combined canned tomatoes, carrots, turnips, onions, celery root, brown sugar, cabbage, salt, paprika, and meat from a soup bone. "Chloe's" "Everyday Onion Soup" featured the usual ingredients but included Parmesan cheese, which was becoming increasingly commonplace in the 1930s.[163] Soup was considered suitable for presidents. Ellen White cooked a difficult "Bouillon a la James Madison," named for her former employer, while "Katie Seabrook, Pres. McKinley's Cook" (elsewhere referred to as "Pres. McKinley's Colored Cook") made a simple but "Delicious Stew" with leftover meat.[164] Canned soups became widely available in the late nineteenth century. Atlanta matrons could purchase soup from the J. H. W. Huckins Company, in Boston, or from the Philip J. Ritter Conserve Co., of Philadelphia, by the mid-1890s in such varieties as tomato, rice tomato, pea puree, oxtail, chicken, barley beef, beef broth, bean puree, and mock turtle. The placement of a Ritter ad opposite the soup page in an Atlanta Presbyterian church cookbook may indicate a clear message: spend hours making soup, or pour it out of a can.[165]

The stereotype of the southern table groaning with side dishes seems to have been true for city families, at least when produce was in season. Some families kept gardens and sometimes expected the cook to work in the "patch." At the very least, she might be expected to go into the garden to pick the vege-

An unidentified cook and a market delivery truck driver in Washington, D.C., 1942.
Photo by Howard Liberman, Farm Security Administration/Office of War Information,
Library of Congress LC-USW3-054159-D.

tables for the day. Beulah Nelson of Washington, D.C., remembered that she
attended to her morning chores, then turned her attention to the vegetables
for the noonday meal: "And then after that you had to go out behind the
house, honey, and pick the garden. And pick what kind of vegetables you got
to have. You got to wash them and cook them. And they had three meals a day.
They would eat they breakfast, and then twelve o'clock they had to have a big
dinner. And then they had supper later in the evening."[166]

Urban merchants as early as 1891 trumpeted the availability of country
produce. In Tyler, Texas, grocer Tom H. Thornton bragged about "vegetables
fresh from the gardens every morning."[167] In Macon, Georgia, in the 1890s,
affluent housekeepers bought assorted vegetables (butternut squash, peas,
corn, okra, beans, butterbeans; root vegetables, including radishes, onions,
Irish potatoes, beets, sweet potatoes, and turnips; leafy vegetables in the form
of collards, cabbage, and spinach; and pecans and peanuts). All of these products were likely grown in Middle Georgia.[168] From Texas to Virginia, merchants advertised their wares as locally grown "country products" well into

the 1930s.[169] In the 1930s, these items included asparagus, "very fancy cabbage," yellow squash, and "extra fancy" green beans.[170] The most desirable produce was grown nearby and was extremely fresh and of very high quality.

While Macon women seem to have bought far more fresh produce than canned, prosperous southerners also had access to national brands of canned goods by the 1890s. Anniston, Alabama, merchants sold canned vegetables from Thurber, Whyland, and Company, one of the nation's largest wholesalers, as early as 1893.[171] Richmond women could buy "California canned goods" in 1895.[172] And in 1901, a Knoxville merchant offered "a very select line of groceries including the best known packers, both domestic and foreign, of canned delicacies."[173] Such marketing continued well into the 1920s, when a Memphis grocer advertised "a full line of Sprague, Warner & Co.'s famous Richelieu Brand of canned and bottled goods," touting goods from the Chicago-based food processor.[174]

Although African American cooks almost surely prepared multiple dishes of vegetables on many days, few of their recipes are extant, indicating, perhaps, that most of the preparations were simple. Southern cooks often let vegetables simmer for hours, giving them flexibility in preparing other foods and in holding the vegetables for indefinite serving periods.

Yet even the plainest vegetables required some labor. Idella Parker remembered, "I especially remember the asparagus. Sand behind each eye, and *so* much trouble to wash. I was really upset whenever Mrs. Rawlings would say, 'Idella, let's have asparagus tonight,' because it was hard work. To this day I cringe whenever asparagus is mentioned."[175]

Emma Jane Christian gave details for three vegetable dishes, all based on the most ordinary of vegetables, made extraordinary through Christian's cooking ability. Corn became hominy, which required twelve hours to process. Christian's personal favorites, onion pudding and fresh corn pudding, each consisted of those respective vegetables, boiled then baked in a custard of milk, egg, and butter.[176] In New Orleans, Ozite made delectable black-eyed peas, highly seasoned with smoked bacon, peppercorns, hot red pepper, green pepper, a can of tomatoes, minced celery, and minced onion.[177]

By far the vegetable recipes most attributed to African American cooks were those for sweet potatoes. In Virginia, Florida, and Mississippi, "Mammy," "old colored Martha," and "Malissa" combined sweet potatoes with sugar or cane syrup and various spices to candy them or make pone.[178] Mildred Council, later proprietor of the highly regarded Dip's Country Kitchen in Chapel Hill, North Carolina, came up with her own well-received recipe for sweet potatoes baked in orange cups.[179] Lowly sweet potatoes became a delicacy in Council's creative hands and launched a cooking career that has spanned seven decades.

Southern cooks also had access to plentiful supplies of fruit. In season, Macon cooks could find in stores locally grown figs, peaches, pears, berries of various types, grapes, tomatoes, cantaloupes, "melon," and apples from north Georgia. Additionally, peddlers sold their products door to door.[180] By the 1890s, affluent families also had access to more exotic fruits. Macon matrons bought citrus fruit—lemons, navel oranges, grapefruit, and oranges; other tropical fruits, such as bananas and pineapples; tropical nuts like almonds and Brazil nuts; coconuts; and cranberries and cherries, American in origin but far from Middle Georgia.[181] Huge growing combinations such as the California Citrus Growers (marketing under Sunkist), Dole Pineapple, and Florida citrus growers were all well established by 1900 and eager to place their wares on American tables.[182] As people and goods continued to move around the globe, still other exotic fruits came into the kitchen. Cleora Butler recalled the first avocado she encountered, in the 1920s, "brought from Mexico by my employer, Charles Robertson." "Mrs. Robertson and I," she wrote, "studied this unusual piece of fruit, and when we cut it open to find the enormous seed inside, we couldn't decide which was the part to be eaten, the pulp or the seed. Finally we decided we had best wait until Mr. Robertson returned home."[183] Some cooks likely welcomed opportunities to expand their repertoires, while others probably regarded new materials as hassles best to be avoided.

Although salads were a common part of the southern diet after the Civil War, very few of them were credited to African American cooks. Sociologist Elizabeth Haynes reported in 1923 that most cooks thought that making salad and salad dressing exceeded their talent.[184] Perhaps the cooks' alleged lack of confidence came from unfamiliar ingredients or the sometimes difficult blending of fats and acids for dressings, although it seems unlikely that a cook who could figure out how to make cookies without eggs would be intimidated by vinegar and oil. Yet only Betty Patterson, writing in the 1920s, attributed salad recipes to African American cooks. "Hulda" made an elaborate salad platter of hard-cooked eggs, fresh tomatoes, lettuce leaf, chilled caviar seasoned with lemon and onion juice, mayonnaise, pimiento-stuffed olives, chilled cooked shrimp, anchovies, pickled beets, pearl onions, cucumber pickles, and "freshly fried potato chips."[185] "Hulda" also composed a salad of snap beans and onions dressed with a combination of bacon grease, flour, and sweet pickle vinegar.[186] "Lucy" made a boiled salad dressing from egg yolks, sugar, flour, salt, lemon juice, orange juice, butter, and whipped cream.[187]

"Mandy" concocted a dressing for fruit salad with egg yolks, sugar, dry mustard, salt, plain vinegar, tarragon vinegar, and whipped cream.[188] It is also possible that cookbook writers considered salads too modern to be attributed to African American cooks and would contradict their sentimental portrayals of stereotypical southern fare.[189]

In addition to salad dressings, southerners used an array of sauces and condiments, both homemade and purchased. African American cooks preserved fruits and vegetables in a number of ways. Women who preserved foods had to squeeze these time-consuming, hot, rather dangerous tasks among their everyday chores, usually during the hottest time of the year in the pre-air-conditioned South. Women pickled vegetables and occasionally fruit in vinegar and stored them in glass jars. Virginian Caroline Pickett created "Aunt Caroline's Own Pickle" from green tomatoes, onions, green and red peppers, and cabbage, salted and left to stand overnight, then seasoned with vinegar, sugar, celery seed, mustard seed, "spice," and cloves.[190] Noted Atlanta food columnist Henrietta Stanley Dull praised "Aunt Ella's Cucumber Pickles," made with brine, apple vinegar, salt, sugar, red pepper, and spices, recommending them for breakfast or with broiled fish.[191] Cleora Butler made chow-chow, a chopped relish with green tomatoes, cabbage, cucumbers, onions, green beans, red sweet peppers, and a plethora of spices, as well as corn relish, a composition of sweet corn, tomatoes, onions, cucumbers, celery, and sweet green peppers.[192] Anne Robertson told the story of Mae, who worked for Robertson's mother, making corn relish. Robertson's mother had Mae drive her to the farmer's market, where the vendors brought the corn and peppers to the car. Robertson recalled that she and her mother took a nap while Mae shucked the corn out in the yard, cut the peppers, and cooked the relish. "We came downstairs," Robertson said, "and there was a big pot of relish on the stove. Mother stirred it and said, 'See, Anne, there's nothing to making corn relish.'"[193] While Robertson saw the irony of the situation, her mother apparently did not, and Robertson did not report Mae's reaction to the denigration of her efforts.

Cooks made jellies and preserves by combining fruit with sugar and heating the mixture and then storing it in glass jars. Made at the height of fruit season, early to midsummer, jellies and preserves required constant stirring over boiling pots of popping, hissing fruit. "Mam Jude" boiled figs in water and sugar to make preserves, and "Chloe" from New Orleans made a simple strawberry preserve from strawberries and sugar; "Chloe," who worked for Elizabeth Pringle, cooked peach preserves from the trees that she guarded assiduously, and Cleora Butler proudly claimed a recipe for pear preserves.[194]

Buying choices also abounded. In 1894, the "Old Virginia Brand" of Wheeling, West Virginia, advertised preserves, jellies, jam, ketchups, sauces, and mincemeat.[195] While Macon women did not purchase jelly, they did buy chowchow and "sauce," which may have been Durkee Famous Sauce, an extremely popular salad dressing developed in 1857, or something similar.[196] They did not buy cucumbers, so any cucumber pickles either were made from their own garden produce or from vegetables bought from peddlers or were purchased readymade.

ONE OF THE MOST DIFFICULT aspects of cooking is bringing all of the dishes to the table at the same time, an outcome that challenges beginning cooks even today. Experienced cooks learned tricks that allowed them to time meals carefully. An anecdote from a 1904 cookbook told of a cleric impressed by the cook in a home he was visiting singing a hymn before breakfast: "On expressing his satisfaction at this act of early devotion, he was told she had discovered that exactly the time needed to sing two verses was that which was required to boil an egg."[197]

Once the food was prepared, cooks sometimes participated in serving it. Idella Parker quickly learned the exact ritual Marjorie Kinnan Rawlings required for breakfast: fresh-squeezed orange juice, a hard-boiled egg, toast if Rawlings requested it, coffee in a silver pot with sugar and cream, and a bowl of milk and a dish of canned cat food for "Smokey," all on a tray with a fresh flower in a silver vase and a linen napkin, brought to Rawlings's bed.[198] In the 1940s and 1950s, Mattie Holmes prepared and served a formal dinner to the Adler family of Memphis every night. To a table set with linen, china, and silver, Holmes carried a mixture of German, Eastern European, and southern dishes, from fried chicken to the stewed carrot dish known as tzimmes.[199]

While everyday meals might be casual, dinner for company was another matter, and serving formal meals could prove frightening to both employer and employee. Employers who were insecure about their places in society could be especially tense about proper meal service, for their status depended on the ability of their servants to properly perform dining rituals.[200] African American women interviewed in Washington, D.C., where social functions reached extraordinarily high levels of complexity, remarked that "wealthy persons wrongly assumed that every servant was born knowing how to function at even the most formal occasions."[201] A woman's lack of training in serving could disappoint her employer just as did her lack of instinctual knowledge of cooking.

Southern households followed custom, and proper hostesses chose to serve their meals either buffet style or, more formally, *à la russe*, in which each seated guest was served individually. An unnamed Knoxville writer observed in 1901, "It is very simple to prepare a dinner served *a la Russe*, as it matters little how many courses there may be. . . . With one or two assistants, and with time between each course to prepare the succeeding one, after a very little practice it becomes a mere amusement." Despite it being a "mere amusement," the formal service required careful orchestration: "Every one must know exactly her own business, so that no questions need be asked at the last moment. The cook can attend to nothing but the cooking, at the risk of neglecting this most important part."[202] Author Marjorie Kinnan Rawlings had dinner presented both styles at her Florida home in the 1940s. A dish such as baked fish might be served whole, passed by "the maid." Most of the time, Rawlings observed, they "had a crowd" and served buffet style. It fell to the cook to replenish the buffet with the proper courses.

At Cross Creek, a cook named 'Geechee appeared to take special pleasure in bringing forth labor-intensive tangerine sherbet, which required owning one's own tangerine trees and, as Rawlings put it, "the patience to squeeze the juice from at least a twelve-quart water bucket of the tangerines." According to Rawlings, 'Geechee served tangerine sherbet often because she knew that it pleased Rawlings's guests. Rawlings recalled with condescending amusement, "'Geechee would race through the farmhouse, cap awry, bearing a loaded tray, and shouting at the top of her strong lungs, 'Tangerine sherbet comin' up! Tangerine sherbet comin' up!'"[203] By the time that 'Geechee squeezed the juice, made the sherbet, and served it, she had spent many hours in its production and might justifiably be proud of her creation. As Rawlings observed with regard to ice cream, 'Geechee might get some of the sherbet if the guests left some.

At times, employers put the finishing touches on dishes prepared by cooks, creating public spectacles or rituals that enhanced the apparent involvement of the hostess in household affairs and thus made her appear more domestic. The cook employed by North Carolinian Julia Manning Jones Marriner—perhaps in the 1930s or 1940s—baked a large popover called yellow cat, and then Marriner made a hard sauce, "patiently creaming the butter, beating in the sugar, pouring in the bourbon, grating a little fresh nutmeg on top." According to Marriner's granddaughter, the dish was considered her specialty, despite the fact that the foundation came from the hands of her African American cook.[204] Cleora Butler prepared elaborate parties for the Howard Whitehill family in Tulsa, also likely in the late 1940s. At one party, "a black-tie bon voyage dinner party for twenty-six friends leaving on an 'Around

the World in Eighty Days' sojourn," Butler recalled, "Mrs. Whitehill personally mixed a special dressing at the table to serve with wedges of lettuce."[205]
In the Geismar household in New Orleans, Rosa Smith did all of the cooking, mastering the family's preferred Alsatian cuisine, but Evelyn Geismar
made desserts and candy, including southern specialties like divinity and pra-
lines.[206] In this way, the employer may have been able to claim credit for the
cook's work, putting her final stamp on a multilayered preparation.[207]

AFTER A LARGE EVENT, cleaning was a major undertaking. Doris Woodson
remembered the duties of her mother, Frances Walker, at Maymont, and the
elaborate service that took hours to clean up: "You had a thousand dishes—a
dish for everything, a piece of eating utensil for every single different thing.
So it was a long, drawn-out process."[208] Washing dishes could be considered
a straightforward task, but in houses without running water, taking hot water
from a cookstove reservoir could prove a risky and dangerous undertaking.
Breakage, particularly of fine dishes, was a major concern of employers, and
many hapless servants saw their meager pay docked to compensate for broken
pieces of household dishware. The servants had their own worries. Frances
Walker bore the responsibility for scouring pots and pans, a hot and miserable task. Her nephew remembered that she sometimes bribed the household
chauffeur with a couple of muffins to help her. But, the nephew recalled, "She
couldn't give him more than two, because everything was watched over."[209]
The appliances, too, had to be cared for, often an onerous undertaking. Dal-
lasite Annie Mae Hunt remembered, "I'd . . . clean a stove, a bad stove. My
hands'd be all messed up. Cleaning an ice box. That's a day's work to clean a
stove."[210] And, finally, the refuse would have to be removed from the kitchen,
whether to a trash heap on the property or a garbage can for centralized
pickup.

The cook could finally get off of her feet, whether in her own home or
in her quarters at her employer's house. But the next morning, the process
would begin again.

DURING THE LATE NINETEENTH and early twentieth centuries, food and
cooking altered dramatically, if unevenly, in the South as in the entire United
States. As the economic effects of the Civil War became less harsh for white
southerners, employers could afford to buy better food for their families.
The development of commercial food industries made available items such
as store-bought yeast bread and chickens ready for cooking, while enhanced
transportation networks expanded the range of fruits and vegetables available

year-round. In some households, however, yeast bread made from scratch and chicken yards remained the standard until the 1940s. Technological changes, including the shift from wood to gas and electricity as fuel and the ever-increasing availability of fresh, pure running water in the house, made many cooks' work significantly less cumbersome. While a cook still needed all of the skill at her command to turn out creative, tasty meals, the labor decreased significantly. By the middle of the twentieth century, some employers became more willing to take on cooking tasks themselves and turn over more unpleasant work, such as cleaning, to the African American women who had once occupied their kitchens. The work hours remained long and the wages low, however, as long as African American women remained in the kitchen.

Long Hours and Little Pay

COMPENSATION AND WORKERS' RESISTANCE

In 1938, Roxanna Hupes of Galveston, Texas, wrote to "President Rosevelt," feeling as many of her peers did that the president was likely to read her entreaties and make needed changes in American society. Detailing her workday, which began at 6:30 in the morning with a mile's walk to her place of employment, Hupes efficiently summarized the situation for most domestic workers in the American South: "The wages that we get, so small and the hours is so long."[1] In an oral history interview, Alice Adams praised her longtime employers in Atlanta in almost all ways: "They was lovely people to work around. They treated you as peoples. I had vacations with pay and sick leave with pay. She was one of the loveliest people you could be around. She'd help me if I needed money for house rent or if I needed money for clothing." But there was a catch, said Adams: "The onliest objection was long hours and little pay. She was willing to do anything to help me—but the money. Four dollars a week. Just no money. And everybody was doing the same."[2] "Long hours and little pay" ruled the days of African American cooks.

Sociologist Mary Anderson published in 1936 the results of a survey of working conditions around the South, aptly titled "The Plight of Negro Domestic Labor." Anderson found wages, hours, and tasks to be extremely uneven, varying erratically between location and employer: "The household employee finds no definite wage scale based on experience, skill[,] or amount of work required." No job descriptions or limitations on tasks existed, resulting in inexact expectations and crazily shifting hours. Anderson observed, "There is no standard for the length of the working day nor for the amount of work to be accomplished during that day. Overtime is rarely computed or paid for. Many workers are expected to perform any service that may be required from the time of getting up in the morning until going to bed at night."[3] For an African American cook working in the home of a white family, the bottom line was that she might be expected to do just about anything, at any time, for very little pay. Historian Ira Katznelson argues that domestic workers were "the most exploited group of workers" in the United States before World War II.[4] Few cooks would disagree with him.

IRRESPECTIVE OF THEIR TRAINING or their skill, cooks worked long days. For some live-in servants, the workday was de facto twenty-four hours. Reconstruction-era contracts sometimes required round-the-clock presence. An 1865 South Carolina statute dictated that "[s]ervants . . . in all the domestic duties of the family shall at all hours of the day and night and on all days of the week promptly answer all calls and obey and execute all lawful orders and commands of the family in whose service they are employed."[5]

The lengthy days played into whites' stereotypical ideas about the strength of African American women. Domestic workers spoke openly about their employers' expectations of superior strength based on race. Katherine Rutherford of Baltimore wrote to President Roosevelt in 1933, "These private familys work the poor woman to death . . . they are harder on the colored woman[;] they seam to think that a colored woman have no feeling of tiredness . . . and if they say they are tired the people they work for will say they are lazy."[6] L. G. Huff, from Fort Worth, said as much in a 1937 plea to Eleanor Roosevelt: "Mrs. Roosevelt if you can help talk or orga[n]ize something that will cause these dear house wives whom we work for will realize we are human even if we are a Black race."[7]

Even at forty-three dollars a month—a fine sum for 1923—Frances Walker worked excruciatingly long hours under extreme pressure at the Maymont estate outside Richmond. Her mornings began early as she set to making bread and rolls at about four A.M. Walker's daughter, Doris Woodson, recalled that the employers "had gourmet meals, with so many courses. It took all day, from morning to dinnertime, to cook *one* meal. It took them 2 to 2½ hours or more to eat a meal. You never got out of the kitchen before 10:00 or 10:30 at night."[8] The cooks at the McFaddin home in Beaumont, Texas, also reported hard work and lengthy toil. Albertine Parker recalled that the McFaddins "were good people. . . . But you didn't go there to sit down." McFaddin employees worked from at least seven in the morning until six or seven at night, with two afternoons off per week.[9] When Idella Parker first began working at Cross Creek in 1940, she went three months without an entire day off. She recalled, "I thought to myself, 'This must be what working on a plantation was like.' It seemed just like what my grandmother had told me about slavery. . . . From six in the morning until dark every day we worked. We spent no time talking, unless it was talk about what we were doing, or what was to be done next."[10]

For women who lived in their own homes, their employers' dining preferences defined their working hours, making it difficult to negotiate a schedule or length of the workday. Few complained about the midday meal, commonly known as dinner, which fell within normal working hours. Breakfast and the evening meal, which was often referred to as supper, were another matter. Arriving early in the morning and staying late into the evening caused workers great anguish.

Getting to work in time to cook the employer's breakfast was a constant challenge. Cooks often left their own homes in the dark to be at their employers' in time for the morning meal.[11] Willie Mae Fitzgerald, from New Orleans, recalled a particularly bad incident in the 1930s:

> I can remember one day I went to work it was so cold the buses weren't running. . . . I was young. I walked to work and I got halfway and I was so cold! I just stopped still and looked back, like I wanted to go back home. My children was small then, and I knew I had to take care of them. I thought of my little children, and I went on to work. The white people they're sitting up there in their heated breakfast room, waiting on me. "And hurry up," they said when I got there, "'cause Mr. Quigley got to be to the office." I was frozen. I was just trembling. I ran the hot water on my hands to try to get them warm. She rushed me out to serve breakfast! I felt like cussing, saying, "Damn you, you get back in here and you fix it for once." I thought of my little children. I stayed. I was quiet. That's how I worked."[12]

Unable to prepare breakfast for her own children, Fitzgerald headed out into the cold to ensure that her own family would have food and shelter. And she held her tongue against the people whose insensitivity so galled her.

Even after twenty years of employment with the same family, Alice Adams knew that she ran the risk of being discharged after missing breakfast duty one morning: "I didn't wake up until six o'clock and I was supposed to be on the job at seven, because I was supposed to have his breakfast ready so he could be at his office at 7:30. There was no way. So, I said, 'God has a way of answering.' I didn't get there until 7:30. He had left. So I thought, 'Well, this is it.'" In this instance, the employer reproached but did not fire her.[13]

Cooks who left after the midday meal could be at home as early as three or four o'clock in the afternoon, making a significant difference in their lives and that of their families.[14] Contemporary sociologists routinely observed that cooks who remained through the evening meal got to rest for an hour or two in the afternoon.[15] Few cooks spoke of such an arrangement, however, and L. G. Huff of Fort Worth directly contradicted this notion: "No rest on the job not an hour to lie down or sit down or rest but we poor Negro women have to work."[16] Other women simply spoke of long, long days. Mrs. Anna Smith in Washington, D.C., wrote to Eleanor Roosevelt, "[W]e all so work from ten to twelve hours a day. No holidays or Sundays."[17] Elizabeth Clyburn, also from Washington, observed, "I works from 8 o'clock in the morning until 25 minutes of 8 at night and I be on my feet all that time just for $7 per week."[18] In Mobile in 1930, Priscilla Butler was on the job fifteen hours a day for a lawyer who paid her ten dollars a week. She remembered, "Oh, that was a lot of money then. But darling! You stayed there. If they wanted to have a conversation around the table, you didn't act sour, didn't rattle those pots and pans. And maybe it be nine-thirty before you'd get out of the kitchen. And oh, my dear, you'd been there since six-thirty in the morning."[19]

In 1913, about two-thirds of cooks fixed evening meals as well as breakfast and midday dinner.[20] "An Interested Colored Friend" in Raleigh, North Carolina, remarked in 1933 that domestic workers' weeks stretched to ninety-one hours: "Most people will not consider eating supper until a certain hr with no feeling as to when you leave or what and with two thirds of the time many guests in the house with no extra money."[21] Idella Parker recalled with disgust the large evening meals that she cooked for her employer, a single woman, even when she dined alone: "I had to prepare fresh vegetables, lavish cuts of meat complete with rich sauces and gravies, fancy desserts, and cook and serve it all just as if there was a house full of company."[22]

Families who entertained at night could be particularly difficult to work for, and numerous women detailed the hardships brought about by such employers. Insecure employers often engaged in a type of performance for their guests' benefit, emphasizing their financial well-being and social gentility as well as their authority over their employees to demonstrate their mastery of the situation.[23] Some employers allowed their workers to wear their own clothing most days but required them to wear uniforms when company came, distinguishing the worker from the employer for the benefit of the outsider in the home.[24]

Willie Mae Wright remembered the Bowers family's unpleasant conduct, evidenced most strongly in the way they treated her around guests: "The Bowers never were my slice of watermelon, but what really got my goat was the ritzy way they had me to serve meals. Which it didn't do them a bit of good anyhow to put on a show for company, not the way they was behaving." She recalled the Bowerses' complaining about her new government-housing apartment in front of their guests, and she defended herself "right while I was serving to the left and taking off at the right."[25] Idella Parker excused Marjorie Kinnan Rawlings's bad behavior because of her guests:

It was different when company was there. That's when I was really treated as a servant. Mrs. Rawlings wanted everything to be just right and would sometimes bark orders at me throughout such a visit. I remember once I was slow (so she thought) bringing in the hot biscuits to the table. Mrs. Rawlings yelled for me in front of the guests. Then, as I was coming through the swinging door, she jumped up from her seat and snatched the biscuits out of my hands. "Why the hell didn't you hurry up with the food?" she hollered. She wouldn't have done that if she hadn't had company, I believe.[26]

Having company also greatly lengthened the cook's workday. Idella Parker recalled, "The days lasted from dawn till cleanup after supper, later if we had dinner guests. On company nights it was often midnight or later before I could rest my weary head."[27] As her employer's dependence on alcohol increased, Parker's days lengthened even further: "There would be a dinner party at Cross Creek, and all the guests would have cocktails. . . . Dinner would have to be rewarmed, and it would be long hours before I could clean up and get to bed, all because of whiskey."[28]

Workers could expect nothing in terms of compensatory time off after working extended hours at their employers' parties. Nannie Thompson of Alexandria, Virginia, wrote in 1933, "The domestic the cook and house worker have put in 12 and 15 hours I myself have and if there was a big function I have put in 16 hours before leaving the kitchen for instance suppose you get up in the morning at 6:30 at 2:30 you have put in 8 hours now dinner at 7 or 7:30 there is around 13 hours by the time you clean up put things in ample [apple] pie order and efficient maid will do this of course she'll probably get to bed around 9:30 or 10 o'clock."[29] Going to bed at 9:30 would have sounded good to L. G. Huff of Fort Worth, who wrote, "If a party is to be given we get to work 7 A.M. of[f] about 1.45 A.M. the next morning and look for us at 7 A.M. on the job only 5 hours to sleep."[30] As art historian Elizabeth Johns has observed, when their employers entertained, African American cooks did "not assume equality in the merriment; instead, they [made] it possible."[31] Their employers were willing to stretch out the employees' working hours for the pleasure of their guests. Employers acted worse, and workdays lengthened, and company was in general a bad deal for cooks all the way around.

Some thoughtful people did pay extra for extended service. Jane Stafford remembered the woman who worked for her at the time of her marriage in 1938: "Nellie lived on the place, and we paid her seven dollars a week. And she'd always get extra if she served a dinner party or a luncheon—both from me and from the other guests. You were taught to leave a little extra for the extra work you'd brought."[32] Celeste King recalled working in Statesville, North Carolina, from 1935 to 1945, for a family that owned a factory: "He owned this factory and men from up the road would come down . . . and he'd call me at the last minute and tell me to put down another plate, you know, he was having so-and-so for dinner, and then they'd leave me good tips."[33] King might have appreciated a little more advance notice, but the extra cash helped smooth the situation for her.

While workdays of twelve to thirteen hours were common, what often grieved cooks the most was the inability to have a Sabbath or attend church. As early as 1870, a South Carolina cook named Ellen refused to kill a chicken on Sunday, although she eventually cooked the bird after her employer's son killed it.[34] In the Birmingham home of Presbyterian minister Sterling Foster before World War I, the cook named Sally could not even attend private morning prayer with the Foster family because she was preparing breakfast.[35] Such hypocritical piety on the part of employers galled Washingtonian Bernice Reeder, who complained about her employer in the 1920s: The husband would "act like Sunday was such a holy day around there. No loud talk, no laughing or nothing. . . . He made it clear Sunday was a day of rest. But us? We'd work like dogs just the same. We didn't get no rest on that day."[36] Letter after letter to the New Deal administration outlined the sadness of cooks who had to work on Sunday. Mildred Brown of Washington, D.C., spoke for many when she pleaded in 1940: "I don't mind working because I know I need to work. But will you please try to do something about working on Sunday we don't even get a chance to attend a church as well as I love to go to church. . . . We would be please to death if you would only help us to have all day Sundays off so we could get to go to church Sunday mornings which every one should go."[37]

After working for the same family for four dollars a week for twenty years, Alice Adams became emboldened to ask for Sundays off. She recalled, "I worked from seven to seven. . . . Now, we was off for half a day on Sunday, the same thing on Thursday. Now, do you know what half a day was? You'd get off at one o'clock, get home around three. Well, I did that for about twenty some-odd years. I couldn't go to church because I had to work." She desired normal activities outside of work: "I wanted to go to church and I wanted to visit friends and take care of my house. . . . What you did, you had to do at night. . . . Every church used to have a service at night, and that was the only time you could go. And then sometimes you'd get to church and the church was so crowded you couldn't get a seat. And I was determined to have Sunday off. . . . Because I was reared up in Sunday school going to church, and I was just tired of it." After praying for a solution, Adams finally threatened to quit, saying, "I wants every Sunday and every Thursday. And it's that or I'll have to quit because I want to go to church." Her employer relented. Adams recalled her triumph: "From then on I stopped working on Sunday and I stopped working on Thursday. If you ask for it and act right and intelligent, you'll get it. But you have to ask for it."[38]

THE RETURNS FOR SUCH working hours often scarcely justified the cooks' efforts. Cooks after 1865 were no longer slaves, but the meager or nonexistent wages that they received must have made them wonder whether conditions had changed. The transition from slave labor to free came only with great difficulty. While the Freedman's Bureau often stipulated wages in their labor contracts, oftentimes women's wages were either below the designated amount or nonexistent. A contract between Emmie Gray and I. A. Gray (likely Emmie Gray's former owner), in Anderson, South Carolina, bound the former to the latter for the year 1867, to do "the cooking washing and all other necessary work about the house." She could not receive visitors or leave the premises without her employer's permission, and she received no cash wages. Emmie Gray might be forgiven if she were unable to distinguish her situation from slavery.[39] State laws reinforced the reluctance of employers to pay cash wages or otherwise make promises to their new employees. The State of South Carolina, for example, passed Reconstruction-era laws exempting employees from work contracts "when servant voluntarily receives no remuneration except for food and clothing."[40]

In a change of huge proportions, former slaves openly contested the system of in-kind payments and demanded cash wages for their work.[41] As Elizabeth Clark-Lewis observed, they "developed the determination to transform a master-servant relationship into an employer-employee relationship."[42] In 1889, Eda Hickman of Missouri sued her former owners for twenty-four years of back wages, saying that they had never informed her of her freedom. The owners/employers claimed that Hickman asked to stay with the family. In any event, no one disputed the fact that Hickman worked a quarter of a century without any wages, receiving only food and shelter as her pay.[43] Although rare, such practices continued well into the twentieth century. An employer paid Lottie Cooksey of Washington, D.C., for example, in old clothes for three days' work preparing for religious holidays.[44]

Decade after decade, wages remained low for most women working as cooks. White housewives paid the lowest wages that they could get away with, priding themselves on their household economy.[45] How they determined these wages is unclear, but they almost surely consulted their friends and neighbors to fix on a prevailing local rate. The 1892 account book of Laura McElwain Jones, the wife of a Methodist minister in Cartersville, Georgia, provides a comparison of what she spent on groceries and the wages she paid "Aunt Sarah," whose name appeared alongside notations for purchases of groceries such as sugar, coffee, and garden seeds. In January, Aunt Sarah earned $2.50, equivalent to the sum that Jones paid for oysters. On February 8, Jones paid Aunt Sarah $0.50, equal to the price of her butter and cabbage purchases the same week. Two weeks later, Aunt Sarah received $1.25, the cost of the household's Irish potatoes. March and April payments to Aunt Sarah each totaled one dollar, equivalent to the price of walnuts. No pay for Aunt Sarah was recorded in May or June. The reader can estimate little about the relative value of Aunt Sarah, for there is no way of determining whether she was paid by the task or by the time. What is quite clear, however, is that her income from the Jones family rose and fell sharply and, even at its highest, would have afforded her family very little cash.[46]

Historian Earl Lewis refers to work that did not provide "economic independence or material advancement" as "underemployment," and such situations abounded in the New South.[47] Wages for domestic work were extremely uneven. Sources from around the South between 1901 and the 1950s graphically demonstrate this point. Auburn, Alabama, had the lowest wages, of about one dollar a week, in 1905, while the wealthy in Tulsa paid seventeen times that in the oil boom years of the 1920s. During the Great Depression, payments in the range of $1.50 per week again appeared in Macon, Atlanta, and LaGrange, Georgia, as widespread unemployment drove down wages,[48] while the fortunes of World War II brought pay in Houston up to thirteen dollars per week. The Appendix reveals the lack of pattern in wages.

With such low pay, the majority of African American families required a "composite income" of several members of the family contributing wages to get by.[49] The situations of two families in Macon illustrate the complexities of obtaining life's necessities among wage earners. In 1880, Maria Gibson was twenty-eight years old. Born in North Carolina, she shared her home with her husband, Jack; fifteen-year-old twin daughters, Julia and Sophia; another daughter, Elizay, age nine; an eight-year-old "adopted daughter," Carry Edwards; and Hilliard Groce, a fifty-year-old man unrelated to the family. The Gibson family members were able to live together, rather than Maria having to be apart from them under her employer's roof. Jack had a trade as a drayman, and Hilliard Groce was a blacksmith. But, despite Jack's earning potential and the possible income from Groce, all of the women in the house worked. Maria was a cook, and both Julia and Sophia were "domestic servants." With all of the adults away from home, finding care for the two little girls may have been difficult.[50] If the family had been able to forego Maria's wages, they likely would have done so, especially as the twins became old enough to contribute to the family income. Maria's salary was essential.

In the 1930s, Macon resident Florence Howard, at about the age of eighteen, advanced to the position of cook in her employers' household, at a salary of three dollars a week. Her mother, Sarah Howard, was frail and could work only three days a week and earned a mere thirty-five cents a day, cleaning and cooking one meal a day for a widow. Sarah Howard's wages were insufficient to support her younger children, whom she consequently sent to live with an aunt. Sarah Howard's husband and eighteen-year-old son were not working in those years of the Great Depression. The Howard family was statistically a nuclear one, with two parents and two teenage children. But this particular nuclear family had been shorn of its younger members and was being supported primarily by the wages of a teenage girl. Florence Howard carried a heavy load of responsibility on her young shoulders as she moved upward through the ranks of domestic service.[51]

In these examples, two households, in the same city fifty years apart, depended on the wages of women cooks to make survival possible for all family members. Maria Gibson left two young children at home to supplement her husband's wages. Florence Howard left her youth behind as she joined the ranks of single women earning cook's pay. And Sarah Howard, despite her bad health, labored to earn a third of what her daughter did. All of the women contributed their wages to a household in which numerous people worked, pooling their meager incomes to try to make ends meet.

Such flexible households enabled people to gain autonomy, to avoid dependence upon a single employer, and thus to resist abusive relationships.[52] Very few cooks were the only wage earners in their families, and those who were, were almost always either widows with young children or the sole supporters of their widowed mothers.[53] Every penny counted. Augusta Swanson, born in 1910 near Mobile, went to work at the age of eight. She recalled: "I made a dollar a week, and Mother was right there every week to get that dollar. I don't care what I wanted—I didn't get it. Poor mother. She thought about that little dollar. I guess that helped her."[54]

CONTRIBUTING TO THE CRAZY quilt pattern of uneven wages and incomes, many employees received several types of in-kind payment in lieu of cash wages, including board, lodging, leftover food, and castoff household goods and clothing.[55] Such payments cost employers little or nothing in hard currency. The worth of in-kind payments was difficult to calculate, and the employer was more likely to place a higher value on them than would the recipient.[56] Payments of this kind were often inconsistent and unreliable, even whimsical, but widespread.

The most common income supplement came in the form of food. Employers often considered meals as part of the domestic worker's pay, yet clearly some of the food would be thrown away if not given to the employee.[57] First, the cook received leftovers for her own sustenance on the job after the employer's family finished its meal. Poor-quality food and insufficient quantities created difficulties for cooks hungry after preparing meals for others. In Gainesville, Georgia, sociologist Ruth Reed remarked that cooks often walked "a mile or two across town" to arrive in time to cook light breakfasts for their employers. The meals were insubstantial for someone who had just trekked across Gainesville, and cooks were "not allowed to prepare anything more substantial for themselves." Housewives might also measure out insufficient amounts of food, so that by the time the family finished eating, the cook had little from which to make her own breakfast.[58] Marjorie Kinnan Rawlings cavalierly described the dispensation of leftover ice cream at Cross Creek: first the guests ate their fill; then the cook, Idella; "old colored Martha and old Will"; and "even the dog a lick or two." In Rawlings's hierarchy, Idella Parker and Martha and Will Mickens occupied a middle ground between the guests and the canines.[59]

As African American cooks increasingly preferred to live in their own homes rather than in those of their employers, many of them received leftover food to take home to supplement cash wages. "Toting," or the "service pan," as the practice of taking leftover food home was called, augmented wages in almost two-thirds of the employers' households in Athens, Georgia, in 1913.[60] Cash-short families depended upon this in-kind wage, as "Negro Nurse" wrote in 1912: "Well, I'll be frank with you, if it were not for the service pan, I don't know what the majority of our Southern colored families would do. The service pan is the mainstay in many a home. . . . Others may denounce the service pan, and say that it is used only to support idle negroes, but many a time, when I was a cook, and had the responsibility of rearing my three children upon my lone shoulders, many a time I have had occasion to bless the Lord for the service pan!"[61]

After her father was injured in a construction accident, thirteen-year-old Willie Mae Wright took a job as a child's nurse in Atlanta to aid her family. She regarded her service pan as a mark of her growing maturity: "I'd get ready to go home about five o'clock, nearly supper-time. She'd go in the kitchen, and whatever we had for dinner she'd take some of all of it and put it in a little pan. It was a good little white enamel pan with a blue ring around it, and not chipped in any place. She'd fix my supper in that pan for me to take home, and she'd tell me to hurry and get there while it was still first dark." The employer doled out the food and instructed the young girl on how to get home safely in the "first dark"—not releasing her earlier so that she could arrive home in the daylight. Wright's pleasure in her unchipped pan likely indicates that some women bore home pans of lesser quality, both in terms of the content and the physical condition. She refers to "her supper," not that of her family, so the amount of food in the pan may have been only enough to feed a thirteen-year-old girl. Nonetheless, Wright was able to relieve her adult relatives of responsibility for her evening meal, and she regarded it as something quite positive: "I thought I was the biggest woman, going with a pan in my elbow—'toting the crooked arm,' folks called it."[62]

Toting carried many negative connotations, however. The quality of the meals varied widely from household to household, and the monetary value of the food undoubtedly did as well.[63] African American families had to accept leftover food on the employer's terms with regard to quantity, quality, and timing. Washingtonian Nellie Willoughby recalled receiving leftover roast beef—the tough, hard ends of the cut.[64] Educator William Henry Holtzclaw, born about 1875, remembered genuine hunger waiting for his mother to return from her cooking job:

My mother cooked for the "white folks," and, her work being very exacting, she could not always get home at night. At such times we children suffered an excruciating kind of pain,—the pain of hunger. I can well remember how at night we would often cry for food until falling here and there on the floor we would sob ourselves to sleep. Late at night, sometimes after midnight, mother would reach home with a large pan of pot-liquor, or more often a variety of scraps from the "white folks'" table (she might have brought more, but she was not the kind of cook that slipped things out of

Easter, the cook for the C. A. Moers family, Fort Bend County, Texas, date unknown. Courtesy the Fort Bend County Museum Association, Richmond, Texas.

the back door); waking us all, she would place the pan on the floor, or on her knees, and gathering around her we would eat to our satisfaction.

One memorable meal consisted solely of piecrust, which the family dog tried to steal. The dog was almost surely hungry too.[65]

White families, furthermore, ate foods strange to some African American palates, and families who relied on the service pan sometimes had to accept foods not of their own choosing. Audrey Smith recalled having to learn to eat the pheasant, lamb, and veal that her mother, Georgia Anderson, brought home from Maymont.[66] And throughout the South, cooks for Jewish families brought home chopped liver, kugel, and other Eastern European delicacies as part of their "hookarm."[67] If the food were good, plentiful, and regular, a cook might gratefully accept the service pan. But if the supply were inconsistent, the cook's family suffered.

Arguments over theft, which will be discussed in detail in Chapter 7, notwithstanding, the custom of toting may have broken down one barrier, as cooks might eventually expect to eat what their own hands had prepared. Knowing that her children might enjoy the food from her employer's kitchen may have spurred a cook to take a little extra care with the preparations. It may also have mitigated the alienation of laboring mightily on a meal that one would never share, lessening the division "between those who prepare the food and those who will enjoy the fruits of their labors."[68]

In-kind benefits came from other sources as well. Marjorie Kinnan Rawlings allowed Idella Parker the use of her car, if grudgingly. Parker remembered, "We couldn't leave the place unless Mrs. Rawlings let us use her car or truck, and we were always told what time to be back." But, Parker said, "I was allowed to drive Mrs. Rawlings' new car as if it were mine." She admitted, "It was a great feeling for me, driving that new-looking, cream-colored Oldsmobile."[69] Rawlings could grant or withhold access to the vehicles and hence to the world outside of her compound at Cross Creek. Parker recognized the car as a privilege, however, and such small benefits kept Parker from leaving a situation that was often miserable.

EMPLOYERS ALSO GAVE GIFTS, particularly of old clothing, to their cooks, or sold them goods inexpensively rather than increasing their cash wages. Sociologist Mary Romero observes that such "unilateral" gift giving "defines an unequal relationship," as both the one-way giving and the types of gifts convey "the message that domestics are needy and further serves to maintain class differences between domestics and their employers."[70] Evelyn Nakano Glenn remarks that employees learned to accept employers' "noblesse oblige" even when they didn't want the goods to keep from seeming "too proud" and tempting their employers to withhold future gifts and bonuses.[71]

Sometimes the line between gift and sale blurred, much to the detriment of the worker, as observer Walter Fleming wrote: "There are a very few women who have the reputation of not being exactly honest with the negro in the matter of wages. When pay day comes, forgotten delinquencies are remembered and deductions made, or the servant may be charged with things which she thought had been given her."[72] Willie Mae Wright recalled one particularly dreadful employer in Newnan, Georgia, who cheated her through inappropriate sales: "One woman I worked for, I'd work all week and then she'd say, 'Here's a nice dress I'd like to sell for fifty cents.' It'd be so big I could have flung a fit inside it and never popped a seam, but I'd be scared to say anything, so I'd get that big old wore-out dress and fifty cents for that week's work." Wright continued ruefully, "Regular, every week, she'd palm off things on me that way. The week she sold me the Rhode Island rooster I didn't get but a quarter in money. It was terrible. I was scared to say no to her. . . . I tucked that rooster under my arm, and he sure was a buster. I got as far as the bridge before he got away from me. So when I got home, I just had that quarter and not even the rooster." On such weeks, Wright's family suffered from the abject shortage of cash. A family simply needed more than twenty-five cents a week to live.[73]

On the other hand, Wright thoroughly enjoyed the gifts from and transactions with her employer, Mrs. Duke. She lovingly detailing the clothing that she bought at a discount from her very wealthy and fashionable employer.[74] When Wright married, Mrs. Duke allowed her to take "whatever she wanted" from the storeroom: "some vases, a solid mahogany chair, two lamps, sheets—not at all bad, just thin—and two bedspreads, brand-new, what had been given to her. And dishes. I always was a fool about odd teacups and saucers, and she give me just a big stack of them."[75] The Dukes charged Wright fairly for the items that they sold to her and gave her household items not as a supplement to her wages but rather as a means of starting her own household.

An astute judge of people, Wright evaluated her favorite gifts from her employers over a forty-year span. They included a pair of pale yellow silk "step ins," a set of dishes from Japan, and a needle threader from a Mrs. Church. Wright commented, "That was what was so nice about Mrs. Church. She'd *think* about you. Plenty of folks will give you something like at Christmastime, even if it's a box of candy or a handkerchief because they don't want to fool with thinking up anything else, but not Mrs. Church. She's give you some little something just whenever it come to her mind here was something you'd need or specially like, and that's why her presents always was the best presents—even if sometimes they didn't cost over fifty cents."[76] Church's selection of gifts meant that she thought of Wright as an individual, not just "the cook."

WITHOUT HEALTH INSURANCE, workers could be forced into extremely difficult situations by ill health, first by their inability to work and then by the costs of medical care. For workers whose employers did not pay their medical expenses, the situation could be dire. Undone by the stress of her husband's abandonment and trying to care for two small sons on her own in Memphis in the years just before World War I, Ella Wilson Wright fell ill. Her son, novelist Richard Wright, wrote, "The problem of food became an acute daily agony. Hunger was with us always. Sometimes the neighbors would feed us or a dollar bill would come in the mail from my grandmother. It was winter and I would buy a dime's worth of coal each morning from the corner coalyard and lug it home in paper bags."[77]

Sometimes employers stepped in to ameliorate cooks' dangerous financial situations, paying for medical or other services. Complications from an appendectomy forced Idella Parker to remain hospitalized for six weeks. Her employer, Marjorie Kinnan Rawlings, paid the entire bill, including a private nurse. Rawlings also gave Parker a direct transfusion of blood.[78] In other situations at Cross Creek, Rawlings twisted her affection for Parker with her need to bind Parker to her through obligation. Perhaps Rawlings herself did not know what motivated her actions around the appendectomy. Hazel Lambert's husband arranged surgery for Mary "Cookie," his family's longtime cook, and in gratitude Mary cooked for him at no charge for the rest of her life, a period of about eleven years.[79] In fairness to Lambert, Mary might well have died without the surgery, and, according to Hazel Lambert, she simply showed up to work afterward; the young white couple did not request it of her. The financial equality of this transaction cannot be calculated from existing information, but one wonders who benefited more from the arrangement.

No workers' compensation insurance existed, of course, although employers sometimes paid for situations that resulted from on-the-job injuries. Willie Mae Wright slipped and broke her foot while throwing out dishwater on an icy day. She was on crutches and unable to work for an entire year. The employer in whose service Wright had become injured, Mrs. Lake, did not pay Wright directly but did collect cash from Lake's boarders and bring it to Wright with food.[80] The problem with such a situation was that the employer was under no obligation to pay for medical expenses and in most instances likely did not. The employee would have no way of knowing what expenses would be covered and which not, and she would also have no way of paying the uncovered expenses on her low wages. Employers' generosity could be capricious, unstable, and highly personal.

In much the same way, white employers sometimes paid funeral expenses for employees' family members. The Duke family funded the funerals of Wright's half sister, who died of tuberculosis, and Wright's first-born son. When the sister died, the Dukes "brought everything to be laid out in—a slip, pants, white socks, the prettiest white dress, and a wide white satin ribbon for her hair." Although the Dukes declined payment, Wright's husband worked off the two-hundred-dollar funeral cost by cutting the grass, washing the car, and performing other tasks on his day off.[81] Some employees feared white people's interference with mourning practices. When a Mississippi doctor insisted on having his maid's funeral at his house, the local African American population stayed away from the funeral.[82]

Munificence such as the Mississippi doctor's and the Lamberts', in particular, point to the complexity of relationships between employer and employee. On the one hand, the white patrons paid for goods and services that the African Americans could not afford. On the other hand, they were often not gifts. The African American families felt compelled to repay their white patrons and were thus tied to them by bonds of financial obligation.

WITH WAGES FOR DOMESTIC work remaining uniformly low, African American women often eagerly supplemented their incomes with other types of labor when time and energy allowed. Mary Patricia Foley remembered their family cook, Delores, in the 1940s: "She could do everything. She could cook and she could cook anything. In the early days—she supplemented her income by catering parties. Imagine working until three or four o'clock and then going home and cooking for forty."[83] In the early 1940s, Annie Mae Hunt supplemented her income by working an additional four hours: "I fried pies after work too. At Nall's Pie Shop on Wall Street, at night from 8 to 12 o'clock."[84]

From the postbellum period until well into the twentieth century, African American women availed themselves of seasonal agricultural work, which paid better than domestic work.[85] Chopping and picking cotton and harvesting tobacco, all labor-intensive activities, required large workforces over short periods of time, and women could earn better money quickly. After emancipation, African American women wanted to remain out of the fields as much as possible. By the turn of the twentieth century, however, the wages for field work attracted their granddaughters, for whom working outside held little stigma. Walter Fleming observed in 1906, "The old 'freedom' prejudice of the women against working in the fields is dying out, and a number of women work on the farm in the spring and fall and go out as house servants in the summer and especially in the winter."[86] White housewives fussed about their domestic workers' seasonal departures but seemed unwilling or unable to raise wages enough to dissuade them from leaving. In 1906, Georgian Magnolia Le Guin wrote of her thirteen-year-old cook, Fannie, "Hope I can keep her till cotton chopping time—and wish I could keep her all the year."[87] Hoping and wishing might not be enough to induce a cook to stay. In Athens, Georgia, one woman declared that she was simply unable to get a servant from September until Christmas, the peak of the harvest season.[88] Some women saved up money so they could take a break from domestic duties in the summer and avoid the worst of the heat, so that they would not have to spend summer days cooking on a stove "too hot for us."[89]

AFRICAN AMERICAN WOMEN sought redress for the negative aspects of their work by banding together with peers for support. One of the worst parts of domestic work was its isolation, as each woman worked in a unique location without a significant opportunity to communicate with anyone except her employer during the day. In their own homes, however, cooks overcame their daily isolation through a "work culture" among female relatives and neighbors that enabled them to "share secrets about how to perform certain tasks, to exchange recipes, and to pass on survival strategies for handling demanding mistresses, long hours, menial work conditions[,] and lack of respect or autonomy."[90] When domestic workers began riding public transportation to their work sites, the buses and streetcars, too, became places to share information.[91] Sociologist Ruth Reed observed that African American women talked "over the different peculiarities of the white women for whom they work" and knew a great deal about "who is 'particular' about house work, who has guests most frequently, who serves the best meals and other matters of interest to employee[s]."[92] Domestic workers used such knowledge to lobby their employers for various reasons, including, according to Warren Fleming, "greater privileges and less work." Fleming averred that the African American women used peer pressure to cajole their employers: "Each servant holds up the conduct of the woman next door as an example to her mistress. 'Mrs. Jones does not have her cook to cook supper,' or, 'she hires extra help, and you must do the same for me.'"[93]

Employers' opposition to organized labor has long prevailed in the United States and in the South in particular. Uneasy housewives feared everything from their employees sharing information to strikes. At the turn of the twentieth century, white women firmly believed that African American women colluded against them, forming clubs or societies and making lists of employers for whom they would not work.[94] A 1912 Atlanta mayoral candidate, arguing for a registry of servants, declared, "Today, if you discharge your cook, every one of that number belong to a negro secret society; they immediately go to the next meeting of that society and blacklist you, and what is the result? You find in a month that your wife will be possibly unable to secure a servant under any consideration. They have organized for their protection, and our little women are made to suffer and worry and fret their souls out trying to handle incompetent, worthless, diseased and irresponsible negroes."[95] In Gainesville, Georgia, around 1920, white women concluded that African American women were acting collectively to discriminate against employers. Ruth Reed wrote, "There seems to exist among the white women of the town a belief that the negro women in their lodges or in some other organization established for that purpose, had formed an agreement as to the amount of work, number of hours, and the wage which they would agree upon with the whites. Some even believe that this organization had prevailed upon its members not to go out to service at all, adopting as its motto the words signified by the title of the organization, W.W.T.K., or White Women to the Kitchen."[96] Reed, however, found no evidence of such a union except in the minds of the white employers, who may have been reading about the growing strength of such activist unions as the Industrial Workers of the World and imagining Wobblies in their own kitchens.[97]

Because they depended so heavily on their cooks and other domestic workers for their daily comforts at home, employers greatly feared direct action, such as a strike. Auburn, Alabama, employers in 1906 believed that a strike was in the offing. Walter Fleming wrote, "At present, the general state of the servant mind has resulted in a club or society, the members of which pay regular dues. As soon as the finances are in a good condition they propose to go on a regular strike, in order to show their employers how dependent they are upon them, and to secure higher wages." Fleming, recognizing the abundance of women seeking work in southern cities, cynically predicted that such a strike would fail, as "the country darkies will come in and take the places of some of the strikers."[98]

According to historian Tera Hunter, a "surreptitious strike" occurred among domestic workers in Rock Hill, South Carolina, in 1919, possibly the effort of a secret society. The "workers identified their affiliation in a euphemistic 'Fold-the-Arms Club'—a slogan identified with the Industrial Workers of the World." In New Orleans at the same time, more than one thousand members joined Ella Pete in her Domestic Servants' Union to demanded higher wages and shorter hours through negotiation rather than a strike.[99] African American women adapted the rhetoric of the large organizations to suit their needs. Although they never struck in Gainesville, Georgia, African American women fed their employers' fears by saying things such as "We's got our Union back of us"; "We gets instructions from our Union every day"; or "We mean for the white women to know what it means to do the work we've been doing."[100]

While actual strikes by household workers were rare, women did in fact organize themselves for collective action across the South. African American women in Houston established the Women's Domestic Union in 1916 and affiliated with the American Federation of Labor, indicating their alliance with other skilled laborers.[101] In Norfolk in 1917, African American domestic workers formed the Working Women's Union to "unite laboring women and bring about a closer relationship between them."[102] The Transportation Workers Association approached domestic workers about organizing, and with TWA encouragement the women threatened to strike for guaranteed wages of one dollar per day and predetermined work hours. One white resi-

dent reported his cook to federal agents because she "had recently been in-
dulging in frequent and lengthy dissertations on the great injustice done the
negroes by the whites." The Norfolk police stopped any action in its tracks,
however, arresting numerous members of the African American working
class.[103]

The Franklin Roosevelt administration's labor-friendly stances spurred
collective action across the South in the 1930s, and numerous African Americans formed organizations and set forth labor guidelines similar to the federal legislation governing hours and wages in other lines of work. In Jackson,
Mississippi, in 1933, Mrs. Z. Elizabeth Moman styled herself as president
of the National Association for Domestic Workers. She and her constituents
presented to the federal government a request for a "Code of Fair Competition for Personal and Domestic Workers." Moman enumerated her group's re-
quests: a work week not to exceed fifty-six hours, with two half days off, one
week paid vacation, and a minimum wage of $14.40 a week. If the employer
provided housing and board, the cost of those was not to be deducted from
wages. Living quarters should have a reception room, a private bath with running water, toilet, and bathtub, "lights (same as used by employer)," heating,
and ventilation. If the servant were required to live in a basement, it should
be "hygienic."[104]

In 1935, seven "prominent Negroes" in Washington, D.C., led by a den-
tist named Garland A. Smyer, met to consider the problems of household
workers. They gathered information and contacted the Women's Bureau of
the U.S. Department of Labor. In March 1935, their group expanded to include members of the Women's Trade Union League, "outstanding Negro
Catholics," leaders of the National Negro Congress, and "several domestic
workers." They met and decided to organize the Domestic Workers' Union
(DWU). To the organizers' disappointment, only five domestic workers showed
up at the first called meeting. Undaunted, Smyer and the first president, Minnie Poole, sent out information to African American churches, wrote to the
African American newspapers, and contacted the Young Women's Christian
Association and night schools. As the union began to grow, members gave
dances and a garden party at the Frederick Douglass house in Anacostia and
provided other entertainments to raise money, which they spent printing cir-
culars and bulletins. The DWU announced its intention to negotiate wages of
at least ten dollars a week, working days of no more than ten hours a day, written employment agreements, overtime pay, decent living quarters for live-in
workers, and training, and to prevent unfair dismissal from the job. By 1940,
the DWU had 500 members, of whom 480 were African American females—a

discouraging total for a city with nearly 20,000 domestic workers. Although the group called themselves Local No. 1, they had not been able to affiliate with the American Federation of Labor or the Congress of Industrial Organizations.[105]

Organizing domestic workers always proved difficult, for a variety of reasons: the isolation of individual workers in homes; the oversupply of willing substitutes; the notorious southern hostility to organized labor.[106] According to sociology student Esther Jackson in the late 1930s, some women were suspicious of unions. One woman had other priorities, declaring that she didn't have time for a union because she spent all her spare time in church work. Others simply were not convinced of the benefit of union membership. Jackson revealed that class differences among domestic workers thwarted worker solidarity. She observed, "Some domestic workers are opposed to the Union. They are often those workers who have been in families for years, and who see no similarity between themselves and other domestic workers." While the seventeen members of a Nashville group called the Pink Carnation Club said that they were interested in improving workers' conditions, they limited their membership to women earning more than eight dollars a week and appeared unlikely to have sympathy with their less-skilled counterparts.[107]

Union organizers, too, suffered from the very conditions that they sought to ameliorate. In Nashville in November 1935, I. L. Dungee, a chauffeur, called together a dozen or more domestics, male and female, and organized the Faithful Workers League. The group started out holding recreational events, then began to think about a placement bureau. But Dungee had insufficient time "for making the contacts necessary to increase membership." The group reorganized in 1939 with one hundred members and in 1940 had meetings ranging in size from "a dozen to fifty or more." Members of the group wanted to use churches as their organizing vehicle, but as full-time employees, they lacked time to visit the churches. As late as 1940, however, Dungee was signing correspondence as president of the "Faithful Domestic Workers League" in Nashville.[108] He was plugging along despite his five-year struggle.

Numerous organizations came and went, with little success, remaining what Esther Jackson termed "paper organizations." She enumerated the disappointing attempts of the Domestic and Industrial Women's Association of the United States, formed in 1936 with headquarters in Washington, D.C., and the National Association of Domestic Workers organized in 1935 with headquarters in Jackson, Mississippi, which "lacked experienced organizers and trade union contacts."[109] From New Orleans in 1942, "A group of Organized Women's [*sic*]" wrote to President Roosevelt, addressing concerns about wages.[110] Although little other evidence of these organizations exists and their lives were probably short, obviously African American domestic workers were paying attention to the federal labor legislation regarding such organizations as the Congress of Industrial Organizations, and they wanted to be a part of the action.

As a result of labor shortages due to World War II, Jean Collier Brown, formerly of the U.S. Women's Bureau, organized the United Domestic Workers' Local Industrial Union 1283, affiliated with the CIO, in Baltimore in 1942. Brown wrote to all of the union members' employers, promising that the local would cooperate with employers and send reliable members to their homes. In return, they requested pay of $3.00 per day, or $1.75 for half a day. A full workday would be nine hours long with a one-hour lunch break. The union made little headway, although in 1944 it also included sick leave and vacation pay in the request to employers. By the end of World War II, the United Domestic Workers' Union was largely gone.[111]

Just as they had during the period before World War I, employers' imaginations remained more active than organizing African American workers in the 1940s. Around the South during World War II, rumors abounded of "Eleanor Clubs . . . supposedly, formally organized groups of black women who took direction from Eleanor Roosevelt's tendency to challenge conventions on racial matters." White housewives feared that "the 'Eleanorites would insist on the right to enter the kitchen by way of the front door'; they might become surly and refuse to don servants' uniforms or work limitless hours, or they might commit an even more grievous error like refusing to answer when addressed by their first names."[112] White women became extremely anxious about the social order turning upside down perhaps even more than the prospect of workers cutting their hours.

So serious a concern to employers were the Eleanor Clubs that the Federal Bureau of Investigation launched a formal inquiry in 1942. One informant reported being told by several sources that "the negroes were organizing 'ELEANOR CLUBS' whose motto was 'No colored maid in the kitchen by Christmas.'" Employers feared that the Eleanor Clubs would foment rebellious behavior as well as incite quitting. An employee of the Naval Research Laboratory in Washington, D.C., reported having a neighbor whose cook was a member of the reviled organization. The employer told the African American woman to set the table for dinner for four. The employee instead set five places, and when asked for the reason, the cook replied that she was "a member of an 'ELEANOR CLUB' and that she was to eat with the guests that evening." Stories of the Eleanor Club included tales of women signing pledges in their own blood and of their intention to beat up scabs. The FBI concluded that "the stories of the so-called 'ELEANOR CLUBS' are the result of widespread rumors without foundation and fact."[113]

The hysteria over the Eleanor Clubs indicated dislike and distrust of domestic workers and their perceived ally, the First Lady. Tennessee congressman Clifford Davis wrote to the mayor of Memphis in 1942, assuring him that there was no concrete evidence of organizing by domestic workers. "I really believe that a few citizens have so thoroughly worked themselves up over their antipathy to Mrs. Roosevelt, and the loss of cooks that they have been honestly misled and are responsible for the rumors," Davis commented.[114]

UNFORTUNATELY FOR THE WOMEN WORKERS, ties between the Roosevelt administration and the cooks was not as strong as some New Deal opponents feared. During the 1930s and 1940s, domestic workers were infuriated by legislation that rendered them "invisible to the law," excluding domestic service and agricultural labor from the federal wage and hour laws that were developed to protect other workers, as well as Social Security.[115] Annie Truitt of La Grange, Georgia, wrote indignantly to President Roosevelt: "As you are fixing prices on labor, please sir remember the poor cooks and wash women it's a dirty shame we can not get but $1.50 to $2.00 per week for cooking keeping house and nursing all in one job."[116]

Many cooks followed closely the 1935 passage of the Social Security Act and were extremely dismayed to find themselves excluded. Anna Smith, a cook in Washington, D.C., appealed to Eleanor Roosevelt in 1938: "Dear Madam: We the domestic find that we are not considered in the wage and hour bill and allso [sic] the social security act. I am writing you asking if you will please consider the domestic[;] after all we are essential we spend all of lives working in one place not getting enough to be able to save anything. So when we grow old we have nothing to go upon."[117] After a lifetime of work, they had little recourse.[118]

Few domestic workers could count on their employers to take care of them in their old age.[119] Occasionally an employer left money in her or his will for a cook. Many times, however, the promise of an inheritance caused only trouble. Ruth Shays remembered cooking for an elderly woman in Chattanooga in 1921 and running afoul of the woman's granddaughter: "The old soul said something about remembering me in her will. Now, I told her not to say that. She asked me why and I told her 'twas foolish to hurry your life away. Now, how was I going to tell that old lady that her granddaughter wanted every cent she had and wasn't above throwing dirt in her face to get it?"[120]

Marjorie Kinnan Rawlings, thinking of an angle to gain her employee's loyalty, tried to bribe Idella Parker to stay with her by promising her an annuity in her will, saying, "Idella, it says right here that if you're with me 'til I die, you'll receive fifty dollars a month as long as you live." Parker remarked, "I do believe she hoped that promise of fifty dollars a month would bind me to her and I would not leave her again." But Parker left shortly thereafter.[121]

At times, white families did care for longtime employees in their old age. Celia Lipscomb remained with the Goodman family of Tyler, Texas, for forty years after emancipation. In 1900, Lipscomb was a seventy-two-year-old widow who had borne six children and had four living. She lived with ninety-five-year-old Samuel Goodman and his grandson in Tyler.[122] Although census data fail to confirm the story, a local historian writes that "Aunt Cely" had "lived in [Goodman's] home for 72 years and had been his regular cook for sixty of those years as slave and free woman." The Goodman family supplied Lipscomb with a house and stipend for her old age.[123] Most women, however, depended on their kin to comfort them in old age.

OVER TIME, COOKS NEGOTIATED some changes in their hours and wages. By refusing to live in with their employers, they put a stop to twenty-four-hour workdays. Long work hours persisted, however, and so did low wages for many women. Domestic workers found their hopes dashed for improvement through either unionization or New Deal legislation. Despite the fears of southern whites, cooks remained unorganized and exploited until World War II.

Creating a Homeplace

SHELTER, FOOD, CLOTHING, AND A LITTLE FUN

With their paltry earnings, cooks provided for their families as best they could. All those hours in front of stoves bought food, clothing, shelter, and sometimes a little recreation for cooks and their loved ones. The small houses of segregated African American neighborhoods sheltered a population working diligently to make their ways in southern society. In meeting the essential needs of the next generation, African American women opposed the dominant culture that slighted the requirements of black children. In the Jim Crow South, survival was tantamount to resistance. Poor pay made providing the basics of food, clothing, and shelter a significant accomplishment. Mrs. H. A. Clement, from Baltimore, summarized the situation in 1939 in a letter to Franklin Roosevelt: "I am a [domestic] worker and have three children no body to support them but my self my husban is dead ben dead 4 years. . . . Core fair [carfare] to pay my rent insurance and three children to clothes and fead. . . . Sometimes supthing to eate and some time nuthing. . . . I am all most to my roes in [rows end]."[1]

In most Western societies, servants have historically lived on the premises of the places that they served, and in the nineteenth-century South, the practice was called "living in." In the lean decades immediately after the Civil War, a significant number of cooks lived on the premises of their employers' homes. Increasingly, however, African American women created a new paradigm for domestic workers, insisting that they live in homes of their own. "Living out," as this new phenomenon was called, had incalculable effects on the lives of southerners, both African American and white. African American women, as never before, had places of their own, however spartan or shabby. Their employers had to adjust to a new type of servant, one who was not at their beck and call around the clock. The process took decades. At first, many emancipated domestic workers needed to live with their employers, for they had no homes of their own and no money with which to acquire them. But in the early years of the twentieth century, more and more women lived away. Living in never went away completely, but it became increasingly rare. Washingtonian Dolethia Otis, born about 1900, remembered the pleasure in leaving her employer's house at night: "The living-in jobs just kept you running; never stopped. Day or night . . . never a minute's peace. But when I went out days on my jobs, I'd get my work done and be gone . . . that's it. This work had a' end."[2]

FOR MANY AFRICAN AMERICAN WOMEN, their own homes represented an autonomy that living in their employers' households simply did not afford. Critic bell hooks has written eloquently on the importance of what she calls "homeplace," or the home as a "small private reality."[3] Having a spot to call one's own was "about the construction of a safe place where black people could affirm one another and by so doing heal many of the wounds inflicted by racist domination." The possession of homes by African Americans had "a radical political dimension" and could create "a community of resistance."[4] When Willie Mae Wright married Dan Workman in the 1920s, Wright's employer asked them to continue living "on the lot." Workman refused, however. Wright recalled, "Dan didn't like to live on white people's places; Dan always said every tub ought to stand on its own bottom."[5]

Living in, conversely, carried over a number of the practices of slavery. For the worker, living in had distinct disadvantages. Cooks remained available to their employers around the clock and had very little personal freedom. In 1933, Mrs. Z. Elizabeth Moman of Jackson, Mississippi, president of the presumably short-lived "National Association for Domestic Workers," wrote, "Very few servants find it desirable to live on the place because of the disregard of personal rights, by the employer. They are called upon to perform duties any time after hours, with no additional compensation."[6] In 1885, Mary Wade's employers expected her to stay near the house in the evenings, but instead she spent time away "nearly every evening, leaving her business and going off to Wilson's home and in the neighborhood and to the Creacys." Leaving after two months, Wade owed her employers for a barrel of flour, for which they collected payment from her cousin. Since a young woman living in would have little need for that much flour, presumably Wade acquired the flour for her family of origin or someone else who needed the provisions that Wade's employment brought.[7] Wade's experience illustrated another difficulty of living in: a domestic worker's transgressions could be visited upon her relatives. Living out, according to Marie Stone of Washington, D.C., meant that a woman didn't have to worry so much about her actions reflecting badly on her family.[8]

Living in isolated African American families from one another. Anne Moody remembered that her mother went to work for the Johnson family in Centreville, Mississippi, around 1948. The Moodys lived in a house on the Johnsons' large lot, on a paved street "near the beginning of gravel." Moody remembered, "We were the only Negros in that section, which seemed like some sort of honor."[9] As a child, Moody did not realize the supreme paradox that being a live-in domestic worker created for her mother. She gained status, and perhaps some convenience, by living in a neighborhood with pavement, but she gave up life among her peers to do so.

That African Americans and whites shared domiciles was one of the key ironies of Jim Crow. As historian Neil McMillen has pointed out, however, "Even in spatially close circumstances a sense of distinction prevailed."[10] Most employers managed to show their racism in the accommodations that they made for their cooks, carrying segregation right into the physical layouts of their households.

The quarters that employers supplied for their cooks varied dramatically, whether in the house or in a separate structure behind the house. Some employers provided comfortable, decent surroundings and others had only the barest spaces, but, regardless of quality, cooks' domiciles were always close at hand. Writer Alice Walker recalled visiting the Georgia home of white writer Flannery O'Connor. She observed that the O'Connor home had a "typical arrangement": "white folks up front, the 'help,' in a far shabbier house, within calling distance from the back door."[11]

Willie Mae Wright lived in with a wide variety of employers before her marriage in the 1920s. Grateful for the simplest quarters if they were clean and somewhat comfortable, she didn't care if they were in the house or "on the lot." The Thompson family used scrap lumber to build a "nice big room" for Wright in their backyard. She had to carry water for her bath from the main house but still considered the room "fixed . . . up nice." A "two-eyed Franklin heater" kept the place toasty in the coldest weather. The Thompsons installed a telephone "when some men tried to break in there on me."[12] Even better was her basement room in the home of her respected employers, the Dukes, which had indoor plumbing: "The bedroom had a cute little new bed in it and a nice dressing-table. And there was a good bathroom with a tub and everything. Just for me. I thought, Lord, if I ain't swimming in deep water now."[13] The bed was "new" and the bathtub "good," and Wright was grateful for small favors. But Wright fumed about another employer, Mrs. Caruthers: "Nothing ever flew all over me the ways that did about her bed. Telling me I needn't sleep on a pallet, just go ahead and be comfortable and sleep in the guest room, she was going to get the mattress cleaned and re-covered anyhow. I wonder what she was aiming to do with the sheets—burn them?"[14] Caruthers's blatant if casual prejudice greatly irritated Wright.

Idella Parker experienced horrific living conditions at Cross Creek when she joined the staff of novelist Marjorie Kinnan Rawlings in 1940. The four other employees, Martha Mickens, her husband Will Mickens, their son Little Will Mickens, and his girlfriend Alberta, all lived in one room of "the tenant house," an "unpainted wood frame house" behind the main house. Parker lived in the other room, separated from the Mickens clan only by a curtain. Initially, Parker's furnishings included an army cot, a straight chair, a small potbelly stove, and a kerosene lantern. The outhouse was behind, "hidden by some trees at the edge of an orange grove, and a number 2 tin washtub hanging on a nail outside the tenant house was our bathtub." Eventually, as Parker toughed it out in poor circumstances, Rawlings bought a nice set of furniture for her and had a real door installed between Parker's room and that of the Mickenses. In 1941, Rawlings expanded the tenant house to add a small apartment just for Parker. The Mickens family gained more space for themselves as well.[15]

Some employers treated servant quarters like storage for any other household appliance. Esther Lawson remembered her first live-in accommodations in Washington, D.C., in 1914: "This woman had me a room fixed up in the basement. Well, it was more like a garage. No door on it, or nothing. They pulled the car right in—just like you have your room, put all your tools and things in, a little room. I guess that's what that was. When I'd go down at night from the kitchen I'd go right in this little room. Car sitting up there. That's where I slept."[16] Lawson rested amid gasoline fumes and road dust, just another tool for her employer.

The number of live-in servants declined sharply across the South after 1880, as African Americans found the means to become autonomous. The desire of cooks to live away from their places of employment caused considerable disagreement with their employers, who valued the control that they exercised over domestic workers living under their roofs.[17] A 1924 survey taken in Baltimore revealed that housewives feared that a cook living away from them might "fail to be regular and punctual in the morning," as they thought that a woman returning to her own home would "do the work [she] must neglect during the day," or would go out to play rather than resting. Sociologist Mary Robinson summarized the housewives' concerns: "In either case [cooks] are trying to burn their candles at both ends and their health suffers, while the employer suffers from a tired servant utterly unequal to the requirements of her day's work."[18] Employers simply preferred that a cook not have her own life.

Moving out of one's employer's house into a place of one's own was a huge step for a domestic worker. Naomi Yates lived in for a year with the same family for whom her brother worked. She recalled, "They made me so tired and sick I just was going to try. Like I said I got set and in near a year I left and started on my own." Any woman who moved out burned bridges as she left, for she and her employers almost always "tacitly agreed" that she would not work for them again.[19]

MANY AFRICAN AMERICAN WOMEN considered the risks of moving out to be worth taking. In their own homes, they could have more freedom and more time to do as they wished, despite the requirements of maintaining separate households.[20] Having one's own place apart from one's employer came at a cost, but it was a price that most African American domestic workers gladly paid.

Although African American neighborhoods might be adjacent to white ones, making for a short commute to work, increasingly they became segregated and often isolated, and, in larger towns and cities, commutes of a mile or more were not uncommon.[21] In larger cities, trolleys and then motor buses shortened the trips, but they brought indignity through their segregated seating and additional costs to already tight budgets.[22]

In southern cities such as Atlanta, the move toward racially segregated neighborhoods began in the late nineteenth century and solidified in the early twentieth century.[23] John Dollard observed that in Indianola, Mississippi, African Americans lived literally on the other side of the tracks, in an area of small, cheap houses known as "nigger town."[24] bell hooks recalled the ramifications of living in segregated neighborhoods in her small Kentucky town. For African Americans, hooks said, "The railroad tracks were a daily reminder of our marginality. Across those tracks were paved streets, stores we could not enter, restaurants we could not eat in, and people we could not look directly in the face. Across those tracks was a world we could work in as maids, as janitors, as prostitutes, as long as it was in a service capacity. We could enter that world but we could not live there. We had always to return to the margin, to cross the tracks to shacks and abandoned houses on the edge of town."[25]

Domestic workers waiting for the streetcar, Mitchell Street, Atlanta, 1939. Photo by Marion Post Wolcott, Farm Security Administration/Office of War Information, Library of Congress LC-USF33-030339-M4.

Rural migrants adapting to the city often found their neighborhoods to be crowded, smelly, and noisy.[26] In most towns, the streets of African American neighborhoods remained unpaved, creating problems with dust, dirt, and mud for tidy housekeepers. Public transportation could be spotty. In Gainesville, Georgia, Ruth Reed observed in the 1920s that "the street car lines do not approach near enough to the negro section of town to be of any great service."[27]

Commuting proved to be a sizeable expense for African Americans living in their own homes. In their letters to the federal government during the New Deal, the expenditure that cooks mentioned most often was for transportation to and from work. Women who lived in relatively small towns often saved transportation costs by walking to work. Roxanna Hupes of Galveston observed: "We don't make enough to ride the bus I walk a mile every morning to get to my work."[28] In larger cities, however, getting from one part of town to another, from neighborhoods populated only by African Americans to those occupied only by whites, took sizeable chunks out of already crowded daily schedules and already slender paychecks. Doris Woodson remembered a familiar scene in Richmond perhaps in the 1940s: "It was usually dark when they left. You'd see all these people standing on the street corners waiting for the streetcars, later buses, with their bags or packages of leftover food—whatever they'd be taking home to their own families. . . . And it took forever, because employers weren't living in the city where you were living."[29] And Willie Mae Wright commented that in a big city like Atlanta, even when one rode the streetcar, the distance on foot to the employer's residence could be considerable: "Walking two miles a day to and from the car line is no plaything."[30]

Women spent a large portion of their wages on transportation. G. S. Ellington, a Baptist pastor in Athens, Georgia, wrote of his wife's situation: "My wife is a splended [sic] cook and can only get $5.00 and pay half of the week's expense for Taxi fare making her only get for salary $4.30 per week." Even sharing taxi fare with another domestic worker, Mrs. Ellington spent approximately 15 percent of her salary on transportation to work.[31] In large urban areas, the costs could be even greater than in Athens: $0.90 a week in San Antonio, and a formidable $1.25 in Washington, D.C. For streetcar or bus fare in Norfolk, Virginia, during the Great Depression, domestic workers paid a whopping $1.25 a week, or 31 percent of an average weekly wage of $4.00.[32]

In Atlanta, some employers sought to ameliorate the situation by paying their workers' bus fare, and the employees chose to keep the extra money by walking home in the evenings. In the 1940s, Jonell Clark's mother worked for ten to fifteen dollars per week plus bus fare. Clark recalled, "A few women lost their right to receive bus fare when their employers discovered that they chose to walk the long trek home to save the ten to fifteen cents bus fare."[33] Even the employers' attempts to help their employees by giving them rides home turned into opportunities for subjection, according to G. K. Butterfield Jr., of Wilson, North Carolina. Many "rich white women" picked up their domestic workers at home, and a few even let them ride in the front seat. Butterfield recalled, "But whenever the husband would bring the maid home, without exception, the maid would have to sit in the back seat, because no white man wanted ever to be seen with a black woman sitting in the front seat of his car with him. So invariably, the maid would be in the back. So that was a symbol in the black community."[34] Similar to Willie Mae Wright's employer who said she would have the mattress recovered, these employers reinforced segregation in their private spaces and insulted their employees in the process.

COOKS WERE WILLING to be inconvenienced, however, and sought to live separately from their employers whenever possible. In the first quarter of the twentieth century, single women in large cities such as Washington, D.C., and Atlanta in increasing numbers lived in boarding or lodging houses. Beulah

Nelson stayed in a boardinghouse in Washington for three years. She fondly recalled the parties she and other female boarders hosted: "Them was my best days, and that's how I met my husband!"[35] In Atlanta, the African American First Congregational Church sponsored a boardinghouse attached to its parsonage for young working women.[36] Lodging houses, which were cheaper and provided no food, could be more beneficial than boardinghouses, which charged for meals, because African American women who received meals as compensation from their employers did not need food from their landladies.[37] On occasion, cooks kept lodgers in their own homes. In addition to her work as a cook, Rilla Jones of Macon sheltered two young male lodgers in her home in the 1920s. Sometimes the individuals whom the census takers classified as lodgers may have in fact had other types of relationships with the people with whom they were living. In 1930, Mattie Drewery lodged with Homer Pitts, a forty-seven-year-old single carpenter who owned a nice home; his two adopted children, ages ten and twelve; and Pitt's single sister. Perhaps Drewery had some other type of relationship with Pitts. Next door to the Pitts household on Broad Street, Dora Hughes, a fifty-five-year-old widow, lodged with Janie Jones, age ninety-two, who also owned her home. Hughes almost surely assisted her landlady in some way, perhaps in return for rent.

Drewery and Hughes numbered among the handful of cooks living in African American–owned homes. Given the low wages of African Americans in general, predictably few cooks owned real estate. From a sample of fifty cooks in Macon in 1930, only Nettie Wright, a sixty-year-old widow, owned property, a house valued at $500. Her twelve-year-old granddaughter lived with her, as did a forty-nine-year-old male roomer, whose rent presumably helped with expenses. Seven other cooks, or 14 percent, lived with people who owned their houses, but the cooks themselves were not the property owners. Three of them lived with their widowed mothers, whose houses were valued at $1,000, $600, and $750, and Drewery and Hughes were lodgers.

A married couple with two incomes had more ability to buy a home than did single people. Two Macon cooks lived with their husbands in houses valued at $1,000 and $600 in 1930. In Lakeland, Florida, in the 1930s, Lucinda and Charlie Robinson were buying their home in the Teaspoon Hill section "from Oxford and Oxford Attorney" for six dollars a month. With both of them working, they could pool Charlie's wages as a laborer and Lucinda's four dollars per week as a cook and make their house payments. According to their interviewer, Teaspoon Hill was a mixture of good and bad houses, of homeowners and renters. The Robinsons' four-room house was unpainted with a small porch across the front. Water came from a pump under an orange tree, and the outhouse sat at the back of the property. The kitchen featured a woodstove and a "large new Ice refrigerator." The floors were bare wood, and only two rooms had "ceiled" walls.[38] The Robinsons, working together, provided simple but adequate housing for themselves. Partnership made their goal more attainable.

Most cooks lived in rental properties, often clustered on alleys, also known as "short streets."[39] Since almost all rental property was owned by white people,[40] cooks found themselves subject to white people for shelter even in their own households.[41] And the rents took huge percentages—anywhere from one-half to two-thirds—of cooks' incomes.[42] In 1937, Elizabeth Clyburn of Washington, D.C., who earned seven dollars a week, wrote to Eleanor Roosevelt describing the difficulty of rent costs: "We cant buy clothes we pay all for rent I don't even have [illegible] a 10 cent policy on my life."[43] Clyburn mourned about housing costs that prevented her from paying for a mutual-aid life insurance policy to help her family.

Just as rents varied widely, so too did the quality of cooks' houses. The worst properties had porous outside walls and floors and only fireplaces for cooking and heat. Electricity remained rare into the 1930s, as did indoor plumbing. In Birmingham, Jackson, and Charleston in 1940, fewer than 10 percent of African Americans had running water in their houses, and the vast majority of African Americans cooked on woodstoves.[44] In the 1930s, Katy Brumby lived in Scruggs Alley in Birmingham, an area of "small, gray, unpainted houses," where several families shared an outdoor privy. Brumby, a fastidious housekeeper, knew that she and her neighbors deserved better: "Dat's bad," she said, "Dat ain't right." She complained that the landlord didn't make improvements to or maintain his property.[45] In Montgomery in the 1940s, seven members of Jonell Clark's family lived in a shotgun house: "seven people cramped, living, loving, and losing in two rooms." She and her brother could lie in bed and see the Big Dipper through the holes in the roof, and each autumn her mother and grandmother saved newspapers to plaster the walls and block the winter wind.[46]

Against such a backdrop of shoddy rental properties, Willie Mae Wright and others were thrilled when public housing became available. Wright delighted in her new apartment in the Edgewood housing project, which opened in Atlanta after World War II. She remembered, "Everybody was so glad and rejoicing for them nice homes that they couldn't rest. . . . [One woman] said the ceilings were so good, which most of them never slept under a stout ceiling in all their born lives before."[47] Jonell Clark's family similarly exulted in Patterson Court in Montgomery, which had running water, electricity, and indoor toilets. Her mother bought on installment living room furniture, a stylish red and white Formica dinette set, and a wringer washing machine to furnish their fine new dwelling.[48]

Willie Mae Wright, ever conscious of her surroundings, carefully recounted the furnishings of her various abodes. As a young woman, she set up housekeeping with her young sisters in a two-room rented house in Tifton, Georgia. Taking an interest in Wright's attempt to provide a home for the orphaned girls, her employer and the employers' friends provided secondhand furniture aplenty. "They just kept on until they had us fixed up," she recalled. "Some evenings when I'd get home there'd be so much piled on the porch I could hardly get in the door—clothes, food, wood, just about anything. And wasn't none of it no junk."[49] When Wright married, another employer helped her and her new husband furnish a three-room apartment, providing a mahogany dining suite and a complete bedroom suite. The bedroom furniture was a little dirty, but, she added, "time I washed it off with Ivory soap it looked like a million dollars." Wright's father-in-law made a five-dollar down payment on a Detroit Jewel gas stove for the newlyweds, who paid for it in installments of five dollars a month. Wright said, "I didn't want no wood stove, because I didn't want to get up and have to make a fire every morning."[50]

With crude sanitation and many people living in small houses, health conditions were sometimes awful in African American neighborhoods. In 1904, sociologist William Elwang complained of "this close herding together of men, women and children, not only members of families, but even boarders, often into a single room under circumstances where modesty must forever be a stranger and in which vice ensures as certainly as physical disease grows out of noxious hygienic situations."[51] As early as Reconstruction, employers began to fret about the sanitary conditions under which their cooks lived, not out of a particular concern about the cooks' welfare but rather because they feared cooks as vectors of disease into their own homes.[52] By the Progressive Era, the hue and cry against servants as disease carriers was in full swing, and white observers viewed tuberculosis as a "Negro servant's disease."[53] Whites, concerned mainly about their own families' health, complained about being "thrown into intimate contact with the negroes, who are employed as cooks, nurses, house servants, laundresses, etc."[54] The public outcry about African Americans and tuberculosis highlighted a number of factors, most notably the poor health care available for African Americans and the quickness with which whites stigmatized them.

Poverty, decade after decade, took its toll. In the late nineteenth century, the death rate among African American children under the age of five was three times that of whites.[55] Jonell Clark recalled the death of her brother Marvin from rheumatic fever in the 1940s: "Marvin died because we were poor Negroes who could not afford medical care for him. We had just enough money for our basic needs." Their mother, she remembered, "went back to work after taking a few days off."[56]

To the extent that they could, cooks cared for and about their living quarters. If a cook were not required to prepare the evening meal, she might have some time in the afternoons to work on her house, and observers thought that the homes of cooks were often the nicest around. Ruth Reed commented that in Gainesville, Georgia, "the homes of the women who 'cook out' presented a much better appearance than those who work away from home during the entire day or than of those who take in washing."[57] Certainly Katy Brumby's home fit that description. She sowed her tiny front yard with winter grass, "struggl[ing] up through the hard-packed black earth in patches." In the backyard, she grew a few vegetables and flowers, greens and dahlias, onions and zinnias, to which, to Brumby's chagrin, "folks in the alley" helped themselves while she was away all day working.[58]

Most of the work of creating "homeplace" fell to the women. Somehow, according to bell hooks, tired mothers found the motivation to make homes: "Their lives were not easy. Their lives were hard. They were black women who for the most part worked outside the home serving white folks, cleaning their houses, washing their clothes, tending their children—black women who worked in the fields or in the streets, whatever they could do to make ends meet, whatever was necessary. Then they returned to their homes to make life happen there." hooks marveled at "the effort of black women to conserve enough of themselves to provide service (care and nurturance) within their own families and communities."[59] When hooks's mother, Rosa Bell Watkins, returned home in the evenings, she greeted her children with warmth, with "the effort it must have taken for her to transcend her own tiredness" and whatever wounds to her spirit that she had suffered during the day.[60]

Women had to squeeze in chores and tasks for their own families around long workdays. L. G. Huff of Fort Worth, Texas, wrote to Eleanor Roosevelt in 1937:

When we give all of our time on a small salary job and have to pay to get our laundry done but still we do laundry for the family whom we work but don't have time to wash for our selves or even cook a decent meal of food at home for our husband until Thursday evening we get what is called one evening out of a week get off at 2.30 P.M. stores close at 5.30 P.M. a very short time to shop clean our own house cook that one decent meal at home all after 2.30 pm no time then to do laundry at home but still our appearance must be superb or we can't work on the job. I ask the lady whom I work for to grant me a few hours to care for some real business and bills that had to be seen after and I was sorry I spoke about it. I was answered with such grievous words.[61]

THE IRONY OF COOKING all day for their employers and coming home to a second shift of cooking for their own families was not lost on African American women. Many, of course, brought leftovers home with them, but "toting" could not ensure a steady supply of food. Families with older daughters might press them into kitchen service while the mothers worked outside of the house.[62] But, if there were no one else available to cook, a tired woman had to think about another set of meals. Lucinda Robinson told her Federal Writers' Project interviewer, "I like to cook, and after I get through cooking for white folks, I have to come home and cook for Charlie."[63]

Cooks' families sometimes suffered from poor nutrition despite the abundance of food women had as raw materials in their employers' homes. At a time when her family had very little money, Willie Mae Wright became addicted to starch. She explained, "If you eat starch, you don't be hungry for anything else much." She ate Argo starch "a pinch at a time" while she was ironing, "and then I wouldn't want no lunch."[64] Cooks were keenly aware of the materials available to feed their own families, for good or for ill. Eva Davis of Vicksburg recalled an exchange with her cook, Matilda: "I told Matilda (my cook) I wanted her to be as economical in cooking for me as she was for herself and she replied, 'lawsy, Miss Eva, I couldn't do dat, you wouldn't eat what we has to eat.'"[65] In the 1950s, Anne Moody noticed the difference: "Sometimes Mama would bring us the white family's leftovers. It was the best food I had ever eaten. That was when I discovered that white folks ate different from us. They had all kinds of different food with meat and all. We always had just beans and bread." Because of their deep poverty, Elmira Moody sometimes fed her children only cornbread and clabbered milk, which she could buy for a quarter a gallon.[66]

Besides not having enough good food, another difficulty in cooking for one's family was simply a matter of time. Since many cooks had to be at their employers' to prepare breakfast, they had scant time to fix early-morning meals for their own families. In 1897, African American minister Joseph E. Smith reported that children had meager breakfasts, perhaps bread or molasses, and quarreled among themselves, wanting their mothers to stay at home.[67] Two decades later, sociologist Ruth Reed fretted that the cook's family breakfast was often food left from the previous day or "some poorly cooked food prepared by a younger member of the family." Reed found that 30 percent of the African American families in Gainesville, Georgia, that she visited had only two meals per day.[68] And in the afternoon, the cook's family's meal often had to be squeezed in around the white family's schedule. In Indianola, Mississippi, John Dollard observed the patterns of traffic between the African American and white sections of town. African American women left their homes between six and seven in the morning and returned home between two and three o'clock, "in the dead heat of the afternoon," to get the "main meal of the day" for their families. They returned to their employers at about five o'clock and came home "again at dusk after the whites have finished supper and the dishes are done."[69]

Meals in cooks' homes were often simple affairs. A young woman living with her mother in the late 1890s reported a breakfast of coffee, wheat bread, "meat" (probably fat pork), and bacon, eaten at 6:30 before she left for her cooking job. The family's evening meal, at around eight P.M., consisted of cornbread and vegetables with meat "now and then."[70] In Athens, Georgia, according to sociologist T. J. Woofter, diets of cornbread and side meat or flour hoecake and pork were still common in the early twentieth century.[71] Turnip greens cooked with fat pork appeared on tables year-round.[72]

In his study of "Farmersville" in 1898, W. E. B. DuBois found that African Americans bought plain foods, "furnished by colored grocers": pork, beef, ham and bacon, chickens, and turkeys; wheat flour, cornmeal, and rice; cabbage, potatoes, green corn, tomatoes, and beans; tea and coffee; sugar; lard; butter; salt and pepper; herrings; eggs; apples; watermelon; milk and buttermilk, as well as wood for cooking.[73] In Athens, Georgia, food expenditures accounted for 29 percent of an African American family's entire annual budget,[74] while DuBois estimated expenditures among Farmersville families of between 38 and 52 percent.[75] In either locale, groceries made up a significant portion of a family's expenses. Families with little access to credit could buy only small quantities of food at a time, raising the cost considerably.[76] And, according to researcher Paul Kenneth Edwards in the early 1930s, African American–owned grocery stores charged higher prices than did white-owned establishments, adding yet one more expense to the tote board of segregation.[77]

Edwards further observed that cooks often bought carefully for their own families, getting "variety just so far as the family budget will permit." He noted that cooks purchased canned fruit and that "fresh fruits and vegetables are consumed when in season and consequently at their lowest prices." Cooks bought turnip greens, mustard greens, cabbage, onions, green beans, and tomatoes in season, eschewing "fancy canned products" and expensive, out-of-season fruits and vegetables.[78] Jonell Clark's family ordinarily ate meat only on Sunday and fish on Friday, but after they moved to the public housing projects, her mother began to use part of her days off to prepare simple but good meals for her children: "delicious meat loaf," cabbage, okra, corn and tomato, rice, pickled beets, and cornbread.[79]

A cook working fifteen hours a day had little time to think about gardening or canning, but if she shared a household with someone who had resources to garden, the family's diet might improve dramatically. From Gainesville, Georgia, at the turn of the twentieth century to Indianola, Mississippi, in the 1930s, African Americans tried to supplement their diets with greens, chickens, and pigs.[80] Charlie and Lucinda Robinson enjoyed a meal of fish, sweet potatoes, strawberry jam, butter, cornbread, and coffee while their interviewer visited them. Charlie Robinson kept rabbits and chickens, and his garden brought forth collard greens, mustard greens, corn, and onions.[81] But having a garden took significant effort, often the labor of the entire family, as well as having a landlord who would permit such activities and a lot large enough to accommodate a garden space. A U.S. Senate report in 1880, the outcome of an investigation of the reasons for African American migration from the South to the North, commented that Joseph Adams of Goldsboro, North Carolina, farmed, his wife cooked for wages, their children kept a productive garden, and still they rarely had a diet of more than fatback and bread.[82] In his study of Columbia, Missouri, William Elwang found that fewer than half of the African American families that he talked to had kitchen gardens or livestock,[83] while T. J. Woofter observed that African Americans in Athens rarely grew anything except collard and turnip greens.[84]

Taking leftovers from one's employer in lieu of cash wages, a practice commonly called "toting," made up important parts of African American cooks' diets. Employers' food choices strongly affected African American families. Annette Coleman recalled that her employer in Georgia in the 1920s expected her to eat table scraps, which had to be shared with the employer's dog.[85] In the 1940s, Marjorie Kinnan Rawlings indirectly commented on the impact that her food choices had on her cook, Idella Parker: "Idella and I alone are likely to eat food that is definitely 'scrappy.'" Rawlings observed that she was likely to eat a poached egg or warmed-over vegetables, "while Idella wanders back to the tenant house with a bit of bread and bacon."[86] Most poignantly, Richard Wright remembered waiting for his mother's employers to finish their meals so that he could learn what his own dinner would be: "If the white people left anything, my brother and I would eat well; but if they did not, we would have our usual bread and tea. Watching the white people eat would make my empty stomach churn and I would grow vaguely angry. Why could I not eat when I was hungry? Why did I always have to wait until others were through? I could not understand why some people had food and others did not."[87] The gross inequalities of the situation piqued Wright's sense of justice, but there was not much that Ella Wright could do to correct the situation.

Regardless of where the food came from, the cost was high for the cook who worked hard for her family on top of her labor for her employers. Florence Ladd wrote fondly of the meals prepared by her grandmother, Florence Virginia Wood Willis, who lived in New Bern, North Carolina, and served as housekeeper and cook for the Roman Catholic priests. "Mama" and "Pa" Willis kept a garden with tomatoes, string beans, new potatoes, and corn. Ladd recalled that a "typical" meal of fried chicken, corn, and biscuits, ended with "luscious" pecan pie. But Ladd realized that the work took a toll on her "often silent" grandmother: "Had years of domestic chores, in the service of others and in her own domain, rendered her quiet (as well as visibly weary)? Had she been silenced, over the years, by the labor required to purchase the land and building materials for a house, acquire furniture, buy a piano, provide piano and organ lessons for my mother, then send her to Winston-Salem Teachers College? After years of rearing her own children, Mama Willis had three grandchildren thrust upon her. Had her voice been stilled by duty and responsibility?"[88]

THE THIRD BASIC ESSENTIAL of human life, clothing, also came at a premium. Mothers struggled in particular to clothe their growing children. Richard Wright started school at a "later age than was usual" because his mother couldn't buy him presentable clothes.[89] In Alexandria, Virginia, Doris Willis wrote to Franklin Roosevelt of the needs of her children: "I am only getting $3 per week with 4 small children to support with no husband. My husband pass away one year ago. . . . This fall I am not able to buy my children cloths for school. Not able to buy them 3 meals a day."[90] Clothing shortages affected many parts of a child's life, but perhaps the inability to attend school had the longest-term effects.

Some cooks, particularly as young women, loved clothes and spent sizeable percentages of their income on their wardrobes. Willie Mae Wright remembered the suit, purchased in Jacksonville, that she was wearing when her husband-to-be proposed marriage: "light-weight, soft blue wool, with big white buttons . . . lined with white silk." For another outfit she bought "gray dropstitch stockings for three dollars and a half," a substantial sum of money.[91] When Bernice Reeder left her employers' home for a place of her own in Washington, D.C., about the time of World War I, she had her photograph taken in the first new outfit that she bought. Her new ensemble included a large hat and a fur coat over a blouse with a large white bow at the neck.[92] And Annie Mae Hunt remembered that her wages, combined with the ten dollars a week that her husband earned at the Sinclair gas station, bought luxuries in Dallas in the early 1940s: "I had a diamond ring, fur coats. The fur coat I remember now was about $45 or $50. Course I didn't know anything about no mink, and I don't know if it was mink or not. I don't know what kind of coat it was. Only I knew it was a fur coat, and everybody was wearing em. It looked good at that time and I made 8 and a half [dollars a week]."[93] Hunt delighted in being outfitted in the latest fashions on her domestic's income.

Some women managed to transform gifts or cast-off attire from their employers into perfectly acceptable wardrobes, marking themselves as respectable urban dwellers.[94] Mary Belle Jordan, who worked for a family with daughters about her size and age, gained a certain status among her peers for the fine — although used — clothing that she received from her employers. Her son recalled, "She was one of the best-dressed ladies at St. Paul Church, wearing clothes that the white girls had tossed away. They called this 'making do'— making the most of what you had."[95] Willie Mae Wright suffered occasionally when employers gave or sold her inappropriate clothes, but she thoroughly enjoyed having access to the castoffs from wealthy, stylish Atlanta women. As a young, single woman, Wright "was really wanting to strut" in such items as a "gray georgette dress and gray slippers" topped with a powder blue evening cape.[96] Wearing finery provided an antidote to days of hard work, and a woman could feel good about turning an employer's castoffs into something of which to be proud.[97]

Hats, too, formed an important part of a cook's off-duty wardrobe, a direct disruption of the caricature of Mammy covering her head with a scarf.[98] In the early part of the twentieth century, South Carolinian Chloe spent thirty-five cents on a showy new hat for the Fourth of July. It was "a very large, black straw trimmed with a wealth of black and white veiling and a huge purple orchid on top," an investment that, according to her condescendingly amused employer, greatly enhanced Chloe's enjoyment of the holiday.[99] Cleora Butler adored hats and in the 1940s bought two "exquisite," expensive hats from a new "and very exclusive store" in downtown Tulsa. She recalled the racism that threatened any shopping trip: "While society in the 1940s had changed to the point where blacks could shop in a few white establishments, it was not usually permitted for one to try on clothing, especially hats and shoes. Occasionally, you might be permitted to try on a hat, but you were given a hand mirror and shown to a back room where 'preferred' customers could not see you trying on your selection." On this particular occasion, Butler became infuriated at the "horrible treatment" that she received and subsequently signed up for a millinery course, "totally resolved never to buy another hat as long as [she] lived." Instead of submitting to the indignity of ill treatment by white salespeople, Butler became proficient at hat making and sold her products to her friends for as much as fifty dollars apiece.[100]

WHEN THE BASIC NEEDS of shelter, food, and clothing were taken care of, many cooks had scant leisure. In part this was because of the length of their workdays and the paucity of time off. Katherine Rutherford of Baltimore wrote to President Roosevelt, "You know the law of health is 8 hours work, 8 hours recreation and 8 hours sleep but the poor women that works in these private familys don't get any recreation they get all work and but very little sleep and if they say they are tired the people they work for will say they are lazy after 16 and 18 hours work in one day that is they work them all day and the best part of the night."[101]

But others, particularly the young and single, did have some fun in their time off. Idella Parker, who never drank alcohol, eschewed the juke joints that proliferated in upper central Florida, but when she and Bernard Young began courting in the early 1940s, they went to "ball games, the drugstore-ice cream parlor, a good movie, a card party, always somewhere."[102] Live performances often drew enthusiastic crowds. Chloe from South Carolina thoroughly enjoyed a trip to the circus, recounting in detail to her employer the activities of the acrobats and other performers.[103] In Birmingham, Katy Brumby liked hearing "one of the Negro swing orchestras that play at the Negro Masonic Temple one night, at the City's Auditorium the next," and she also attended the circus.[104] Cooks also went to movies in segregated theaters. Willie Mae Wright and her husband celebrated their marriage by attending the show at the Grand Theatre in Atlanta, for "colored people could go there then."[105]

As radio became more common, African American cooks received pleasure in listening to broadcasts. Katy Brumby listened to the radio at her employers', taking in broadcasts by President Roosevelt and Marian Anderson. At her own house, however, she had only a broken radio, in addition to an old Victrola.[106] In a sample of the 1930 U.S. Census, not a single household in the African American neighborhoods in Macon had a radio.[107] For women without their own radios, access to information about the outside world was fil-tered through their employers' media.

By the late 1930s, radio became the basis for community gatherings. On the occasion of the Joe Louis–Max Schmeling boxing match in 1937, Cleora Butler's parents hosted a picnic for a large group, complete with fried chicken and homemade ice cream. The Cab Calloway orchestra, for which Butler's brother played saxophone, entertained before the fight. The guests gathered before the radio, and, when Louis won, Butler recalled, "[t]he blacks of North Tulsa literally danced in the streets. This was a most special occasion. We didn't often get a chance to cheer about anything, let alone a hero of our very own."[108]

Lack of cash kept the amusements for many African Americans simple. Into the 1930s, many people found their greatest pleasure in visiting with friends and family.[109] Idella Parker remembered dating her first husband: "Bernard and I became a twosome, and we had many happy times playing cards with friends at his mother's house."[110] Henrietta Elizabeth Sellers found relaxation at the end of a fishing pole, according to the Federal Writers' Project interviewer: "I likes to fish, too, and every week when I gets my Thursday afternoon off, I goes fishin' out here on the wharf. Sometimes I catches one, sometimes a lot, and then again I don't catch none—just sets there all evenin' hopin' to get a bite."[111] Fishing gave Sellers a rare opportunity to sit down and be quiet. In the event that she actually caught something, she would then have the pleasure of augmenting her family's diet with fresh fish.

Some cooks belonged to lodges or other mutual-aid societies, including the organizations known as "penny savers clubs."[112] Tera Hunter commented, "From Reconstruction onward, African American women led and joined secret societies to pool their meager resources to aid the sick, orphaned, wid-owed, or unemployed, and to create opportunities for personal enrichment as well as broader race advancement."[113] In 1870 Richmond, eighteen-year-old Camilla Mayo, who lived at home and worked full time as a cook for a white family, was elected an officer in the Daughters of Elijah, a beneficial society affiliated with the Second African Baptist Church. Despite her youth, Mayo received a position of responsibility from her peers.[114] Alice Reed, "a popu-lar woman, respectable and thrifty," from Waco, Texas, belonged to a "colored benevolent order and had a policy on her life." Thirty-year-old Reed was shot and killed, allegedly by her "lunatic" lover, George Dewberry, in 1902, and the newspaper reporting the incident may have mentioned the life-insurance policy as evidence of Reed's respectability or possibly as a motive for her mur-der.[115] Such organizations divided themselves by class, and club work would have been an occasion on which a cook could socialize with other domestic workers and working-class African American women.[116]

For many African American cooks, their churches provided their main social outlets, and working on Sundays was a source of considerable dissension between them and their employers. Although Katy Brumby thought that drinking and smoking were permissible and even fun, she believed in keeping the Sabbath as a day of rest.[117] As poor as Richard Wright's mother was, she took her sons to Sunday school and on at least one occasion invited the minister of the church and one or two neighbors to a fried chicken lunch. Wright recalled the "talking and laughing adults" and that the preacher picked out the choice pieces of chicken.[118] Even when Georgia Sutton's mother had to work on Sundays, she got her children ready and a Sunday school teacher picked the children up and took them to church. Sutton remembered, "Some Sundays my mother worked, but there wasn't any doubt about where we were going."[119]

In addition to theological and spiritual uplift, at church cooks received refreshment for their spirits that were battered all week. Vernon Jordan pointed out the impact of his mother's ushering at her Sunday services: "The maid or a cook, hostage most of the time to other people's whims or cruelty, could be an usher and tell people where to sit so that the program could proceed as planned."[120]

The requirement of work on Sundays prevented many women from attending worship regularly, and so they turned inward to their religious impulses. Dianne Swann-Wright commented on the faith of Ethel Bolden and her foremothers: "She did what her mother and her mother's mother had done—she cooked in the Caryswood Plantation kitchen and prayed to the Lord to make her way easier in this world, keep her children safe, and save them all from sin."[121] In the 1930s, Annie Squire explained her faith simply: "Well, all I can say is trust in the Lord and pray. The Scripture say prayer will sho' take us where we goin'. And I'm bound for the Promise Land."[122] Mrs. H. A. Clement, a widow with three children from Baltimore, shared her faith with Franklin Roosevelt in a 1939 letter: "We pore culard peaple is rely [really] having it hard expechull [especially] the women but I relize that [God] has his time set and I shall indever to lean on him. . . . Yrs in Crist, H. A. Clement at 1805 Penn Ave."[123] These women asked for relief in this world and rewards in the next.

THROUGHOUT THE END OF the nineteenth century, cooks increasingly created homes of their own as they moved out of their employers' houses. With increasing urban segregation, they often found themselves living in neighborhoods composed entirely of African Americans. The continued growth of southern cities resulted in longer commutes and increased transportation costs. Most cooks considered these costs worth bearing, however. With leftover food and cast-off clothing, stretching their dollars as far as they could, they made do, and they made homes for themselves and their families.

Mama Leaps off the Pancake Box

COOKS AND THEIR FAMILIES

Ain't chure Mama on the pancake box?

Mama Mama
Get off that box
And come home to me
And my Mama leaps off that box
She swoops down in her nurse's cape
Which she wears on Sunday
And for Wednesday night prayer meeting
And she wipes my forehead
And she fans my face
And she makes me a cup of tea
And it don't do a thing for my real pain
Except she is my mama
—Kate Rushin, "The Black Back-ups"

In her 1993 poem "The Black Back-ups," Kate Rushin depicts a child's fantasy: that in response to its request, its mother will leave her work in the white people's space, come home, and take care of its needs instead of her employer's. In reality, for more than a century, mothers obligated to work for wages as cooks found themselves with limited choices in balancing work and family. Among American women in the late nineteenth and early twentieth centuries, African Americans were by far the most likely to work after marriage and childbearing. Irish women, who formed the largest group of domestic workers in the nineteenth-century North, tended to work until marriage and then become stay-at-home housewives.[1] But because wages for African

American men were so low and jobs so inconsistent, women had to step into the breach. The majority of African American families simply had to have the wages that a mother could bring in. Paradoxically, preserving and providing for the family frequently meant leaving it for long hours, days, or even weeks. All too often, love equaled absence.

TO COMPREHEND THE LIVES of African American cooks, one must understand the strong ties of family that encompassed them, for, as historian Leslie Alexander has observed, "the concept of family, community, and kinship" is integral to the study of African American women.[2] Their responsibilities, including financial support and physical care, reached not only to the immediate family but also to an extended network of relatives and fictive kin.[3] The family and community at large, in turn, provided strong bases from which women gathered strength to face the indignities of life and work in the Jim Crow South.

Putting the needs of their families foremost had major ramifications for African American women. Primarily, it meant that cooks constantly risked conflict with their employers, for the best interests of the cook's family often were diametrically opposed to those of the employer. Cooks negotiated for shorter hours, better pay, and better quantity and quality of foodstuffs to take home, while employers tried to get more hours at lower pay and to decrease the amount of food carried out. Motherhood affected women's work performance; because they juggled paid work and child care, cooks sometimes brought children to the workplace or fretted about what was happening at home in their absence.[4] Employers, predictably, resented any impediment to their workers' full attention.

Employers tried to disregard the fact that their cooks had lives outside the boundaries of the employers' homes, preferring to view their cooks as workers rather than as wives, mothers, or daughters. Expecting their employees to leave behind their own homes and children to care for those who paid their wages, they considered unmarried cooks to be a boon and actively discriminated against women with children.[5] White employers congratulated themselves on finding single cooks. In 1871, Richmond resident Maria Louisa Carrington hired "a very good cook, without husband, or children, and a chamber maid in the same happy state,"[6] and Virginian Gertrude Thomas kept an "indifferent cook" at least temporarily, declaring, "She has no children which has been the one reason why I have tolerated her."[7] Such negative attitudes continued well into the twentieth century. In the 1940s, author Marjorie Kinnan Rawlings cited the fact that her cook, Idella Parker, wasn't "interested in men" as one of her positive attributes.[8] In disparaging African American women's childbearing, white women denied their employees access to the ideal of domesticity and tried to disrupt their families' continuity.[9] Instead, they conflated their cooks with the work that the cooks did.[10]

In this matter as in many others, African American women refused to accept white people's views of them, relying instead on their inner compasses to guide them.[11] In historian Sharon Harley's words, African American "wage-earning women tended to view themselves as self-sacrificing mothers, wives, aunts, and sisters or as race uplifters rather than as workers." Harley observes that domestic workers tended to "de-emphasize the importance of their paid work lives to their everyday life and self-perception."[12] African Americans scorned the notion that they were merely cooks. May Anna Madison, who grew up in Kentucky, commented, "One very important difference between white people and black people is that white people think that you are your work. . . . Now, a black person has more sense than that because he knows that what I am doing doesn't have anything to do with what I want to do or what I do when I am doing for myself. Now, black people think that my work is just what I have to do to get what I want."[13] As critic Elizabeth Janeway has noted, such disbelief, or the "refusal to accept the definition of oneself that is put forward by the powerful" is a significant form of power among the disadvantaged.[14] A cook might be on call twenty-four hours a day, but she still would think of the needs of her own family, and putting one's own family in front of the needs of one's employer's family constituted a major form of resistance.[15]

LIKE WOMEN EVERYWHERE, most African American women married at some point in their lives. But in the late nineteenth century, perhaps as many as a third of domestic cooks were single, and most of these women were under the age of thirty. While single women may not have had spouses or children to concern themselves with, most women nonetheless belonged to kin groups. First, they were often the daughters of parents who cared deeply about them. In Macon, Georgia, from Reconstruction through the Great Depression, almost all single women lived with their parents or relatives.[16] In 1900, for example, Dana White still lived with her mother and brother, even though she had reached the age of thirty-three, and in 1920, Nellie Broadles, age thirty-nine, lived with her younger sister and the sister's family. Also during the latter part of the nineteenth century, about a quarter of single cooks in Macon and Atlanta had children of their own.[17] Few single women struck out on their own to create their own households. Surrounded by kin, these unmarried women lived amid limitations as well as support, as their families often had high expectations for their behavior and their contributions to the household.

The daily lives of single women away from their families tended to run in two directions. Many single young women had conservative lifestyles, finding lodging with other families or sometimes older people, as the situations of women in Macon show. In 1880, twenty-one-year old Fannie Pitts lived with a married couple and the couple's four children. In 1900, twenty-seven-year-old Lou Chappel boarded with an elderly African American couple whose eight children had all died. Young people who lived together often came under the watch of an older woman. In 1910, for example, Tressa Evans and three other single young people lived in the home of a widow. In Macon, only rarely did young women set up housekeeping together. In 1930, Madie P. Solomon, who was twenty-eight and single, and Sallie Bell Stanford, a nineteen-year-old widow, lived together in an all–African American neighborhood on Middle Street in Macon, likely splitting the six-dollar rent.

Other young women, free and on their own in the city, availed themselves more of the good times to be had with their peers. In Washington, D.C., historian Elizabeth Clark-Lewis found that while young women frequently lived with relatives when they first moved to the big city in the period between 1910 and 1940, within a year or two they often left the homes of their kin and moved into boardinghouses or "the homes of friends from their rural birthplaces."[18] Bernice Reeder relocated into a boardinghouse and didn't see her sister for months. She remembered, "I just liked being with these girls who was single, nice—not wild or drinking—and doing things. I guess that's when I started to feel I'd finally left home." Beulah Nelson concurred: "I liked the girls, and we was all from different places too. And nobody was bad. We had fun and the best old parties; full of people."[19]

Even when they were not living with their families, however, many single women thought of the needs of their relatives; oftentimes many domestic workers placed their families' collective requirements above their own desires as individuals.[20] Like the current-day immigrants who send remittances to their kin back home, cooks helped to support their distant families with cash, food, and household goods. South Carolinian Marva Woods started a job living with her employers in 1938 when she was sixteen. She recalled taking food to her family: "The husband [of her employer] would go hunting and kill rabbits and bring one for me. I'd take it to my mother's."[21] In Birmingham in the 1930s, Katy Brumby sent clothes to her family in rural Alabama and assisted in any way possible, saying (in words transcribed by her Federal Writers' Project interviewer), "I'm de oldest, and dey needs it bad, Miss

Mary. Dey got children, I haven't." Even though Brumby lived apart from her family members, they clearly occupied her thoughts and affections, and she shared her resources with them.[22] From farther away, women could send mainly cash, and almost all of the migrants to Washington, D.C., faithfully dispatched parts of their minuscule salaries home. Young women's responsibilities to the homefolks occupied the minds of those yearning to switch jobs. Weida Edwards commented that she had to be careful when she quit her first job, around the time of World War I, because "you had to be able to get work to help yourself and help Mama down home."[23] Self-support was not the only concern.

LIKE WOMEN EVERYWHERE, at some point in their lives, most cooks found themselves in relationships with men and, often, bearing children. In the late nineteenth century, African American women often married in their teens, sometimes but infrequently as young as twelve or fourteen but, by 1930, more typically at eighteen or nineteen.[24] In cities large and small, the percentage of women working as cooks who were married increased between 1880 and 1930, while the number of single women similarly employed declined.[25] After 1900, fully three-quarters of women employed as cooks were under the age of forty, the peak years for marriage and childbearing. Their lives were complicated, as they labored to balance the needs of their families with the requirements of their employers. Their days were unending rounds of "caring for and waiting on others," both at work and at home.[26]

Living situations varied widely among married women. At times, as many as two-thirds of married cooks lived with their husbands and had their own households. But a significant number did not, especially in the twentieth century. Typically, married women living apart from their husbands might have their own households, stay with relatives, or board or lodge with unrelated individuals. From the 1860s forward, African American women were significantly more likely to be heads of households in the urban South than in rural areas.[27] An unmarried woman had difficulty supporting a family in a rural setting, and opportunities for employment were substantially larger in the city. In many southern cities, the African American female population outnumbered the African American male population. In Atlanta between 1880 and 1930, the ratio of women to men was roughly five to four, while in Norfolk between 1910 and 1930, it was roughly eleven to ten.[28] At any given point, females could be expected to be heads of households if only because fewer males were present. Women working as cooks were highly likely to reside in households in which all of the adults were female.

Physical separations from spouses were probable due at least in part to the ongoing difficulties of African American men in finding gainful employment in cities.[29] Cooks who lived with their employers rarely had husbands present; perhaps the husbands lived in another location (on a farm, for example), or perhaps employers simply forbade conjugal relationships under their roofs. Those spouses who did live as couples in the homes of their employers often both worked for the same family, but such a situation still proved less than ideal. Elizabeth Clark-Lewis told of her aunt who with her husband went to great lengths to obtain some privacy in the early 1920s. Both of them lived with their employer, but they rented a room that "they slept in together maybe four times a month—if they were lucky! Most months they went there together just twice. But [her aunt] said she slipped away to her apartment every opportunity she got, with or without him. She would cook on a tiny stove in the room, relax, and 'have a few minutes of peace to myself.'"[30]

Although the phenomenon of married cooks living with their employers decreased sharply in the twentieth century, it did not disappear completely.[31] Marva Woods remembered living apart from her husband in the late 1930s and 1940s: "I worked days and evenings. I saw my husband on weekends and some afternoons. I'd go home on Saturday morning and didn't have to go back until Monday morning. I'd see him then." The union produced two children but eventually ended.[32] The strain of separation could easily have exacerbated any other tensions present in the relationship, and the marriages of many live-in cooks likely suffered from their living situations.

While research can never disclose how many marriages were happy and how many were miserable, long marriages might serve at least as an indication of stable relationships.[33] The 1900 and 1910 census takers for Macon more often than not left the survey field blank for length of marriage, but clearly lengthy relationships occurred. In 1900, Anna and Coatney Sims, for example, had been wed sixteen years, since Anna was sixteen; and Mattie Reid, at fifty-eight, had been married to her husband, Carry, since 1868. Mary Houser married Pete when she was fourteen, and in 1910 they had been together thirteen years. Lizzie Driskell did not marry Eugene until she was twenty-four, but in 1910 they had been united fifteen years. These couples were able to balance the wife's work with their home life, and perhaps they found contentment with one another.

Like Marva Woods and her husband, some couples could not remain together. Although few statistics exist on the number of broken marriages and desertions, relationships definitely disintegrated. Having work of one's own gave women the means to leave unhappy relationships, and a significant number exercised their autonomy despite possible negative social consequences.

In some marriages, tensions arose over money. Mandy Long Roberson, a former slave, began cooking and housekeeping for white families in her youth, perhaps in the 1880s, in North Carolina. The Federal Writers' Project interviewer who talked with Roberson in the 1930s observed that she had been "thrifty and industrious, and in the course of a few years, had saved up a considerable sum of money . . . money earned cooking and housekeeping for well-to-do white families." Roberson's fiscal conservatism created conflict with her first husband, Joe Goodman, a worker in a cotton brokerage warehouse. She remembered, according to the interviewer, "Dat scound'el was de mos' wu'thless scamp I evah seed. We hadn't bin hitched two days when he up an' quit his job at de warehouse, an' commenced loafin' 'round de house, wid me payin' all de bills an' doin' all de work. I said to myself, 'dis won't nevah work.'" She packed her bags and moved to the home of a wealthy uncle in Atlanta, finding refuge among her kinspeople and in her ability to make her own living.[34]

In other situations, marital infidelity caused breaches. In Indianola, Mississippi, "Mrs. S." married right out of elementary school, perhaps about 1900, and soon had three children. After many years of marriage, her husband, a sharecropper, began cheating on her. So she left her husband and the farm and took her youngest son with her to Indianola, where her married daughter was living. Sociologist Hortense Powdermaker reported, "She found a good job in town as cook, with living quarters and fuel in addition to her wages. She did not remarry. She wasn't going to support any man. She wanted to save for herself and her daughter's little boy, whom she had taken to raise after his mother died."[35] "Mrs. S." became a part of the migration to urban areas, as the presence of her daughter gave her a toehold in the city, and her cooking talent gave her a way to support herself and her grandson.

Both wives and daughters suffered physical abuse. In 1869, Cornelia Shelman displeased her employer, Gertrude Thomas, in just about every way possible, but Thomas was reluctant to dismiss her, commenting: "Her father whips her so much and so often I do not like to complain to him."[36] In the 1930s, a cook named Edwina fled to her employer's home to escape her husband's rage.[37] In both of these instances, employers assisted their cooks in escaping, at least temporarily, the fury of their family members. As the employers recalled it, the workplace became a refuge. Other women took matters into their own hands. Nancy White not only left her husband, James

Tucker, to escape his abuse in 1922, but she also departed the region where he lived. She told interviewer John Gwaltney, "Nancy Sawyer Tucker White is not going to have no man beating on her after she is out from under her parents' rule! That is my law and I live by that law first!" The first time Tucker hit White, she was pregnant, and she told him not to do it again. For a while, Tucker behaved, but several years later, after drinking away their hard-earned assets, he hit White again. She left him in Tennessee and went to Chicago. "I have not seen him since," she said, "and don't want to see him! That's why I came up here, because I wanted to put some states between me and my children and James Tucker."[38] White had the courage and the resourcefulness to flee permanently a bad marital situation.

Women sometimes exhibited violent or malevolent behaviors as well. Mary Howard, who lived in Plaquemines Parish, Louisiana, in the late nineteenth and early twentieth centuries, was a "splendid cook" who "could turn her hand to anything, even to swinging a side of salt meat against the head of her husband."[39] Willie Mae Wright, a longtime Atlanta cook, referred to her sister, Emma, as "the devil's handiwork." Sometime around World War I, Emma's husband developed tuberculosis and at his birth family's insistence substituted his mother for Emma as the beneficiary of his substantial insurance policy. Emma became cruel to him and, the family believed, brought on his death prematurely by casting him out in the rain, much to her relatives' mortification.[40]

At times the domestic violence became deadly. In 1886, Pattie Scott of San Antonio served dinner to her employer's family at six o'clock one evening and then was brutally murdered in the "small pine outhouse used as a dormitory" behind her employer's house. Her estranged husband, who had already been fined several times for beating her, was accused of killing Scott with a hatchet and a crowbar. Virgie Lee, of Conroe, Texas, died after having her throat cut "from ear to ear" in 1906, and her husband was the chief suspect.[41]

With or without violence, death came frequently to southern African American homes before World War II. From the beginning of urban migration, African American males had a higher death rate and shorter life expectancy than African American females, and an African American woman was four times more likely to be a widow than an African American man was to be a widower.[42] A woman could lose her husband at any age, and widows comprised about 40 percent of the cooks in Macon between 1880 and 1930. Most of the women were in their thirties, forties, and fifties. Widows worked as cooks longer than women with husbands, with many more widows remaining on the job into their fifties, and a small number of them cooked into their sixties or seventies. Financial need kept them in the kitchen, whereas women who had access to their husband's incomes could do other types of work or possibly even leave the workforce altogether.[43]

In 1880, two-thirds of widowed cooks in Macon lived with their employers, perhaps finding a modicum of security in having a roof provided with their job. Most of the others lived with relatives, and a few headed their own households. By 1900, the number of widows living with their employers had dropped by 75 percent, and a third of Macon widows were heads of their own households. Another third lived with family members. Mallie Kendrick, for example, found herself at the age of forty-eight residing in the home of her adult son and his family. As with single women, widows were far more likely to live with their kin than to set up housekeeping with nonfamily.

In addition to relationships with African American men, cooks also had sexual and occasionally affectionate associations with white men, although much more often the former than the latter. While sexual abuse of African American women by white men was a topic of particular concern to families and reformers alike, some long-term biracial relationships existed that may have been consensual or at least nonviolent if coerced. Determining the sources of such relationships is almost impossible. Some may have been completely coerced, coming from threats of violence or other types of punishment. Others may have been the products of genuine affection or love.[44] Still others might have been the result of calculated choices on the parts of African American women who decided that acquiescing to the desires of white men might make their lives somehow easier. African American women criticized sharply the last group of women. "Negro Nurse," writing in 1912, spoke harshly of African American women who compromised their morals and developed relationships with white men: "Those who tamely submit to these improper relations live in clover. They always have a little 'spending change,' wear better clothes, and are able to get off from work at least once a week— and sometimes oftener." The benefits that "Negro Nurse" details are not particularly impressive; getting time off once a week was not much of a break, and "tamely submitting" to a relationship hardly sounds like a romantic liaison. But these perquisites indicate how severe working conditions could be and the lengths to which some women were willing to go to mitigate them.

The white men's wives, said "Negro Nurse," sometimes encouraged such relationships because they feared their husbands would develop relationships with "outside white women. . . . The white wives . . . preferred to have their husbands do wrong with colored women in order to keep their husbands straight!" Presumably a husband would be unlikely to leave his white wife for an African American woman, whereas he might depart for a white rival, whom he could legally wed. "Negro Nurse" adamantly declared the commonplace nature of these situations: "I know at least fifty places where white men are positively raising two families—a white family in the 'Big House' in front, and a colored family in a 'Little House' in the backyard. In most cases, to be sure, the colored women involved are the cooks or chambermaids or seamstresses, but it cannot be true that their real connection with the white men of the families is unknown to the white women of the families."[45]

Whether they were consensual or not, such relationships might last for decades. Author Vertamae Smart-Grosvenor wrote of her cousin, who was rebuffed publicly by her white employer who was also the father of her children: "One cousin of mine who lives in a small town in Tennessee was a cook for a Mr. & Mrs. Brooks for over twenty years. My cousin lived in a little house in back of the big house. She had six children, all of whom were fathered by Mr. Brooks. . . . When my cousin passed Mr. Brooks on the street she was not allowed to speak. She was obliged to step aside for him."[46] Two decades and six children could not earn Smart-Grosvenor's cousin the right to acknowledge publicly the man who fathered her children. Any claim that she had on him remained tenuous and impermanent.

By the 1940s, sociologist Charles Spurgeon Johnson wrote that "the early practice of 'keeping' Negro 'second wives'" was continuing in rural areas longer than in the city. For an African American woman, a long-term relationship with a white man still might bring benefits such as those outlined by "Negro Nurse" three decades earlier, but the costs continued to be high. Johnson recounted the story of a city woman who "was referred to as the cook." In an ongoing relationship with her white employer, she actually hired others to do the cooking and housework, and she, the employer, and their two children all took their meals together, breaching a taboo far stronger than interracial sex. Her "paramour" left his property to her when he died. However, the woman, in her virtually widowed state, found herself rejected by both African Americans and whites and moved about town "like a neglected ghost."[47] Her inheritance, which would be passed to her mixed-race children, challenged whites' most cherished ideals about segregation. Casual intimate relationships between white men and African American women were expected, even encouraged, in polite white society; permanent relationships with conveyance of property were not.[48]

In Indianola, Mississippi, in the 1930s, one brave woman who tried to assert the rightful place of her mixed-race child paid a heavy price. According to sociologist John Dollard, the woman "insisted on calling the child by the name of its father, a member of a prominent family." Dollard commented that the woman had worked as a cook for her employers for more than ten years, possibly indicating that she was a person of character and reliability, and the father was apparently not a member of the employer's family. Dollard did not comment on the woman's motivation; perhaps she was trying to shame the father, or perhaps she was trying to claim a patrimony for her child. The family of the father became "indignant" and, Dollard observed, "the cook was forced to leave town." Her employers gave her money to go away with, apparently trying to smooth the path for the woman who had given them a decade of work. She wanted her child called by his or her rightful name, but the father's family in no way would grace their descendant with their proud name. The father himself seems to have remained silent throughout the incident.[49]

AS THE EXPERIENCES OF the women above indicate, childbearing and child-rearing were extremely important in the lives of cooks as they were almost all women. By the end of the nineteenth century, African Americans in urban settings were carefully limiting their family size. Atlanta University researchers found that in 1897 the average size of the African American family was 4.1, and Eugene Harris of Fisk University worried that the African American population was "barely more than reproducing itself."[50] By 1945, the African American birthrate had dropped by more than half, and the average number of children per woman was 2.5. Additionally, childlessness had "reached unprecedented proportions."[51] The African American press carried abundant information about birth control, and barrier methods of contraception, such as plugs of Vaseline and quinine, were popular.[52] Access to birth control remained somewhat spotty, however. Annie Mae Hunt did not use birth control until her employer, Mrs. Norrell, took Hunt to a physician in the early 1930s to have her fitted for a diaphragm. With four miscarriages, three children dying as infants, and six living children, Hunt had been pregnant thirteen times. Hunt recalled, "Fixing to have those babies I was having, didn't know what else to do. The white woman I was working for, Mrs. Norrell, she's dead now, say to me, 'Annie Mae, I don't want you to have any more babies. . . . It's going to kill you.' She got me my first diaphragm. Took me to the doctor herself." A privileged white woman had easier access to information than Hunt did, and she shared it freely.

When contraception failed, some African American women resorted to abortions, at times self-induced with pencils, nails, or hat pins.[53] Annie Mae Hunt recalled such practices in Texas in the 1920s: "When I got to be a young woman, the women began to—they called it *throwing away babies*. So-and-so, that woman *throwed away* three babies. They would do things to theirself. . . . So many of our colored women died, because their mamas would do it themselves. . . . They would take things, and open theirselves up, go up in theirselves. Take bluing, and put it all in their hands. Take this quinine, a big dose of it, and kill theirself. They done it. A lot of times they'd mess up. Oh, it's a sad story."[54]

Even with birth control and abortion, cooks did bear children, and they continued to work throughout their cycles of pregnancy and childbirth. Presumably employers of freedwomen would have had little incentive to afford their employees any consideration in light of their pregnancies or postpartum status, and one can imagine the backaches and swollen legs and feet women suffered from standing in the kitchen all day. In the late nineteenth century, the number of stillbirths among African American women was double those of whites. H. R. Butler, a highly regarded Atlanta physician, blamed the mortality on domestic work: "Why should we be surprised at the great number of still-births among our women, since they do most of the work that is liable to produce this state of things? They do the cooking, the sweeping, the lifting of heavy pots; they carry the coal, the wood, the water; carry heavy burdens on their heads; they do heavy washing, make beds, turn heavy mattresses, and climb the stairs several times during the day, while their more favored white sister is seated in her big arm-chair, and not allowed to move, even if she wanted to."[55] By 1920, the situation had improved little. In Norfolk, the mortality rate for African American infants was six times greater than for whites.[56] Even after World War II, the difficulties of cooking while pregnant continued. Willie Mae Wright had to be hospitalized twice during her first pregnancy as the doctors, she explained, "said I was having trouble because I'd worked too hard after I was pregnant."[57] And in 1957, a cook named Margaret went into labor at her employers' house and then gave birth alone in "her shanty" to her tenth child, which was stillborn.[58]

Childbearing provided professional as well as personal challenges to cooks. Sometimes just being pregnant cost them their jobs. As late as the 1950s and 1960s, employers in Houston and Hickory, North Carolina, fired their cooks when learning of their pregnancies, not wanting to deal with the inconveniences of their employees' pregnancies, childbirths, and motherhood.[59] From emancipation on, employers reacted negatively after their employees had their babies, too. The most tightfisted employers forced women with small children to accept lower wages, on the grounds that they could not give their full attention to their work.[60] Gertrude Thomas wrote of her servants shortly after the Civil War: "I have a girl Anna who cooks milks the cows & sweeps the yard whom I give four dollars to. She wished me to raise her wages this morning but I would not do it as she has a baby with no nurse who occupies a good deal of her time."[61]

Child care presented huge trials for working mothers, and they coped with their difficulties in a variety of ways. Women who lived with their employers encountered particular sets of difficulties. At times, children lived on the employers' properties with their families.[62] In Macon in 1880, however, only six of twenty-four live-in cooks had children present; of those, three women had children under the age of ten. The children could be made useful: Marian White's eight-year-old son lived with her as a "servant" to the Isaacs family and their seven boarders. After 1880, no small children lived with their mothers who resided with their employers. Being a twenty-four-hour employee as well as a parent apparently became impossible.

Rather than trying to keep their children with them at their employers', more commonly, live-in servants placed their children with relatives or boarded them with other families.[63] Relatives and friends could help a woman keep her family together. As sociologist Evelyn Nakano Glenn has pointed out, African American women have "historically relied on a larger network of extended kin, including fictive relatives and clan associations, for goods and services." Child care was high on the list of ways that women helped one another. Such familial ties could be "a source of resistance to oppression from outside institutions," socializing children and providing identity for its members.[64]

Grandmothers in particular provided for their daughters' children. Zelma Powell's grandmother cared for her from Powell's birth in 1898 until the grandmother's death in 1905. Powell recalled, "Mama did live-in work. She'd leave Sunday and be working at the Wills' till late Saturday." When the grandmother died, Powell's mother had to leave her domestic work and take in washing and sewing. Without child care, she could no longer maintain the schedule demanded by her employer.[65] Winnie Hefley, widowed when her daughter was only three weeks old, described life in rural Alabama in the 1930s. Finding employment keeping house and cooking for an elderly couple, Hefley lived on her employers' farm by herself: "I had a little house on the place, and I stayed there. My mother and them they lived further up in the country—up in the woods, on the farm. And they kept my child. She was just a baby about six months old when I left her. Yes, my mother and father took care of her. She was happy with them. And I had to go. . . . I had her and I loved her, and I could go home on weekends. I could walk up."[66] As a widow,

Hefley needed the assistance of her parents to assure that her child had a good place to live.

At times, women might leave their children with people who were not related by blood but might have been fictive kin. During Reconstruction, Gertrude Thomas wrote about two of her servants with children living apart from them. Hannah "has a child two years old & expects soon to have another. Her old mistress has her eldest child. Diania went in town with me taking her little boy whom she leaves with a married coloured woman whom she calls Miss Green."[67]

With the demanding hours of their work, even mothers who had their own households sometimes sent their children to live with other families.[68] Frances Walker, born in 1904, grew up with extended family in Richmond while her mother worked for various employers. When she herself became a cook in the 1920s, she boarded her children with several different families and saw them about once a week. Her daughter, Doris Woodson, recalled, "I would only see her on Thursday afternoons, and maybe every other Sunday."[69] Walker spent the typical cook's days off visiting with her children. During the Great Depression, Sarah Howard's two youngest children went to live with an aunt when their mother's wages were insufficient to support them.[70]

The practice of putting children with relatives lasted well into the twentieth century. Margaret, the woman who lost her last baby, had had nine children, all of whom lived with her mother in Mandeville, across Lake Ponchartrain from Margaret's New Orleans employers. The daughter of her former employer recalled Margaret as a kind person who worked two jobs, coming to their house at two o'clock in the afternoon to cook supper. Each Friday she called her family to get their grocery list, and she and her husband, Sam, bought food and took it to the family in Mandeville. Margaret worried about her mother, who was "elderly," with the responsibility for so many youngsters.[71]

Sometimes women creatively pooled their assets to find child care. Isetta Peters remembered that in Washington, D.C., in the 1920s and 1930s, recent urban immigrants asked younger women to come to the city to watch their babies while they worked: "No, in them days a man didn't do no mindin' for no child. Maybe a half hour or so, but somebody'd be over there quick 'cause he wasn't staying in there with childrens long. No sir. So the womens has girls come up from home. Whoever had somebody that's where all them left they babies. See, they all had to work so they all helped bring up somebody to watch the babies."[72] The young assistants likely had roomsful of toddlers and infants to tend for many hours a day.

In Dallas in the 1930s, Annie Mae Hunt relied on friends to watch her children while she worked. Hunt would get the girls ready for school before her departure: "I'd get up before day and comb my children's hair. I dressed a many a one of those girls asleep. Lay them back down. Go tell my neighbor, Miss So and So, 'They're already ready. Will you wake them up? And see that they get to school in time?' Many a day, I had to leave for work before they were up." Hunt mused about the importance of such relationships: "You got to have somebody that cares. I always lived around somebody that cared. I would leave my children asleep, and they would go ahead and wake those children up." In the evenings, Hunt relied particularly on her neighbor Lusettie Williams, popularly known as "Big Mama." As Hunt's children waited for her to arrive home from work, they fell asleep on the front porch of their rent house, and Williams watched them through the window. Hunt recalled, "I always told them to go in the house, or go next door to Big Mama, my neighbor. But sometimes they chose not to; I'd come home late at night and see Big Mama's window cracked like that. She'd be sitting at her window looking at them. Now she cared about my children. That's the reason I love her. . . . She set in there looking at those kids and stay there until I come, and nobody didn't bother them. 'Well, I was watching them. . . . I was watching you come. I'm going to bed now.'"[73] Hunt worked late, and Williams postponed her own rest to make sure that the single mother's children stayed safe.

The severity of the child-care situation deeply affected some children, who later recalled it with bitterness. Attorney Jonell Clark, who grew up in Montgomery after World War II, recalled, "My mother was one of a cadre of colored women who, like her mother before her, worked to keep white folk up, while we were left to practically raise ourselves."[74] Mississippi civil rights activist Anne Moody similarly told of her mother, Elmira Moody, deserted by her husband, leaving her two younger children alone while she worked as a cook and Anne attended school.[75]

Novelist Richard Wright, raised in Memphis before World War I, wrote starkly of a "crowd of black children—abandoned for the day by their working parents."[76] Wright's father deserted his family when they moved to Memphis about 1914. The situation for the family, according to Wright, was desperate: "My mother finally went to work as a cook and left me and my brother alone in the flat each day with a loaf of bread and a pot of tea." Perhaps even worse than physical want was Ella Wilson Wright's psychological distress at her and her children's plight: "When she returned at evening she would be tired and dispirited and would cry a lot. Sometimes, when she was in despair, she would call us to her and talk to us for hours, telling us that we now had no father, that our lives would be different from those of other children, that we must learn as soon as possible to take care of ourselves, to dress ourselves, to prepare our own food; that we must take upon ourselves the responsibility of the flat while she worked."[77] According to Wright's memoir, his mother forced him to become tough, making him brave neighborhood bullies by locking him out of the house.[78] When the preschooler Wright began begging at a saloon near the family's home, he recalled, "[m]y mother was in despair. She beat me; then she prayed and wept over me, imploring me to be good, telling me that she had to work, all of which carried no weight to my wayward mind." Finally, Ella Wright had to part with some of her tiny income for child care, placing her boys "in the keeping of an old black woman who watched me every moment to keep me from running to the doors of the saloons to beg for whiskey."[79] Her makeshift plan to leave the boys alone while she worked was simply untenable.

The length of a mother's day made a significant difference in her life and those of her children. Most employers expected their cooks to arrive at their houses early to prepare and serve them breakfast. The cooks might have to roust their own children out of bed in the wee hours and try to feed them before they left between five and six o'clock. Around World War I, researcher Ruth Reed found in Georgia that women who went to work early and cooked only two meals a day could be home by about three o'clock. This schedule, according to Reed, gave the women a chance to put their own homes in order and to be at home when the children returned from school.[80] Sometimes, however, the separations could last for days. Cecelia Gaudet, born in 1897, remembered, "My grandmother she was also one of those Creole cooks. She'd go to big fine jobs like that, and sometimes she'd be gone two or three days cooking."[81]

Jonell Clark remembered the difficulty that her mother's employers caused through their carelessness and self-centered focus on their party guests, unexpectedly separating her mother from her children for more than a day and a half sometime in the 1940s: "Little Mama worked from ten o'clock in the morning until seven at night, with Wednesday and every other Sunday off. On Saturday she normally got off around two; but if she worked late on Friday, she only had to serve breakfast on Saturday and would leave around ten." One Friday night, Clark's mother served a party and arrived home late. Thinking that her employers would release her early the next day because of her long day, she promised the children that she would take them on a picnic. Instead of being home at ten o'clock on Saturday morning, however, she did not return for another full day: "Little Mama didn't come home until ten-thirty

Sunday morning. We learned that she had to keep the white folks' children. They had forgotten to tell her that they were going to the lake with some of their guests from the Friday night party." Arriving home twenty-four hours late to a houseful of worried and disappointed children, Clark's mother cried and sang the hymn "His Eye Is on the Sparrow," consoling herself that Jesus was her "constant friend" and that he was watching her.[82]

Cooks' hours pushed some women beyond their limits. Sarah Hill told the Federal Writers' Project interviewer about leaving the kitchen and taking in washing, which allowed her to work at her house and tend her own children at the same time: "I have been working every since I knowed what work was. I maided and cooked befo' I married, I maided a while and cooked a while. After I married and started having chillun I couldn't do no good at working out. So I stayed home and tuk in washing."[83] Other mothers persevered, continuing to leave their homes and work at the white people's houses.

As early as the 1890s, social reformers were calling for day nurseries and kindergartens for the children of domestic workers, and African American women quickly established a handful of institutions in the larger cities of the South.[84] In Washington, D.C., the Woman's League created seven kindergartens between 1892 and 1898, although most of the teachers worked for no salary.[85] By 1911, mothers in Richmond could pay ten cents a day to leave their children at the Richmond Working Woman's Home.[86] White women, too, established day care centers, such as the Tanyard Bottom Mission of the First Congregational Church of Atlanta, for the children of domestic workers.[87] Such progressive places provided children with daytime activities, meals, and recreation.

In extreme cases, desperate mothers might place their children in orphanages, as Ella Wright did when she fell ill. The competing demands upon her as single mother, breadwinner, and full-time domestic worker, without a kin network to assist, simply exceeded her abilities. Her son, Richard Wright, commented, "My mother hated to be separated from us, but she had no choice."[88] By 1898, orphanages for African American children existed in Charleston, South Carolina; Americus, Georgia; Atlanta; Baltimore, Maryland; and Petersburg, Virginia. In its first eight years of existence, the Carrie Steele Orphanage, founded in an abandoned boxcar in 1886 in Atlanta, sheltered more than 225 children.[89] Some of the children's parents had died, but others, like Ella Wright, simply were unable to make enough money to feed, clothe, and house their young ones.

At times, cooks brought their children to work with them, usually with the employer's permission.[90] Some employers frowned on their cooks nurs-

Mati, the cook for the W. W. Wilkes family, Waco, Texas, date unknown. Courtesy the Texas Collection, Baylor University, Waco, Texas.

ing their infants on the job, and Orra Langhorne observed tartly in 1901 that "few employers will tolerate negro children about the kitchen nowadays."[91] White South Carolinian Margaret McDow MacDougall remembered that her family's cook brought her small son into the kitchen with her: "And he slept in the woodbox. . . . You had a woodstove and then a kerosene stove. And the wood for the stove would be in the kitchen. And Sam, her little boy, would sleep in that woodbox because she didn't have anybody to leave him with."[92] Richard Wright recalled going to work with his mother, envying the fine foods of the employer that might well never touch his lips: "To keep us out of mischief, my mother often took my brother and me with her to her cooking job. Standing hungrily and silently in a corner of the kitchen, we would watch her go from the stove to the sink, from the cabinet to the table."[93] The presence of a famished child, standing silently in the corner of a white family's kitchen, likely challenged the child's mother in many ways as she worked to try to get some food to feed that child, even amid the abundance of her employer's larder.

WHILE CHILD CARE WAS often a woman's primary concern, some cooks also balanced care of ill or elderly relatives with their work. Sometimes the cook had an elderly spouse. Nannie Pharis remembered "Aunt Mary," who cooked for Pharis's family in North Carolina while caring for her husband, a former slave named "Uncle Jim": "He just stayed there for her to look after him. She couldn't leave him alone. . . . And then him and her would spend Saturday night and Sunday with her son."[94]

More typically, younger women cared for their parents or their in-laws. Creola Wilson, at age sixteen, took her ailing mother's place in a New Orleans kitchen. She recalled, "I took care of my mamma off of five dollars a week. Talkin' about making a dollar stretch!"[95] Two examples from Macon in 1930 further illustrate the complex lives of women providing elder care. A twenty-seven-year-old cook named Julia Hutchins lived with her in-laws, ages ninety-nine and seventy-five, as well as her husband and their six children, ages one to twelve. Her mother-in-law may well have been able to care for the household, including the children, but, if she were not, Hutchins's workload could have been heavy indeed. Laura Glover, a twenty-four-year-old married woman, lived in a household headed by her twenty-one-year-old brother, who worked in a garage. Also living with them were their parents, ages seventy-six and sixty, with no occupations listed; Glover's twenty-eight-year-old married sister, a washerwoman whose husband also was not in evidence; the sister's four-year-old son; Glover's six-year-old son; and a thirteen-year-old niece. Living apart from their spouses, Glover and her siblings supported two elderly parents and three members of the next generation.[96]

COOKING WAS HARD ON one's body, standing on one's feet all day, in a hot room. Anne Moody recalled, "That white lady Mama was working for worked her so hard that she always came home griping about backaches. Every night she'd have to put a red rubber bottle filled with hot water under her back."[97] Few women reached old age working as cooks, although one anonymous writer in the 1930s helpfully pointed out to potential employers that age was not a handicap: "Quite an old woman can often cook excellently well."[98] Some cooks continued well past the age of their maximum energy and effectiveness. Georgia employer Magnolia Le Guin referred to "old Aunt Susan Tarpley." On a day when Le Guin was about to give birth, she wrote in her journal, "Suse Tarpley is getting dinner. Mrs. Bartie is assisting her some. Mrs. B. is so kind that she sympathizes with Suse and will help her. Suse has rheumatism and is getting somewhat old."[99] Katy Brumby's employer observed, "Katy is getting older and cannot do what she did when younger; her weight, too, is a handicap."[100] Elderly, arthritic, overweight, and possibly diabetic and hypertensive, these women merited consideration, but they continued to work.

Often, African American women aged in poverty. The Federal Writers' Project recorded the life of Harriet Sanders of Starkville, Mississippi, who had spent her lifetime serving "many of the best families in town." As an old woman, Sanders was "in the usual condition of most all old negroes. Just existing, at the mercy of her grandchild and kindness of the city."[101] Family was the only thing that stood between a cook and the poorhouse. Katy Brumby regarded her sister's home in Montgomery as her next residence, threatening her employers by saying, "Y'all be sorry when I goes to Mon'gomery. My sister wants me to live with dem. Y'all be sorry."[102] Elderly cooks' lives returned full circle when they went back to live with family and no longer had households of their own.

THROUGHOUT CYCLES OF BIRTH, life, and death, African American cooks maintained intimate relationships with the people nearest and dearest to them, from birth families to husbands to children. Family size declined, and so did the number of long-term relationships with white employers. Many conditions persisted, however, in the personal lives of African American cooks. Across the years, many struggled with child care and remained responsible for members of their extended families. They worked diligently to maintain their personal integrity in the face of harassment and coercion. While some women were able to find less physically taxing work as they aged, others cooked into their last decades, finding little rest for their weary bodies.

Gendering Jim Crow

RELATIONSHIPS WITH EMPLOYERS

Under any circumstances, relationships between domestic workers and their employers are extremely complex, including in the mix "power, dependence, deference, care, gift-giving, erotic involvement, love and hate."[1] Around the world, across time, conflict has been integral to the domestic employer-employee connection. The relationship, "inherently asymmetrical," can never be made equal.[2] Power and domination, conflict and struggle all occur in people's lives. In an association such as that between a housewife and a domestic worker, everyday actions both control and oppose.[3]

A historic structure of subjugation and prejudice made an already complicated situation even more difficult in the postemancipation American South. The people involved in domestic worker and employer relationships were former slaves, their daughters, granddaughters, and great-granddaughters, and, often, former slave owners or their descendents. Connections between employees and employers, intrinsically vexed, became even more tangled when old expectations clashed with current realities and race remained an overriding consideration.[4]

In all such relationships, the more conspicuous power lay with the employer, who guarded her right to set hours, wages, and tasks and could easily terminate the employee if affairs did not suit her. Across space and time, employers expected "obedience, meekness, deference and competence in those who performed personal services. Through superiority of wealth, social position and often age, they could demand these qualities and punish those who failed them."[5] For workers, relationships tended to be marked by "ambivalence, latent hostility, and *ressentiment*," which sociologist Judith Rollins defines as "a long-term, seething, deep-rooted negative feeling toward those whom one feels unjustly have power or an advantage over one's life."[6]

For their part, African American cooks, like domestic workers everywhere, sought to master their working conditions. They struggled to control their work processes, their hours, and their wages, to make their labor more task-oriented and less personal and affective.[7] But a cook also had to work within the confines of her circumstances. While the powerless do exercise agency, material conditions affect their lives nonetheless.[8] Historian Leonore David-off observes: "The overwhelming fact is that the whole of the life of the servant and wife, from material support to human surroundings, depends on the household of which she happens to be a member: its resources, physical setting, technical equipment and above all the temperament and taste of the master (mistress)/husband."[9] Each cook had to calculate how far she could push for her own advantage without creating an open confrontation with a daunting opponent.[10]

DOMESTIC SERVICE IS USUALLY highly gendered, as two women, some-times near the same age, occupy space under the same roof. But the roof covers the home of the more privileged woman; the less privileged woman is there to work at the more privileged one's behest. Historically, critic bell hooks notes, "[t]he person who directly benefited from a servant's work was the white woman, since without the servant she would have performed do-mestic chores. Not surprisingly, the black female domestic tended to see the white female as her 'boss,' her oppressor, not the white male whose earnings usually paid her wage."[11] The domestic worker carries out services that the employer usually could, if forced to, perform for her own family but that the employer finds demeaning or belittling. Often the domestic worker is doing tasks for pay that she would prefer to perform for her own family. Her need for wages, however, requires that she do this labor for someone else.[12] In the American South, even as they shared the characteristic of sex, the women in the household differed dramatically from one another in their daily lives: the space that they occupied within the house, the chores that they did (divided into ladylike and unladylike tasks), the ways that they dressed.[13] As a rule, sex did little or nothing to mitigate the differences between the women.

ONE OF THE PARTICULAR liabilities of domestic work was that of having a housewife as a supervisor. To be a middle-class woman in America in the nine-teenth century "was to be a manager of servants."[14] Yet, despite the efforts of

Catharine Beecher and others in the domestic science movement, few women had any education as managers or as housekeepers themselves.[15] As Leonore Davidoff observes, housework is an art, a mixture of traditional maxims and "empirically proven rules of thumb."[16] Southern cookbook writers studied domestic manuals and frequently quoted from prominent northern domestic authorities,[17] but it appears that the ordinary women of the house relied mostly on themselves and friends and relatives to figure out how to manage their employees. An unnamed member of the Cameron family, among the largest landholders in North Carolina, gave sisterly advice in 1884: "And now let me give you a piece of advice yes I must use that word although I know it is *peculiarly obnoxious* to the ears of *young* people like yourself always give out sufficient *materials* and if your cook happens not to make them to suit exactly don't say 'I think you are the most provoking negro I ever laid my eyes upon.'"[18] More self-reflective than most housekeepers, Georgian Magnolia Le Guin grieved about her own shortcomings in 1903: "Mentally, too, how unfitted I am to raise children and govern the careless negroes who help me. I'm not firm enough with negroes at one time and the next, I think, too impatient, etc."[19] The inconsistency of Le Guin's supervision made her employees' work even more difficult.

As managers, white women wielded enormous power over the lives of their African American employees. Well into the twentieth century, the only people over whom the typical white housewife had any control were her children and her employees.[20] Women took a variety of approaches to household management, with fluctuating amounts of trust and supervision. Richmond housewife Martha Branch set the menu each morning with her cook, but she herself never cooked. Fellow Richmondite Martha Valentine Cronly remembered that her mother set the menus and doled out food supplies: "My mother 'gave out' the provisions each day from the pantry; then they were put on the 'dumb waiter' and pulled by rope to the kitchen, which was in the basement."[21] Helen Kahn, a New Orleans housewife in the middle of the twentieth century, was "a pointer," according to her daughter-in-law Catherine Kahn. She pointed her finger and instructed domestic staff on the work to be done in her home and garden.[22]

Employers often were vague about their expectations, both in terms of the tasks to be completed and in the ways in which they were to be done. As historian Elizabeth O'Leary comments, "Terms of employment were typically verbal and frustratingly fluid."[23] Famed North Carolina restaurateur Mildred Council recalled her initial foray into cooking for a family named Patterson:

My first job doing family cooking was for a Mrs. Patterson on Wilson Court in Chapel Hill. (All I ever knew her as was 'Mrs. Patterson'; at that time, blacks used only the last names of their employers.) . . . One day Mrs. Patterson told me to cook some sweet potatoes. She didn't say they were for a pie for dessert, but I just assumed that they were and boiled them. I guessed wrong, however, as she wanted them for the main dinner (though I never knew exactly how she wanted them cooked). When I realized my mistake, I decided to try something—I was never given recipes or a cookbook on my cooking jobs—so I mashed them and then put butter, Karo syrup, canned milk, orange juice, a handful of sugar, and a pinch of salt in them. The thought came to me to squeeze the oranges and put the potato mixture in the orange peel cups, then bake them.

Council feared the worst from her experiment: "At supper time, I set the table and put the food on, but I was so afraid of what I had done with the sweet potatoes that as they sat down I went to stand at the swinging door to hear if I was going to get fired. But what I heard them say was that the potatoes were sooo good. My heart said, 'Yes, yes, yes, Dip.' And I've been making up my own recipes and cooking them ever since."[24] Council successfully turned her employer's hazy instructions into a culinary tour de force. The incident could just as easily have gone against her favor, however, and would have almost surely done so with an employee less talented than Council, who would not have had the creativity to switch from dessert to side dish with facility.

Because they typically changed jobs so often, cooks had to learn to please many different types of employers.[25] Letters of recommendation generated by employers in the 1920s point to both the characteristics that white women desired and the difficulty of making happy a disparate set of employers. Positive references praised women for their cooking ability, their effort, their kindness to the children in the family, their honesty and reliability, their cleanliness, and their adventurousness in trying new dishes. But the same woman might garner employers' opinions directly in conflict with one another. One Baltimore cook received one reference announcing, "Is not a good cook" and a second one remarking, "Very good cook. Efficient, clean, honest."[26] What satisfied one employer might not satisfy another. It was up to the cook to figure out the differences and negotiate them.[27]

IN THE JIM CROW SOUTH, race as well as sex affected relationships between employer and employee, as it did nearly everything else.[28] The employer and employee involved in domestic work typically were of different races. Until after World War II, almost all employers of domestic workers in the South were white. Although a very few wealthy African Americans hired domestic workers, researcher Carter Woodson observed in 1933, "The Negroes of today are unable to employ one another."[29] Middle-class African Americans did not seek the status of having hired workers as white southerners did. Because of the desire of white southerners for domestic workers, an African American cook's relationship with her employer hit her with race and racism almost every minute.

The noxious combination of race and sex compounded negative situations. As bell hooks wrote, African American women were on the bottom rung of southern society. While African American men and white women could be oppressed themselves, both groups looked down on African American women. African American women experienced the world differently from the way either white women or African American men did.[30] As former slave owners who were now employers grudgingly accommodated themselves to the new social order, white women actively participated in creating this difficult situation. Historian Jennifer Ritterhouse points out, "The enforcement and perpetuation of racial etiquette was one of white women's chief forms of collusion in the Jim Crow system." While women were not in the "legal and political dramas of segregation," the daily performance of segregation affected everyone.[31]

Intimidation existed at many levels. On a broad scale, African American women knew about and were affected by the threat of racial violence that lurked everywhere in the South. Cleora Butler's parents let her move to Tulsa in 1923, but the terrible race riot that occurred there in 1921 lingered in their minds as a serious matter. Butler wrote, "There was some concern because of the racial disturbances in Tulsa two years earlier. But since both Aunt Minnie and my brother George would be close by, it was considered safe."[32] For Butler's parents, the presence of nearby family—a young male and an older female—lessened their anxieties about their daughter going to a big, hostile city.

Idella Parker's mother likewise voiced grave concerns at her daughter's intention of working near the town of Island Grove, Florida. The year was 1940 and Parker was twenty-six years old: "She was almost shouting now. 'You know you can't go work in no Island Grove, Child. They'll kill you!' I knew what Mama was talking about. I'd been hearing stories about how sometimes colored folks mysteriously disappeared in Island Grove ever since I was a child, and those scary tales came rushing into my mind. Island Grove was a white man's town, a place where colored people were not welcome." Parker saw the racist town as a symbol of the worst possibilities: "We all feared Island Grove, that cold fear we all had of whites in those days. Mama was fearful for my safety, of what might happen to me if I so much as set foot in Island Grove."[33] But Parker had accepted an advance check from her new employer, and so off to Island Grove she went, over her mother's protests.

If violence formed the backdrop against which African American women lived, banal racial prejudice shaped their daily actions. Racism proliferated throughout the South despite the close encounters among domestic workers and employers. Journalist Oswald Garrison Villard traveled to the South in 1905, and he commonly found "the overbearing mistresses who feel that their Colored help is trash and do not conceal their feeling in the matter from those who serve them." Villard observed that no economic relationship could be happy or even satisfactory "on which one side thoroughly despises the other, and insists on rubbing in upon the lowly their inferiority."[34] Such attitudes openly continued well into the twentieth century. Bertha Whitridge Smith, a white woman who was president of the Domestic Efficiency Association in Baltimore, wrote in the 1930s that employers needed to be more patient with their servants because the former didn't realize that "they are dealing with very limited brain power." A servant, easily confused, "would like to do better if she knew how." While Smith conceded that the "better class of Negro" was "faithful, intelligent, willing, and with a real native genius for cooking," she believed that the overwhelming majority of African Americans were "little more than irresponsible children, and not infrequently either vicious or feeble-minded."[35] Domestic workers had to cope with employers with just such attitudes, who believed them stupid, faithful, and innately talented cooks.

One way that employers demonstrated their discrimination against African American women was by creating both physical and emotional boundaries between themselves and their cooks. The employer set the tone and distance that she desired, and she expected the cook to follow her lead. Swedish sociologist Gunnar Myrdal wrote in 1944: "Negroes often complain about the uncertainty they experience because of the fact that the initiative in defining the personal situation always belongs to the white man. It is the white man who chooses between the alternatives as to the character of the contact to be established." Such a dynamic, Myrdal observed, constantly kept African Americans off balance.[36]

White people expected certain highly proscribed behaviors from their African American employees. As William Faulkner put it most succinctly in *Intruder in the Dust* (1948), a white person might like African Americans just fine: "All he requires is that they act like niggers."[37] White people accepted African Americans as good cooks; that was a suitable activity for them. James Larkin Pearson observed the transformation of Sudie Holton, a caterer whom he and his wife had hired for an evening in 1939 in Guilford, North Carolina. A superb cook, Holton was provoked by a rude dinner guest into exposing her fluency in French and Spanish and her previous career as a teacher. After Holton spoke of her husband's wounds in World War I and their ambitions for their daughters, Pearson wrote, "Here Sudie realized that she had been the center of attention for some time and she picked up the plate of cold biscuits. There was a wicked twinkle in her black eyes as she looked at the crestfallen young would-be linguist and then dropped into a rich dialect. 'Bress yo' hearts, folkses, the biscuits am cold an' old Sudie done talked her fool head off. 'Scuse me, suh. 'Scuse me, Ma'am, an' I'll fotch some hot ones.'"[38] After speaking inappropriately as an intelligent, well-educated human being, superior to one of the white dinner guests, Holton quickly reverted back into a "nigger" persona and resumed her expected stance as a baker and fetcher of biscuits.

And yet the white employers needed the very physically intimate services that an African American domestic worker performed, from child care to cooking their food. As historian Tera Hunter has commented, domestic service "represented contradictory desires among urban whites striving to distance themselves from an 'inferior' race, but dependent on the very same people they despised to perform the most intimate labor in their homes."[39] While employers demanded that domestic workers remain confined within their limits, the employers usually felt no such obligation to respect any limits on their interference with their workers.

Employers demanded obedience from their employees. As Jennifer Ritterhouse has observed, they expected subordination, manifested in "not only civil but often servile behavior," shown "in a wide array of verbal and physical cues."[40] Throughout much of the twentieth century, patterns of "domination and deference prevailed even as they had in the late nineteenth century."[41] Idella Parker described the behaviors that had been instilled in her growing up in the 1920s and 1930s: "We didn't enter white people's houses by the front door, and we were taught to address white people with 'yes, sir' and 'no, ma'am,' not just 'yes' or 'no.' We sat in the back seats on public buses and separate cars on trains."[42] Fear of white people permeated the lives of African Americans in Parker's hometown of Reddick, Florida: "A white person might strike you or trip you up or anything, just going up and down the street. If you came to two white people talking on the sidewalk, you just had to wait until they finished or go around. I wouldn't dare go through or say, 'Pardon me,' or 'Please let me pass.' It was rough back then; it wasn't pleasant."[43] The fear that she felt toward her white employer led her to unquestioning obedience: "These were the days of the Depression, when most black people were afraid of whites. I was one of those that feared. I think fear caused us to be obedient and do as we were told. I say 'told,' because even Mrs. Rawlings, kind as she was, never asked her workers to do anything, she *told* them. In our first years together Mrs. Rawlings was just like other white people; she talked *at* me, not *to* me. Whatever she said do, I did."[44] Rawlings's employees had little reason to fear her physically, but she controlled their livelihoods and hence could command obedience through threats to their economic well-being.

One of the great sources of employers' power was their ability to discipline their cooks. Punishment—whether for tardiness, performance, attitude, or a myriad other possibilities—came mostly in verbal reprimands and, often, dismissal.[45] In 1871, Macon, Georgia, housewife Jennie Akehurst Lines recorded her expectations of her new cook, Caroline. On the first day, Lines wrote in her diary, "I like her so far and hope she will prove to be a faithful efficient and willing servant and I will try to be a kind, patient and reasonable mistress." The next day, Lines expressed reservations about Caroline's ironing but praised her cooking and her agreeability: "[She] seems willing to do as I direct so I will try to be patient and bear with her shortcomings hoping she will improve." On the third day, Lines reflected that Caroline had but to bend to Lines's way of doing things to be satisfactory: "I like Caroline so far, better than any servant I have ever had, but still she needs a great deal of watching and directing to do work as I want it done. I think when we get entirely settled and she becomes accustomed to doing work *my way* (which is very different from what she has been used to) she will be able to go through the regular routine of duties without quite so much vigilance on my part. I always systematize my household arrangements so that a servant knows what work is to be done each day." Lines expected Caroline to perform according to Lines's standards and not to question Lines's authority. By the end of the second week, however, Caroline disappointed Lines in every possible way: "She has been slow and careless about the work for several days, not the best by any means, and today she adds sullenness to her list of misdemeanors. I think I shall discharge her to-night although I do not yet know where I shall get another, and am not able to be without one."[46] In exactly two weeks, Caroline had gone from being the servant whom Lines liked better than any others to being a woman without a job.

While dismissal brought the loss of one's livelihood, cooks also sometimes faced the violation of their bodies through corporal punishment. Physical abuse had been a constant in slave women's lives, and it continued, although in a more limited way, after emancipation.[47] Some employers did exercise more restraint under the new regime than they would have under the old. Around 1875, Georgian Dolly Burge complained, "I declare I get so bothered with [the servants'] wants & ways sometimes that I want to run off & never see or hear of them any more—Dink is 'worser' than Aunt Lydia & so slow. Mattie is the waiting girl & she is right provoking some times—She needs a whipping badly."[48] Burge declared that Mattie needed a whipping but, even in the days of Reconstruction, did not mention that Mattie actually received any corporal punishment. By the early twentieth century, corporal punishment was less common. Activist Katharine Du Pre Lumpkin reflected on an incident that occurred around 1910 in which her father beat the unnamed family cook with a stick for being impudent: "It was not the custom for Southern white gentlemen to thrash their cooks, not by the early 1900's. But it was not heinous. We did not think so. It had once been right not so many years before. Apparently it could be. Given sufficient provocation, it might be argued: and what recourse did a white man have? All would have assumed, and no doubt did on this occasion, that the provocation on the Negro cook's part had been very great."[49] Respectable white people such as Lumpkin's father still believed that it was acceptable to beat an African American like a disobedient or disrespectful child—even like a recalcitrant horse—and they likely would not have made a similar assumption about an adult white woman.

And, as in slavery, employers could be horrifically creative in their punishments for their employees. In 1888, white Atlanta writer Maud Andrews approvingly quoted an unnamed woman who complained about her cook: "The cook boiled fish with the scales on and my husband made her eat it all up herself. He also compelled her to eat a whole turkey which she had baked without removing the craw." The cook paid for her ignorance or carelessness by being forced to eat large quantities of inedible food. Such a punishment echoed the imaginative penalties from slavery.[50]

Although they stood little chance of winning any given battle, African Americans sometimes stood up for themselves against their punishers. When William Lumpkin began beating the cook, the woman screamed loudly, according to Katharine Du Pre Lumpkin: "I was certain they could be heard for blocks, 'Mister Sheriff! Mister Sheriff! He's killing me! Help!'" Despite the cook's protests, Lumpkin did not stop the beating, and "nothing was heard from the sheriff." She expected the law to protect her, and it did not.[51] On occasion, cooks would not tolerate physical violence and considered it proper provocation to leave a position. Members of the Gregory family, who worked at the estate called Belmont in Richmond, ended a thirty-year relationship in 1895 because of physical abuse. Sarah Woodson, the cook at Belmont, had an argument with twenty-one-year-old Stephen Trent, nephew of Belmont's owner. Trent slapped Woodson, and Sam Gregory, her beau, stood up for her, fighting and beating Trent. Both Woodson and Gregory left their employer as a result of the incident.[52]

AS AFRICAN AMERICANS were expected to behave in a certain way, whites considered themselves exempt from any limitations. The proximity of white men to African American women in the households where the women worked created enormous tensions for all of the women concerned, black and white. Sexual harassment by and nonconsensual sexual relationships with males living in the employer's house was one of the most difficult aspects of domestic service.[53] No matter how great her virtue, an African American woman was often considered fair game by white men, and her very body became a site of struggle, between the races and between the sexes.[54] The psychological impact of sexual abuse was staggering. Writer Gloria Anzaldúa referred to it as "intimate terrorism," observing that "the world is not a safe place to live in. . . . Woman does not feel safe when . . . the males of all races hunt her as prey."[55] Neither black men nor white women, points out critic bell hooks, came to the defense of exploited African American women.[56] Such vulnerability shaped African American women's place in society, "Negro Nurse" wrote in 1912, making African American women "little more than pack horses, beasts of burden, slaves!"[57]

Racialized sexual violence continued unabated from the time of slavery, as Lydia Anderson experienced in postwar Mississippi. When Anderson rejected her employer's advances, he began coercing her teenage daughter.[58] At the turn of the twentieth century, witnesses both African American and white decried the situation. Journalist Oswald Villard observed, "In far too many southern homes the Colored waitress or cook is not morally safe."[59] And in the early twentieth century, William Henry Holtzclaw discussed the placement of young women who graduated from his school in Mississippi. Most of them found satisfactory situations, but Holtzclaw followed up with those who did not stay in their new positions as long as he thought they should have. The two reasons that the young women gave were insufficient wages and not receiving "sufficient protection." Holtzclaw commented, "Respectable Negroes will trust their daughters in the future in the homes of only such white men as they can trust to protect them."[60] Sociologist John Dollard, writing about

Indianola, Mississippi, thirty years later, remarked, "There is no doubt that household servants are more exposed to sexual approaches than are women who stay at home. . . . I encountered two cases where Negro women with high personal standards left employment in houses where the husband or son was 'always bothering' them."[61] This concern continued well into the late twentieth century. Historian Elsa Barkley Brown, born in the 1950s, recalled, "Many of us were painfully aware that one reason our families worked so hard to shield us from domestic and factory work was to shield us from sexual abuse."[62]

Women tried their best to minimize their vulnerability, teaching one another how to avoid sexual assault. Washington, D.C., resident Odessa Minnie Barnes recalled, "Nobody was sent out before you was told to be careful of the white man or his sons. They'd tell you the stories of rape . . . hard too! No lies! You was to be told true, so you'd not get raped. Everyone warned you and told you to 'be careful.'" Weida Edwards corroborated Barnes's observation: "You'd know how to run, or almost not be in the house with the white man or big sons."[63]

In the early twentieth century, after literally centuries of endurance, African American women began to speak out about the situation. "Negro Nurse," writing from Georgia in 1912, recounted being fired because she stood up for herself:

> I remember very well the first and last place from which I was dismissed. I lost my place because I refused to let the madam's husband kiss me. He must have been accustomed to undue familiarity with his servants, or else he took it as a matter of course, because without any love-making at all, soon after I was installed as cook, he walked up to me, threw his arms around me, and was in the act of kissing me, when I demanded to know what he meant, and shoved him away. I was young then, and newly married, and didn't know then that what has been a burden to my mind and heart ever since: that a colored woman's virtue in this part of the country has no protection.

Naively, she turned to her husband to set the matter straight: "I at once went home, and told my husband about it. When my husband went to the man who had insulted me, the man cursed him, and slapped him, and—had him arrested! The police judge fined my husband $25. I was present at the hearing, and testified on oath to the insult offered me. The white man, of course, denied the charge. The old judge looked up and said: 'This court will never take the word of a nigger against the word of a white man.'" "Negro Nurse" concluded that such situations were all too common: "Many and many a time since I have heard similar stories repeated again and again by my friends. I believe nearly all white men take, and expect to take, undue liberties with their colored female servants—not only the fathers, but in many cases the sons also. Those servants who rebel against such familiarity must either leave or expect a mighty hard time, if they stay."[64]

Nancy White, who grew up in Tennessee in the early twentieth century, also spoke of leaving a job to avoid sexual harassment: "Now, I have worked for some nice people and some rotten ones. I've had to ask some hands off me and I've had to just give up some jobs if they got too hot behind me. . . . In one job I had I could see this young boy who was just able to pee straight making up his mind whether he was going to try me. I told the woman some lie and got my money and got out of there fast!" White castigated the boy's mother, who had to be aware of what was happening but "had spoiled that fool little boy of hers" and would not correct him. The cost of leaving such a situation, according to White, was worth it: "Now, I have lost some money that way, but that's all right. When you lose control of your body, you have just about lost all you have in this world!"[65] Determined to keep her physical integrity, White took her leave.

While each of these women spoke out against her would-be assailant, others acceded to or resisted aggression differently. White people had so much control over African American cooks, from paying their wages to owning the houses that they lived in, that many women may have felt that they had no choice but to cooperate. A white man had dozens of ways at his disposal to make an African American woman who spurned him suffer. Carolyn Chase spoke vividly of witnessing her mother's sexual assault by a white man, Mr. Gilford, in rural Arkansas in the 1940s. Although it is unclear whether her mother actually worked for the Gilfords, Chase's mother's defenselessness in the situation shows plainly. Chase recalled, "I had never seen my mother helpless or very silent. She always seemed to know what she should do and what other people should do too." In the face of Gilford's relentless advance, however, the normally confident woman shook and asked her assailant to stop, but "she did not strike him or push him." The mother and daughter never mentioned Gilford's actions to Chase's father. Chase observed, "I think she was afraid everything would fall down if she did the wrong thing or if she did anything at all."[66] Fear of reprisal also kept a Georgia family from protesting the attempted rape of their thirteen-year-old daughter, Zipporah. Zipporah substituted at work for her mother, Sarah, one afternoon, and her employer's husband tried to rape her. Sarah's first words were, "Child, for God's sake, don't tell your father. You'll get him killed." Sarah believed that there was nothing that "a poor black man" could do to "a rich white man" and "get away with—alive." Hence, Zipporah's father never learned of his daughter's violation, lest he try to avenge or somehow settle the trespass. Sarah was forced to tolerate the assault of her daughter to avoid the murder of her husband.[67]

NUMEROUS SCHOLARS HAVE documented the lengths to which white southerners went to keep the lines drawn between the races during the Jim Crow era. In their homes, white women used a variety of tools to segregate the African American women who worked there. Language served as a common weapon, particularly the practice of referring to the African American by first name while the white employer was called by a courtesy title and family name.[68] Author Vertamae Smart-Grosvenor observed, "Nothing depresses me more than to see a woman who could be my grandmother on a first name basis with some snotty-nose kid."[69] "Negro Nurse" wrote bitterly, "Another thing it's a small indignity, it may be, but an indignity just the same. No white person, not even the little children just learning to talk, no white person at the South ever thinks of addressing any negro man or woman as Mr., or Mrs., or Miss. The women are called, 'Cook,' or 'Nurse,' or 'Mammy,' or 'Mary Jane,' or 'Lou,' or 'Dilcey,' as the case might be, and the men are called 'Bob,' or 'Boy,' or 'Old Man,' or 'Uncle Bill,' or 'Pate.'"[70] Later in the twentieth century, May Anna Madison recalled one employer who deliberately inverted her name: "I worked for a lady for five years, and do you know that woman always called me Anna May? She used to say that she depended on me for everything and that I was just like one of the family, but she didn't want to call me by my name. After I had been working for them for about three years I asked her why she did that, and she said it was just easier for her to call me Anna May. So that's what she did." Madison concluded that the name symbolized the relationship: "That's what I was there for—to make things easier for her."[71]

Segregation was also spatial. Domestic work, including cooking, almost always took place in the employer's home, bringing the African American woman into a white family's intimate physical space.[72] Whether she lived with her employer or in her own home, when she came into the home of her employer, the African American cook entered a culture other than her own. Usually the only African American person on the premises, she often suffered from isolation, prevented from ongoing contact with others in similar situations that would have established a healthy work culture. Critic Trudier Harris has captured the dilemma of an African American woman leaving her own space and entering that of a woman of a different race and different social and economic class: "In moving from her home to that of the white woman, the black woman connects two racially and spatially distinct worlds in one direction—she goes into the white world." Harris continues, "The black woman is presumably at home in her own environment; but when she enters the white woman's kitchen, she moves into a culture which is at least apart from her own, if not alien or openly hostile."[73] Writer Gloria Anzaldúa calls such spaces "borderlands," places where "two or more cultures edge each other, where people of different races occupy the same territory." Living on the edges, says Anzaldúa, causes a person to work hard at keeping her "shifting and multiple identity and integrity." The "alien" place may become "familiar—never comfortable."[74]

For a cook, the kitchen sometimes became the least hostile place in this alien environment, but being in the kitchen could also enhance a cook's sense of segregation and separation. As Leonore Davidoff has observed, access to various parts of the house carried with it shifts in status: "Who has access to which parts of the house and when becomes a marker of gender and age categories as well as permitted intimacies."[75] Often cooks remained isolated in the kitchen, the most private part of the household. The floor plan for an 1867 Victorian house, copied in Texarkana, Texas, placed the kitchen at the very back of the house, with the dining room separating the kitchen and the parlor.[76] The space between the kitchen and parlor doors measured more than twenty feet; no cook would find herself in the parlor by mere accident. The dining room might serve as a sort of middle ground, in which the cook served the food that she cooked to her employer's family and guests.[77] In the dining room, an African American woman's role as social inferior would be reinforced by her dress, her role as servant, and her exclusion from the pleasantries of the white people's table. But the parlor (later, living room) would be strictly off-limits except in serving situations.

Although a cook may indeed have felt a sense of belonging in the kitchen—with its heat ("hotter than Dante's Inferno," said Frances Walker[78]) and food smells—there was no question that the ultimate ownership of the space and authority remained with the housewife/employer.[79] Martha Plant Ross reiterated this point in discussing her family's home in Macon: "Old Anne—I don't suppose she was really so very old—would not let us stay in 'her' kitchen, and who could blame her?" While the cook named Anne had the authority to chase children from her workspace, the quotation marks around Ross's possessive leave no doubt that the white family knew very clearly who was, in the final analysis, the owner of the kitchen.[80]

Yet another form of segregation existed in the taboo against African

Americans and white people eating together. For cooks, one of the most bitter ironies was that they were good enough to prepare food but not good enough to eat it in the company of their employers. As critic Psyche Williams-Forson remarked, for an African American woman to "share in the consumption of the food, especially in the presence of whites, meant that culinary (and social) boundaries would have to be broken."[81] According to sociologist Charles Spurgeon Johnson, the taboo against eating together was so strong that it was "rarely broken." Eating together was "thoroughly prohibited and severely punished" because it suggested "social intimacy which is universally banned."[82] The very strong southern proscription against commensality became even more paradoxical when the person being denied the right to eat the food was the very one who had cooked it. Idella Parker recalled the elaborate preparation of a ham, and she commented, "It was a lovely sight to see, and *without even tasting it* I knew it was good."[83]

Prohibitions extended even to cooks' contact with cooked food. Beulah Nelson quit her first job, perhaps in 1910, after three days over the issue of her handling bread. Disgusted with her employer's prohibition against her touching the hot bread to transfer it onto the dining table, she simply refused to bring the loaf from the kitchen and then left before her employer could fire her.[84] Anna Mae Dickson remembered, "You would go in the kitchen and make biscuits and rolls for people because they weren't buying bread in those days. Now you know you got to put your hands in it to make it. All right you'd make the bread and then after it would get brown and ready to eat, but they wouldn't want you to put your hands on it. And it was the same thing with meat. You could touch the meat before it was cooked, but after it was done, don't touch it! Oh, that would get me mad!"[85] In such households, it was acceptable for cooks to come into contact with the crude raw ingredients but not with the finished products.

If a cook were in fact allowed to dine in the house, she could eat the food that she prepared only in the kitchen, and she had to wait until everyone else had eaten. Her isolation thus spanned both space and time. Idella Parker remembered the distance that existed between her and her employer: "She usually took her dinner in the dining room, and I would serve her each course just as I did when guests were there. Then I would go in the kitchen to eat my dinner. Even though it was only the two of us, I still had my place as servant; she never once invited me to sit at the table with her to eat."[86] Employers reinforced such discrimination with their children. A young white woman from near the Mississippi River observed in 1954: "I came in late to lunch one day. Everyone had eaten except the cook, and I started to sit at the table with her and eat. Mother asked her to move. I didn't understand it." In the employer's mind, the cook's lunch took third place—after the family's main meal and after the tardy teenager.[87]

Even the dishes from which cooks ate could be separated. Writer Maya Angelou, who grew up in Arkansas, recalled that in the 1930s a cook named Miss Glory had a glass "that sat on a separate shelf from the others."[88] In Olive Ann Burns's novel *Cold Sassy Tree*, the cook Queenie drinks from a quart jar and eats from a pie pan in her employer's kitchen; her employer considers even the plainest dishes too fine for her.[89] Willie Mae Wright recalled one especially awful employer who expected her to eat out of the dog's dish: "She thought it was dirty to use the same dish a dog had done eat out of, but still and yet she thought it was good enough for me." Wright quit that particular household after two days' employment.[90]

Clothing labels people by status and rank, and employers who required their cooks to wear uniforms attempted to set apart the women visually.[91] Although the practice of having servants wear uniforms or livery extends back at least to eighteenth-century France, in the American South it seems to have been a late-Victorian affectation that extended well into the twentieth century, illustrating a method of control and a craving for conspicuous consumption.[92]

While uniforms may have been part of the Victorian social order that also required twelve pieces of silver per guest at a formal dinner, they also played a fearsome part in delineating a cook's acceptable place in her employer's world and reinforcing the Jim Crow society, which was growing ever stronger across the South in the early twentieth century. Not only did her race make an African American woman stand out in a white enclave, but the type of clothing that her employer expected her to wear also marked visually her low position within the household. Wearing a uniform negated a woman's individuality. When she removed her own clothing and donned a uniform, a domestic worker became someone whose primary function was to serve the family that had stripped her of her own identity.[93] They might be white, green, or gray, but, no matter their color, uniforms clearly marked a woman as a domestic servant.[94] Cooks recognized the uniforms for what they were, signs of attempted subordination, and some refused to wear them in public. Idella Parker arrived at Marjorie Kinnan Rawlings's house with two uniforms in her suitcase, but she eventually made it abundantly clear that she would not leave the premises without changing into her own clothes first.[95] According to Astor Smith, his grandmother Frances Walker went on errands with her employer: "She didn't mind that, except she did not like to be out in public wearing that uniform."[96]

Cooks and servants in the South often regarded uniforms as pretentious and ostentatious, evidence of their employers' skewed values. They sometimes got the last laugh, turning the tables on their employers' attempts to debase them with uniforms, and they told the stories with glee. In Louisville, Martha Poole's employer had extremely high standards for Poole's uniform, requiring three changes per day, but she expected Poole to care for the uniforms (which the employer owned) on her own time, despite the fact that she served breakfast, lunch, and dinner at the employer's home. This particular employer required a white uniform in the morning, a black-and-white one in the afternoon, and "in the evening[, one] the color of the dining room paper. It was beautiful. It was the color of rose." In her pink uniform the same hue as the wallpaper, the cook became a part of the household décor. Poole pointed out that when she first started working in the 1930s, "everybody didn't have washers and dryers," and she recalled, "One day I was washing my uniforms and she said to me, 'Oh, are you washing your uniforms here?' I said, 'Well, I wear them here, don't I?' She said, 'Well, I don't like for you to be using my electricity to wash your uniforms here. . . .' When I left I left every one of them dirty. I stayed long enough to dirty them and then I left them all stacked up in the closet."[97] Discarding an employer's precious uniform was Anna Mae Dickson's last act of defiance the day she quit: "I took off her dainty little apron and her dainty little hat piece and folded them up in the drawer. Then I put on my old straw hat, and I walked out."[98] Dickson contrasted her own serviceable straw hat with the flimsy ornamental headgear expected by her employer. On her own time, she would wear her own hat.

OBLIGATED TO DO WORK that she likely would prefer not to do, under difficult circumstances, a cook had to figure out ways to improve her lot. Managing the relationship with her employer was a means by which a domestic worker gained some control over her work.[99] One way that African American women mastered the situation was by cultivating dissemblance, a careful concealment of what she actually thought and felt.[100] As historian David Goldfield has written, tone of voice, gesture, and what was said and not said "became parts of the rituals of southern personal relations. It was theater."[101] Anna Mae Dickson spoke of the lessons she learned through decades of cooking for other women: "They may keep you from speaking out, but they can't keep you from thinking. It's something on the inside. And you learn to be two persons to live through it all."[102]

Sociologist Hortense Powdermaker observed the phenomenon of dissemblance repeatedly in Indianola, Mississippi, in the 1930s: "Almost every white woman feels that she knows all about her cook's personality and life, but she seldom does. The servant is quite a different person Across the Tracks and is not as a rule communicative about the life she leads there."[103] Such a lack of communication was often a deliberate ploy on the part of the employee to keep her life separate from her employers'. In Washington, D.C., with the anonymity of a big city, Nellie Willoughby took great pride in the fact that her employers "didn't even know where I lived."[104]

Employees concealed information about their personal lives and also about their feelings concerning their employers. Georgia Sutton spoke candidly of the situation that she witnessed growing up in North Carolina:

> You talk to just about anyone who grew up in a segregated situation, you're going to find those people [were] readily adaptable to certain situations. You had to have strength in order to have survived. My mother used to say, "That lady that I work for is foolish enough to believe that I really like her. I'm not thinking about her one way or the other. Just pay me what she owes me." What I am saying is that it has been in recent years that the average white has discovered that blacks do not love them per se because all along they thought years ago, "She's just crazy about me. She works for me. She does this for me, and she's this, that, and the other." We've learned over the years to survive.

Sutton took the lessons from her mother to heart: "And I learned, too, that I could smile on the outside. My mother told me, 'Nobody ever knows what goes through your head. You can afford to smile on the outside. Get what you want and go on.'" Sutton recalled her mother tried to make light of her need to fool her employers: "[This] used to be an interesting thing to us. Mama would always come home and tell what she said and what she had done [at work] and have a big laugh about it. It'd be a big joke to us. But my mother learned to survive. She had two girls to rear and she did what she had to do."

Sutton observed that whites played into the dissemblance by discounting the intelligence of African Americans: "But you see, that's a side of black life that whites never see. They never felt that a black was a thinker. Never thought that blacks thought about anything, but you can sure believe they did. And a lot of them who worked in their kitchen laughed about some of the things that went on. And they'd laugh about it and say, 'Didn't I fool her.' It was always a big joke to us. And I used to enjoy it. Well, it used to sort of make me feel better about some of the things that I had to suffer."[105] Whether she gained genuine pleasure from fooling her white employers, Sutton clearly found recompense for the slights and slurs of segregated life.

As Sutton commented, white women often fancied that they knew what their cooks were thinking and feeling. Gertrude Thomas observed in February 1880, "Altogether I have felt more like old times during the past month. Dinah my cook is a treasure. I believe she likes me and she mingles with her service so much interest in my welfare that it touches me." Dinah stayed for less than a year, however, for by January 1881, Thomas was unhappy with a cook named Della.[106]

Marjorie Kinnan Rawlings thought that she understood the varying attitudes of her sometime cook, Martha Mickens: "We call Martha 'old-timey.' That means specifically that to our white faces she presents a low-voiced deference, to our backs an acute criticism."[107] Rawlings's reference to "old-timey" might indicate that she considered Mickens a vestige of a time when African Americans were more respectful to their employers' faces. And yet Rawlings proved far less astute than she believed herself to be. Idella Parker recalled Rawlings as almost willfully ignorant of employees' lives. Thinking of a story about her sister Hettie, Parker wrote, "Mrs. Rawlings did not know anything about this story in my life. All she was interested in was whether I could cook and keep her house, hold quiet, and let her do her work."[108] Years later, Parker was outraged when she saw what Rawlings had written about her in a 1941 letter: "[Idella] is the answer to a prayer. Not only a marvelous cook, but doesn't drink, isn't interested in men, borrows my books, likes the same movies I do, and adores having company and protests when I pay her extra after a heavy week." Parker responded to Rawlings's comments: "Of course, I didn't read that until sometime after her death, and when I did my friends and I had quite a laugh. My friends told me, 'She's sure got the wrong Idella. I can tell she didn't know you.'"[109] The assumptions of white women about their domestic employees sometimes proved harmful, if the employers incorrectly imagined bad things. Sometimes they simply made the white women look silly, incorrectly assuming that they knew things that they did not.

In addition to dissemblance, African American workers had other means of resisting the oppression and overwork that their employers meted out. As historian Jessica Millward observed, "Black women confronted the power system with the tools available to them and did so with both measured and phenomenal successes."[110] Across the South, domestic workers were "particularly proficient in their protest tactics and small-scale negotiations to alter the balance of power between employer and employee."[111] These small battles are what historian Robin D. G. Kelley calls the "everyday nature of workplace resistance."[112]

One of the easiest ways for a domestic worker to resist her employer was simply by acting grumpy. Free and easy to make, a sour face could cause friction in the household and remind the white housewife that one could not always be jolly. Cooks leaving home in the wee hours, standing on their feet all day, cooking food for other people surely had plenty to be cross about, but their employers expected them to ignore or rise above all circumstances to be affable and agreeable at all times. Any other behavior occasioned comment or chastisement.

In 1869, Gertrude Thomas tried to punish her cook, Cornelia Shelman, for her sullen attitude by dismissing her. "She is the most utterly worthless of all the indolent race—Since breakfast she has added the crowning annoyance of impertinence to her other aggravations and I have dismissed her," Thomas wrote. "I have told her to go home two or three times before but this time I think I will insist upon her leaving."[113] By 1881, the situation had improved but little at the Thomas house, and Gertrude Thomas remarked, "I have but one woman, the cook (Della) and she is as annoying as it is possible for a servant to be. She teases Kathleen [Thomas's five-year-old daughter], is very disrespectful and noisy but she is the best I can command the services of."[114] Such behaviors continued well into the twentieth century. Katy Brumby, a longtime cook in Georgia, muttered to herself while she cooked. The Federal Writers' Project interviewer reported, "Her chief complaint is that she has too much work to do. 'Y'all just got one somebody to do all de work. Need two somebodies.'"[115]

Jane Stafford remembered the long tenure of Beatrice Walters in her parents' household: "She had a cute little sense of humor, and she could be fun. But she could also be as mean as a snake. She had a real strange side sometimes."[116] A woman who excelled at cooking could get away with more than an unskilled worker could. Edith Whitney recalled her cook named Mildred: "I had Mildred. And she wasn't a part of the family! I'd forgotten Mildred. She was my cook. The meanest one! She couldn't get along with anybody.... But she made the most beautiful little flowered mints and cheese straws, for parties and all. She was mean as the devil, but I kept her. When the children had all been gone, though, I let Mildred go."[117] Mildred didn't fit the stereotype—she "wasn't a part of the family." Mildred's perceived poor disposition finally outweighed her value as a cook. Her job became more vulnerable than perhaps she realized, or perhaps she did not value the job enough to act as Whitney wanted her to.

Simply not showing up for work was another way of thoroughly annoying one's employer, who either had no meal or had to cook it herself when the cook did not appear. This particular weapon had to be used with great care, however, for it could result in one's summary dismissal. Magnolia Le Guin lamented her cook's absence: "I am worried. Hired a negro girl and let her get in debt to me for a pr shoes and tobacco—she was nearly barefoot. She helped me 2 ½ days—went home Sun. A.M. Now 'tis Tuesday P.M. and no negro yet—and Quarterly meeting is to come off next Friday and I'm looking for company and a whole lot of cooking for me to do and no one to help now—I try not to worry, but I can hardly cook a meal unless baby cries and cries." If the unnamed cook wanted to cause her high-strung employer maximum distress, she picked her time well, with the impending presence of guests making Le Guin even more nervous than usual.[118]

Abusing the work tools—particularly appliances and household goods—was another type of resistance. Stoves came in for their share of trouble, for even a skilled, careful cook could have difficulty with a temperamental stove. Jennie Akehurst Lines suspected that the ill-fated Caroline was simply not trying to use her stove appropriately: "Caroline either can not or will not manage the stove so that the oven will bake. I have showed her and told her so much too."[119] Sixty years later, Frenise Logan reported that African American cooks caused stoves to clog with soot and to "'burn out' in half the time they ought to last."[120] An anonymous writer from Knoxville, Tennessee, in 1901 also condemned servants' carelessness with the good dishes:

See how she handles it; piling glass, silverware and china, thick or thin, into one promiscuous heap in a not over-clean dish-pan; pouring a kettleful of water over it, the water boiling hot, or barely warm, as may happen to suit her convenience and the state of the kitchen fire; sloshing the whole around, chipping and cracking it more or less in the process; draining the dishes, one upon top of another, without regard to weight or decoration, while the greasy water dries in streaks on their dull surfaces; and finally wiping them, two or three at a time, upon a dingy, musty towel.[121]

Employers reacted sharply to the destruction of their property. During Reconstruction, Kentuckian Nancy Johnson suffered a beating from her employer for breaking a teacup.[122] Twenty years later, Anne Ruffin Cameron, a member of the wealthiest family in Durham County, North Carolina, doled out harsh monetary punishment for breakage: one dollar, or four days' wages, for each broken dish.[123] Employers feared even the destruction of dish towels. In the 1870s, cookbook writer Marion Tyree recommended that housewives hem their dish towels so that the servants would be "less likely to throw them away."[124]

And of course, the cook could sabotage the food itself, usually without the employer's knowledge. Aunt Delia, who had cooked as a slave, told activist Pauli Murray's grandmother, "How many times I spit in the biscuits and peed in the coffee just to get back at them mean white folks."[125] When Beulah Nelson quit her first job, she taunted her former employers: "I said, 'These two days I been in your house. . . . You could be done ate a lot of my spit [in your food]. I could have done did anything I want to do to it, and you wouldn't have never known nothing about it.'"[126] Even the rare well-to-do African American employer feared the worst, as a turn-of-the-century etiquette book demonstrated the harm that an unhappy employee could cause: "The cook that's in a good humor when she is preparing a meal is more careful that her hands are kept clean, and into what she slings the sweat which runs in ringlets down her glossy cheeks, and where the nose drips fall, than she who's in ill humor."[127]

Quitting was one of the greatest prerogatives of an African American woman in the postbellum South. Historian Tera Hunter comments, "Quitting did not necessarily guarantee a better situation elsewhere (and often did not), but it reinforced workers' desire for self-determination and deprived employers of the ascendancy to which they were accustomed as slaveholders."[128] Willie Mae Wright exercised this option frequently in her ongoing search for a good employer: "I'd go from one job to another when I had to. Sometimes I'd get a sorry one. I'd always tough it out for a right smart spell, but finally I'd think, Lord, can't nothing be worse than this; so I'd quit and go someplace else, and sometimes I'd come to find out I'd done got out of the sandspurs and fell into the poison oak."[129] Between jobs, her cousin Mary provided lodging for her and other relatives in similar fixes: "That's where we'd all go when we got out of a job—provided we had a little money. Cousin Mary would sleep you free, but she wouldn't feed you the first bite."[130] In Columbia, Missouri, at the turn of the twentieth century, sociologist William Elwang reported that thirty-three white families had 141 servants in a period of three years, with the average tenure being nine months. Among other families, Elwang observed, "the general average term of service is much shorter." One family reported having twenty-four servants in three years; another seventeen; and still another, twelve.[131] In Athens, Georgia, before World War I, a homemaker complained, "Before they can learn where to put cooking vessels they just fail to come back and then another is to be taught the same things." World War I increased unsettledness, as the war made other types of employment temporarily available. One Athens housewife had five different cooks during the nineteen months of war, and she claimed not to be unusual. In a volatile economy with new opportunities, cooks stayed only a few months.[132] Similar narratives emerged across the South in the 1920s.[133]

Quitting might have been a cook's ultimate weapon, but it had to be used with care because, for many African American women, employment was absolutely essential to the welfare of their own families.[134] A woman could not do without income for long. Still, many servants went ahead and left. In Gainesville, Georgia, servants listed their top reasons for quitting, in order of frequency: better wages, violation of contract, overwork, unkindness, tired of work, to remain at home, and "just for a change."[135] An anonymous worker in Knoxville in 1941 said that she had had eighty jobs in ten years. For a fourth of those, she observed, "I'll take the blame, due to their nerves, a restless dissatisfied nature, and due to my own ideas of right and wrong, which is common to all idealists." Another twenty she blamed on "a *bad system* with *set customs.*" And for half she attributed the loss to "the 'cussedness of human nature' in my employers. This is the crux of the matter." She listed her employers' offenses: "1. Too long hours with too short pay. 2. Overcritical of trifling details. 3. Laziness and pride. 4. Too many guests to dine. 5. Failure to discipline children. . . . 6. Treating maids as *inferior* in various ways. 7. Under priviledging [sic] maids who show ear marks of being of much better family."[136] Only two of the complaints, about hours and pay and "too many guests," dealt with the actual work. Another, the failure to discipline children, pointed to inferior working conditions. Most of the complaints, then, had to do with the employers' attitudes toward their workers.

DOMESTIC WORKERS WERE most likely to switch jobs frequently in their early years of work, for, as young people, they chafed under close supervision.[137] Living in their employers' homes proved particularly difficult for young women with social interaction on their minds. Like Virginian Mary Wade, who owed her employers for a barrel of flour when she left, they wanted to be out and about "in the neighborhood."[138] Magnolia Le Guin complained of Fannie's inconsistency: "My negro girl Fannie came back and stayed 7½ days and left again yesterday." Fannie was thirteen years old.[139]

Even seasoned workers had their breaking points. Anna Mae Dickson told the story of leaving an employer who expected perfection in cooking for and serving a crowd: "Like this banker's wife, one day I was serving a lunch for her. She had all the bankers there, and she was the only woman. She had her meal served in courses. We had got to the dessert and coffee. I came in with the coffee cups—I used to be able to tote 12 cups of coffee on one hand and serve with the other. . . . When I set the first cup of coffee down, Mrs. Thompson hollered: 'Anna Mae, goddamnit it, you're serving the coffee on the wrong side!' Boy, I just started to shake." Dickson went back to the kitchen and then out the back door, leaving the banker's wife with a living room full of bankers and a kitchen full of dirty dishes. Dickson left another employer when a child spit on the back of her dress, and another time when she was accused of stealing a handkerchief.[140]

Rather than walking out like Dickson, many cooks simply failed to show up for work, never saying goodbye. As Tera Hunter points out, "Quitting as a tactic thrived because it did not require such direct antagonism."[141] Utterly disgusted with the filth of one new employer's home as well as the woman's crude prejudices, Willie Mae Wright observed: "When I left out of there late that afternoon she said she'd meet me at the car line in Buckhead the next day at eight in the morning, and I said: 'Yes'm, I'll be right there at Miller's filling-station.' I let her drive that whole eight miles the next morning; and if I was there, Mrs. Joe Louis was there."[142] John Dollard reported from Indianola, Mississippi, that white women complained about their cooks disappearing the day after payday. He theorized, "The only explanation of such behavior is that the Negro woman views leaving as an aggressive act and fears to confess her intention lest she be stopped somehow or argued out of going."[143] It was better to simply disappear rather than risk a confrontation.

Dorothy Bolden quit out of principle in 1959, at the time that Martin Luther King Jr. was leading civil rights demonstrations in Atlanta: "This one lady I was working for, I had been working there four or five years, and she was just against these demonstrations. One day her little girl came back and told me, 'Oh, Mama's glad you're not with those niggers out there demonstrating.' And that just really got to me, so I quit. Before that, she seemed real nice, but it was always two-faced. It didn't bother me, I went and did my work and came on out, but I knew it was two-faced and when it really came out it hurt to see this."[144]

Some cooks and their employers developed relationships in which the cook would quit or be fired, rehired, and quit or be fired again. Idella Parker abandoned working for Marjorie Rawlings three times over a ten-year span, returning twice: "Those were the times she would realize she had treated me badly, and she would come looking for me, all apologies, and promising it wouldn't happen again. I believed her in the beginning, and I went back knowing she needed me. Each time she would give me money, and because she knew I liked new clothes, she would tell me to go buy a new dress or something. That was her way of trying to appease me. Mama grew to hate her for the way she treated me, saying, 'I don't know why you keep going back to that woman.'"[145] An Indianola, Mississippi, woman named Opal "was repeatedly taken back after being fired under the most tempestuous circumstances and money was loaned to her when it was unlikely that she would return it." John Dollard observed that the white employer gained psychological benefit from the situation, as she loved "to play the forgiving role."[146]

In addition to having the psychic satisfaction of leaving a bad situation, the repeated departures of cooks had a cumulative effect, according to Tera Hunter: "The instability created in the labor market strengthened the bargaining position of domestic workers since employers persisted in thinking of the pool as scarce, though, in absolute numbers, the supply of domestic workers available to the employing population in Atlanta was virtually endless."[147] Women like Magnolia Le Guin, who could barely cope with their own households in the absence of paid labor, thought of cooks as scarce because they had such difficulty keeping one in service. Hunter concludes, "The incongruence between the perception of a dearth and the reality of an abundance suggests that black women's self-assertion had indeed created a shortage of workers with the attributes employers preferred."[148] Employers desired workers who would come and stay regardless of circumstances. African American cooks refused to be that kind of worker.

IN ADDITION TO RACE AND SEX, strains within the employer-employee interaction arose from class differences, manifested in the contrasts between the home and food of the employer and the home and food of the employee. French food scholar Claude Grignon speaks of "conspicuous waste . . . the excess of which insults the poor without even thinking of it."[149] More than any other type of worker, domestic workers had "intimate acquaintance with the possessions, priorities, and financial affairs of their employers" and were "well aware that their employers consumed luxuries while they claimed to be unable to afford decent wages."[150] The members of the Club of the Colored Maids in Kannapolis, North Carolina, demonstrated their awareness of the inequality in a letter to Franklin Roosevelt, commenting that their employers "make more in one day than we make in two weeks labor."[151] Anna Mae Dickson expressed eloquently her grasp of the disparity between her income and that of her employers:

It was like leading two lives. I'd be down there all day working in those houses and then I'd come back home and I'd look around and think: "Oh my God, why do I have to live this way?" I'd walk around and look at my floors when all we had were those little patches of linoleum, and I'd think of their floors. Then I'd have to haul and heat our dishwater when right down there where I'd been all day they'd have more hot running water than they could use. Sometimes when I was driving home, I'd be saying to myself: "Now if I just had such and such a thing. And oh, my God, if I could only have a bathtub." But you did what you had to and didn't feel sorry for yourself. We just had to make a living and that was the only way to do it.[152]

Dickson, well aware of the inequality and injustice of the situation, nonetheless bowed her neck to do what she had to do to earn her living.

With such glaring inequity in living standards, one of the most constant sources of tension between housewives and cooks was theft, whether real, imagined, intentional, accidental, or through misunderstanding. Many white people believed that all African Americans were potential, if not actual, thieves. Katharine Du Pre Lumpkin recalled her upbringing in an upper-class white home: "We verily believed that a Negro could not help but steal. So we acted accordingly. We must lock up our valuables. We children should never leave the key in the food pantry door, but turn it and put it back in its hiding place. Let something be missing; we suspected the cook, unless it was found; maybe even then, for she could have 'got scared' and returned it. It was not serious with us; just a disability of the race, we said, that only we Southerners understood and took charitably."[153]

While, as Lumpkin points out, African Americans might be accused of stealing anything and everything, including jewelry and money, food created the most friction.[154] Psyche Williams-Forson posits that theft of food may not have been as common as believed but that whites may have used the threat of being stolen from as a tool of control. Treating an employee as a potential thief would create a cloud of suspicion that would shadow her every move.[155]

Stealing food was an extension of the widely sanctioned practice known as "toting," in which cooks received leftover food as part of their pay, in lieu of cash. The system of toting had advantages for the employers. Most notably, it meant that they could pay less in cash wages, and they might hope that, because her family would have some at the end of the day, the cook would take extra care with the food, producing a finer result. In addition to the cash savings, employers also received psychological benefits from allowing toting, for the practice of employees removing food from the home "reinforced the stereotype of African Americans as morally bankrupt and shifty characters and reinforced the notions of black inferiority and dependency and white paternalism."[156] Virginian Daniel Staples observed in 1879 that the Staples family cook was "stealing her pro rata share of a dinner fixed for the preacher," with ample leftovers.[157] If everyone concerned knew that the cook would receive a certain portion—"pro rata"—of the dinner, labeling the cook's action as "stealing" served to shore up white feelings of superiority.

Frugal (or stingy) housewives carefully oversaw what left their house, controlling their cooks' food supplies. Kathleen Claiborne, a boardinghouse keeper in Indianola, Mississippi, allowed the "servants" to tote, but any leftover turkey or chicken had to be saved to be turned into croquettes for another meal for the Claibornes and their boarders.[158] Some domestic workers received food on site but were not allowed to take it home. One Athens woman reported that two of her employees quit "because I required them to eat their meals here instead of taking them home," while another observed, "My cook feeds her son from my table, but it is with my consent."[159] Such employers used food as a very strong method of control, repeatedly asserting their authority over their cooks' access to surpluses.

Employers became outraged when employees took home cooked food without permission and when they prepared food in quantities larger than the white families needed, thereby resulting in healthy surpluses for the cooks' own families. Some African Americans considered such actions as a matter of course and viewed them simply as being resourceful. Novelist and cookbook author Dori Sanders recalled her family's attitude toward her aunt's toting: "Aunt Vestula worked at a time when the 'pay and tote' system was in effect. It was just a little Southern thing. 'Pay' was the amount of money you received for your services, 'tote' was the extra food you carried home to your own family. Cooks during that time always prepared a little bit more food than necessary for the family they worked for. That way they were guaranteed to have some food to tote home. They simply added a little more sugar to the pound than necessary."[160] Sarah Harris Anderson methodically created a clever system for slipping food from her employers' houses. Her granddaughter, singer Ethel Waters, remembered that Anderson "sewed little pockets in an apron and filled the pockets with neatly done up parcels of food—sandwiches, pieces of pie or cake, sugar, and eggs. Then when she was ready to take her day off on Thursday, she'd put on the heavily laden apron under her petticoat. Mom could sneak any kind of food out of her boss's house except soup."[161] Some astute African American women considered taking food simply as retribution for past wrongs. "A White Woman" writing in the *Independent* in 1902, said, "I was provoked into chiding the cook for stealing too much of the salad, '*Why* do you take things, Mary?' 'Hit's dis way, Miss Sarah, *we* all thinks we is got the right to take from *you* all dis as much as our daddies and mammies was worth endurin' slavery times!'"[162] It would take a lot of salad to compensate for centuries of enslavement.

In addition to "toting" leftovers without permission, housewives feared that cooks would remove staple goods, usually out of the pantry and usually without permission.[163] Thus, they sought to limit cooks' access to food supplies. Some locked their pantries between meals, a process that must have been a headache for all concerned parties.[164] Orra Langhorne observed in 1901 that households in Washington, D.C., an urban area with numerous stores and generous delivery policies by those stores, kept their larders in short rations to discourage theft: "Such people usually employ negro cooks; and as it is well known that the cook will, if possible, supply her own family from her employer's stores, the custom has become general to buy food in very small quantities,—just enough to last from day to day, thus putting the only available check on the servants."[165]

With her own family in mind, a cook might run through household supplies more quickly than her employer thought she ought. During World War I, a white Dallas writer cracked, "There is no more wasteful human on earth than the average transient colored woman who poses as a cook."[166] Such accusations made Chloe, who cooked for Elizabeth Pringle in South Carolina, fear her employer's displeasure at her generous gesture of baking a surprise fruitcake for Pringle's birthday. Pringle wrote, "She seemed afraid I might accuse her of extravagance and assured me she had only used up the odds and ends of fruit which were left in the storeroom and the fresh butter and fresh eggs which I was not at home to eat."[167] In Chloe's worldview, even African Americans' kindnesses could create suspicion in the minds of their employers.

Other women justified their removal of small amounts of staple goods from their employers' larders. "Negro Nurse" observed: "I do not deny that the cooks find opportunity to hide away at times, along with the cold 'grub,' a little sugar, a little flour, a little meal, or a little piece of soap; but I indignantly deny that we are thieves. We don't steal; we just 'take' things—they are a part of the oral contract, exprest [sic] or implied. We understand it, and most of the white folks understand it."[168] And a South Carolina cook commented to a Federal Writers' Project interviewer in the 1930s, "You just have to help de chillum to take things, and while you doin' dat for them, you take things for yourself. I never call it stealin'!"[169]

Conversely, some African American mothers, aspiring to white people's standards of respectability, taught their children never to steal, lest they be branded with the racial stereotype. Educator William Henry Holtzclaw recalled his mother's careful tutelage. Once he found a nest of hen's eggs that belonged to the white people who owned the farm where the Holtzclaw family lived and worked. He took "a few" but ashamedly told his mother. He recalled, "She told me it was wrong to steal from the 'white folks,' that 'white folks' thought all negroes would steal, and that we must show them that we would not. She said she knew I did not steal them, but that it would look that way, and that I must show that I did not by taking them right back to the white lady and giving them to her." Holtzclaw "spent an hour in going a distance of 300 yards" and upon reaching the "big house" confessed to the "white lady." She responded with a lecture about stealing and gave him two of the eggs.[170] The employer took full advantage of the situation to remind the boy to whom the eggs belonged.

WORKING IN THE HOME of a white family, a domestic worker gained "a close, oftentimes unbearably intimate look" at her employer.[171] As Leonore Davidoff and her coauthors comment, it was "hard to hide the most intimate secrets from those who came into the bedroom every morning to open the curtains, bringing tea or a breakfast tray."[172] The cook knew family members' likes and their habits, and so she could see through them, in sociologist Patricia Hill Collins's words, with a "curious outsider-within stance, a peculiar marginality."[173] Such familiarity worked to the cooks' advantage, for in seeing their employers' most personal flaws, they gained firsthand evidence that white people were not in fact superior to African American people, and this knowledge helped keep their internal compasses straight amid the misinformation of Jim Crow.[174] Despite their fears of exposure, employers revealed their inner selves and their secrets.[175] Perhaps they underestimated their employees' powers of observation and discernment. Hortense Powdermaker wrote in the 1930s that the domestic worker "has ample opportunity to know intimate details concerning her mistress's life and family. Under her mild 'Yes, Ma'am,' and 'No, Ma'am,' there is often a comprehension which is unsuspected and far from mutual."[176]

In close quarters with their employers, cooks had to deal with the white women's emotional ups and downs. Cooks sometimes bore the wrath of their employers simply because they were available and vulnerable. A cook from Indianola, Mississippi, told Hortense Powdermaker that "everyone has to be cross sometimes," but that "people should 'keep to themselves' when they are like that. If a woman is 'hot' at her husband in the morning, she should just say she is in a bad mood and not come near the cook, instead of 'taking it out on her.'"[177] Willie Mae Wright remembered a couple named Bowers for whom she worked for nine years. She tried to "handle" Mrs. Bowers "like she was made of tissue paper." Wright pondered, "You never could tell about them. Most usually she was the meanest woman ever put a shoe on her foot, but still she was nice in lots of ways. . . . She'd do something nice for you, then turn right around and be hissing and spitting like a viper."[178]

Georgia author Corra Harris demonstrated a temper that made life difficult for her cook, Aunt Mary, who suffered from rheumatism so acute that at times she could barely walk. Mary's coworker, Alma Brown, wrote in her journal, "We had quite a stir this morning, breakfast was a little late and Mrs. Harris got riled up. When I went in to carry her small tray and to fix table for her she asked, 'What in the hell was the matter with the coffee.' She dashed out as mad as rip—raked Aunt Mary over good about the percolator being stopped up when it really was due to sobby [soggy] wood—no heat to make coffee boil. Mrs. Harris is so good and kind but my! She has a temper. It seems such a pity too for one so good as she to allow herself to go all to pieces in such a way."[179]

In addition to subjecting them to unmerited angry outbursts, employers sometimes expected their cooks to provide "emotional labor," to provide listening ears and sympathetic words whenever their employers were having a rough time.[180] Needy white children often found solace with African American women.[181] But adults also turned to their domestic workers as confidantes, regardless of whether the African American women wanted to hear them unburden themselves.[182] Sociologist Mary Romero observes that class differences make domestic workers safe listeners, "giving the middle-class mistress little fear of rebuttal, retaliation, or disparagement."[183] Emotional relationships developed, furthermore, because the domestic worker was a regular presence in the employer's life.[184]

Idella Parker bore much of the brunt of Marjorie Kinnan Rawlings's mood swings and alcohol abuse throughout the 1940s. Parker recalled: "Her demands on me were enormous. I'm not talking about work, now, I'm talking about emotional demands. . . . She would go through depressions and bouts of sickness, dark moods and terrible drinking sprees, and here was Idella, trying to cope with her day and night." Parker observed the toll that Rawlings's emotional outbursts took on her: "At times we would hug and cry together when there was nothing else to be done. These times when she would cling to me, sobbing out all her fears and anxieties, were the times that were hardest for me. She told me things I am sure she would never have told anyone else, and leaned on me in ways that few people ever knew." Parker tried to excuse Rawlings's behavior but found herself exhausted: "She was a good, kind woman who never meant anyone any harm. The person she hurt the most was herself.

Our relationship was a close one, but it was one that often felt burdensome to me. Still, I did my best to protect her and help her. I loved her then, and I love her still, but what could I do? A person gets weary carrying another person's misery and woe, and gradually I was beginning to feel that I could not carry Mrs. Baskin's [Rawlings's name after her marriage] much longer."[185] While the Parker-Rawlings relationship was extraordinarily convoluted, it demonstrates the extent to which an employer could impose psychologically upon an employee without reciprocation.

Domestic workers were uniquely positioned to see human nature at its worst, and they were exposed up close to their employers' unhappiness.[186] Willie Mae Wright shrewdly observed a variety of employers in Atlanta between 1920 and 1960, including their violence toward one another. She liked her employers the Thompsons until "they went to boozing and fighting." One night an argument about the husband's taste in food escalated into a two-hour episode of "pots and pans . . . zooming around the kitchen" as well as the beef and rice that Wright had cooked for their dinner. In another incident, Mrs. Thompson, who had at least two extramarital lovers simultaneously, hit Wright while attempting to beat her eight-year-old stepson, Buddy. Wright remembered: "I got beat my own self, because he'd run to me and they'd be wrassling around me, him trying to get away and her strike out. I cried harder than he did, and I'd holler: 'Wait! You hitting me!' But she didn't quit. She gave us both a bad time that day."[187] Wright eventually left that employer on the recommendation of "Old Maria," who came to do the wash and said, "Willie Mae, you're too nice and young a girl to work for people like this. The Thompsons always have plenty of something-to-eat and they pay good and they're good in lots of ways, but it ain't worth this."[188] Even more dramatically, Wright witnessed another employer, Mrs. Prewitt, murder her cheating husband with the little hatchet that they used to cut kindling. In the attack, Prewitt ruined Wright's new shepherd's plaid coat, which Prewitt had borrowed. Wright's cousin Mary, to whom Wright went every time she left a job, observed, "I hope next time you get in with some plain ordinary good folks, because you sure been having the by-Godest jobs I ever heard of."[189]

Across the South, white people who behaved badly—engaging in extramarital affairs, child abuse, and murder—also employed domestic workers. Cooks saw it all and told what they knew on the witness stands in their former employers' trials. Presumably, because the crimes were perpetrated by white people against other white people, the courts took into account the words of African American women.[190] Emma Levelle of Atlanta told of seeing "Mr. Annis in Captain Hains' home with his arms around Mrs. Hains and kissing her" in a 1909 trial in which Captain Hains was being tried for the murder of Mr. Annis.[191] Mattie Fisher, of Columbia, South Carolina, witnessed Belle Graddick giving her husband, J. W. Graddick, "medicine" from a certain bottle "hidden between the woodwork and bricks of the fireplace." The "medicine" turned out to be arsenic, and Fisher testified in Belle Graddick's trial for murder.[192] And in Birmingham, Ellen Moore told the court that Laura Howe was "very cruel" to her three-year-old stepson. According to Moore, Howe finally "beat and choked and thumped [the child] to death."[193] Although the employers ignored their domestic workers, perhaps oblivious to their presence,[194] the courts considered them as credible witnesses who had intimate knowledge of the goings-on in the household.

Just as domestic workers observed behaviors that they would prefer not to see, the cooks, particularly those who lived with their employers, were also "exposed . . . unable, at least in principle, to shield their private lives from the scrutiny of the employer" and were "constantly observable not only when they work[ed] but even when they [did] not."[195] While some employers evidenced interest in their employees' personal lives, the relationship between the two were rarely equal or reciprocal. Many mistresses responded to the workers as though they were children, giving unsolicited advice or even scolding them.[196] Home economist Ava L. Johnson observed in 1932 that employers wanted "perfection in five different lines of endeavor, and they assume the role of moral arbiter over the creature, besides."[197]

Cooks' sexuality in particular merited employers' observation and attempts at regulation. Activist Virginia Foster Durr remembered her mother's concern in Birmingham about the time of World War I:

> Mother was always worried about the cooks having men in the basement. The cook always lived in the servants' rooms in the basement of the house on Niazuma so that she could rise early to cook breakfast. The servants were paid five or six dollars a week with room and board. We had a succession of cooks, and I remember the terrific anxiety about the men in the basement. . . . If Mother or Daddy knew there was a man in the basement, there was always a big row and sometimes the cook would leave. The men would creep out early in the morning, and Mother would say, "I see a man going down the alley. I bet he spent the night here."[198]

Durr does not speculate about why her mother stayed so concerned about the men in the basement, but the older woman seems to have believed that she had a say in the sexuality of a woman living under her roof, much as a mother might try to regulate a teenage daughter. The sexual exploitation of domestic workers by employers rendered white women's concerns about the purity of their employees highly ironic. As activist Frances Ellen Watkins Harper and other African American observers pointed out, white women considered white men's sex with domestic workers—consensual or not—to be permissible within their households.[199] According to Durr's mother, that of black men was not.[200] Idella Parker simply sneaked visitors, both male and female, into Cross Creek: "They'd come in over the cattle guard and follow the road around back to the tenant house."[201] Cooks apparently wanted to treat their living quarters as "home" and asserted their right to behave in those quarters as they chose and have any visitors that they wanted. With employers' vigorous contestation of this right, ongoing conflict could be assured.

Willie Mae Wright was very fond of her employer Mrs. Duke, but the two women disagreed when Wright married Dan Workman. Duke called Wright a fool for marrying a man she deemed unsuitable. Wright observed, "I wanted to tell her and I didn't want to tell her. I didn't want to hear her fuss no more. . . . When I did tell her, she just sat there. Then she said, 'I don't know exactly what to think, but I don't appreciate this.'" Mrs. Duke then "pouted around two or three days" but finally came around. Wright knew that Duke did not want her to move out (which meant that her work hours would lessen): "She knew I wasn't going to be working any more like I had been." But Wright also gave Duke the benefit of the doubt, acknowledging that Duke truly believed that she had Wright's best interest at heart: "And then too I believe she really didn't think me and Dan matched up very well."[202] Irrespective of motives, Duke clearly felt free to pass judgment on her employee's decision to marry and her choice of spouse.

The Federal Writers' Project interviewee dubbed "The Lil' Black Girl" immigrated to Atlanta at the age of seventeen, and she was grateful for the training that her employer provided for her. But she lost patience at the white woman's overfamiliarity and left the job: "I started going with a boy and my employer didn't approve of it, for she didn't like the boy. I felt I was deeply in love with him and didn't want to stop my attentions to him. My employer insisted that I do just that, and being young, ignorant, and inexperienced, I thought she was doing me an injustice in forbidding me to see the boy." In a fit of anger, the young woman boarded a train to Birmingham and did not return for a year.[203]

White women's disapproval also extended to African American women's childbearing. "A White Woman," writing in 1902, more or less excused a cook named Mary for illicitly taking food home to her family, but she clucked her tongue over one other aspect of Mary's life: "She is also the mother of two illegitimate children, one black, the other yellow."[204] Forty years later, Idella Parker observed the judgmental attitude of Marjorie Kinnan Rawlings toward her predecessor: "Martha's daughter Adrenna had been cook before me. To hear Mrs. Rawlings tell it, Adrenna cared more about running after men than working. When Adrenna came back to Cross Creek some months after I came, with a fair-skinned baby, Mrs. Rawlings refused to take her back."[205] It is impossible to know how much of the white women's outrage was over the mixed races of the babies, how much was over their mothers' unmarried status, or how much was over the fact that the mothers would have something to think about besides their work. Whatever the source of the white women's disapproval, the young mothers certainly took the force of it.

At times, white people carried over behavior from the antebellum period and tried to become involved with African American workers' public rituals to an uncomfortable extent. Frances Butler Leigh put on extravagant weddings for the freedwomen on her Georgia plantation, perhaps wanting to thrust the values of Victorian morality upon them, or make them indebted to her for fine parties.[206] And in the twentieth century, Mississippian Mittie Price kept her employer, Ethel Mohamed, at bay with a cautionary tale about another woman whose boss assumed too much. Mohamed recalled that Price refused to move into the Mohameds' home: "She said, 'Oh, no, I bet I don't. You do me just exactly like Dr. Bell did.' That was a doctor here in town. He had a maid that he just loved, and when she died he had her funeral from his house. He was not gonna put her in a poor church. They wanted to put her away nice. So naturally the colored folks didn't come to the funeral much. She said, 'I wouldn't do that for anything in the world. You do me just like Dr. Bell did her, and I don't want any of that. I want to be buried in my church.' So she never gave up her house."[207] Price regarded Bell as a usurper, improperly engaged in the private life of his employee, and she would not tolerate such intrusion from her own employer.

AGAINST STRONG ODDS, at times deep affections arose between African American and white people. White people wanted to believe that affection existed in all relationships. The author of "The Story of Katy Brumby" for the Federal Writers' Project wrote: "Katy is loyal above all persons I know, and absolutely an individual. She is not only a friend, but a member of the family, which, despite the accusation of 'paternalism,' is the only way to describe a relationship at once so intricate and so simple."[208] To be sure, bonds of mutual affection did exist, particularly in situations where the employer and employee knew each other for many years. As sociologist Mary Romero observed, "In general, the longer the period of employment, the more informal the employer-employee relationship tends to be, as well as the more likely it is that a personal relationship will emerge."[209] W. E. B. DuBois commented that in the best scenario, "I have seen children who were spiritual sons and daughters of their masters, girls who were friends of their mistresses, and old servants honored and revered. But in every such case the Servant had transcended the Menial, the Service had been exalted above the Wage."[210]

Examples from the African American perspective are few, but some African American women did profess affection for their employers. In the 1930s and 1940s, Annie Mae Hunt was very fond of her employer, Mrs. Norrell, who took enough interest in Hunt to take her to a doctor to be fitted for a diaphragm. Although she could have viewed such an activity as negative interference, Hunt was in fact grateful for the attention and time that Norrell took to help her avoid future unwanted pregnancies. Hunt recalled, "I worked for Mrs. Norrell for years and years and years. . . . She was very good to me." They were not peers, however, and Hunt always referred to her employer by her courtesy title, Mrs., and her family name. Hunt indicated that she owed Norrell a great deal. "I couldn't have made it if it hadn't been for Mrs. Norrell," she said—but then she caught herself: "Oh, I guess I would have made it."[211]

Emma Jane Christian worked for the family of Blanche Elbert Moncure in Williamsburg, Virginia, for more than fifty years. According to the 1900 U.S. Census, that household consisted of Moncure's parents; her unmarried sister; Moncure, who was already a widow; her three small children; and Christian, who had never married and could not read or write. In the 1930 U.S. Census, the same household was composed of Moncure, her daughter who worked as a stenographer, two teachers as boarders, and Christian. With the flow of the generations, as family members aged and died or grew up and moved out, Moncure and Christian, two unmarried women, remained constants in each others' lives. If her employer's rendition of Christian's comments is reliable, Christian herself was proud of her long tenure with the Moncure family. "Of cose, I been cookin' fur a purty long time when you come to think of it," Christian reportedly said. "When a pusson has cooked fur de same fambly fur over fifty years, dey has done a purty good job I thinks—an' dat is what I has done, as you knows. Over fifty years, mont' in, mont' out."[212] Tellingly, Christian does not use the word "love." Rather, she stresses the repetitive cycle of the months and the years.

The U.S. Census traces Emma Jane Christian's career with the Moncure family. In 1880, she was seventeen and living with her parents and older brother in Black Creek, New Kent County, Virginia.[213] This African American neighborhood was home to dozens of Christians, probably aunts, uncles, and cousins, possibly providing a warm community for young Emma Jane to grow up in. By 1900, Christian, now an unmarried woman in her middle thirties, had moved the twenty-five miles to Williamsburg and had begun her long association with the Trevillian family, which included a daughter, Blanche Moncure, a young widow with three children.[214] Ten years later, the household remained the same, with the senior Trevillians now in their seventies.[215] By 1920, the senior Trevillians were absent—presumably deceased—and Blanche Moncure was listed as head of household; Emma Jane Christian remained as a servant in the house on Richmond Avenue. Two of Moncure's children had moved out, and they now had one boarder, a forty-year-old white male college professor.[216]

When Moncure published *Emma Jane's Souvenir Cookbook* in 1937, Christian was in her early seventies. She and Blanche Moncure were only about six years apart in age, and both were single—Christian evidently never married and Moncure remained a widow.[217] Sharing the same household for forty years, the two women must have known each other well and perhaps shared affection.

Even as individual cooks served single families for multiple generations, generations of the same families served in the same households. White cookbook writer Marion Brown described the workers at Glenwood Plantation House in Napoleonville, Louisiana, as "servants whose ancestors served for generations."[218] At Maymont, in Richmond, Frances Twiggs Walker served as cook for the Dooley family between 1919 and 1925. During the 1920s, six of her grown children also joined the Maymont staff.[219] Recommending one's employer to one's children may have meant that the parent found the situation acceptable for the child.

For an employer, having a cook who stayed for years or decades was almost always positive. The employer avoided the hassles of hiring and training, and the cook learned the family's preferences and tastes.[220] White women prided themselves on their abilities to keep cooks. One Athens housewife observed that she had "a 'black mammy' servant for 23 years and have the same servant now that I had after the death of an old servant." Another remarked that she had "had no occasion to discharge a servant for twenty years," perhaps indicating her superiority as an employer.[221]

The adjective that many white employers used to describe such servants was "faithful." Morning in and morning out, they could depend on "Aunt Sophie" or "Beppie" to be there with biscuits or egg pie on the table.[222] "Aunt Mollie" or "Nursie" would have fried chicken and hominy ready for the midday meal known as dinner.[223] "Nursie" was Hattie Crumwell of Macon, who did in fact work for the John J. McKay family for more than fifty years. "Beppie" cooked for the family of Mrs. Walter Monroe Brown of Burlington, North Carolina, for three generations. But we learn nothing else of the women with the diminutive names in quotation marks, nor do we know anything further about Aunt Mollie or Aunt Sophie. Because they lived apart from the families for which they cooked, the census gives us few hints as to their identity. And their employers, the Davis and Whitaker families of Mississippi, give no clue about their personae outside of their employment. Their names are not Davis or Whitaker. They have lives of their own. But in the records written by their white employers, those lives remain hidden from view.

To Carter G. Woodson, the longevity of African Americans' tenure as domestic workers pointed to a lack of economic mobility for African Americans. In *The Mis-Education of the Negro*, he blasted the establishment that kept African Americans in the same position for decade after decade: "Tradition fixes his status . . . and both races feel satisfied. . . . Thoughtless Negro editors, instead of expressing their regret that such a life of usefulness was not rewarded by promotion, take up the refrain as some great honor bestowed upon the race."[224]

Contrary to appearances, long years of service may have blunted but did not eliminate friction. Ruth Margon of New Orleans wrote to a government worker in 1942 that older people were asking her about wage and pension laws. Margon observed, "They all tell me it is hard to get along with employee after they stay so long with them. It seems to me that it art [*sic*] to be easy to work for a family for so many years." But clearly it was not.[225] Although Nellie Willoughby worked for the same Washington, D.C., family for fifty years, she called her employers "them people I hate." When pressed, she told of the father who likely abused his daughters, of the mother who depended on Willoughby for emotional support, and of the grown children who despised their parents. Willoughby told her interviewer that "her hatred for her employers helped her keep her life in perspective."[226]

Rather than genuine affection toward their employers as people, African Americans sometimes expressed their gratitude toward them in terms of what the white people were able to do for them in return for their services. Anna Mae Dickson observed, "Conditions changed from family to family. I've worked for people I would go back and work for anytime because they treated me as a member of the family. They didn't treat me like a servant. You'd try to find the people who seemed like they'd help you get ahead."[227]

For African American women, domestic work was, first and foremost, a job—a job that, in most cases, took them away from their own homes for long hours to earn low pay. Relationships, they knew, were generally temporary, and their employers most likely would not care for them in sickness or old age. Family members of the employees at Maymont, a large household in Richmond, were forthright about the transactional nature of the relationships. Doris Woodson, descendent of two generations of Maymont employees, observed, "They came there to work to make some money to take home to their *own* families. . . . They weren't caring so much about whether Mrs. Dooley, for instance—or whomever—loved them."[228] W. E. B. DuBois summed up the situation: "[White employers] exact, not a natural, but a purchased deference."[229]

Esther Jones worked for a family with eight children in the 1940s. She recalled, "I liked the job because the kids were very, very nice. I didn't feel like I was working. I felt like I was in the family then," using the phrase commonly uttered by sentimental white people. She was satisfied with her wages of four dollars a week, which were "enough money to live off at that time. And you know, that was what they were paying." She viewed positively the in-kind gifts that supplemented her salary: "And they gave you so much more! I mean, they gave you food. I don't mean just scraps, but good food. And you could get what you wanted. They didn't mind if you took it home, so mostly I didn't have any food to buy. At holidays, they would give me money. And they would give me used clothes because they was *good*. And, at that time, I was happy to get them; they seemed new to me! [laughter] Yes, they really treated me well." Jones felt that she "was in the family then," but she then ticked off the benefits that she received: salary, food, good used clothing. She does not say that she liked or loved the family members, but she "liked the job."[230]

Women's tributes to their employers, on examination, sometimes contained veiled criticism and often damned their employers with faint praise. Annie Squire of South Carolina remarked to the Federal Writers' Project interviewer, "I'm cookin' for a fine family of folks now. I been workin' for Mrs. Sallie Jenkins for three years, Mis' Sallie sho' good to me. She give me clothes and food and lets me off ever other Sunday."[231] Given the minimal perquisites that Squire recited, one wonders if she were not being sarcastic. Every other Sunday off was not generous, and food and clothing often came with one's pay. Winnie Hefley, a single mother, received welcome assistance from her white employer in Mobile. "I worked for Miz Watts from 1942 to 1972," she said. "I liked it there. I was the head cook. Salaries, at that time, were pretty low unless you were working on defense jobs or something like pertaining to the war. But Miz Watts was just such a sweet, good lady until I didn't even want to try to work for nobody else." Watts scored points with Hefley by thinking about Hefley's daughter: "And by me not having a husband, she helped with my child, helped me to raise her up. She would give me things for her, and she would make her clothes and send them and give me something extra when I go home to take to my parents and all. And I got a vacation with pay. Everybody wouldn't give you a vacation with pay."[232] Hefley's employers paid less than defense jobs, and their kindness did not extend to letting her keep her child with her. The girl remained with Hefley's parents.

WHITE WRITERS OFTEN PROCLAIMED the cook's power in the household. The stereotype of the African American woman as a powerful authority figure in the white household arose alongside the sweet accommodation of Aunt Jemima. Yet, as critic Doris Witt has commented, there is a "disjunction between the minimal power that African American women have wielded in the United States and the often exaggerated perceptions of their power."[233] The figure of the cantankerous, bossy cook served to enhance the contrast between the physically unattractive, masculinized African American woman and her coy, delicate employer.[234] Poorly paid, subject to being fired on a moment's notice, with brutally long working hours, few cooks were in a position to exert their wills in a white home.

Critic bell hooks deconstructs the childhood recollections by white women regarding powerful African American women, confronting author Lillian Hellman's offhanded assertion that "All my life, beginning at birth, I have taken orders from black women."[235] hooks finds such a statement to be highly disingenuous and manipulative: "Hellman places power in the hands of these black women rather than acknowledge her own power of them; hence she mystifies the true nature of their relationship. By projecting onto black women a mythical power and strength, white women both promote a false image of themselves as powerless, passive victims and deflect attention away from their aggressiveness, their power (however limited in a white supremacist, male-dominated state), their willingness to dominate and control others."[236]

Employers sometimes liked to talk about the power that cooks had in their households. White people's perceptions of the authoritarian African American cook arise from at least two sources. First, cooks do seem to have had permission to discipline children and at least keep their feet clear of small distractions. Young children who were sent marching from the kitchen later wrote of the imposing African American women who chastised them. Mrs. John W. Brookfield, from Woodbridge, Virginia, remembered being "chased

An unidentified cook with her employer's daughter, San Augustine, Texas, 1943.
Photo by John Vachon, Farm Security Administration/Office of War Information,
Library of Congress LC-USW3-025195-D.

out of the basement kitchen by Aunt Mahala, with a switch, for swiping"
ginger cookies made from her grandmother's recipe.[237] Kate Page, also from
Woodbridge, remembered "Aunt Esther Mason" at Greenwood plantation,
Charlotte County, who would say (according to Page), "Ef yo don't go out of
dis kitchen, I'se gwine pin disyear dishrag on yo'."[238] Jennie Benedict, later a
revered caterer in Louisville, "as a very small girl" got underfoot of her "dear
old black Mammy," who would say (in the recollections of Benedict), "Lor'
bless my soul, chile, why don' you git outen dis kitchen, an' stop pesterin'
me 'bout dat cake? You knows I ain't got no time ter fool wif you!"[239] These
writers carried impressions of powerful African American cooks with them
into adulthood.

Second, African American cooks possessed skills that white women often
had not troubled themselves to learn. An undetermined number of white
women in the South simply did not know how to cook and were thus in-
capable of putting an edible hot meal on the table for their families. Mary
Hunt Affleck, from near Brenham, Texas, had constant turnover in cooks

because of a rumored ghost in her house. Affleck characterized herself as "handicapped by inexperience of domestic economy" and recalled her family, in the absence of a trained cook, "far[ing] sumptuously, on tinned things."[240] Into the twentieth century, some white women still did not learn to cook. When Alice Adams was negotiating for days off in the 1940s, her longtime employer at first refused to give her the Thursdays and Sundays off that she was requesting. Adams recalled, "I said, 'Well, I'm telling you now. I'm not going to work anymore on Sunday, not anymore on Thursday. I want every Sunday off and every Thursday off.' She said, 'No, I can't do it because I never had to cook, I've never had to wash dishes, and I'm not going to do it. Now, if you want to be off every Sunday and Thursday you get somebody to work in your place.' I sat down. I said, 'Now, listen. That is your job. You get them.'"[241] Because she had knowledge that her employer did not, Adams negotiated from a position of strength and her argument carried the day. Some white families had substitute cooks so that when the regular employee was gone, the family would not have to fend for itself.[242]

Some women did gain the trust of their employers enough to achieve autonomy within the sphere of cookery. Many factors, particularly skill and longevity, affected a cook's independence. The better cook a woman was, the more likely the white family was to let her have her way about things. The Whitney family tolerated, at least for a while, what they considered meanness on the part of Mildred because of the quality of her flowered mints and cheese straws.[243] In Belzoni, Mississippi, Ethel Wright Mohamed reprimanded her new employee Mittie Price for cutting the green part off a bunch of scallions. Price, resenting Mohamed's interference, threw the scallions at her boss. Mohamed quickly fired her, even though her first week of work had been exemplary until she pitched the onions. Price was talented enough, however, that Mohamed quickly wanted her back and rehired her, observing, "Honey, I never said another word to her. . . . Nobody went in that kitchen back there but her."[244]

At times, African American cooks taught younger white women to cook. Revered Louisville caterer Jennie Benedict, for example, gained much from the tutelage of her "old black Mammy."[245] *Emma Jane's Souvenir Cookbook*, featuring the recipes of Emma Jane Christian, was framed as a cooking lesson for a bride-to-be. In the cookbook, Christian, speaking through her employer Blanche Moncure, demurs about her own ability, observing, "I aint no cookin' teacher! I is jes a plain undedicated cook-o'man, what can't even read her own name, much less a 'ceat book!" Nonetheless, Christian admits fifty years' experience and counsels cooking with boldness.[246]

Absent genuine affection, some employers truly liked the food that their employees prepared. Although cooking is more "frequently criticized in its shortcomings than praised in its successes—based upon the unforgiving premise that one who cooks is consistently and quietly good at it,"[247] some employers commended their cooks directly, and some cooks won acclaim for their cooking. Sudie Holton's employer said, "We were soon to learn that Sudie could swing a wicked skillet. Her biscuits were delectable morsels of feather-lightness and her fricasseed chicken and gravy beggared description."[248] Cookbook author Natalie Scott in the 1920s wrote that an excellent dish could win acclaim for an African American, even "fame," as she observed, "Aunt Melissa is famous for her cabbage."[249] Frances Twiggs Walker cooked at Maymont in the 1920s; according to Maymont historian Elizabeth O'Leary, Walker's reputation was "made on the elaborate French dishes that her ladies required for luncheons and dinner parties."[250] In a moment of candor, white Richmond resident Maria Hoar admitted that domestic employees "had much more talent, much more ability than most of us."[251] Cooking was an arena in which African American women were allowed to succeed.

As an increasing number of white women learned to cook and commercially processed foods became more readily available, the importance of having an African American cook diminished across the South. Elements of competition arose between two women in the same household, sometimes manifested in the struggle over the preparation or sharing of a recipe.[252] When Mary Hunt Affleck's cook refused to try the recipe for a new cake, Affleck made the white loaf cake herself and observed that it turned out beautifully. She could do just as well as her cook could, Affleck believed.[253] In the 1930s, advertisers used the scenario of conflict between employee and employer to sell cookware. An ad for a Pyrex dish in a 1939 *Ladies' Home Journal* depicted an African American woman in a maid's cap looking at a pie being held by a fashionably dressed white woman. The African American woman exclaims, "Lawsy[,] how you make such chicken pie?" The white woman replies, "It's your recipe[,] Bessie . . . and my Pyrex dish!" This exchange underscores the white woman's ownership of the home's cookware and of the home itself. The white homemaker can also make a chicken pie, one good enough to arouse envy in her cook.[254] By using the African American woman's recipe and technology unavailable to the cook, the housewife beats the cook at her own game.

ACROSS THE DECADES, cooks managed their relationships with their employers as best they could. They controlled their physical environments by living away from their employers' homes, and they used their power to quit as leverage. Within the employers' homes, however, cooks often remained segregated, experiencing Jim Crow inside the workplace as well as on the outside. Tensions frequently remained high, often undiminished by the passage of time. As technology made cooking simpler, employers tended to replace cooking with other, more arduous tasks for their employees. Employees, seeing opportunities outside white people's homes, departed for better conditions.

If I Ever Catch You in a White Woman's Kitchen,
I'll Kill You

EXPANDING OPPORTUNITIES AND THE DECLINE
OF DOMESTIC WORK

In Langston Hughes's 1949 poem "Graduation," his prediction for postwar America, he contrasts the old and new types of employment for African American women. Mrs. Jackson—"Mama"—has toted home chicken and has put her daughter Mary Lulu through secretarial school with her wages as a cook. Being a typist may not be the best job in the world, but for the Jackson family, it is a big step out of the kitchen, and that hope is enough to spread stardust over the two women. Mama looks forward to the day when "the colored race shall rise," but, tired from cooking in the white woman's kitchen, she sighs with weariness.[1]

Like Mrs. Jackson, from the early part of the twentieth century, real-life cooks envisioned brighter futures for their young female relatives.[2] Frances Twiggs Walker was a skilled cook who prepared elaborate French cuisine for her Richmond employer, Sallie Dooley. Walker's niece, Virgie Payne, visited her aunt at Maymont, the Dooleys' estate, in 1923. Dooley addressed the little girl: "I hope, young lady, that when you grow up, you'll be a fine cook like your aunt." Walker, by then a seasoned servant at age sixty, placed her hands on Payne's shoulder, looked her employer of four years in the eye, and said, "Thank you, ma'am, but I don't want her to be a cook." Later, she told her niece, "You learn something besides cooking, because they'll cook you to death." Walker anticipated days of opportunity and potential for her young relatives, times to come with education, suffrage, and employment that did not involve working in someone else's home.[3]

Like Walker, other African American cooks were not afraid to tell employers that they had better things in mind for the young women in their lives. Zelda Green, born in 1915 and herself the daughter of a domestic worker, remembered white people's assumptions and her own determination to change the future: "A lot of people told me they were scared to let the white people know they were sending their children to college. . . . I'll tell you the way white people used to be long time ago. They would say, 'Well, if your mother used to work for me, you grow up, and then after she got too old, the children will work for me.' They would just keep it coming on down from generation to generation. I say, it's going to stop right there! My daughter she won't need to think she need to do that days work for a living."[4] Green would have none of the employers' low aspirations for her child.

Young women also received the message that they needed to take advantage of the opportunities that were slowly beginning to come their way. North Carolinian Georgia Sutton, who grew up in the 1940s, remembered her mother's words: "She was telling me, 'You need to work. You've got to have the money to go to school. You do what you have to do [to] earn the money.' She said, 'Then when you earn your money, go where you have to go, do what you have to do. You don't have to tell anybody, 'I'm going to scrub your floors.'"[5] Carole Brown's grandmother minced no words in telling her granddaughter what she expected: "If I ever catch you in a white woman's kitchen, I'll kill you."[6]

BY THE EARLY TWENTIETH CENTURY, doing domestic work for white people had become the least desired employment for urban African American women. Sociologist T. J. Woofter observed in 1913 that African Americans held domestic service jobs, which they had found more desirable than field work immediately after emancipation, in the lowest regard.[7] In the twentieth century, African American women abandoned domestic work just as quickly as they could. Between 1880 and 1930, the percentage of African American women wage earners performing household labor dropped dramatically: by more than half in Atlanta, Baltimore, and Richmond, and by more than two-thirds in Washington, D.C.[8]

In the South as a whole, changes in African American women's jobs outside of domestic work developed slowly. Entrepreneurship provided many women with avenues out of white people's kitchens. Between 1900 and 1910, the proportion of domestic workers declined slightly while the numbers of African American seamstresses, dressmakers, tailoresses, and milliners increased. Some former domestic workers ran businesses: boardinghouses, lunchrooms, restaurants, groceries, secondhand clothing stores, hairdressing shops, dry goods stores, and ice cream and cold drink parlors. Some peddled on the streets. The underground economy created jobs for women as gamblers, bootleggers, and prostitutes. African American women also made gains in clerical posts and sales jobs in African American–owned insurance companies and retail shops.[9]

Gradually, African American women found limited employment in manufacturing, usually in the lowest-status, lowest-paid jobs.[10] A plug tobacco factory in Iredell County, North Carolina, employed a hundred African American women in skilled and unskilled positions as early as 1894.[11] In Atlanta, the number of African American women in the textile industry grew steadily until World War I, with the Fulton Bag and Cotton Mill employing 121 African American women by 1914.[12] About 11 percent of the African American women in Norfolk worked in manufacturing as early as 1910, although these jobs were mostly low wage and piecework. Most were tobacco stemmers at the American Cigar Company; others worked for small clothing manufacturers.[13] Around Durham, North Carolina, African American women worked in tobacco factories and occasionally in textile mills.[14]

World War I presented the "first substantial competition" from industries seeking to hire African American women, as white women took jobs previously occupied by men.[15] During World War I in Atlanta, African American women found employment, heretofore unavailable to them, in a variety of businesses, including producers of cotton seed oil and chemicals, furniture, lumber, excelsior (wood shavings used as packing materials), wooden boxes, other wood products, metals, pencils, and caskets, and the Atlanta Gas Light Company.[16] World War I, of course, also presented a way out of the South, as labor shortages opened opportunities in the cities of the urban North. Dozens of letters to the *Chicago Defender* declared women's willingness to cook—but not in the South. Their culinary skills would find them jobs away, in the words of a cook from Biloxi, Mississippi, from "a land of starvaten. . . . this land of sufring."[17] More than half a million African Americans found their way to the urban North between 1916 and 1921.

After World War I, the trend away from domestic work continued in many areas of the South. By 1920, 26.3 percent of African American female workers in Louisville worked in factories, and they comprised more than a third of the women working in the tobacco products industry there.[18] In Norfolk in 1920, 18 percent of African American women had employment other than domestic work, holding virtually all of the women's positions in the tobacco jobs. Other women in the area left domestic work for positions as dressmakers in non-factory situations and, eventually, for work in textile and garment factories.[19] Unlike their white counterparts, African American women did not depart the labor force after the wartime economy ended; rather, they shifted to other areas of the economy.

As the African American middle class grew during the 1920s and 1930s, racial segregation created opportunities for African American women in a range of "urban occupational entrepreneurial options that required little capital and minimal special training." These options included keeping boardinghouses, running cafés, and becoming beauticians.[20] In Dallas and elsewhere, African American women departed cooking jobs to run lodging houses, boardinghouses, small neighborhood grocery stores, and beauty parlors. They branched out into hotels and restaurants, applying their domestic skills on a larger scale.[21] By the late 1930s, almost sixteen thousand African American women in the United States were making their living as hairdressers.[22]

When educational opportunities for young African American women increased, the daughters of domestic workers found other types of employment. Teaching was one avenue for improvement. Florence Virginia Wood Willis cooked for the Catholic priests in New Bern, North Carolina, and with her earnings she bought a piano as well as piano and organ lessons for her daughter, who subsequently attended Winston-Salem Teachers College.[23] In the early twentieth century, Sudie Holton made her own way up from the kitchens where her mother worked: "I wanted something better for myself than my poor mother had. She was just somebody's Negro cook and I lived in a shanty 'on the lot' with her. She was contented enough with her fate but my father had been white and I was always restless and dissatisfied. Mammy sent me to school whenever it was possible and I saved every penny I could and worked my way through college, cooking, dishwashing, sweeping, hairdressing, mending, anything I could get to do. I loved to study and lessons were easy." Holton majored in Spanish at Bennett College and took a year of French and music at Columbia University, becoming a language teacher at the high school and college levels. After her husband became disabled during World War I, Holton found that she could make more money as a caterer, and she left teaching. Her daughters, however, were following in her footsteps through college and into teaching.[24] With rising teachers' salaries, they would not be domestic workers.

The Great Depression hit domestic workers hard, as employers either cut their wages or dispensed with household help altogether.[25] In Atlanta between 1930 and 1940, as domestic jobs declined, African American women's employment in manufacturing doubled and in the professions rose slightly.

In New Orleans and San Antonio, however, domestic jobs declined without a corresponding rise in manufacturing or the professions.[26] African American women in those two cities found difficulty in holding jobs of any kind.

WORLD WAR II CONTINUED the trend out of the kitchen, as federal law for the first time forbade racial discrimination in defense industries and opened employment never before available to African Americans.[27] In Memphis, African American domestic workers protested vociferously employers' non-compliance with regulations established by the new President's Committee on Fair Employment Practice. In Kannapolis, North Carolina, the "Club of the Colored Maids" contacted President Roosevelt to report that their employment opportunities were limited because of their race: "We can't get a job in the factory where we could make something because we are colored."[28] Altha Sims wrote to both President Roosevelt and the mayor of Memphis in 1942, complaining, "I want a Job but I don't [want] no cook Job." Women such as Sims longed to be out of domestic work. They were willing to voice their discontent, and they fostered a "palpable climate of dissent" in Memphis.[29] The defense industry jobs that opened for African American women tended to be few in number, low paying, and unpleasant, but they were not domestic work.[30] More African American women than African American men were hired at Bell Aircraft in Atlanta during World War II, however, to work as assemblers, riveters, and drill press operators.[31]

African American women, perceiving a sea change, seized their new opportunities. In Richmond, women preferred to go unemployed rather than take domestic jobs. Their new avenues of employment included war work, working at bottling companies, needlework, operating elevators, sewing bags, working at the railway, and waiting counters and tables at soda fountains and restaurants. According to historian Megan Taylor Shockley, "Grant's Drug Store hired African American women as night clerks and cashiers, and major department stores hired them as billing clerks and customer service clerks for $15 to $25 per week." Thalhimer's, the largest department store in Richmond, "had to promote African American women to better jobs when white women left to enter defense industries." New jobs had shorter hours and increased freedom, and domestic positions went unfilled. Those women who did accept domestic jobs tried hard to limit their hours and, according to the Richmond Urban League, "practically refuse[d] any work that called for time on Sunday." The average education of domestic workers dropped from 9.5 to 7.2 years of schooling, while the average age of domestic workers dropped to twenty-four years. Older, better-educated workers found employment that they preferred over cooking and cleaning. Of those who settled for domestic work, 75 to 80 percent insisted on eight-hour workdays and at least 1.5 days off per week.[32]

While downplaying the impact of World War II on the domestic workforce in New Orleans, contemporary researchers found that "the better types of servants were going into war industry, and . . . many of those who remained were becoming 'independent,' 'impudent and impertinent,' 'rude and undependable,' 'sassy,' and 'unappreciative.'" Housewives complained that "defense jobs" were creating rising wages and a shortage of "really competent Negro women."[33] Wartime opportunities actually did provide more pay for some cooks. Anna Mae Dickson moved from the tiny town of Navasota, Texas, to the booming city of Houston and quadrupled her wages, to thirteen dollars a week, working at a boardinghouse.[34] After the war, however, Dickson returned to Navasota, and her wages fell to the point that by the end of the 1950s she was making only ten to twelve dollars per week.[35]

Dorothy Bolden remembered her own exit from domestic work as other jobs became available in the 1940s: "I worked all over the city of Atlanta. About that time you were always looking for a little more money, so if you heard of a job making more, you'd quit and go get another one. So I worked domestic a lot, but I worked public jobs some too. I've been an elevator operator, I've been a waitress, a trucker. At Sears Roebuck I was the first chute girl they hired, to keep other girls supplied with work."[36] Annie Benning, who lived in Alabama, left cooking for a job at Belkes' Cotton Mill around the beginning of World War II. When asked whether she preferred mill work to cooking, Benning responded, "Oh yeah, Lord, yeah, Lord, because I had them eight hours—I made them and went on home and took care of my house." The set hours of factory work enabled Benning to care for her aging mother and her half-siblings.[37]

Desegregation of the federal civil service led to further employment opportunities. Anna Graves took typing in high school even though she knew she would find work only as a cook or a maid. After World War II, her training qualified her to become the first African American clerical worker at Kelly Field in San Antonio, Texas.[38] As historian Laurie B. Green has observed, African American woman "protested their designation as natural, permanent servants," realizing that they should not be restricted to service and agricultural employment only.[39] Even though southern racial mores limited African American women's access to the opportunities brought about by the war, wartime conditions did provide a crack in Jim Crow, and African American women eagerly stepped through.[40]

Economists worried that the gains of World War II would be eradicated in the transition to a peacetime economy but soon concluded that their fears were unfounded.[41] In the 1940s, average real weekly wages of African American women nearly doubled. The proportion of employed African American women holding "formal sector" jobs—that is to day, jobs outside of agriculture and domestic service—increased from 27 to 50 percent.[42] According to economists Martha J. Bailey and William J. Collins, the 1940s proved to be "a watershed decade for African-American women's integration into formal sector employment and marked a turning point in the growth path of their wages relative to those of white women." The market gains "were not a continuation of pre-existing trends," and they were "sustained," as wages did not revert back to their pre–World War II levels. African American women increasingly worked in positions covered by "formal contracts and benefits, minimum wage legislation, and collective bargaining."[43] Women would take the opportunities afforded them.

THE NUMBER OF AFRICAN AMERICAN domestic workers continued to decline dramatically in the second half of the twentieth century. In 1940, 59.5 percent of employed African American women were in domestic service; by 1960, that number had dropped to 36.2 percent, and by 1980, 7.4 percent. After 1950, African American women's employment in professional-technical, clerical, and sales employment rose significantly.[44]

In the late 1940s and early 1950s, sociologists C. Arnold Anderson and Mary Jean Bowman found that the availability of other employment changed the nature of domestic work for those women who remained: "Where other opportunities multiply, the subservience of maid to mistress is undermined."[45] As the number of African American women in domestic service dropped, furthermore, the nature of the employers changed, and wealthier families were much more likely to retain household help than were their less-affluent counterparts.[46] Increasingly, African American women also did "day work," where they worked for a variety of families for only one or two days per week. While day work required piecing together an income, it also allowed women more flexibility and gave them more independence, with their livelihood coming from more than one source.[47]

As women increasingly shifted to day work, their tasks also changed. The more employers a woman had, the less likely her employers were to ask that she cook as part of her duties. Rather, employers preferred that she handle the cleaning and laundry.[48] Over the course of the twentieth century, food preparation had shifted from among the most labor-intensive, unpleasant household jobs to one of the easier jobs. With food processing becoming increasingly widespread, no woman needed to cut up a raw chicken or wash clumps of mud from a bunch of radishes. Significant increases in the presence of so-called convenience foods meant that factory workers, not domestic workers or housewives, did much of the prep work in putting meals together.[49] More and more, housewives preferred to prepare their families' dinners themselves and to hire someone else to scrub their toilets. While cooking became less labor-intensive, cleaning remained as time-consuming and distasteful as ever.

The civil rights movement of the 1950s and 1960s spurred further changes in the lives of African American domestic workers. In Montgomery, Alabama, domestic workers supported the bus boycott for a long twelve months, choosing to walk to work rather than tolerate segregated buses any longer. According to civil rights activist Jo Ann Robinson, the women gained more than seats on the buses; they acquired dignity and confidence along with their hard-won rights.[50]

Title VII of the Civil Rights Act of 1964 outlawed discrimination in hiring on the basis of race, color, religion, sex, or national origin, and it established the Equal Employment Opportunity Commission to oversee the new provisions.[51] For all intents and purposes, the age of African American domestic work was dying by 1960 and dead by 1970. The proportion of African American white-collar workers rose from 6 percent in 1940 to 17 percent in 1960 and to 32 percent in 1970, and the number of blue-collar workers rose from 7 percent to 14 percent to 17 percent by 1970.[52]

AS THE INSTITUTION OF domestic work by African American women expired, African American artists quickly seized the visual representation of Aunt Jemima, seeking to reconstrue those onerous images into more satisfying depictions. During the 1960s and 1970s, African American artists such as Jeff Donaldson, Joe Overstreet, and Faith Ringgold turned the supposedly nurturing Aunt Jemima stereotype on its head, showing the image in angry and aggressive postures.[53] Perhaps the most trenchant of the representations was Betye Saar's mixed-media work, *The Liberation of Aunt Jemima* (1972). Saar's shadow box uses as a background the silk-screened face of Aunt Jemima, taken directly from the pancake mix box and repeated in a pattern. The figure of Aunt Jemima in Saar's shadow box once served as a base for a kitchen notepad and features every type of negative stereotype: "bulging eyes; thick, intensely red lips; and a smile that is more grimace than grin. . . . Embedded in the place of the notepad on the front of her skirt is another variation on the theme—a third 'Mammy,' who also smiles as she holds a white

Betye Saar's The Liberation of Aunt Jemima, *1972, mixed media. University of California, Berkeley Art Museum and Pacific Film Archive. Purchased with the aid of funds from the National Endowment for the Arts (selected by The Committee for the Acquisition of Afro-American Art). Photograph by Benjamin Blackwell. Used by permission.*

infant in her left arm." The dress on the third figure "is in actuality a magnified black fist. . . . The infant she holds is resting on the apex of that fist. The baby cries, its face is smudged with dirt, and its brows are deeply furrowed with anxiety."[54] According to Saar, the baby is a mulatto and represents how African American women were "sexually abused or misused" in white households. Aunt Jemima's right hand holds a broom and a pistol, and the left hand holds a military carbine.[55] Saar took an Aunt Jemima image and recontextualized it, suggesting that harmless objects "were in fact very dangerous."[56] Most African American women, of course, did not commit violence on their white employers. They simply left. But Saar's powerful iconography may in fact portray emotions that many departing cooks shared.

WHEN AFRICAN AMERICAN WOMEN left the kitchens of their employers, they usually took employment in the public sector. No longer did they disappear into other people's homes to do their work. New employers often had more regular hours and wages. Their families could expect them home at set hours. Their employers took on the work of cooking for their own families and, like many Americans, relied increasingly on packaged, convenient foods. The labor-intensive meals of the past became occasional or celebratory.

Idella Parker gets the last word. After Parker left the employ of Marjorie Kinnan Rawlings, she remarried and became a hairdresser and then a teacher of vocational homemaking. She did not return to domestic work. In her memoir published in 1992, she wrote, "Cross Creek does not fill me with longing for the 'good old days.' It stands as a reminder to me of how far we have come from those days of hard work and segregation."[57] Parker speaks for millions of women who cooked for their livings. They worked hard, they carved out space for themselves in every way possible, and they often gave their best to their families. Given a choice to leave other women's kitchens, they did not go back.

Acknowledgments

I have been looking forward to acknowledging the help of the many people who have shared this path with me.

Librarians and archivists make almost all historical research possible. I am indebted to the amazing people in the Rare Books and Special Collections Division, Library of Congress; the New York Public Library; the Schomburg Center for Research in Black Culture; the Arthur and Elizabeth Schlesinger Library on the History of Women in America, Harvard University; the Hargrett Rare Book and Manuscript Library, University of Georgia; the Southern Historical Collection, University of North Carolina at Chapel Hill; the Robert W. Woodruff Library, Emory University, particularly the Manuscript, Archives, and Rare Book Library; the Center for American History, University of Texas at Austin; and the Mary Couts Burnett Library, Texas Christian University. I owe individual thanks to Tab Lewis at the National Archives; Dawn Letson at the Woman's Collection, Blagg-Huey Library, Texas Woman's University; Muriel Jackson and Christopher Stokes at the Middle Georgia Archives, Macon-Bibb County Public Libraries; and especially Steven Fisher, at the University of Denver Penrose Library Special Collections, who has been particularly generous with his time and resources in their fabulous culinary collection.

The Baylor University libraries have provided invaluable materials and comfortable work space, year in and year out. Interlibrary Services has been incredibly helpful, fast, and important. Billie Peterson-Lugo obtained the *Atlanta Constitution* online for me, while Sinai Wood helped track down census data. In the Texas Collection, Aimee Oliver, Tiffany Sowell, and Michael Toon found rare and uncataloged sources. For these and hundreds of other services and kindnesses I am profoundly grateful.

Other individuals have generously shared their research and sources with me, as well as their friendship, enthusiasm, and support for this project. I thank Stephanie Cole for her vast knowledge of slaves as domestic workers and their context; Karen Cox for her work on Aunt Jemima; Shennette Garrett for sources on African American women and work; Daphne Carr Henderson for East Texas family stories; Lu Ann Jones for the oral history of Ethel Mohamed; Jamie Murray of the Brazoria County [Texas] Historical Museum for oral history interviews; Terri Jo Ryan for photos; Antoinette van Zelm for her research on black and white women at the time of emancipation; and Erik McDuffie for his studies of women and organized labor. Nancy Grayson and others at the University of Georgia Press searched their records for information on Willie Mae Wright.

I've received constructive feedback from a number of quarters. The Dallas Area Social Historians group and the TCU Department of History research seminar gave lively critiques. Tera Hunter and Kimberly Wallace-Sanders responded thoughtfully to my queries. Gaines Foster and Ted Ownby commented on parts of the study as conference papers, while Linda Shopes and Melissa Walker read the entire manuscript. I am grateful to Lu Ann Jones and Julia Kirk Blackwelder for their thoughtful, perceptive readings on behalf of the press.

At the University of North Carolina Press, I am grateful to editor-in-chief David Perry for his years of patience and his thoughtful assistance in shaping the project, to director Kate Douglas Torrey for her steadfast support and enthusiasm, to assistant editor Zachary Read for his competence and reassurance, and to Mary Caviness for her careful copyediting and overall kindness.

The Baylor University Institute for Oral History provided a warm professional nest for thirteen years. BUIOH student worker Michael Barrera and graduate assistants Nalani Hilderman and Taryn Whittington spent many hours compiling census data. I am unspeakably thankful for the enduring love and sustenance from my BUIOH colleagues Elinor Mazé, Lois Myers, and Becky Shulda. The Baylor University Research Committee funded the research on cookbooks and Macon, and Vice Provost Dianna Vitanza arranged for a summer sabbatical.

In the Department of History at Texas Christian University, my academic home since 2006, I thank all of my outstanding colleagues, in particular former chair Ken Stevens and current chair Peter Worthing for their unstinting affirmation; Jodi Campbell for her ready ears, brain, and feet; and Kathy McDorman for her encouragement. Dana Summers and Stacey Theisen have been logistical goddesses.

Some friends share their affection and support across the miles. They've been part of my life for decades, and I thank each of them lavishly for all that they give to me: Ann Short Chirhart, Suzanne Marshall, Theresa Furgeson McClellan, Linda Shopes, and Kyle Wilkison. Equally dear and long-suffering, Sharlande Sledge, minister of poetry and soup bowls, and Ashley Thornton deal with me on a daily basis. Ashley and I have walked enough miles together to get from Texas to New York. Melissa Walker is friend; colleague; co-author; cheerleader; sharer of conference hotel rooms, music, pottery, poetry, recipes, dreams, hopes, and fears. She is on every page of this book.

Another pillar of my life is my brother, Lester Sharpless. He often knows me better than I know myself, and I am overwhelmed with gratitude for his constant friendship as well as our kinship. Our family's younger generation—Amanda Sharpless; Nathan Sharpless; Jennifer, Joshua, Kayley, and Trey Ables; and Jan, Richard, Elizabeth, Sarah, and Hannah Charlton—fill our lives with energy and laughter.

It's impossible to summarize the gifts of Tom Charlton—husband, friend, mentor—to my life and my work. In the past ten years, we've spent lots of difficult time together in the valley of the shadow. How good it is to stand together in the light as well. This is for him. *Siempre juntos*, indeed.

Appendix

COOKS' WAGES, 1901–1960

Year	Cook's Name, If Known	State	Wages
1901		Georgia	$2.03/week
1901		Texas	$4.00/week
1904		Columbia, Missouri	$4.00/week
1905		Auburn, Alabama	$4.00–5.00/month
1913		Athens, Georgia	$10.00/month [$2.50/week] with service pan $12.00/month [$3.00/week] without service pan
1913		Athens, Georgia	Average $2.72/week
1919		Clarke County, Georgia	Before World War I: $1.5–2.00/week After World War I: $3.00–4.00/week
1921		Gainesville, Georgia	$3.00–5.00/week
1923		Richmond, Virginia	$43.00/month [$10.85/week]
1923–24	Cleora Butler	Tulsa, Oklahoma	$14.00–17.50/week
1924		Baltimore, Maryland	$12.00/week
1930		Mobile, Alabama	$10.00/week
1930s	Mittie Price	Belzoni, Mississippi	$5.00/week
1933	Doris Willis	Alexandria, Virginia	$3.00/week
1933	Nora Ruddy	Kansas City	$14.00/month [$3.50/week]
"The Depression"		Norfolk, Virginia	$4.00/week
1936		Lynchburg, Virginia	$5.00–6.00/week
1937	Annie W. Truitt	LaGrange, Georgia	$1.50–2.00/week

Year	Cook's Name, If Known	State	Wages
1937	Elizabeth Clyburn	Washington, D.C.	$7.00/week
1937	G. S. Ellington	Athens, Georgia	$2.50–3.00/week
1937	L. G. Huff	Fort Worth, Texas	$8.00/week
1937	Miss A. L. Graves	Houston, Texas	$3.50–6.00/week
1938		Louisiana	$7.00/week
1938		Navasota, Texas	$2.50–3.00/week
1938		San Antonio, Texas	$2.50–3.00/week
1938	Roxanna Hupes	Galveston, Texas	$3.00/week
1939	Catherine L. Wood	Atlanta, Georgia	$1.50–2.00/week
1939	Mrs. H. A. Clement	Baltimore, Maryland	$10.00/week
1939	O'Neal	Memphis, Tennessee	$8.00/week
1939	Lucinda Robinson	Lakeland, Florida	$4.00/week
Late 1930s	Katy Brumby	Birmingham, Alabama	$6.00/week
Late 1930s	Lucinda Robinson	Lakeland, Florida	$4.00/week
Late 1930s	Nannie Hawkins	Macon, Georgia	$1.50/week
1940	Corine Colman	Anniston, Alabama	$3.00/week
1940		Greensboro, North Carolina	$8.00/week
1940		South Carolina	$2.00/week
1940	Alice Adams	Atlanta, Georgia	$4.00/week
1941	Geneva Dawkins	Concord, North Carolina	$3.00–4.00/week
1941	Annie Mae Hunt	Dallas, Texas	$8.50/week
1941		Hampton, Virginia	$5.00–7.00/week
1941		Kannapolis, North Carolina	$3.00–3.50/week
1941	"A Negro Cook"	Pine Bluff, Arkansas	$3.50/week
1941		Washington, D.C.	$7.00–8.00/week
1941		Washington, D.C.	$6.00–10.00/week
1942		Dyersburg, Tennessee	$3.00/week
1942	Anna Mae Dickson	Houston, Texas	$13.00/week
1943		Memphis, Tennessee	$5.00–6.00/week

Year	Cook's Name, If Known	State	Wages
1943	Idella Parker	Cross Creek, Florida	$5.00/week
1944		New Orleans	$9.26/week
1955		Montgomery, Alabama	$20.00/week (a "good" cook)
1955		Montgomery, Alabama	$25.00–30.00/week ("truly excellent cooks")
Late 1950s	Anna Mae Dickson	Navasota, Texas	$10.00–12.00/week

Sources: Fleming, "Servant Problem," 8; Laughlin, "Domestic Service," 748; Elwang, "Negroes of Columbia," 24; Woofter, "Negroes of Athens," 46, 47; Ruth Reed, *Negro Woman of Gainesville*, 28; Robinson, *Domestic Workers*, 52; O'Leary, *From Morning to Night*, 111; Tucker, *Telling Memories*, 24, 178; Watriss, "It's Something Inside You," 78, 80; Mary Anderson, *Plight of Negro Domestic Labor*, 68; Cleora Butler, *Cleora's Kitchens*, 40; Parker, *From Reddick to Cross Creek*, 129; Long, *Negroes of Clarke County*, 37, 40; Mrs. Daniel's Folder, undated typescript, "Household Employment: The Problem of 2,000,000 Workers," NARA; Mrs. Daniel's Folder, undated typescript, "Wages of Domestic Workers," NARA; Katy Brumby and Charlie and Lucinda Robinson, American Life Histories: Manuscripts from the Federal Writers' Project; Gilmore and Wilson, "Employment of Negro Women," 321; Hunt, *I Am Annie Mae*, 79; Robinson, *Montgomery Bus Boycott*, 107.

Notes

Preface

1. Cleora Butler, *Cleora's Kitchens*, 39.
2. See, for example, Dubert, "Modernity without Modernisation," on Spain, 1752–1900; Maza, *Servants and Masters*, 6, 17, and Fairchilds, *Domestic Enemies*, 59, 60, 61, 62, for discussions of eighteenth-century France; Hecht, *Domestic Servant Class*, 177–99, and Hill, *Servants*, 135–36, for eighteenth-century England; Davidoff, "Mastered," 408, and Horn, *Rise and Fall*, 36–38, for nineteenth-century England; Stansell, *City of Women*, 155–66, for early-nineteenth-century New York City; Broom and Smith, "Bridging Occupations," 321–34, for nineteenth- and twentieth-century Britain; McBride, *Domestic Revolution*, for nineteenth- and twentieth-century England and France; Kousha, "Best Friends," 4, for twentieth-century Iran; and Chang, *Disposable Domestics*, and Hondagneu-Sotelo, *Doméstica*, on late-twentieth-century America.
3. On domestic work in the United States in general, see Dudden, *Serving Women*; Katzman, *Seven Days a Week*; Palmer, *Domesticity and Dirt*; Rollins, *Between Women*; and Sutherland, *Americans and Their Servants*. For African American women specifically, see Tucker, *Telling Memories*, and Clark-Lewis, *Living In, Living Out*.
4. Swann-Wright, *Way Out of No Way*, offers this apt phrase as the title for her study of her ancestors' new lives after emancipation in Virginia.
5. Gabaccia, *We Are What We Eat*, 6. See also Revel, "Culture and Cuisine," 244; Charles Camp, *American Foodways*, 23, 29; De Silva, *In Memory's Kitchen*, xxvi; Bentley, *Eating for Victory*, 85; Flandrin and Montanari, Introduction, 6; and Bardenstein, "Transmissions Interrupted," 353–61.
6. Gabaccia, *We Are What We Eat*, 8, 51; Douglas, *World of Goods*, 66; Munro, "Food in Catherinian St. Petersburg," 33; Pilcher, *Que Vivan los Tamales*, 2.
7. Douglas, *World of Goods*, 57, 72.
8. See, for example, Jessica B. Harris, *Welcome Table*; Jessica B. Harris, *Iron Pots*; Spivey, *Peppers, Cracklings*; and Hess, "What We Know."
9. For example, in 1920, the Bureau of the Census reported that the data on cooks was inaccurate: "'In the occupation returns, especially the returns for the colored females of the South, a careful distinction was not made,' the bureau stated, 'between cooks and general servants'" (Katzman, *Seven Days a Week*, 301).
10. African American men tended to cook in restaurants, not private homes, and many more women were employed in private homes than in public venues like restaurants (Mary V. Robinson, *Domestic Workers*, 4–5; Tippett, "Economic Activities of Women," 118).
11. Goldfield, *Black, White, and Southern*, 9–10; Neil R. McMillen, *Dark Journey*, 27.
12. Collins, "Learning from the Outsider Within," S16–S19.
13. In recent years there has been a significant outpouring of high-quality scholarship about representations of African American women in the late nineteenth and twentieth

centuries. See, for example, Witt, *Black Hunger*; Williams-Forson, *Building Houses Out of Chicken Legs*; Turner, *Ceramic Uncles and Celluloid Mammies*; Goings, *Mammy and Uncle Mose*; Haug, "Myth and Matriarchy"; Michael D. Harris, *Colored Pictures*, 83–124; Morgan, "Mammy the Huckster"; Lee A. Hunter, "Myth of the Mammy"; Joan Marie Johnson, "'Ye Gave Them a Stone'"; McElya, *Clinging to Mammy*; Wallace-Sanders, *Mammy*; and Wallace-Sanders, "Southern Memory, Southern Monuments."

14. Visual representations of African American women as rotund figures with head rags began as early as the 1840s in the minstrel impersonations of George Christy and in the circa 1842 painting *The Bashful Cousin* by Francis William Edmonds (Morgan, "Mammy the Huckster," 90).

The plantation legend in novel form developed during the antebellum era in the work of John Esten Cooke, John Pendleton Kennedy, and William Gilmore Simms, followed in 1866 by E. A. Pollard's *The Lost Cause*. The so-called plantation genre of literature arose by the 1890s; it included such writers as Joel Chandler Harris, Francis Pendleton Gaines, and Walter Hines Page. As Jane Turner Censer has observed, these writers "specialized in colorful mammies" who bullied the white folks and loved white children. See Clinton, *Tara Revisited*, 192, 196; Censer, *Reconstruction of White Southern Womanhood*, 270; Goings, *Mammy and Uncle Mose*, 10; and Fienberg, "Charles W. Chesnutt," 164.

In the twentieth century, the depiction of the African American cook by white authors continued through the civil rights movement, often as a sympathetic companion to a frightened white child. The most prominent examples include Dilsey Gibson in *The Sound and the Fury* (William Faulkner, 1929), Delilah Johnston in Fannie Hurst's *Imitation of Life* (1933), Bereniece Sadie Brown in *The Member of the Wedding* (Carson McCullers, 1946), Narciss in *The Ponder Heart* (Eudora Welty, 1954), and Calpurnia in *To Kill a Mockingbird* (Harper Lee, 1960). Most of these novels were turned into movies: *Imitation of Life* in 1934 and 1959 with Louise Beavers playing Johnston in the first production and Juanita Moore in the second version; *The Member of the Wedding* in 1952 with Ethel Waters in the role of Brown; and *To Kill a Mockingbird* in 1962 with Estelle Evans portraying Calpurnia. *The Ponder Heart*, filmed in 2001, featured Jenifer Lewis as "Narcissa."

15. The conflation of "mammy" with "cook" occurred in the twentieth century. Herbert Gutman pointed out that slave "mammies" caring for white children were fairly rare. The typical urban house slave, according to Gutman, "was a young and unmarried black woman" under the age of twenty (Gutman, *Black Family*, 443, 631). See also Lee A. Hunter, "Myth of Mammy," 4, 7–8; and Parkhurst, "Role of the Black Mammy," 359–69. White southerners also rolled together the myth of mammy and that of the cook. Although their tasks differed significantly, the mammy and the cook both engaged in nurturing, the mammy by caring for the children and the cook by providing food for them. When white southerners recalled their cooks, they frequently made the two women into one composite.

A visual representation of such a relationship is a 1905 photograph of Celia Lipscomb and Sallie Goodman LeGrand of Tyler, Texas. The photograph shows Lipscomb, the longtime cook for the Goodman family, seated in a chair wearing a dark dress with a large white collar, a white apron, and wire-framed glasses. The young white woman is apparently seated on the floor beside her, her hair in a pompadour. Her head is against the older woman's breast, and the older woman's left hand rests on her shoulder. LeGrand is clearly positioned as a child taking comfort in Lipscomb's physical presence, a comfort she felt compelled to commemorate and make permanent through the medium of photography (Pollan, "Goodman Family," 12).

16. Witt, *Black Hunger*, 57.

17. Lancaster, "Simmering Stew," viii; Grossman, "Trauma, Memory, and Revenge." See also George, "Recycling," 3, 16.

18. Litwack, *Trouble in Mind*, xiii.

19. Hale, *Making Whiteness*, 7; quotation from Litwack, *Trouble in Mind*, xiv, xvi.

20. Janeway, *Powers of the Weak*, 6, 14.

21. Langhorne, "Domestic Service in the South," 169; Card "used by M.C.W. speech in Newark, NJ, Feb. 15, 1933," Record Group 86, Women's Bureau, Office of the Director, General Correspondence of the Women's Bureau, 1919–48 (hereafter RG 86), Box 286, "Domestic Workers Household Employment (1912–1956)": Domestic Workers—Census Data, National Archives and Records Administration (hereafter NARA); Katzman, *Seven Days a Week*, 63, 289–90.

22. Sally McMillen, "Mothers' Sacred Duty," 333, 334. In her appeal to the sympathies of abolitionist women, Harriet Jacobs also played up the relationship between slave wet nurses and their white charges (Jacobs, *Incidents in the Life of a Slave Girl*, 6–7, 130). See Wallace-Sanders, *Mammy*, 1, 36–37, for comments on Jacobs and wet nursing.

23. Witt, *Black Hunger*, 25–32; Cox, "From Aunt Jemima to Scarlett O'Hara."

24. Goings, *Mammy and Uncle Mose*, 28, 64–65. For trenchant discussions of the images of African American women in advertising, see Deck, "'Now Then—Who Said Biscuits?,'" 70–93, and Morgan, "Mammy the Huckster."

25. McElya, *Clinging to Mammy*, 20.

26. Michael D. Harris, *Colored Pictures*, 122.

27. Cleora Butler, *Cleora's Kitchens*, 40.

28. Janeway, *Powers of the Weak*, 23; quotation from Michael D. Harris, *Colored Pictures*, 122.

29. Christine Stansell observes that domestic workers in New York had to deal with the rising expectations of the cult of domesticity. By the 1840s, servants "also had new obligations in fulfilling their mistresses' developing conceptions of the home. Much of the servant's labor was in service to her mistress's imagination" (Stansell, *City of Women*, 161). The expectations for African American women included not only domesticity and gentility but also alleged memories of the nonexistent Old South.

30. Brundage, *Southern Past*, 33; quotation from Joan Marie Johnson, "'Ye Gave Them a Stone,'" 73–75. For an extended discussion of the proposed monument and African Americans' reactions to it, see McElya, *Clinging to Mammy*, 116–206.

31. Woodson, "Negro Washerwoman," 269.

32. Walker, *Living by the Word*, 59–60, 61, 62. See also hooks, *Ain't I a Woman*, 84.

33. Rushin, "Black Back-Ups," 20.

34. Michael D. Harris, *Colored Pictures*, 84.

35. Williams-Forson, *Building Houses Out of Chicken Legs*, 38. Numerous African American women historians have called for studies that look at actual women who did genuine work. See Brewer, "Theorizing Race, Class and Gender," 16; Hine, "Black Women's History," 127; and Alexander, "Challenge of Race," 56.

36. Bay, *White Image in the Black Mind*, 5.

37. See ibid., 5–6, for a discussion of the risks to African Americans publicly critiquing white Americans.

38. For an extended discussion of the Federal Writers' Project, its strengths and weaknesses, see Hirsch, *Portrait of America*. For the slave narratives in particular, see Blassingame, "Using the Testimony," and Glymph, *Out of the House of Bondage*, 14–16.

39. Kytle, *Willie Mae*, xvii.

40. My attempts to verify Wright's identity have been futile to date. In the 1993 University of Georgia Press reprint of *Willie Mae*, Kytle revealed her subject's family name to be Wright (xvi). The University of Georgia Press has no information on Willie Mae Wright. A search through Atlanta city directories of the 1940s and 1950s showed a number of women named Willie Wright, one of whom lived on Edgewood Avenue, but there is no way to conclude that that person is the person in Kytle's book.

41. For a discussion of Butler's memoir, see Haber, "Cooking to Survive."

42. Although many books on African American cookery have appeared since the 1960s, for example the remarkable work of Jessica Harris and Edna Lewis, few have extended discussions of cooks as domestic workers in the South. For a complete bibliography through 1999, see Witt, *Black Hunger*, 220–28. For a discussion of the use of African American cookbooks to fight stereotypes, see Inness, *Secret Ingredients*, 105–25.

43. The literature on cookbooks as cultural productions continues to grow. The most thoughtful work to date is Theophano, *Eat My Words*. See also Bower, *Recipes for Reading*; Goldman, "'I Yam What I Yam'"; Leavitt, *From Catharine Beecher to Martha Stewart*; and Romines, *Home Plot*. For discussions of the meanings of cookbooks to white southerners, see Grubb, "House and Home in the Victorian South," and Stanonis, "Just Like Mammy Used to Make," 210–16.

44. Fisher, *What Mrs. Fisher Knows*, 72.

45. Ibid., 50.

46. Bowers, *Plantation Kitchen*, 9–10.

47. Ibid., 45, 142, 143.

48. Heldke, *Exotic Appetites*, 131.

49. Hess, "What We Know," 90. See also Witt, *Black Hunger*, 60. While Hess points out that white women stole recipes from African American women, southern cookbook writers read and freely borrowed from a wide variety of sources, including other cookbooks. As Damon Fowler notes in his introduction to *Mrs. Hill's Southern Practical Cookery and Receipt Book*, cookbook writers frequently lifted recipes from one another and occasionally engaged in "outright plagiarism" (Fowler, "Historical Commentary," xxvi). Annabella Hill, for example, cited recipes from English and American cookbook writers (Fowler, "Historical Commentary," xxiv). By the 1890s, writers were quoting at will from northern cookbook writers such as Sarah Tyson Rorer and Maria Parloa. (See, for example, Glover, *Warm Springs Receipt-Book*.) And southern women swapped recipes among themselves, as the earliest community-based cookbooks will attest. (See, for example, Augusta, Ga., Second Presbyterian Church, *Choice Recipes*, and *Household Manual and Practical Cook Book*.)

50. Walker, *Living by the Word*, 32. Lisa Heldke discusses the harm done to cooks in taking their recipes. First, the "language of property" is not useful because cooks haven't

laid claim to recipes by publishing them themselves; second, the recipes are common, and cooks are not likely to think of them as things that can be owned. Recipes can be lifted out of the public domain and copyrighted as the author's own (Heldke, *Exotic Appetites*, 136, 139).

51. Doris Smith, "In Search of Our Mothers' Cookbooks," 23.

52. Ibid., 24.

53. Flexner, *Dixie Dishes*, 125–26.

54. Cleora Butler, *Cleora's Kitchens*, 49.

55. Doris Smith, "In Search of Our Mothers' Cookbooks," 26, cites Viola Lampkin, *Viola's Favorite Recipes* (Olathe, Kans.: Cook Book Publishers, 1988) as an instance of a contemporary cookbook that usurps the voice of an African American woman. To Smith's example I would add Rankin and Callender, *Cookin' Up a Storm*, published in 1998.

56. Wynter, "Sambos and Minstrels," 149, 155.

57. Illiteracy among cooks declined steadily in the late nineteenth century. In 1880, only 20 percent of the cooks in a sample of the U.S. Census in Macon, Georgia, could read, but by 1900, that number had increased to 76 percent.

58. "Negro Nurse," "More Slavery at the South," 197. Mary Virginia Terhune (writing as Marion Harland) discusses her cook Emily's "getting her hand out" in making bread (Harland, *Marion Harland's Autobiography*, 340–45).

59. Parker, *Idella*, 69.

60. Ibid., 68–69.

61. Lustig, Sondheim, and Rensel, *Southern Cook Book*, unpaged introduction; Flexner, *Dixie Dishes*, x–xi; Duncan Hines, *Food Odyssey*, 1955, quoted in Egerton, *Southern Food*, 41; Mary Stuart Harrison Smith, *Virginia Cookery-Book*, 19; Natalie Scott, *Mirations and Miracles*, unpaged preface; Patterson, *Mammy Lou*, ix; Davidoff, *Worlds Between*, 76–77.

62. Patterson, *Mammy Lou*, 39, 170. Lisa Heldke observes that for many cookbook writers, "the writing down of the recipes was a second step. And it is that second step that is all important—so important that it apparently eclipses the work of actually perfecting the recipes in the kitchen" (Heldke, *Exotic Appetites*, 133).

63. Deck, "'Now Then—Who Said Biscuits?,'" 70–71. According to Mary Procida, English citizens living in India attributed the same ability to their Indian cooks: "As with other clever Indian artifices, such as snake-charming, the rope trip, and fire walking, Anglo-Indians expressed their amazement at Indians' culinary prowess and generally declined to investigate these mysteries further" (Procida, "Feeding the Imperial Appetite," 133).

64. Doris Smith, "In Search of Our Mothers' Cookbooks," 24.

65. Witt, *Black Hunger*, 63.

66. Marion Brown, *Southern Cook Book*, 157. This recipe does not appear in the revised edition published in 1968.

67. Parker, *Idella*, 69. According to Parker, Rawlings also took verbal credit for Parker's work: "It was a joy serving her guests and hearing them exclaim over the different dishes, asking, 'Marge, how did you fix this?' Sometimes she would call me and ask, or other times Mrs. Rawlings would say she had put this or that in it. It didn't matter too much that I didn't get the credit. Both Mrs. Rawlings and I were good cooks, and we en-

joyed and often worked together on planning and cooking the meals" (Parker, *From Reddick to Cross Creek*, 106).

68. Fienberg, "Charles W. Chesnutt," 164.

69. Clinton, *Tara Revisited*, 121. In filmmaker Marlon Riggs's apt words, "My mouth moves, but you hear your own words" (Riggs, "Unleash the Queen," 103).

70. *Household Manual and Practical Cook Book*, 51, 53, 142, 143.

71. *Lone Star Cook Book*, 68; Stoney, *Carolina Rice Cook Book*, 25, 41, 57, 76. For the most prominent examples of the "mammy cook" in cookbooks, see McKinney, *Aunt Caroline's Dixieland Recipes*; *Aunt Jemimy's Southern Recipes*; Howard, *Fifty Years in a Maryland Kitchen*; Eustis, *Cooking in Old Creole Days*; Fox, *Blue Grass Cook Book*; McCulloch-Williams, *Dishes and Beverages of the Old South*; Patterson, *Mammy Lou*; and Natalie Scott, *Mirations and Miracles*.

72. McCulloch-Williams, *Dishes and Beverages of the Old South*, 35.

73. Heldke, *Exotic Appetites*, 137.

74. Michele Birnbaum, "Dark Dialects: Scientific and Literary Realism in Joel Chandler Harris's Uncle Remus Series," *New Orleans Review* 18, no. 1 (1991): 36–45, quoted in Minnick, *Dialect and Dichotomy*, 10; Minnick, *Dialect and Dichotomy*, xiv.

75. Yuhl, *Golden Haze*, 12, 13.

76. Ibid., 17, 131.

77. Natalie Scott, *Mirations and Miracles*, unpaged preface, 7, 23, 38, 48, 57.

78. Patterson, *Mammy Lou*, ix.

79. Breckinridge, *From Soup to Nuts*, 8, 13.

80. Moncure, *Emma Jane's Souvenir Cook Book*, 5.

81. Ibid., 10, 68.

82. The David Walker Lupton African American Cookbook Collection at the W. S. Hoole Special Collections Library, University of Alabama, has more than 450 titles written by African Americans, mostly since the 1970s. See ⟨http://www.lib.ua.edu/lupton/luptonlist.htm⟩.

Introduction

1. Stephanie Cole, in her study of five antebellum border cities, demonstrates convincingly that between 1800 and 1850 "cooks were, by and large, African American, enslaved, and female" (Cole, "White Woman, of Middle Age," 85). After the Civil War, some white women in the South worked as domestics, but it is not possible to determine how many of them were cooks, and the percentage of African American cooks increased over time. In the Deep South in 1890, the census counted 206,549 domestic employees, of which 166,305, or 80.13 percent, were "colored." In the "border states," there were 251,544 total, of which 61.73 percent were "colored." The rest were largely "native white," with 3 percent in the South and 6 percent in the border states being "foreign white." By 1930, the percentage of African Americans as domestic servants in the South had increased to 84 percent (Card "used by M.C.W. speech in Newark, NJ, Feb. 15, 1933," Record Group 86, Women's Bureau, Office of the Director, General Correspondence of the Women's Bureau, 1919–48 (hereafter RG 86), Box 286, "Domestic Workers Household Employment

(1912–1956)": Domestic Workers—Census Data, National Archives and Records Administration (hereafter NARA). See also Glymph, *Out of the House of Bondage*, 160–62.

2. Davidoff, *Worlds Between*, 75.

3. For sweeping histories of food, see Toussaint-Samat, *History of Food*; Tannahill, *Food in History*; Flandrin and Montanari, *Food*; and Braudel, *Structures of Everyday Life*. For general histories of American food, see Charles Camp, *American Foodways*; Gabaccia, *We Are What We Eat*; and Andrew F. Smith, *Oxford Encyclopedia*. The best overviews of food in the American South are Egerton, *Southern Food*, and Edge, *Gracious Plenty*.

4. Romines, *Home Plot*, 69.

5. Symons, *History of Cooks and Cooking*, 107.

6. Ibid., 130.

7. Davidoff, *Worlds Between*, 88; Symons, *History of Cooks and Cooking*, 130.

8. Short, *Kitchen Secrets*, 55–59. See also Abarca, *Voices in the Kitchen*, 51.

9. Heldke, "Foodmaking," 219.

10. Fowler, *Damon Lee Fowler's New Southern Kitchen*, 14.

11. Heldke, "Foodmaking," 207–8; Davidoff, "Mastered," 412.

12. Symons, *History of Cooks and Cooking*, 4.

13. Davidoff, *Worlds Between*, 77.

14. Ibid., 5, 74, 87; Davidoff, "Mastered," 412–13.

15. Egerton, *Southern Food*, 13, 14.

16. Spruill, *Women's Life and Work*, 68, 71–72.

17. Ravenel, *Eliza Pinckney*, 245. Pinckney is referring to the definition of a good woman in Proverbs 31 of the Hebrew Bible. Presumably by keeping her workers busy, Pinckney somehow also made them virtuous.

18. Genovese, *Roll, Jordan, Roll*, 328.

19. Hess, "What We Know," 78–79.

20. Smedes, *Memorials of a Southern Planter*, 80–81.

21. Genovese, *Roll, Jordan, Roll*, 541.

22. McCulloch-Williams, *Dishes and Beverages of the Old South*, 10–15.

23. Ibid., 17–19.

24. Burwell, *Girl's Life in Virginia*, 40–41, 71–72. As far as I can determine, the baked goods that Burwell names are all types of quick bread, made without yeast. "Loaf bread" might have been made with yeast.

25. Egerton, *Southern Food*, 15–16; Daina Ramey Berry, *"Swing the Sickle,"* 35, 46, 48. For a selection of antebellum holiday menus, see Queenie Woods Washington, *Sewanee Cook Book*, 222–24.

26. E. N. Noland to Ella Mackenzie, Glen Ora, Middleburg, Va., November 14, 1849, quoted in Hooker, *Colonial Plantation Cookbook*, 32.

27. Fannie Berry, American Life Histories: Manuscripts from the Federal Writers' Project.

28. Thomas, *Secret Eye*, 268. The documentation of white women complaining about their slaves' transition to freedom is substantial. See Weiner, *Mistresses and Slaves*, 193, 197, 199, 201, 204, 212; Censer, *Reconstruction of White Southern Womanhood*, 7,

59–67; Zimmer, *Robert E. Lee Family*, 48; King Diary, August 12, 1866; January 4, 1867; March 14, 1867, Hargrett Library, University of Georgia, Athens; Katzman, *Seven Days a Week*, 193; and Thomas, *Secret Eye*, 319, 349.

29. Haviland, *Woman's Life-Work*, 266.

30. Schwalm, *Hard Fight for We*, 208; Morsman, "Big House after Slavery," 30.

31. Bruce, Jones, and Murchison Family Papers, quoted in Weiner, *Mistresses and Slaves*, 211.

32. Diary of Miss Emma Holmes, 488, quoted in Weiner, *Mistresses and Slaves*, 226.

33. Schwalm, *Hard Fight for We*, 208.

34. Thomas, *Secret Eye*, 272–73. See also Sutherland, "Special Kind of Problem," 158. Glymph, *Out of the House of Bondage*, 156–57, discusses Leah's situation at length.

35. Williams-Forson, *Building Houses Out of Chicken Legs*, 46; O'Donovan, *Becoming Free*, 174–75.

36. Megginson, *African American Life*, 205.

37. Van Zelm, "On the Front Lines of Freedom," 195–96.

38. Logan, *Negro in North Carolina*, 87. Logan points out similar situations in other North Carolina cities: New Bern, 48.0 percent; Asheville, 77.0 percent; Wilmington, 57.3 percent; and Charlotte, 79.0 percent.

39. Edwards, *Southern Urban Negro*, 2; Logan, *Negro in North Carolina*, 86.

40. Lewis, *In Their Own Interests*, 10. See also Jones, *Labor of Love*, 73–74.

41. Janiewski, *Sisterhood Denied*, 56, 57; Maclachlan, "Women's Work," 256; Jones, *Labor of Love*, 74–75.

42. Litwack, *Trouble in Mind*, 483.

43. Clark-Lewis, *Living In, Living Out*, 5.

44. By leaving their families of origin and going to town to seek paid work, these young women became a part of the widespread "family wage economy" described by Joan Wallach Scott and Louise A. Tilly: "A daughter's departure served not only to relieve the family of the burden of supporting her, but it might help support the family as well" (Tilly and Scott, *Women, Work, and Family*, 109).

45. Clark-Lewis, *Living In, Living Out*, 51–66; Cleora Butler, *Cleora's Kitchens*, 39.

46. Jordan, *Vernon Can Read*, 16. In his study of rural migrants to Nashville between 1890 and 1930, Louis M. Kyriakoudes points out that lack of education and racial discrimination limited almost all African American female immigrants to domestic work (Kyriakoudes, *Social Origins of the Urban South*, 138–39).

47. Jordan, *Vernon Can Read*, 20.

48. Although an undetermined number of cooks persisted on the old plantations, domestic service was primarily an urban phenomenon. In 1897, the U.S. cities with the largest proportion of domestic employees to the population were all in the South: Washington, D.C., a 1:13 ratio; Richmond, Virginia, also 1:13; Atlanta, Georgia, 1:14; Memphis, Tennessee, 1:15; and Nashville, Tennessee, 1:16 (Salmon, *Domestic Service*, 84–85). In Atlanta in 1880, there were 331 servants per 1,000 families, while in the rest of Georgia, the ratio was only 85 servants per 1,000 families. In other words, 33 percent of Atlanta families could theoretically have had a servant, while outside of Atlanta, only 8 percent could have. If domestic workers were also common in smaller Georgia cities, like Augusta, Savannah, and Macon, that means that they were almost nonexistent—or at

least invisible to enumerators—in the countryside (Katzman, *Seven Days a Week*, 59–61, 286). As urban populations grew, so did the number of domestic workers. In Atlanta in the 1920s, for example, seven out of ten new jobs for African American women were in household work (Maclachlan, "Women's Work," 257).

49. Watriss, "It's Something Inside You," 78.

50. O'Leary, *From Morning to Night*, 88.

51. Haynes, "Negroes in Domestic Service," 411.

52. Letter from Anonymous to Mrs. Roosevelt, October 15, 1941, RG 86, Box 294, "Domestic Workers Household Employment 1941": File 1941 Anonymous, NARA.

53. Letter from Ida Trail to Mrs. Eleanor Roosevelt, April 17, 1941, RG 86, Box 294, "Domestic Workers Household Employment 1941": File 1941 T–U–V, NARA.

Chapter One

1. Katzman, *Seven Days a Week*, 302; Romero, "Sisterhood and Domestic Service," 328. An extreme example of this arose in Cleora Butler's life. In 1932, her employer, the Sneddens family, bought the Tulsa home of Arthur Hull, with eighteen rooms and thirteen acres. The Sneddenses fired most of the Hulls' staff of eleven, including Butler's mother, who was the cook; Butler therefore replaced her own mother (Butler, *Cleora's Kitchens*, 43–44).

2. Clark-Lewis, *Living In, Living Out*, 152.

3. Woofter, *Negroes of Athens*, 45.

4. Interview of "The Lil' Black Girl," 3414, Federal Writers' Project Files, Southern Oral History Project, Southern Historical Collection, University of North Carolina at Chapel Hill.

5. Kuhn, Joye, and West, *Living Atlanta*, 116.

6. Linsley, "Main House, Carriage House," 32; O'Leary, *From Morning to Night*, 99; Parker, *Idella*, 14, 16; Parker, *From Reddick to Cross Creek*, 89.

7. Tucker, *Telling Memories*, 178.

8. Thomas, *Secret Eye*, 273.

9. *Houston Civic Club Cook Book*, 20. The 1870, 1880, and 1900 censuses do not reveal any live-in domestic workers in the Affleck household, so presumably this unnamed woman lived in her own home.

10. Tucker, *Telling Memories*, 175.

11. Letter from Elizabeth Collins to Miss Dahlia Wood, November 12, 1877, Grisham Family Papers, Woodruff Library, Special Collections, Emory University, Atlanta, Ga.

12. Letter from Elizabeth Collins, Dalton, Ga., to Miss Dahlia Wood, Chattanooga, June 25, 1886, Grisham Family Papers, Woodruff Library, Special Collections, Emory University, Atlanta, Ga.

13. Clark-Lewis, *Living In, Living Out*, 100.

14. Davidoff et al., *Family Story*, 166; O'Leary, *From Morning to Night*, 83.

15. Watriss, "It's Something Inside You," 79.

16. Hunt, *I Am Annie Mae*, 68 (emphasis in the original). Hunt is making a pun on the word "pickaninny," an often disparaging term for a small African American child, derived from the Spanish *pequeño*, meaning small, or Portuguese *pequinino*, meaning very little.

17. Fleming, "Servant Problem," 14. Ray Stannard Baker (*Following the Color Line*, 53) observed the same phenomenon in Atlanta in 1908.

18. Raper, *Tragedy of Lynching*, 262. See also Tera Hunter, *To 'Joy My Freedom*, 108–11, and Kytle, *Willie Mae*, 133, 134–35, for a discussion of similar practices in Atlanta.

19. A 1904 survey of Columbia, Missouri, found thirty-nine servants in thirty-three families, "all of them negroes, as housegirls, cooks, nurses, and men-of-all-work" (Elwang, "Negroes of Columbia," 27). No more than six, or 20 percent, of the families in the Columbia sample had multiple servants, and that number doubtlessly decreased with time. See also Chaplin, "Domestic Service," 104.

20. Tucker, *Telling Memories*, 264.

21. Plant Family Reminiscences by "Mrs. Ross (Martha Plant)," 1, Southern Oral History Project, Southern Historical Collection, University of North Carolina at Chapel Hill.

22. Schwalm, "Sweet Dreams," 28. See also Sutherland, "Special Kind of Problem," 159, and Glymph, *Out of the House of Bondage*, 151–52.

23. Tucker, *Telling Memories*, 111. See also Mary V. Robinson, *Domestic Workers*, 15, 34.

24. Sarah Howard, Drury Ave., Macon, Georgia, interview by Annie A. Rose, Macon, pp. 3238–39, Federal Writers' Project Files, Southern Oral History Project, Box 13, Folder 247, Southern Historical Collection, University of North Carolina at Chapel Hill.

25. Mary V. Robinson, *Domestic Workers*, 15, 34.

26. In 1918, Robert Brooks (*Sanitary Conditions*, 23) observed that because washer-women frequently made more money than cooks did and worked in their own homes, women often preferred to do laundry.

27. In Athens, Georgia, in 1913, T. J. Woofter (*Negroes of Athens*, 47) found that cooks averaged $2.50 per week, while maids averaged between $2.00 and $2.25.

28. Kytle, *Willie Mae*, 120.

29. Perkins, "Forgotten Victorians," 122–23.

30. Clipping of "The Housemaid's Boss: A Striking Presentation of a Present-day Problem" by Ava L. Johnson, *Home Economics News* 3, no. 5 (May 1932): 91–92, in RG 86, Box 288, "Domestic Workers Household Employment 1912–1932: Domestic Workers—1933," NARA.

31. Letter from Catherine L. Wood to Secretary of Labor, April 18, 1939, RG 86, Box 292, "Domestic Workers Household Employment 1936–1939": File 1939 W–X–Y–Z, NARA.

32. Letter from "A Negro Cook" to President Roosevelt, February 13, 1941, RG 86, Box 294, "Domestic Workers Household Employment 1941": File 1941 Anonymous, NARA.

33. Redwine, "Brief History of the Negro," 36.

34. Wilkins, "Dr. Thomas Hunt Hall's Life," 25.

35. Diary of Jennie Akehurst Lines, October 18, October 19, October 20, October 30, 1871, Akehurst-Lines Collection, Box 3, October 17–November 3, 1871, Hargrett Library, University of Georgia, Athens.

36. Kuhn, Joye, and West, *Living Atlanta*, 113, 118. The "wash lady" did the laundry, probably in her own home.

37. Kousha, "African American Private Household Workers," 214. See also Nannie Pharis interviews by Allen Tullos, December 5, 1979, and January 8, 1979, Burlington,

N.C., UNC H-39, p. 68, Southern Oral History Project, Southern Historical Collection, University of North Carolina at Chapel Hill; and Tucker, *Telling Memories*, 87.

38. Tucker, *Telling Memories*, 267.

39. Letter from Anonymous to Mrs. Roosevelt, October 15, 1941, RG 86, Box 294, "Domestic Workers Household Employment 1941": File 1941 Anonymous, NARA.

40. Parker, *From Reddick to Cross Creek*, 95. See also Parker, *Idella*, 31–32, 50–51; Cleora Butler, *Cleora's Kitchens*, 43; and Tarr, *Private Marjorie*, 247, 297, 359.

41. Parker, *Idella*, 38; Welty, *Ponder Heart*, 31, 32, 42–43; Tucker, *Telling Memories*, 134. Parker's employer, Marjorie Kinnan Rawlings, often drank to excess, and Parker often drove to keep her off the roads at those times (Parker, *From Reddick to Cross Creek*, 118).

42. Pringle, *Woman Rice Planter*, 327, 338.

43. Parker, *From Reddick to Cross Creek*, 104.

44. Clark-Lewis, *Living In, Living Out*, 187–88.

45. Kytle, *Willie Mae*, 121. Neither Kytle nor Willoughby discussed traveling under Jim Crow conditions, but train travel would have entailed either being segregated into a "colored car" or being one of a few African Americans with their employers in the first-class car, neither a pleasant prospect. See Bay, "From the 'Ladies Car' to the 'Colored Car.'"

46. Dickson, "Help! Help! Help!," 66.

47. Clipping of "The Housemaid's Boss: A Striking Presentation of a Present-day Problem" by Ava L. Johnson, *Home Economics News* 3, no. 5 (May 1932): 91, in RG 86, Box 288, "Domestic Workers Household Employment (1912–1932): Domestic Workers—1933," NARA.

48. Powdermaker, *After Freedom*, 331.

49. Mary V. Robinson, *Domestic Workers*, 22.

50. Villard, "Negro and the Domestic Problem," 10.

51. Dickins, "Negro Food Habits," 524.

52. Parker, *Idella*, 9–10. See also Clark-Lewis, *Living In, Living Out*, 44, and Boehm, *Making a Way Out of No Way*, 50.

53. Kytle, *Willie Mae*, 24–25.

54. "Bea, The Wash Woman," American Life Histories: Manuscripts from the Federal Writers' Project.

55. Byerly, *Hard Times Cotton Mill Girls*, 36.

56. Council, *Mama Dip's Kitchen*, 3–4.

57. Children performed tasks such as simple cooking in many societies (Davidoff, *Worlds Between*, 75).

58. Interview with Mary Tuck, 1974, Mississippi Department of Archives and History and the Yazoo County Library System Oral History Project, Yazoo City Public Library, Yazoo City, Miss., quoted in Litwack, *Trouble in Mind*, 49.

59. Tucker, *Telling Memories*, 113. See also Swann-Wright, *Way Out of No Way*, 130.

60. Watriss, "It's Something Inside You," 78.

61. Kousha, "African American Private Household Workers," 224.

62. Parker, *From Reddick to Cross Creek*, 60.

63. Tucker, *Telling Memories*, 130.

64. Antoinette van Zelm comments that after emancipation, some white women con-

tinued "to see household workers' labor as a resource she could occasionally share with friends and relatives" (van Zelm, "On the Front Lines of Freedom," 214).

65. O'Leary, *From Morning to Night*, 7.

66. Swann-Wright, *Way Out of No Way*, 132.

67. Benson, *Counter Cultures*, 143; Barringer, *Dixie Cookery*, 3; Salmon, *Domestic Service*, 174; Ruth Reed, *Negro Women in Gainesville*, 25; Langhorne, "Domestic Service in the South," 171; Long, *Negroes of Clarke County*, 40; Woofter, *Negroes of Athens*, 61; Mary V. Robinson, *Domestic Workers*, 6.

68. Censer, *Reconstruction of White Southern Womanhood*, 78. See Bay, *White Image in the Black Mind*, 119–20, 127–49, for a discussion about comparisons of slaves to animals and African Americans' recoil against such notions.

69. Tucker, *Telling Memories*, 113.

70. Ibid., 251.

71. Kytle, *Willie Mae*, 120.

72. Ibid., 120–21. See also Claiborne, *Feast Made for Laughter*, 26; Watriss, "It's Something Inside You," 78; and Moncure, *Emma Jane's Souvenir Cook Book*, 28.

73. Kousha, "African American Private Household Workers," 224.

74. Interview of "The Lil' Black Girl," 3414, Federal Writers' Project Files, Southern Oral History Project, Southern Historical Collection, University of North Carolina at Chapel Hill.

75. Parker, *Idella*, 13–14; Parker, *From Reddick to Cross Creek*, 33.

76. Charles Camp, *American Foodways*, 51. See also Glenn, "Dialectics of Wage Work," 448.

77. *Atlanta Constitution*, November 11, 1897, p. 11.

78. Rosie Lee Smith, who cooked for the Gayle family in Angleton, Texas, in the mid-twentieth century, recalled having to avoid breaking egg yolks to keep from angering the youngest Gayle child, "a ring-tailed toot" (Wing-Leonard, "Figs, Flappers, and Fignolias," 63).

79. Leah Chase, *Dooky Chase Cookbook*, 186–87.

80. Swann-Wright, *Way Out of No Way*, 130.

81. Henrietta Elizabeth Sellers, American Life Histories: Manuscripts from the Federal Writers' Project.

82. Cleora Butler, *Cleora's Kitchens*, 53.

83. Ferris, *Matzoh Ball Gumbo*, 16, 41, 67, 69, 70–71, 72, 109–10, 206–7, 238–39.

84. Zimmer, *Robert E. Lee Family*, 52; Thomas, *Secret Eye*, 315–16; Diary of Jennie Akehurst Lines, October 29, 1871, Akehurst-Lines Collection, Box 3, October 17–November 3, 1871, Hargrett Library, University of Georgia, Athens.

85. Haynes, "Negroes in Domestic Service," 411.

86. Neverdon-Morton, *Afro-American Women*, 49.

87. Mrs. Booker T. Washington, "What Girls Are Taught," 71, 80; Rouse, "Out of the Shadow of Tuskegee," 31–32.

88. Dotson, "Story of a Teacher of Cooking," 203, 205. For discussions of the domestic curriculum at Hampton Institute and Tuskegee within the overall context of African American education, see Neverdon-Morton, *Afro-American Women*, 21, 26–27, 36–37.

89. Bowen, "Woman's Work," 220. See also Neverdon-Morton, *Afro-American Women*, 99.

90. McCluskey, "'We Specialize in the Wholly Impossible,'" 411.

91. Barnett, "Nanny Helen Burroughs," 101.

92. Higginbotham, *Righteous Discontent*, 212. See also Palmer, "Household Work," 83.

93. Harley, "Nanny Helen Burroughs," 64; McCluskey, "'We Specialize in the Wholly Impossible,'" 420; Wolcott, "'Bible, Bath, and Broom.'"

94. Harley, "Nanny Helen Burroughs," 65–66. Deborah Gray White points to the work of Burroughs and others as evidence of the class divide among African American women, in which the more privileged women simply could not imagine the lives of domestic workers (White, *Too Heavy a Load*, 132–33).

95. Palmer, "Household Work," 84; Higginbotham, *Righteous Discontent*, 219–20. For other examples of industrial training at the secondary level, see Neverdon-Morton, *Afro-American Women*, 79, 98.

96. Holtzclaw, *Black Man's Burden*, 189.

97. Doris Smith explores the juxtaposition of domestic training and Howard Weeden's poem "Beaten Biscuit," published in 1899, in "In Search of Our Mothers' Cookbooks," 22–27.

98. For an example of Dooley's racial attitudes, see Isma Dooly, "Permanent Cooking School Badly Needed in Atlanta," *Atlanta Constitution*, March 5, 1907.

99. Patton, "Moonlight and Magnolias." For discussion of the Black Mammy Memorial Institute, see McElya, *Clinging to Mammy*, 217–21, and Wallace-Sanders, *Mammy*, 105–6.

100. Woofter, *Negroes of Athens*, 32.

101. Holtzclaw, *Black Man's Burden*, 154.

102. "Negro High School Cooks in Demand," *Dallas Morning News*, May 30, 1913.

103. Cleora Butler, *Cleora's Kitchens*, 35–36.

104. Dotson, "Story of a Teacher of Cooking," 210; Neverdon-Morton, *Afro-American Women*, 93, 134.

105. Parker, *From Reddick to Cross Creek*, 18.

106. "Colored Cooks Are Given Lessons in Culinary Art," *Atlanta Constitution*, February 29, 1916.

107. "Special Lecture for Negro Cooks Tomorrow," *Dallas Morning News*, March 15, 1917. According to the *Dallas Morning News*, the audience for the white women's series ranged from members of the City Federation of Women's Clubs to "school girls" ("Many Attend Opening of Cooking School," *Dallas Morning News*, March 13, 1917).

108. Haynes, "Negroes in Domestic Service," 399; McElya, *Clinging to Mammy*, 221.

109. Penn, "Educational Progress," 83; Mrs. Booker T. Washington, "What Girls Are Taught," 71.

110. James Anderson, *Education of Blacks in the South*, 55, 56; Hoffschwelle, *Rosenwald Schools*, 1.

111. Burley, "Reconceptualizing Profession," 110.

Chapter Two

1. Letter from Sylvanus Lines to Jennie Lines, October 18, 1868 (quotation), and November 8, 1868, Akehurst-Lines Collection, Box 1, Folder 1:6, Letters 1868, Hargrett Library, University of Georgia, Athens.

2. For a discussion of the importance of southern food to its culture, see Stanonis, "Just Like Mammy Used to Make," 209, 217–33.

3. Edge, *Mrs. Wilkes*, 70.

4. Letter from L. G. Huff to Mrs. Franklin D. Rosevelt [*sic*], January 5, 1937, Record Group 86, Women's Bureau, Office of the Director, General Correspondence of the Women's Bureau, 1919–48 (hereafter RG 86), Box 291, "Domestic Workers Household Employment 1935-1937": File Domestic Workers 1937, National Archives and Records Administration (hereafter NARA).

5. O'Leary, *From Morning to Night*, 29–30.

6. Ibid., 29.

7. Parker, *Idella*, 36; Parker, *From Reddick to Cross Creek*, 106.

8. McIntosh and Zey, "Women as Gatekeepers," 317–19. See also Dudden, *Serving Women*, 136.

9. Southern women were part of a national trend that began in the late eighteenth and early nineteenth centuries in the urban Northeast. See Lubar, "Men/Women/Production/Consumption," 9.

10. Jones & Willaford Grocery Account Book, p. 318, Middle Georgia Archives, Washington Memorial Library, Bibb County Library, Macon, Ga. (hereafter MGA).

11. "Beating Her Employer," *Atlanta Constitution*, February 26, 1885.

12. Thomas, *Secret Eye*, 445.

13. Tucker, *Telling Memories*, 134. See Procida, "Feeding the Imperial Appetite," 137, for a comparison with British India.

14. Moncure, *Emma Jane's Souvenir Cook Book*, 8.

15. Ibid., 9.

16. Tucker, *Telling Memories*, 51.

17. Kytle, *Willie Mae*, 200.

18. Angelou, *Hallelujah!*, 46.

19. *Tyler Journal*, October 23, 1925, p. 5; Piggly Wiggly LLC, "Where It Began."

20. Charles Spurgeon Johnson, *Patterns of Negro Segregation*, 64–65. White housewives also bought food from itinerant peddlers, both African American and white, and from curb markets sponsored by rural cooperatives. Little evidence exists that African American cooks went to the curb markets, but it is conceivable that they would have dealt with the peddlers, who came directly to the house. Their purchasing power would have depended greatly on the amount of trust that their employers gave them. For a discussion of urban women's buying habits, see Sharpless, "'She Ought to Taken Those Cakes.'" An Office of War Information photograph taken in Washington, D.C., in 1942 shows an African American cook speaking with a grocery deliveryman, indicating interaction with the marketplace that came to prosperous white homes (LC-USW3-054160-D).

21. DuBois, *Negro American Family*, 66.

22. Diary of Jennie Akehurst Lines, October 29, 1871, Akehurst-Lines Collection, Box 3, October 17–November 3, 1871, Hargrett Library, University of Georgia, Athens.

23. Weiner, *Mistresses and Slaves*, 213. In South Africa under apartheid in the 1970s, employers denied employees the use of vacuum cleaners (Cock, *Maids and Madams*, 24–25).

24. Tera Hunter, *To 'Joy My Freedom*, 55. See Cole, "Servants and Slaves," 125–28, for a discussion of antebellum cooking technology, and Censer, *Reconstruction of White Southern Womanhood*, 78–80, for the transition from fireplaces to stoves after the Civil War. See Cowan, *More Work for Mother*, 53–62, for a general discussion of nineteenth-century stoves.

25. "In Everyday Life," *Dallas Morning News*, September 28, 1911.

26. "Rescuers Badly Burned," *Dallas Morning News*, November 12, 1906. See also "Girl Fearfully Burned," *Dallas Morning News*, March 31, 1900; "Burns Fatal to Negress," *Dallas Morning News*, April 30, 1909; "Cook Fatally Burned; Poured Oil in Stove," *Atlanta Constitution*, July 1, 1910.

27. Henderson, "'Ace of Clubs,'" 79; Cowan, *More Work for Mother*, 129–30. Newspapers in Texas noted the creation of ice plants in the 1880s in medium-sized towns such as Denison and San Angelo ("The State Capital," *Dallas Morning News*, February 24, 1886; "Denison," *Dallas Morning News*, March 8, 1886). The distribution of ice was apparently uneven, however. An 1890s Virginia cookbook included a hint to "keep fish or beefsteak overnight when you have no ice": wrap it in cloth soaked in vinegar (*Handy Housekeeping*, 113).

28. Cowan, *More Work for Mother*, 93; Enstam, *Women and the Creation of Urban Life*, 137; "Corsicana Cullings," *Dallas Morning News*, October 15, 1885; "Fort Worth Affairs," *Dallas Morning News*, October 8, 1885; "The News from Waco," *Dallas Morning News*, October 17, 1885; personal conversation with Kenneth Hafertepe, July 2008.

29. In estimating a family's wealth and its ability to employ a domestic worker, I determined each husband's occupation through the city directories published annually in Macon, beginning with *Sholes' Directory of the City of Macon*, 1878. Like Macon, Tyler represents an ordinary southern town, away from the state capitals and coastal areas.

30. Hall, "Food Crops"; Hall, "Africa," 29. For discussions of the diaspora of African foods along with African people, see Spivey, *Peppers, Cracklings*; Jessica B. Harris, *Welcome Table*; Jessica B. Harris, *Iron Pots*; Jessica B. Harris, *Africa Cookbook*; and Opie, *Hog and Hominy*, chaps. 1, 2, and 3.

31. Ferris, *Matzoh Ball Gumbo*, 235; O'Leary, *From Morning to Night*, 2; Patterson, *Mammy Lou*, 202.

32. For a basic introduction to grain and its cookery, see Sokolov, *With the Grain*.

33. Jones & Willaford Grocery Account Book, p. 162: Mrs. Sal Waxelbaum; p. 198: Mrs. Wm. H. Ross; p. 240: Mrs. R. M. Seymour; p. 318: Mrs. N. M. Block, MGA.

34. *Lone Star Cook Book*, 68; Eustis, *Cooking in Old Creole Days*, 53; Gibson, *Mrs. Charles H. Gibson's Maryland and Virginia Cook Book*, 17; Glover, *Warm Springs Receipt-Book*, 214; Patterson, *Mammy Lou*, 172.

35. Moncure, *Emma Jane's Souvenir Cook Book*, 14–17.

36. McCulloch-Williams, *Dishes and Beverages of the Old South*, 31; Vaughn, *Culinary Echoes from Dixie*, 126; Patterson, *Mammy Lou*, 162–63.

37. Eustis, *Cooking in Old Creole Days*, 52.

38. McKinney, *Aunt Caroline's Dixieland Recipes*, 7.

39. Patterson, *Mammy Lou*, 174.

40. *Household Manual and Practical Cook Book*, 294, 309, 310, 316, 318.

41. Gibson, *Mrs. Charles H. Gibson's Maryland and Virginia Cook Book*; McPhail, *F.F.V. Receipt Book*, 286; *Housekeeping in Alabama*; Knoxville Woman's Building Association, *Knoxville Cook Book*, unpaged advertising; Vaughn, *Culinary Echoes from Dixie*; *Story of a Pantry Shelf*, 189–91.

42. Rawlings, *Cross Creek Cookery*, 21–22; Eva Davis, *Mississippi Mixin's*, 95; Warren, *Art of Southern Cooking*, 135; Breckinridge, *From Soup to Nuts*, 13; Glover, *Warm Springs Receipt-Book*, 211; *Guild Cook Book*, 47; Lustig, Sondheim, and Rensel, *Southern Cook Book*, 33.

43. Mary Stuart Harrison Smith, *Virginia Cookery-Book*, 8; Moncure, *Emma Jane's Souvenir Cook Book*, 14; Patterson, *Mammy Lou*, 166–67. Fox, *Blue Grass Cook Book*, has two photographs demonstrating the use of a machine for making beaten biscuits (facing pages 216 and 224). Doris Witt discusses at length Howard Weeden's poems "Beaten Biscuit" and "The Old Biscuit Block" in *Black Hunger*, 54–56 and 62.

44. Sanders, *Dori Sanders' Country Cooking*, xiii, 147.

45. Patterson, *Mammy Lou*, 170; Young Men's Christian Association, *Old Virginia Cook Book*, 85; *Selected Southern Recipes*, 45; Eustis, *Cooking in Old Creole Days*, 56.

46. McCulloch-Williams, *Dishes and Beverages of the Old South*, 33; Smitherman, *Louisiana Plantation Cook Book*, 109.

47. Porter, *Mrs. Porter's New Southern Cookery Book*, 165.

48. Moncure, *Emma Jane's Souvenir Cook Book*, 11–12. In the first years of Reconstruction, white housewives moaned over their freed cooks' inability to make "light bread." Frances Elizabeth Greer King, a new boardinghouse keeper in Athens, Georgia, wailed to her diary in 1866, "I have suffered so much today in mind my cook cant or wont make bread we can eat, cooks meat just as well as I wish her to but we cant eat her bread, what must I do I am in much trouble, bless me O my father and help me" (King Diary, August 12, 1866, Hargrett Library, University of Georgia, Athens).

49. *Housekeeping in Alabama*, 141.

50. *Story of a Pantry Shelf*, 99–102; Morgan, "Mammy the Huckster," 99–100, 102.

51. Tyree, *Housekeeping in Old Virginia*, 20.

52. *Handy Housekeeping*; *Housekeeping in Alabama*; Young Men's Christian Association, *Old Virginia Cook Book*; Gibson, *Mrs. Charles H. Gibson's Maryland and Virginia Cook Book*; Central Presbyterian Church, *Southern Housekeeper*, [146]; *Tyler Daily Courier*, March 18, 1902.

53. Central Presbyterian Church, *Southern Housekeeper*, [44]; Stone, *Roanoke Cook Book*; *Tyler Daily Courier*, April 21, 1902; Knoxville Woman's Building Association, *Knoxville Cook Book*; *Tyler Daily Courier Times*, November 27, 1918.

54. *Tyler Morning Telegraph*, April 7, 1934; "Light Crust Doughboys," Handbook of Texas Online.

55. *Housekeeping in Alabama*, 141–42. Harland's instructions are voluminous and detailed. See Harland, *Common Sense*, 256–61. For Harland's description of learning to bake bread, see Harland, *Marion Harland's Autobiography*, 333–45.

56. Gwaltney, *Drylongso*, 145–46.

57. *Tyler National Index*, September 23, 1880.

58. Knoxville Woman's Building Association, *Knoxville Cook Book*.

59. Cleora Butler, *Cleora's Kitchens*, 29.

60. Stone, *Roanoke Cook Book*.

61. *Tyler Morning Telegraph*, April 7, 1934.

62. Jones & Willaford Grocery Account Book, pp. 178–79: Mrs. Chas. Wachtel, MGA; U.S. Census, 1880, Bibb County, Georgia.

63. Jones & Willaford Grocery Account Book, pp. 166–67: Mrs. Floyd Ross, MGA; U.S. Census, 1900, Bibb County, Georgia.

64. Mary Stuart Harrison Smith, *Virginia Cookery-Book*, 27.

65. O'Leary, *From Morning to Night*, 78, 107.

66. Flexner, *Dixie Dishes*, 13–14; Ethel Farmer Hunter, *Secrets of Southern Cooking*, 2; Parker, *From Reddick to Cross Creek*, 95.

67. Mary Stuart Harrison Smith, *Virginia Cookery-Book*, 16.

68. *Housekeeping in Alabama*, 115. The quotation by the Alabama author, from Harland, *Common Sense*, 299, is accurate.

69. *Handy Housekeeping*; *Housekeeping in Alabama*; Vaughn, *Culinary Echoes from Dixie*; McPhail, *F.F.V. Receipt Book*, 278; Cringan, *Instruction in Cooking*.

70. For example, Central Presbyterian Church, *Southern Housekeeper*, [147]; *Handy Housekeeping*; Young Men's Christian Association, *Old Virginia Cook Book*; Gibson, *Mrs. Charles H. Gibson's Maryland and Virginia Cook Book*; and Boston Historical Society and Museum, "Sweet History."

71. *Household Manual and Practical Cook Book*, 292, 297, 326.

72. Hess, *South Carolina Rice Kitchen*, 76–77; Patterson, *Mammy Lou*, 219.

73. Patterson, *Mammy Lou*, 218–19, 227.

74. McKinney, *Aunt Caroline's Dixieland Recipes*, 111.

75. Flexner, *Dixie Dishes*, 115.

76. Ibid., 115.

77. Augusta, Ga., Second Presbyterian Church, *Choice Recipes*, 89.

78. McKinney, *Aunt Caroline's Dixieland Recipes*, 47.

79. Hervey, "Saints in My Kitchen," 368. Although Hervey likely lived in New York at this time, I have taken the liberty of including this story because it demonstrates the abilities of a woman who almost surely grew up in the South.

80. *[Cookbook] Compiled by the Woman's Club of South Jacksonville*, 87; Patterson, *Mammy Lou*, 206. See also McKinney, *Aunt Caroline's Dixieland Recipes*, 105.

81. Moncure, *Emma Jane's Souvenir Cook Book*, 10; Warren, *Art of Southern Cooking*, 198.

82. Patterson, *Mammy Lou*, 207.

83. Ibid., 210.

84. Ibid., 202.

85. Moncure, *Emma Jane's Souvenir Cook Book*, 10.

86. Studio, Charleston, S.C., *Charleston Recipes*, 9; Patterson, *Mammy Lou*, 234.

87. Patterson, *Mammy Lou*, 217.

88. *Houston Civic Club Cook Book*, 20. See also Flexner, *Dixie Dishes*, 61–62.

89. Patterson, *Mammy Lou*, 236.

90. Ibid.

91. Ibid., 233. See also Cleora Butler, *Cleora's Kitchens*, 69, 70.

92. Moncure, *Emma Jane's Souvenir Cook Book*, 35.

93. Patterson, *Mammy Lou*, 234; *Guild Cook Book* (Abingdon), 75–76.

94. For a general history of meat consumption in the United States, see Horowitz, *Putting Meat on the Table*.

95. King Meat Market Ledgers, MGA, Folder 1 1888–90, primarily pp. 17–18: Mrs. A. P. Tennille; pp. 33–34: Miss H. C. Tracy; pp. 57–58: Mrs. Dr. Walker; pp. 179–80: Mrs. T. Guernsey; p. 190: Mrs. G. B. Dettre; and Folder 2 1891–95, primarily p. 21: Mrs. J. C. Curd; pp. 27–28: Mrs. G. B. Dettre; pp. 29–30: Mrs. W. E. Dunwoody; pp. 153–54: Mrs. Joe Dasher, Mrs. Willie Cornell; p. 214: Mrs. J. T. Callaway.

96. *Tyler National Index*, May 20, 1880, p. 3.

97. *Household Manual and Practical Cook Book*, 312.

98. McPhail, *F.F.V. Receipt Book*, 282.

99. Gibson, *Mrs. Charles H. Gibson's Maryland and Virginia Cook Book*; *Housekeeping in Alabama*.

100. *Guild Cook Book* (Abingdon); *Tyler Daily Courier Times*, May 19, 1926.

101. *Tyler Journal*, June 19, 1925.

102. Young Men's Christian Association, *Old Virginia Cook Book*, 43.

103. Breckinridge, *From Soup to Nuts*, 8.

104. Patterson, *Mammy Lou*, 122–23.

105. Parker, *Idella*, 83.

106. Ibid., 69.

107. Williams-Forson, *Building Houses Out of Chicken Legs*.

108. Jones & Willaford Grocery Account Book, MGA, p. 144: Mrs. A. W. Earnest; p. 162: Mrs. Sal Waxelbaum; p. 165: Mrs. Jas. L. Anderson; pp. 166–67: Mrs. Floyd Ross; pp. 172–73: Mrs. Sal Hoge; pp. 174–75: Mrs. E. D. Cherry; p. 176: Mrs. F. A. Daugherty; pp. 178–79: Mrs. Chas. Wachtel; pp. 188–89: Mrs. A. Chambers; p. 190: Mrs. Jno. R. Courtney; p. 198: Mrs. Wm. H. Ross; p. 200: Mrs. Sam Altmayer; pp. 202–3: Mrs. W. T. Ross; p. 210: Mrs. Shinholser; p. 212: Mrs. Joe Bond; p. 213: Mrs. William Wolff; p. 226: Mrs. J. H. Ray; p. 227: Mrs. T. M. Butner; p. 229: Mrs. Evans; p. 232: Mrs. W. B. Sparks; p. 235: Mrs. J. W. Wilcox; p. 237: Mrs. B. Ohlman; p. 239: Mrs. J. W. Robert; p. 240: Mrs. R. M. Seymour; pp. 254–55: Mrs. James H. Smith; p. 256: Mrs. J. B. McNiece; p. 315: Mrs. P. W. Edge; p. 323: Mrs. H. Newman; p. 324: Mrs. Popper; p. 332: Mrs. M. Nussbaum; p. 366: Mrs. L. Wyche.

109. Pringle, *Woman Rice Planter*, 173, 183, 186, 197.

110. Rawlings, *Cross Creek Cookery*, 102–3.

111. While Idella Parker did the vast majority of cooking at Cross Creek in the 1940s, Mickens tended and killed the poultry and cared for the cows. See Tarr, *Private Marjorie*, 102, 110, 158, 222, 281, 295, 419, 420.

112. Williams-Forson, *Building Houses Out of Chicken Legs*, 3.

113. Le Guin, *Home-Concealed Woman*, 57.

114. Parker, *Idella*, 71.

115. Central Presbyterian Church, *Southern Housekeeper*, opposite fish page. A 1938

photograph from the National Archives shows six African American women plucking chickens in a St. Louis industrial setting. The women, dressed in white with rubber boots and white headpieces, stand side by side while the chickens dangle before them at head height. A V-shaped rack with dozens of plucked chickens stands nearby (Jones, *Labor of Love*, 46).

116. *Tyler Morning Telegraph*, April 7, 1934; *Tyler Morning Telegraph*, May 19, 1934.

117. John T. Edge, director of the Southern Foodways Alliance, declines to determine the origins of fried chicken. He notes that frying in deep oil probably has West African antecedents, then says, "Perhaps it will suffice to observe that, in the eighteenth century—while cooking for and sometimes under the direction of white slaveholders—women of African descent honed a dish we now know as fried chicken. And then just leave it at that" (Edge, *Fried Chicken*, 55).

118. Kytle, *Willie Mae*, 208.

119. Vaughn, *Culinary Echoes from Dixie*, 60.

120. *Recipes of the Deep South*, 106–7. See also Sanders, *Dori Sanders' Country Cooking*, 2, 10.

121. Marion Brown, *Southern Cook Book*, 132.

122. Marion Brown, *Marion Brown's Southern Cook Book*, 221–22.

123. Patterson, *Mammy Lou*, 98; Eustis, *Cooking in Old Creole Days*, 31.

124. Sanders, *Dori Sanders' Country Cooking*, 70–71.

125. Moncure, *Emma Jane's Souvenir Cook Book*, 8.

126. Jones & Willaford Grocery Account Book, MGA, p. 162: Mrs. Sal Waxelbaum; pp. 172–73: Mrs. Sal Hoge; pp. 178–79: Mrs. Chas. Wachtel; p. 324: Mrs. Popper; p. 332: Mrs. M. Nussbaum.

127. Patterson, *Mammy Lou*, 106.

128. Eustis, *Cooking in Old Creole Days*, 30–31.

129. Plant Family Reminiscences by "Mrs. Ross (Martha Plant)," 2, Southern Oral History Project, Southern Historical Collection, University of North Carolina at Chapel Hill; Patterson, *Mammy Lou*, 110; Warren, *Art of Southern Cooking*, 107.

130. Watriss, "It's Something Inside You," 137.

131. Pringle, *Woman Rice Planter*, 14–15.

132. Cleora Butler, *Cleora's Kitchens*, 53.

133. King Meat Market Ledgers, MGA, Folder 1 1888–90, primarily pp. 17–18: Mrs. A. P. Tennille; p. 20: Mrs. Floyd Ross; pp. 21–22: Mrs. A. G. Butts; pp. 31–32: Mrs. J. L. Cook; pp. 33–34: Miss H. C. Tracy; pp. 57–58: Mrs. Dr. Walker; p. 190: Mrs. G. B. Dettre; and Folder 2 1891–95, primarily p. 21: Mrs. J. C. Curd; pp. 29–30: Mrs. W. E. Dunwoody; pp. 125–26: Mrs. J. L. Cook; pp. 153–54: Mrs. Joe Dasher; p. 214: Mrs. J. T. Callaway.

134. McKinney, *Aunt Caroline's Dixieland Recipes*, 71, 79.

135. Eustis, *Cooking in Old Creole Days*, 35.

136. Ibid., 5.

137. Mary Stuart Harrison Smith, *Virginia Cookery-Book*, 31.

138. Logue, *Oral Memoirs*, 12–13, The Texas Collection, Baylor University, Waco, Texas; *Atlanta Constitution*, November 16, 1889; *Tyler Daily Courier*, April 12, 1902; "Stray Cows to Bring Money," *Atlanta Constitution*, July 5, 1902; *Atlanta Constitution*, January 8, 1913; *Atlanta Constitution*, May 16, 1926; Welty, "Little Store," 639.

139. Van Zelm, "On the Front Lines of Freedom," 213; Kytle, *Willie Mae*, 25; Pringle, *Woman Rice Planter*, 313. Shortly after the Civil War, a Ku Klux Klan member complained that his "colored servant woman" refused to milk his cow when it rained. He griped, "She would not do it; she thought that thing was 'played out,' and that I must go and milk the cow myself" (Rio, "From Feudal Serfs to Independent Contractors," 32–33).

140. Sanders, *Dori Sanders' Country Cooking*, 33.

141. *Household Manual and Practical Cook Book*, 295; Jones & Willaford Grocery Account Book, MGA.

142. *Tyler Evening Democrat-Reporter*, October 14, 1891.

143. "Milk Supply Depends on Dairymen Uniting on the Marketing of Product," *Tyler Daily Courier Times*, November, 15, 1918; *Calvary Church Circle Cook Book*, 34.

144. Jones & Willaford Grocery Account Book, MGA, p. 144: Mrs. A. W. Earnest; pp. 172–73: Mrs. Sal Hoge; pp. 174–75: Mrs. E. D. Cherry; p. 176: Mrs. F. A. Daugherty; p. 182: Mrs. A. W. Bramion; pp. 202–3: Mrs. W. T. Ross; p. 210: Mrs. Shinholser; p. 229: Mrs. Evans; p. 237: Mrs. B. Ohlman; pp. 260: Mrs. J. M. W. Christian; p. 321: Mrs. L. Wyche; Cringan, *Instruction in Cooking*.

145. *Story of a Pantry Shelf*, 147–50.

146. Pringle, *Woman Rice Planter*, 14, 298.

147. *Household Manual and Practical Cook Book*, 301; Young Men's Christian Association, *Old Virginia Cook Book*; Cringan, *Instruction in Cooking*, unpaged ads; Stone, *Roanoke Cook Book*. See Kirby, *Mockingbird Song*, 192–94, on late-nineteenth-century oyster harvesting in Chesapeake Bay.

148. Central Presbyterian Church, *Southern Housekeeper*, unpaged ad opposite beginning of fish chapter.

149. Jones & Willaford Grocery Account Book, MGA, pp. 172–73: Mrs. Sal Hoge; pp. 178–79: Mrs. Chas. Wachtel; pp. 213: Mrs. William Wolff.

150. Cleora Butler, *Cleora's Kitchens*, 48–49. Butler was also very impressed by McIntyre's generosity in addition to his culinary daring. When the guests ate all of the trout, leaving no leftovers for the servants, McIntyre ordered another dozen trout just for the disappointed employees.

151. Eustis, *Cooking in Old Creole Days*, 28.

152. Patterson, *Mammy Lou*, 24. Worcestershire sauce from the Lea and Perrins Company of England was first imported into the United States in 1839 (Lea & Perrins, "About Lea & Perrins"). Tabasco sauce came from the McIlhenny Company of Avery Island, Louisiana, beginning in 1868 (McIlhenny Company, "History of McIlhenny Company and Tabasco").

153. Patterson, *Mammy Lou*, 29.

154. Ibid., 143–44.

155. Stone, *Roanoke Cook Book*, 10.

156. *Coastal Cookery*, 57.

157. Patterson, *Mammy Lou*, 39–40.

158. Parker, *Idella*, 70.

159. Patterson, *Mammy Lou*, 31.

160. Ibid., 36.

161. Ibid., 160.

162. Ibid., 160–61.

163. Ibid., 9, 14.

164. Eustis, *Cooking in Old Creole Days*, 4–5, 21.

165. Wilson, *Tested Recipe Cook Book*, n.p.; Central Presbyterian Church, *Southern Housekeeper*, opposite soup page.

166. Weiner, *Mistresses and Slaves*, 210; Clark-Lewis, *Living In, Living Out*, 65.

167. *Tyler Evening Democrat-Reporter*, October 14, 1891.

168. Jones & Willaford Grocery Account Book, MGA, p. 144: Mrs. A. W. Earnest; p. 162: Mrs. Sal Waxelbaum; pp. 166–67: Mrs. Floyd Ross; pp. 172–73: Mrs. Sal Hoge; p. 198: Mrs. Wm. H. Ross; p. 200: Mrs. Sam Altmayer; pp. 202–3: Mrs. W. T. Ross; p. 210: Mrs. Shinholser; p. 212: Mrs. Joe Bond; p. 213: Mrs. William Wolff; p. 226: Mrs. J. H. Ray; p. 229: Mrs. Evans; p. 230: Mrs. Dr. Winchester; p. 232: Mrs. W. B. Sparks; p. 233: Mrs. J. W. Hooks; p. 235: Mrs. J. W. Wilcox; p. 237: Mrs. B. Ohlman; p. 239: Mrs. J. W. Roberts; p. 240: Mrs. R. M. Seymour; p. 246: Mrs. J. H. Ray; pp. 250–51: Mrs. Floyd Ross; p. 256: Mrs. J. B. McNiece; p. 258: Mrs. Dr. Winchester; p. 260: Mrs. J. M. W. Christian; pp. 262–63: Mrs. Floyd Ross; p. 266: Mrs. J. W. Hooks; p. 267: Mrs. Evans; p. 315: Mrs. P W. Edge; p. 381: Mrs. Shinholser; p. 387: Mrs. Shinholser; pp. 174–75: Mrs. E. D. Cherry; p. 176: Mrs. F. A. Daugherty; pp. 178–79: Mrs. Chas. Wachtel; p. 180: Mrs. C. T. Chappell; pp. 188–89: Mrs. A. Chambers; p. 190: Mrs. Jno. R. Courtney; pp. 192–93: Mrs. J. B. McNiece; pp. 254–55: Mrs. James H. Smith; p. 321: Mrs. L. Wyche; p. 322: Mrs. Thorner; p. 323: Mrs. H. Newman; p. 324: Mrs. Popper; p. 332: Mrs. M. Nussbaum; p. 373: Mrs. P W. Edge; p. 379: Mrs. P. W. Edge.

169. See, for example, *Handy Housekeeping*; Stone, *Roanoke Cook Book*; *Tyler Morning Telegraph*, May 19, 1934; *Tyler Semi-Weekly Courier-Times*, October 26, 1909; *Tyler Semi-Weekly Courier-Times*, November 13, 1909; *Tyler Semi-Weekly Courier-Times*, July 28, 1906.

170. *Tyler Morning Telegraph*, April 7, 1934; *Tyler Morning Telegraph*, May 19, 1934.

171. *Housekeeping in Alabama*.

172. Cringan, *Instruction in Cooking*.

173. Knoxville Woman's Building Association, *Knoxville Cook Book*.

174. *Calvary Church Circle Cook Book*, 32.

175. Parker, *Idella*, 71.

176. Moncure, *Emma Jane's Souvenir Cookbook*, 28, 29.

177. Patterson, *Mammy Lou*, 77.

178. McKinney, *Aunt Caroline's Dixieland Recipes*, 143; Rawlings, *Cross Creek Cookery*, 183; Warren, *Art of Southern Cooking*, 59.

179. Council, *Mama Dip's Kitchen*, 22.

180. Villas, *My Mother's Southern Kitchen*, 142.

181. Jones & Willaford Grocery Account Book, MGA, p. 144: Mrs. A. W. Earnest; p. 162: Mrs. Sal Waxelbaum; p. 165: Mrs. Jas. L. Anderson; pp. 166–67 Mrs. Floyd Ross; pp. 172–73: Mrs. Sal Hoge; pp. 174–75: Mrs. E. D. Cherry; p. 176: Mrs. F. A. Daugherty; pp. 178–79: Mrs. Chas. Wachtel; p. 180: Mrs. C. T. Chappell; pp. 188–89: Mrs. A. Chambers; p. 190: Mrs. Jno. R. Courtney; pp. 192–93: Mrs. J. B. McNiece; p. 198: Mrs. Wm. H. Ross; p. 200: Mrs. Sam Altmayer; pp. 202–3: Mrs. W. T. Ross; p. 210: Mrs. Shinholser; p. 212: Mrs. Joe Bond; p. 213: Mrs. William Wolff; p. 226: Mrs. J. H. Ray; p. 229:

Mrs. Evans; p. 230: Mrs. Dr. Winchester; p. 232: Mrs. W. B. Sparks; p. 233: Mrs. J. W. Hooks; p. 235: Mrs. J. W. Wilcox; p. 237: Mrs. B. Ohlman; p. 239: Mrs. J. W. Roberts; pp. 254–55: Mrs. James H. Smith; Jones and Willaford: 260: Mrs. J. M. W. Christian; p. 315: Mrs. P. W. Edge; p. 321: Mrs. L. Wyche; p. 322: Mrs. Thorner; p. 324: Mrs. Popper; p. 332: Mrs. M. Nussbaum. See also *Tyler Daily Courier*, March 18, 1902.

182. *Story of a Pantry Shelf*, 48, 103.

183. Cleora Butler, *Cleora's Kitchens*, 76.

184. Haynes, "Negroes in Domestic Service," 411.

185. Patterson, *Mammy Lou*, 177–78.

186. Ibid., 179.

187. Ibid., 194–95.

188. Ibid., 195–96.

189. For comments on the modernity of salads in the 1920s, see Timlin, *Sandwiches, Salads and Desserts*, unpaged foreword.

190. McKinney, *Aunt Caroline's Dixieland Recipes*, 83.

191. Dull, *Southern Cooking*, 286.

192. Cleora Butler, *Cleora's Kitchens*, 70.

193. Tucker, *Telling Memories*, 134.

194. Patterson, *Mammy Lou*, 248, 249; Pringle, *Woman Rice Planter*, 366; Cleora Butler, *Cleora's Kitchens*, 69.

195. Gibson, *Mrs. Charles H. Gibson's Maryland and Virginia Cook Book*.

196. ACH Food Companies, "Durkee Famous Sauce."

197. Mitchell, introduction to Eustis, *Cooking in Old Creole Days*, xiii.

198. Parker, *Idella*, 27–28; Parker, *From Reddick to Cross Creek*, 90.

199. Ferris, *Matzoh Ball Gumbo*, 235.

200. Bentley, *Eating for Victory*, 62.

201. Clark-Lewis, *Living In, Living Out*, 3.

202. Knoxville Woman's Building Association, *Knoxville Cook Book*, 14–15.

203. Rawlings, *Cross Creek Cookery*, 97, 206. Meals at Cross Creek were in fact elaborate affairs. In 1944, Rawlings detailed the menu for a weekend with four guests, prepared by Idella Parker: Friday dinner: baked sherried grapefruit, roast venison, wild rice, creamed scalloped celery, braised onions, wine jelly, tangerine sherbet, fruit cake, and coffee; Saturday breakfast: orange juice, country sausage and hot cakes, maple syrup, honey, and coffee; Saturday luncheon: egg croquettes, beets in orange sauce, jellied tomato and artichoke salad, biscuits, and Utterly Deadly Pecan Pie; Saturday night: consommé, broiled chicken, stuffed potatoes, carrot soufflé, celery hearts, cranberry jelly, frozen custard and mangoes, and coffee; Sunday breakfast: orange juice, sautéed lamb kidneys and mushrooms, toast, marmalade, and coffee; Sunday dinner (likely the midday meal): tomato bouillon, roast loin of pork, baked sweet potatoes, succotash, green beans, spring onions, corn muffins, pumpkin pie with whipped cream, and coffee. Parker did receive an entire weekend off from work in return for her labors. For another dinner for three guests, which Rawlings described as "all right but nothing superb," Parker prepared cold turkey, scalloped oysters, fried stuffing patties, broccoli with Hollandaise (neither done to Rawlings's taste), muffins, jelly, celery, radishes, onions, and banana ice cream

and orange cake (Tarr, *Private Marjorie*, 230–31, 238, 253). For other Parker-Rawlings menus, see Tarr, *Private Marjorie*, 259, 273, 274, 294, 296, 369, 384.

204. Buttenheim, "Shared Sensuality," 77, 79.

205. Cleora Butler, *Cleora's Kitchens*, 51.

206. Ferris, *Matzoh Ball Gumbo*, 111. See also Enstam, *Women and the Creation of Urban Life*, 48. Employers' efforts in the kitchen could also create cleaning headaches for their cooks. Marjorie Kinnan Rawlings once left the pits from dates that she used to make stuffed dates on the kitchen counter for ten days while awaiting Idella Parker's return to Cross Creek (Tarr, *Private Marjorie*, 222).

207. Similar situations existed between English women and their Indian servants during the Raj. See Procida, "Feeding the Imperial Appetite," 123–24, 125, 127, 128, 130.

208. O'Leary, *From Morning to Night*, 83. For an explication of Western table rituals, see Visser, *Rituals of Dinner*. For a discussion of dinnerware, see Blaszcyk, "Cinderella Stories."

209. O'Leary, *From Morning to Night*, 110.

210. Hunt, *I Am Annie Mae*, 68.

Chapter Three

1. Letter from Roxanna Hupes to Mr. President Rosevelt [*sic*], December 12, 1938, Record Group 86, Women's Bureau, Office of the Director, General Correspondence of the Women's Bureau, 1919–48 (hereafter RG 86), Box 292, "Domestic Workers Household Employment 1936–1939": File 1938 H, National Archives and Records Administration (hereafter NARA).

2. Kuhn, Joye, and West, *Living Atlanta*, 113, 118.

3. Mary Anderson, "Plight of Negro Domestic Labor," 66. See also Coser, "Servants," 32. Alma McLain Coleman Brown was not African American, but she nonetheless experienced the difficulty of working under indefinite conditions. She and her husband, Claud, went as newlyweds to work in the home of the novelist Corra Harris in January 1919. By the end of March, "Mrs. H." had changed the rules of engagement, and Brown grew frustrated: "Mrs. H. would have breakfast at 7:30 sometime when we had been having it at 8:00 by old time. I don't know her motive but she is trying me for some reason. I've never worked so hard. She said a week or two ago that she wouldn't require any one to get up before daylight[,] now when I am not well and need rest she requires me to have breakfast at 6:00 sometime. I have to get up before five which is before day to do this." Later that afternoon, Harris came to their room to sit but made a point to say, "I have no conscience about a person's job when I hire them. I pay them and they must do everything I demand of them and that will be a plenty I tell you" (Alma McLain Coleman Brown Diary, March 24, 1919, Harris Papers, Ms. 734, Box 101, Hargrett Library, University of Georgia, Athens).

4. Katznelson, *When Affirmative Action Was White*, 33.

5. Fleming, *Documentary History of Reconstruction*, 1:304.

6. Letter from Mrs. Katherine Rutherford to Mr. President Roosevelt, July 15, 1933, RG 86, Box 289, "Domestic Workers Household Employment 1933": File 1933 R, NARA.

7. Letter from L. G. Huff to Mrs. Franklin D. Rosevelt [*sic*], January 5, 1937, RG 86, Box 291, "Domestic Workers Household Employment 1935–1937": File Domestic Workers 1937, NARA.

8. O'Leary, *From Morning to Night*, 83, 107, 111.

9. Linsley, "Main House, Carriage House," 33.

10. Parker, *Idella*, 40.

11. For white women's complaints about tardy cooks, see Thomas, *Secret Eye*, 358, and Woofter, *Negroes of Athens*, 62.

12. Tucker, *Telling Memories*, 154.

13. Kuhn, Joye, and West, *Living Atlanta*, 119.

14. Ruth Reed, *Negro Women of Gainesville*, 16, 28, 30. See also Fleming, "Servant Problem," 6.

15. Woofter, *Negroes of Athens*, 46–48.

16. Letter from L. G. Huff to Mrs. Franklin D. Rosevelt [*sic*], January 5, 1937, RG 86, Box 291, "Domestic Workers Household Employment 1935–1937": File Domestic Workers 1937, NARA.

17. Letter from Mrs. Anna Smith to Mrs. Franklin D. Roosevelt, April 6, 1938, RG 86, Box 292, "Domestic Workers Household Employment 1936–1939": File 1938 S, NARA.

18. Letter from Elizabeth Clyburn to Honorable Mrs. Roosevelt, November 1937, RG 86, Box 291, "Domestic Workers Household Employment 1935–1937": File Domestic Workers 1937, NARA.

19. Tucker, *Telling Memories*, 24–25.

20. Woofter, *Negroes of Athens*, 46–48.

21. Letter from "An Interested Colored Friend" to Frances Perkins, August 23, 19[33], RG 86, Box 289, "Domestic Workers Household Employment 1933": File 1933 Anonymous, NARA.

22. Parker, *Idella*, 69; Parker, *From Reddick to Cross Creek*, 107.

23. Chaplin, "Domestic Service," 104.

24. Romero, "Sisterhood and Domestic Service," 332.

25. Kytle, *Willie Mae*, 187–88.

26. Parker, *From Reddick to Cross Creek*, 107–8. For disappearing before company arrived as a means of resistance by slaves, see Cole, "Servants and Slaves," 245.

27. Parker, *Idella*, 32.

28. Ibid., 80–81.

29. Letter from Nannie Thompson to Frances Perkins, [July 1933], RG 86, Box 289, "Domestic Workers Household Employment 1933": File 1933 T, NARA. See also Tucker, *Telling Memories*, 175–76, and Kytle, *Willie Mae*, 201.

30. Letter from L. G. Huff to Mrs. Franklin D. Rosevelt [*sic*], January 5, 1937, RG 86, Box 291, "Domestic Workers Household Employment 1935–1937": File Domestic Workers 1937, NARA.

31. Elizabeth Johns, *American Genre Painting: The Politics of Everyday Life* (New Haven: Yale University Press, 1991), 105, quoted in Michael D. Harris, *Colored Pictures*, 41.

32. Tucker, *Telling Memories*, 178.

33. Byerly, *Hard Times Cotton Mill Girls*, 90.

34. Towles, *World Turned Upside Down*, 653.

35. Durr, *Outside the Magic Circle*, 13.

36. Clark-Lewis, *Living In, Living Out*, 125.

37. Letter from Miss Mildred Brown to Mrs. Franklin Roosevelt, March 18, 1940, RG 86, Box 293, "Domestic Workers Household Employment 1940": File 1940 A–B, NARA. See also letter from Mrs. Katherine Rutherford to Mr. President Roosevelt, July 15, 1933, RG 86, Box 289, "Domestic Workers Household Employment 1933": File 1933 R, NARA; letter from Mrs. Anna Smith to Mrs. Franklin D. Roosevelt, April 6, 1938, RG 86, Box 292, "Domestic Workers Household Employment 1936–1939": File 1938 S, NARA; letter from Anonymous to Mrs. Jean Collier Brown, July 21, 1938, RG 86, Box 292, "Domestic Workers Household Employment 1936–1939": File 1938 Anonymous, NARA; letter from "The cook" to Mrs. Roosevelt, February 12, 1940, RG 86, Box 292, "Domestic Workers Household Employment 1936–1939": File 1939 Anonymous, NARA; and Clark-Lewis, *Living In, Living Out*, 125, 169, 171–72.

38. Kuhn, Joye, and West, *Living Atlanta*, 118–19.

39. Sterling, *We Are Your Sisters*, 327–28. See also Sutherland, "Special Kind of Problem," 158.

40. Rio, "From Feudal Serfs to Independent Contractors," 27.

41. Weiner, *Mistresses and Slaves*, 197, 198, 205; Tera Hunter, *To 'Joy My Freedom*, 30–31.

42. Clark-Lewis, *Living In, Living Out*, 5. For a comparison with western Europe, see Davidoff, "Mastered," 414–15, and Fairchilds, *Domestic Enemies*, 5, 17.

43. Schreck, "Her Will against Theirs."

44. Clark-Lewis, *Living In, Living Out*, 157.

45. Ibid., 107.

46. Diary of Laura McElwain Jones (Mrs. Samuel Porter Jones), 1892, Jones Papers, Hargrett Library, University of Georgia, Athens.

47. Lewis, *In Their Own Interests*, 13–14.

48. According to sociologist Mary Anderson, writing in 1935, three-fourths of the 81,000 unemployed servants in twelve U.S. cities were African American (Anderson, "Plight of Negro Domestic Labor," 67). In Norfolk during the Great Depression, more than 1,800 domestic workers lost their positions (Lewis, *In Their Own Interests*, 113).

49. Ruth Reed, *Negro Women of Gainesville*, 30.

50. U.S. Census, 1880, Bibb County, Georgia.

51. Sarah Howard, Drury Ave., Macon, Georgia, interview by Annie A. Rose, Macon, pp. 3238–39, Federal Writers' Project Files, Southern Oral History Project, Southern Historical Collection, Box 13, Folder 247, University of North Carolina at Chapel Hill.

52. Bercaw, *Gendered Freedoms*, 115.

53. U.S. Census, 1880, 1900, 1910, 1920, 1930, Bibb County, Georgia.

54. Tucker, *Telling Memories*, 113.

55. Salmon, *Domestic Service*, 89.

56. In 1908, Warren Fleming estimated that the value of food taken away doubled cash wages (Fleming, "Servant Problem," 8). In his 1914 study of African Americans in Athens, Georgia, T. J. Woofter likewise estimated that feeding the cook, giving her leftovers, and paying for wasted food, fuel, and electricity doubled the household expense of having a

cook, from $2.72 cash per week to $5.30, or an annual total of $300.00 (Woofter, *Negroes of Athens*, 46–48). By 1921, in some places, women with higher wages were much less likely to "tote." With more cash available, employers preferred to pay in ways that could be carefully accounted for, rather than in food, which was hard to quantify (Ruth Reed, *Negro Women of Gainesville*, 16, 28, 30).

57. Romero, "Sisterhood and Domestic Service," 332.

58. Ruth Reed, *Negro Women of Gainesville*, 27.

59. Rawlings, *Cross Creek Cookery*, 188.

60. Woofter, *Negroes of Athens*, 47.

61. "Negro Nurse," "More Slavery at the South," 199.

62. Kytle, *Willie Mae*, 62–63.

63. O'Leary, *From Morning to Night*, 112.

64. Clark-Lewis, *Living In, Living Out*, 188.

65. Holtzclaw, *Black Man's Burden*, 18–20.

66. O'Leary, *From Morning to Night*, 115. Mari Evans's 1970 poem "When in Rome" captures a domestic worker's distaste for the foodways of her employer (Evans, *I Am a Black Woman*, 56–57).

67. Ferris, *Matzoh Ball Gumbo*, 16, 174.

68. Charles Camp, *American Foodways*, 71.

69. Parker, *From Reddick to Cross Creek*, 95, 104.

70. Romero, "Sisterhood and Domestic Service," 333.

71. Glenn, "Dialectics of Wage Work," 455.

72. Fleming, "Servant Problem," 14.

73. Kytle, *Willie Mae*, 116–17.

74. Ibid., 140–41.

75. Ibid., 151.

76. Ibid., 239, 240, 241–42. See also Kytle, *Willie Mae*, 106, 143.

77. Wright, *Black Boy*, 24–25.

78. Parker, *Idella*, 90.

79. Tucker, *Telling Memories*, 95–96.

80. Kytle, *Willie Mae*, 113.

81. Ibid., 155–58.

82. Ethel Wright Mohamed, oral history interview by Lu Ann Jones, Belzoni, Mississippi, October 23, 1987, An Oral History of American Agriculture, Archives Center, National Museum of American History, Smithsonian Institution, Washington, D.C. See also Pringle, *Woman Rice Planter*, 342, 344.

83. Tucker, *Telling Memories*, 53. While most domestic workers had little occupational mobility, a few cooks opened their own businesses as caterers and restaurateurs. See Dill, *Across the Boundaries*, 19; Ruth Reed, *Negro Women of Gainesville*, 23–24; Enstam, *Women and the Creation of Urban Life*, 80. Memoirs of domestic workers turned restaurateurs include Council, *Mama Dip's Kitchen*, and Cleora Butler, *Cleora's Kitchens*.

84. Hunt, *I Am Annie Mae*, 79.

85. Woofter, *Negroes of Athens*, 46.

86. Fleming, "Servant Problem," 16–17. See also Salmon, *Domestic Service*, 110.

87. Le Guin, *Home-Concealed Woman*, 203, 205.

88. Woofter, *Negroes of Athens*, 61.

89. Fleming, "Servant Problem," 13.

90. Kousha, "Best Friends," 11–12, 129.

91. Premilla Nadasen ("'Maids' Honor Day'") points out that domestic workers in present-day New York City use buses as sites for organizing labor.

92. Ruth Reed, *Negro Women of Gainesville*, 46–47.

93. Fleming, "Servant Problem," 15.

94. Woofter, *Negroes of Athens*, 45; Fleming, "Servant Problem," 15.

95. "Many Cooks are Menace to Health," *Atlanta Constitution*, September 15, 1912.

96. Ruth Reed, *Negro Women of Gainesville*, 46–47. Robin Kelley ("Not What We Seem," 89) states that such blacklists did in fact exist. The Industrial Workers of the World peaked in membership in 1923.

97. Ruth Reed, *Negro Women of Gainesville*, 46–47.

98. Fleming, "Servant Problem," 15–16.

99. Tera Hunter, "'Women Are Asking for BREAD,'" 72.

100. Ruth Reed, *Negro Women of Gainesville*, 46–47.

101. Tera Hunter, "'Women Are Asking for BREAD,'" 72.

102. Lewis, *In Their Own Interests*, 56.

103. Ibid., 56–57.

104. Letter from Mrs. Z. Elizabeth Moman to "Dear Friend," 1933, RG 86, Box 289, "Domestic Workers Household Employment 1933," File 1933, NARA.

105. Jackson, "Negro Woman Domestic Worker," 32–37; letter from Dr. A. G. Smyer to Mary Robinson, December 19, 1935, RG 86, Box 291, "Domestic Workers Household Employment 1935–1937," File 1935 (Domestic Workers of America), NARA.

106. Organizing domestic workers remains challenging into the twenty-first century, as the work of Premilla Nadasen and Eileen Boris points out. See Nadasen, "'Maids' Honor Day,'" and Boris, "Cleaning and Caring for the Welfare State."

107. Jackson, "Negro Woman Domestic Worker," 35, 38.

108. Ibid., 72–73; letter from I. L. Dungy [Dungee], RG 86, Box 293, "Domestic Workers Household Employment 1940": File 1940 C–D, NARA.

109. Jackson, "Negro Woman Domestic Worker," 39, 72.

110. Letter from "A group of Organized Women's [*sic*]" to President Roosevelt, August 24, 1942, RG 86, Box 295, "Domestic Workers Household Employment 1942–1944": File 1942 W–X–Y–Z, NARA.

111. Terborg-Penn, "Survival Strategies," 145–46.

112. Odum, *Race and Rumors of Race*, 73–80; Lewis, *In Their Own Interests*, 191; Simon, "Fearing Eleanor," 83–101; Greene, *Our Separate Ways*, 15–17. In New Orleans, employers feared groups called "Disappointment Clubs" and "Aggravating Clubs" (Gilmore and Wilson, "Employment of Negro Women," 322).

113. Federal Bureau of Investigation report 100-11347, January 25, 1943, Public Broadcasting System, "American Experience/Eleanor Roosevelt/FBI Files—Eleanor Clubs." See also Dowdy, "White Rose Mammy," 310.

114. Tyler, "'Blood on Your Hands,'" 102–5; quotation from Green, "'Where Would the Negro Women Apply,'" 106.

115. Reddy, "Home, Houses, Nonidentity," 363; Chaplin, "Domestic Service," 99.

116. Letter from Annie W. Truitt to Mr. President, 1937, RG 86, Box 291, "Domestic Workers Household Employment 1935–1937": File Domestic Workers 1937, NARA.

117. Letter from (Mrs.) Anna Smith to Mrs. Franklin D. Roosevelt, April 6, 1938, RG 86, Box 292, "Domestic Workers Household Employment 1936–1939": File 1938 S, NARA.

118. Charlotte Hawkins Brown's 1919 novella, *"Mammy": An Appeal to the Heart of the South*, tells the story of a woman who gives her life to her employers only to be severely neglected in her old age.

119. Davidoff et al., *Family Story*, 166.

120. Gwaltney, *Drylongso*, 35.

121. Parker, *From Reddick to Cross Creek*, 142.

122. U.S. Census, 1900, Smith County, Texas, Tyler Ward 1, District 95, sheet 18.

123. Pollan, "Goodman Family," 12.

Chapter Four

1. Letter from Mrs. H. A. Clement, 1805 Pennsylvania Ave. in Baltimore, to Mr. President, December 1939, Record Group 86, Women's Bureau, Office of the Director, General Correspondence of the Women's Bureau, 1919–48 (hereafter RG 86), Box 292, "Domestic Workers Household Employment 1936–1939": File 1939 C–D, National Archives and Records Administration (hereafter NARA).

2. Clark-Lewis, *Living In, Living Out*, 147.

3. hooks, *Yearning*, 46.

4. Ibid., 42, 45.

5. Kytle, *Willie Mae*, 150.

6. Letter from Mrs. Z. Elizabeth Moman to "Dear Friend," 1933, RG 86, Box 289, "Domestic Workers Household Employment (1933)," File 1933, NARA. See also Helmbold, "Making Choices, Making Do," 303.

7. Swann-Wright, *Way Out of No Way*, 65.

8. Clark-Lewis, *Living In, Living Out*, 153.

9. Moody, *Coming of Age*, 36.

10. Neil R. McMillen, *Dark Journey*, 12.

11. Walker, *In Search of Our Mother's Gardens*, 57.

12. Kytle, *Willie Mae*, 121–22.

13. Ibid., 140.

14. Ibid., 236.

15. Parker, *Idella*, 22–25, 37; Parker, *From Reddick to Cross Creek*, 88, 116. See Parker, *Idella*, 48, and Parker, *From Reddick to Cross Creek*, 113, for discussions of the accommodations at Rawlings's beach home.

16. Clark-Lewis, *Living In, Living Out*, 99.

17. Davidoff, "Mastered," 409.

18. Mary V. Robinson, *Domestic Workers*, 31, 34.

19. Clark-Lewis, *Living In, Living Out*, 133, 157.

20. Glenn, *Unequal Freedom*, 106; O'Leary, *From Morning to Night*, 104; Katzman, *Seven Days a Week*, 84.

21. Woofter, *Negroes of Athens*, 11; Fleming, "Servant Problem," 6; Charles Spurgeon Johnson, *Patterns of Negro Segregation*, 10; Lewis, *In Their Own Interests*, 18, 67; Megginson, *African American Life*, 351.

22. Neil R. McMillen, *Dark Journey*, 8. For a moving account of the indignities that African Americans suffered on segregated buses, see Jo Ann Robinson, *Montgomery Bus Boycott*, 32–37.

23. Maclachlan, "Women's Work," 278, 329.

24. Dollard, *Caste and Class*, 3.

25. hooks, *Feminist Theory*, unpaged preface.

26. Clark-Lewis, *Living In, Living Out*, 75.

27. Ruth Reed, *Negro Women in Gainesville*, 14.

28. Letter from Roxanna Hupes to Mr. President Rosevelt [*sic*], December 12, 1938, RG 86, Box 292, "Domestic Workers Household Employment 1936–1939": File 1938 H, NARA.

29. O'Leary, *From Morning to Night*, 104–6.

30. Kytle, *Willie Mae*, 183–84.

31. Letter from G. S. Ellington to Hon. Mr. Franklin D. Roosevelt, June 2, 1937, RG 86, Box 291, "Domestic Workers Household Employment 1935–1937": File Domestic Workers 1937, NARA.

32. Letter from Anonymous to Mrs. Jean Collier Brown, July 21, 1938, RG 86, Box 292, "Domestic Workers Household Employment 1936–1939": File 1938 Anonymous, NARA; letter from Anonymous to Mrs. Roosevelt, October 15, 1941, RG 86, Box 294, "Domestic Workers Household Employment 1941": File 1941 Anonymous, NARA; Mary Anderson, "Plight of Negro Domestic Labor," 68.

33. Clark, *From Fatback to Filet*, 15.

34. Chafe, Gavins, and Korstad, *Remembering Jim Crow*, 132.

35. Clark-Lewis, "'This Work Had a End,'" 205.

36. Judson, "'Leisure Is a Foe to Any Man,'" 95.

37. Somerville, "Domestic Renovations," 239. For a comparison with migrants to Chicago, see Meyerowitz, *Women Adrift*, 73–91.

38. Charlie and Lucinda Robinson, American Life Histories: Manuscripts from the Federal Writers' Project.

39. Clark-Lewis, *Living In, Living Out*, 73. For a study of life in alleys in Washington, D.C., see Borchert, *Alley Life*. In 1880, 51 percent of the women living in alleys in Washington worked as domestics (Borchert, *Alley Life*, 168–69). For a similar study of Galveston, see Beasley, *Alleys and Back Buildings*.

40. Megginson, *African American Life*, 349–50. Borchert traces patterns of ownership and absentee landlords in *Alley Life*, 32 and 36.

41. Rio, "From Feudal Serfs to Independent Contractors," 57.

42. U.S. Census, 1930, Bibb County, Georgia; letter from "A Negro Cook" to President Roosevelt, February 13, 1941, RG 86, Box 294, "Domestic Workers Household Employment 1941": File 1941 Anonymous, NARA.

43. Letter from Elizabeth Clyburn to Honorable Mrs. Roosevelt, November 1937, RG 86, Box 291, "Domestic Workers Household Employment 1935–1937": File Domestic Workers 1937, NARA.

44. Katznelson, *When Affirmative Action Was White*, 33.

45. Katy Brumby, American Life Histories: Manuscripts from the Federal Writers' Project. See also Dollard, *Caste and Class*, 3; Woofter, *Negroes of Athens*, 18; Ruth Reed, *Negro Women of Gainesville*, 15, 16; Eugene Harris, "Physical Condition of the Race," 21; and DuBois, *Negro American Family*, 61.

46. Clark, *From Fatback to Filet*, 7.

47. Kytle, *Willie Mae*, 186.

48. Clark, *From Fatback to Filet*, 54–55.

49. Kytle, *Willie Mae*, 110–11.

50. Ibid., 153.

51. Elwang, "Negroes of Columbia," 50. For a discussion of North Carolina cities, see Logan, *Negro in North Carolina*, 196–200.

52. Censer, *Reconstruction of White Southern Womanhood*, 74.

53. Tera Hunter, *To 'Joy My Freedom*, 187–218; quotation on 195.

54. "How White Plague Scourges Blacks," *Atlanta Constitution*, March 14, 1909. See also Weatherford, *Negro Life in the South*, 7–8.

55. Thomas N. Chase, *Mortality among Negroes*, 13–16.

56. Clark, *From Fatback to Filet*, 58–59.

57. Ruth Reed, *Negro Women of Gainesville*, 16.

58. Katy Brumby, American Life Histories: Manuscripts from the Federal Writers' Project.

59. hooks, *Yearning*, 42.

60. Ibid., 46.

61. Letter from L. G. Huff to Mrs. Franklin D. Rosevelt [*sic*], RG 86, Box 291, "Domestic Workers Household Employment 1935–1937": File Domestic Workers 1937, NARA.

62. Byerly, *Hard Times Cotton Mill Girls*, 36; Kaplan, "'I Don't Do No Windows,'" 99.

63. Charlie and Lucinda Robinson, American Life Histories: Manuscripts from the Federal Writers' Project.

64. Kytle, *Willie Mae*, 194–95. South African women under apartheid said that the skills that they learned in making sweets were of no use to them because they lacked the money to make those items for their own families (Cock, *Maids and Madams*, 56).

65. Eva Davis, *Mississippi Mixin's*, 9.

66. Moody, *Coming of Age*, 34, 43, 45.

67. Joseph E. Smith, "Care of Neglected Children," 41.

68. Ruth Reed, *Negro Women of Gainesville*, 35–36.

69. Dollard, *Caste and Class*, 5.

70. DuBois, *Negro American Family*, 142. This diet differed from that of whites not in basics but in niceties. For example, the wife of Macon merchant B. Ohlford in 1893 bought many of the same items as the African Americans to whom DuBois refers, but she also purchased cinnamon, vanilla, and salmon (Jones & Willaford Grocery Account Book, p. 237, Middle Georgia Archives, Washington Memorial Library, Bibb County Library, Macon, Ga.). Numerous scholars have pointed out the enduring similarities between African American and Anglo food in the South. See, for example, Edge, *Gracious Plenty*, 208–9.

71. Woofter, *Negroes of Athens*, 53.

72. Edwards, *Southern Urban Negro*, 58.

73. DuBois, *Negroes of Farmersville*, 27. By 1930, there were 650 African American–owned grocery stores in nine southern cities, in addition to one poultry dealer, seven produce dealers, thirty-one fish dealers, six bakeries, and twenty-eight meat markets (Edwards, *Southern Urban Negro*, 121).

74. Woofter, *Negroes of Athens*, 50.

75. DuBois, *Negroes of Farmersville*, 27–28.

76. Ruth Reed, *Negro Women of Gainesville*, 30–31.

77. Edwards, *Southern Urban Negro*, 131.

78. Ibid., 58.

79. Clark, *From Fatback to Filet*, 47.

80. Powdermaker, *After Freedom*, 132–33; Ruth Reed, *Negro Women in Gainesville*, 15.

81. Charlie and Lucinda Robinson, American Life Histories: Manuscripts from the Federal Writers' Project.

82. Senate Report 693, February 18, 1880, 397, quoted in Holt, *Making Freedom Pay*, 20.

83. Elwang, "Negroes of Columbia," 25.

84. Woofter, *Negroes of Athens*, 31.

85. Yentsch, "Excavating the South's African American Food History," 76.

86. Rawlings, *Cross Creek Cookery*, 216. Rawlings's comments about "scrappy" food contrast with those of Parker, who recalled Rawlings eating fine foods every night even when she dined alone (Parker, *Idella*, 69).

87. Wright, *Black Boy*, 17.

88. Ladd, "She Walked in Silence," 65, 67, 69.

89. Wright, *Black Boy*, 21.

90. Letter from Doris Willis to President Roosevelt, 1933, RG 86, Box 289, "Domestic Workers Household Employment 1933": File 1933 W, NARA.

91. Kytle, *Willie Mae*, 141, 146.

92. Clark-Lewis, *Living In, Living Out*, 151.

93. Hunt, *I Am Annie Mae*, 79.

94. Wolcott, *Remaking Respectability*, 57.

95. Jordan, *Vernon Can Read*, 16–17.

96. Kytle, *Willie Mae*, 140–41.

97. Stephanie M. H. Camp, *Closer to Freedom*, 78–87, discusses clothing as resistance among slave women. See also Enstad, "Fashioning Political Identities," for an extended discussion of clothing as resistance among working-class women.

98. Michael D. Harris, *Colored Pictures*, 94–96.

99. Pringle, *Woman Rice Planter*, 86. See also ibid., 342.

100. Cleora Butler, *Cleora's Kitchens*, 52.

101. Letter from Mrs. Katherine Rutherford to Mr. President Roosevelt, July 15, 1933, RG 86, Box 289, "Domestic Workers Household Employment 1933": File 1933 R, NARA.

102. Parker, *From Reddick to Cross Creek*, 92–93; Parker, *Idella*, 99.

103. Pringle, *Woman Rice Planter*, 46–47.

104. Katy Brumby, American Life Histories: Manuscripts from the Federal Writers' Project.

105. Kytle, *Willie Mae*, 146, 149; Tarr, *Private Marjorie*, 475; Parker, *From Reddick to Cross Creek*, 33.

106. Katy Brumby, American Life Histories: Manuscripts from the Federal Writers' Project.

107. U.S. Census, 1930, Bibb County, Georgia.

108. Cleora Butler, *Cleora's Kitchens*, 46–47.

109. Edwards, *Southern Urban Negro*, 7.

110. Parker, *From Reddick to Cross Creek*, 123.

111. Henrietta Elizabeth Sellers, American Life Histories: Manuscripts from the Federal Writers' Project.

112. Clark-Lewis, *Living In, Living Out*, 136, 166.

113. Tera Hunter, "Domination and Resistance," 349.

114. Rachleff, *Black Labor in the South*, 17.

115. "Waco Negress Assassinated," *Dallas Morning News*, July 14, 1902.

116. White, *Too Heavy a Load*, 17. Neil McMillen discovered more than fifty African American benefit societies in Mississippi. Afro-American Sons and Daughters and Knights and Daughters of Tabor functioned until World War II (McMillen, *Dark Journey*, 183).

117. Katy Brumby, American Life Histories: Manuscripts from the Federal Writers' Project.

118. Wright, *Black Boy*, 22, 23.

119. Chafe, Gavins, and Korstad, *Remembering Jim Crow*, 127.

120. Jordan, *Vernon Can Read*, 17.

121. Swann-Wright, *Way Out of No Way*, 139.

122. "Miss Sallie's Cook," American Life Histories: Manuscripts from the Federal Writers' Project.

123. Letter from Mrs. H. A. Clement to Mr. President, December 1939, RG 86, Box 292, "Domestic Workers Household Employment 1936–1939": File 1939 C–D, NARA.

Chapter Five

1. Irish immigrants, like African American women, suffered from discrimination and stereotyping, but they were able to leave the ranks of domestic work more quickly than African Americans, and their daughters typically did not become domestic workers. See Diner, *Erin's Daughters*, and Dudden, *Serving Women*.

2. Alexander, "Challenge of Race," 53.

3. Gutman, *Black Family*, 201–29.

4. Jones, *Labor of Love*, 3–6, discusses the intertwining of work and family. Di Leonardo, "Women's Work, Women's Culture," refers to the "double consciousness" of women as workers, concerned with both their families and their employment (494–95).

5. Kaplan, "'I Don't Do No Windows,'" 93; Schwalm, "'Sweet Dreams,'" 28; Clinton,

"Bloody Terrain," 141; Coser, "Servants," 35, 36. Stephanie Cole ("Servants and Slaves," 207–9) cites similar discrimination against slaves, although she finds that slaveholders were more willing to make exceptions when it came to excellent cooks. A comparable situation existed in Brazil, where, in one case, a mother negotiated lower wages in return for the right to keep her "infant on her hip" (Graham, *House and Street*, 79).

6. Censer, *Reconstruction of White Southern Womanhood*, 75.

7. Thomas journal, quoted in Weiner, *Mistresses and Slaves*, 210–11.

8. Parker, *From Reddick to Cross Creek*, 95–96.

9. Janeway, *Powers of the Weak*, 172.

10. *Guild Cook Book of Tested Recipes*, 51, 53, 142, 143.

11. Janeway, *Powers of the Weak*, 208.

12. Harley, "When Your Work Is Not Who You Are," 48; Harley, "For the Good of Family and Race," 337.

13. Gwaltney, *Drylongso*, 173–74.

14. Janeway, *Powers of the Weak*, 167.

15. Ibid., 212.

16. U.S. Census, 1880, 1900, 1910, 1920, 1930, Bibb County, Georgia. Herbert Gutman found that in 1880, unmarried black women lived with their parents in "far greater numbers" than not in Beaufort, South Carolina; Natchez, Mississippi, Richmond, Virginia; and Mobile, Alabama (Gutman, *Black Family*, 445). Dolores Janiewski discovered that in Durham, North Carolina, in 1880 and 1900, most females lived with either their husbands or their parents. About 10 percent lived with other relatives (Janiewski, *Sisterhood Denied*, 59).

Census data for this study is drawn from a random sample of the census returns for Macon, Georgia. I chose fifty cooks in each of the census returns for 1880, 1900, 1910, 1920, and 1930. (The 1870 census listed all domestic workers rather than dividing them by task.) The census study is designed to be suggestive, not definitive.

17. U.S. Census, 1880, Bibb County, Georgia. See also Eugene Harris, "Physical Condition of the Race," 27. In his analysis, Gutman found that most single women with children later married (*Black Family*, 445).

18. Clark-Lewis, *Living In, Living Out*, 154.

19. Ibid., 163.

20. Tilly, "Comments," 458.

21. Rollins, *Between Women*, 136.

22. Katy Brumby, American Life Histories: Manuscripts from the Federal Writers' Project. In South Africa under apartheid in the 1970s, almost a third of domestic workers sent part of their salaries elsewhere (Cock, *Maids and Madams*, 42).

23. Clark-Lewis, *Living In, Living Out*, 133, 153.

24. U.S. Census, 1880, 1900, 1910, 1920, 1930, Bibb County, Georgia.

25. U.S. Census, 1880, 1900, 1910, 1920, 1930, Bibb County, Georgia; Maclachlan, "Women's Work," 386.

26. Kaplan, "'I Don't Do No Windows,'" 93.

27. Bercaw, *Gendered Freedoms*, 120; Glenn, *Unequal Freedom*, 108; Gutman, *Black Family*, 444; Jones, *Labor of Love*, 73–74; Blackwelder, "Women in the Work Force," 341.

28. Between 1880 and 1930, the majority of African American cooks in Macon lived in households headed by a female. See Maclachlan, "Women's Work," 2, 3, 4; and Lewis, *In Their Own Interests*, 30.

29. Jones, *Labor of Love*, 111.

30. Clark-Lewis, *Living In, Living Out*, 4. Although this is the only example that I have found of such a practice in the U.S. South, in Brazil in the 1880s and 1890s, live-in servants sought their own space so often that employers specifically forbade it in work agreements (Graham, *House and Street*, 60–61).

31. A significantly lower number of women lived with their employers in the South than in the North, and the numbers declined over the years. By 1920, in Atlanta, 17.6 percent of servants lived with their employers, in New Orleans, 17.3 percent, and in Louisville, 25.8, compared to 78.8 percent in Fall River, Massachusetts, and 69 percent in Providence, Rhode Island. Never-married women were most likely to live with their employers, followed by widows or divorcees, with married women most likely to live away (Katzman, *Seven Days a Week*, 296, 297).

32. Rollins, *Between Women*, 135–36.

33. Gutman, *Black Family*, 449.

34. "Ole an' Broke," American Life Histories: Manuscripts from the Federal Writers' Project.

35. Powdermaker, *After Freedom*, 158.

36. Thomas, *Secret Eye*, 313.

37. Tucker, *Telling Memories*, 133.

38. Gwaltney, *Drylongso*, 148.

39. Tucker, *Telling Memories*, 266.

40. Kytle, *Willie Mae*, 38–40.

41. "A Murdered Cook," *Dallas Morning News*, January 31, 1886; "Negress Dead with Throat Cut," *Dallas Morning News*, February 2, 1906; "Waco Negress Assassinated," *Dallas Morning News*, July 14, 1902.

42. Furstenberg, Hershberg, and Modell, "Origins of the Female-Headed Black Family," 211–33; Lewis, *In Their Own Interests*, 102.

43. Julia Blackwelder ("Women in the Work Force," 338) has documented that in 1930, African American widows were more likely than married or single women to be employed. In Atlanta, 64.2 percent of black single women, 56.5 percent of married women, and 76.6 percent of widows held jobs. In New Orleans, the percentages were 61.6 percent of single women, 43.2 percent of married women, and 66.5 percent of widows. And in San Antonio, 56.0 percent of black single women, 50.1 percent of married women, and 74.4 percent of widows were employed.

44. Lynch, *Reminiscences of an Active Life*, 6; Parker, *From Reddick to Cross Creek*, 54.

45. "Negro Nurse," "More Slavery," 198.

46. Smart-Grosvenor, *Thursdays and Every Other Sunday Off*, 60.

47. Charles Spurgeon Johnson, *Patterns of Negro Segregation*, 148. See also Neil R. McMillen, *Dark Journey*, 18.

48. Cole, "'Neither Matron nor Maid,'" 5. Johnson does not say what state the couple lived in, but antimiscegenation laws would almost surely have prevented their marrying.

Thirty of the forty-eight United States had such laws during the early twentieth century, and all of the states of the former Confederacy kept them on the books until they were found unconstitutional in *Loving v. Virginia* in 1967.

49. Dollard, *Caste and Class*, 142. In addition to the social stigma of having a mixed-race child, the father's family may have feared that acknowledging paternity would make them vulnerable to claims on their property by the child.

50. Eugene Harris, "Physical Condition of the Race," 25.

51. Rodrigue, "Black Community," 244.

52. Ibid., 246; Charles Spurgeon Johnson, *Patterns of Negro Segregation*, 149.

53. Rodrigue, "Black Community," 248. For a discussion of abortion among slaves, including the use of herbal abortifacients, see Sterling, *We Are Your Sisters*, 40.

54. Hunt, *I Am Annie Mae*, 63 (emphasis in the original).

55. Thomas N. Chase, *Mortality among Negroes*, 13–16.

56. Lewis, *In Their Own Interests*, 80–81.

57. Kytle, *Willie Mae*, 156.

58. Tucker, *Telling Memories*, 56.

59. Watriss, "It's Something Inside You," 80; Elondust Patrick Johnson, "Performance, Cultural Identity, and Feminist Practice," 89, 254.

60. Van Zelm, "On the Front Lines of Freedom," 209.

61. Thomas journal, quoted in Weiner, *Mistresses and Slaves*, 210.

62. Swann-Wright, *Way Out of No Way*, 85.

63. Davidoff et al., *Family Story*, 175.

64. Glenn, "Racial Ethnic Women's Labor," 102–3.

65. Clark-Lewis, *Living In, Living Out*, 14, 18. The difficulty of child care was likely one of the main reasons that married women with children preferred washing to domestic work (Gutman, *Black Family*, 630–31).

66. Tucker, *Telling Memories*, 28. See also Boehm, *Making a Way Out of No Way*, 56.

67. Thomas, *Secret Eye*, 319.

68. Ibid., 316.

69. O'Leary, *From Morning to Night*, 103, 143.

70. Sarah Howard, Drury Ave., Macon, Georgia, interview by Annie A. Rose, Macon, pp. 3238–39, Federal Writers' Project Files, Southern Oral History Project, Southern Historical Collection, Box 13, Folder 247, University of North Carolina at Chapel Hill.

71. Tucker, *Telling Memories*, 56.

72. Clark-Lewis, *Living In, Living Out*, 79–80.

73. Hunt, *I Am Annie Mae*, 69, 72.

74. Clark, *From Fatback to Filet*, 15.

75. Moody, *Coming of Age*, 32.

76. Wright, *Black Boy*, 16–17.

77. Ibid., 13–14.

78. Wright, *Black Boy*, 14–16. Psychologist and anthropologist Allison Davis wrote in 1939, "The type of accommodation which a child is taught . . . usually depends, to a degree, upon the *social class* [his emphasis] of his parents in the Negro society. . . . In lower-class families, a child is taught that he is a 'nigger' and that he must be subservient to white people, since he must work for them. He is trained to fight, however, if he is

attacked." Middle-class families taught their children to avoid white people, a luxury that many working-class families could not afford since they were obliged to work for white people (Davis, "Socialization," 270).

79. Wright, *Black Boy*, 19.

80. Ruth Reed, *Negro Women of Gainesville*, 16.

81. Tucker, *Telling Memories*, 80.

82. Clark, *From Fatback to Filet*, 15–16.

83. "Bea, the Wash Woman," American Life Histories: Manuscripts from the Federal Writers' Project.

84. See, for example, Selena Sloan Butler, "Need of Day Nurseries," and Bass, "Need of Kindergartens." A list of institutions appears in DuBois, *Some Efforts of American Negroes*, 30–31. See also Perry, "Carrie Steele Orphanage," and Neverdon-Morton, *Afro-American Women*, 142–43, 171–72.

85. DuBois, *Some Efforts of American Negroes*, 30–31. See also Cook, "Work of the Woman's League," 57–58.

86. O'Leary, *From Morning to Night*, 106.

87. Maclachlan, "Women's Work," 295.

88. Wright, *Black Boy*, 24–25.

89. Brundage, *Southern Past*, 214; DuBois, *Some Efforts of American Negroes*, 30–31; Perry, "Carrie Steele Orphanage"; Maclachlan, "Women's Work," 295; Neverdon-Morton, *Afro-American Women*, 143–44, 181–83.

90. O'Leary, *From Morning to Night*, 106.

91. Van Zelm, "On the Front Lines of Freedom," 209–10; Langhorne, "Domestic Service in the South," 171.

92. Margaret McDow MacDougall interview by Mary Frederickson, April 1977, Southern Oral History Project, Southern Historical Collection, University of North Carolina at Chapel Hill, quoted in Ritterhouse, *Growing Up Jim Crow*, 156.

93. Wright, *Black Boy*, 17.

94. Nannie Pharis interviews by Allen Tullos, December 5, 1978, and January 8, 1979, Burlington, N.C., UNC H-39, p. 69, Southern Oral History Project, Southern Historical Collection, University of North Carolina at Chapel Hill.

95. Sterling, *We Are Your Sisters*, 360. The time frame for this quotation is unclear, although editor Sterling places it in the postbellum period.

96. U.S. Census, 1930, Bibb County, Georgia. See also letter from Miss Imogene Coleman to Mr. President, RG 86, Box 292, "Domestic Workers Household Employment 1936–1939": File 1939 C–D, NARA.

97. Moody, *Coming of Age*, 36.

98. Typescript, "A Supplementary Article on Domestic Service Workers by the President of the Domestic Efficiency Association [Mrs. R. Manson Smith [Bertha Whitridge(?) Smith], 4 East Biddle Street, Baltimore," RG 86, Box 20, correspondence regarding Bulletin 39, NARA.

99. Le Guin, *Home-Concealed Woman*, 198–99.

100. Katy Brumby, American Life Histories: Manuscripts from the Federal Writers' Project.

101. Neil R. McMillen, *Dark Journey*, 163.

102. Katy Brumby, *American Life Histories: Manuscripts from the Federal Writers' Project*.

Chapter Six

1. Davidoff et al., *Family Story*, 182.
2. Coser, "Servants," 36; Ritterhouse, "Etiquette," 25.
3. Glenn, *Unequal Freedom*, 16.
4. For a discussion of the interpersonal relationships between slaves and female owners, see Fox-Genovese, *Within the Plantation Household*, 137–39, 152–66. For a telling exploration of ongoing awkwardness around the employee-employer relationships into the twenty-first century, see Wallace-Sanders, *Mammy*, xiii–xvii.
5. Davidoff et al., *Family Story*, 170.
6. Coser, "Servants," 39; Rollins, *Between Women*, 227.
7. Romero, "Not Just Like," 36–37; Glenn, "Dialectics of Wage Work," 457; Anzaldúa, *Borderlands*, 43.
8. Faust et al., "Interchange," 590.
9. Davidoff, "Mastered," 422.
10. Janeway, *Powers of the Weak*, 202.
11. hooks, *Ain't I a Woman*, 155.
12. Davidoff et al., *Family Story*, 158; Rollins, *Between Women*, 178.
13. Kaplan, "'I Don't Do No Windows,'" 93.
14. Sutherland, *Americans and Their Servants*, 11; Neuhaus, *Manly Meals*, 13, 14.
15. Cooks enabled their employers to adhere to the notion of domesticity that pervaded American society. As articulated by Catharine Beecher and other nineteenth-century writers, and expanded by twentieth-century advertisers, food preparation equaled love and concern for the eater's well-being. While literary critic Mary Titus argues that slavery made "the application of northern domestic ideology to the southern family life less than perfect," clearly many southern women internalized at least parts of the domestic message (Titus, "'Groaning Tables,'" 14; Titus, "Dining Room Door," 245). They wanted to be perceived as exemplary wives and mothers, deeply concerned with the well-being of family members in their charge. (See, for example, *Housekeeping in Alabama*, 235, and Cole, "White Woman, of Middle Age," 76–82). Marli Weiner, in *Mistresses and Slaves*, asserts the applicability of domesticity to antebellum southern white women. Thavolia Glymph argues that "the ideals of nineteenth-century domesticity proved to be as pervasive in the South as in the North" (Glymph, *Out of the House of Bondage*, 64–65, 84, 85). Rather than participating in the domestic ideal herself, a cook enabled her employer to do so. The family meal held an exalted position in the cult of domesticity, and a cook made it possible for her employer's family to enjoy mealtime together (Short, *Kitchen Secrets*, 3). She, however, did not get to have a relaxed meal with members of her own family.
16. Davidoff, *Worlds Between*, 93.
17. The most notable of the cookbooks that borrow at will from other sources is E. T. Glover of Richmond, author of the 1897 *Warm Springs Receipt-Book*. Glover lifts dozens and dozens of recipes from the cookbooks of culinary experts Sarah Tyson Rorer and Maria Parloa as well as *Table Talk's Illustrated Cook Book* and *The Century Cook Book*.

18. "A sister to sister letter," May 18, 1884, Cameron Collection, Cameron Family Papers, Southern Historical Collection, University of North Carolina at Chapel Hill (emphasis in the original), quoted in Neal, *Biscuits*, 246.

19. Le Guin, *Home-Concealed Woman*, 94.

20. Helmbold, "Making Choices, Making Do," 304.

21. O'Leary, *From Morning to Night*, 29–30. The date on these recollections is unclear.

22. Ferris, *Matzoh Ball Gumbo*, 120. See also Witt, *Black Hunger*, 60–61, and Le Guin, *Home-Concealed Woman*, 204–5.

23. O'Leary, *From Morning to Night*, 81.

24. Council, *Mama Dip's Kitchen*, 22.

25. In 1921, researcher Elizabeth Haynes found 90 percent turnover in one year (Haynes, "Negroes in Domestic Service," 395), while in 1924 Mary Robinson found that the average cook's tenure in Baltimore was less than one year (Robinson, *Domestic Workers*, 37).

26. Haynes, "Negroes in Domestic Service," 408.

27. Mary V. Robinson, *Domestic Workers*, 43–46.

28. Collins, "Gender," 44; Collins, "Learning from the Outsider Within," S19–S21.

29. Woodson, *Mis-Education of the Negro*, 38.

30. hooks, *Feminist Theory*, 14. This concept of African American women's unique point of view is, of course, the basis for the theory of intersectionality, first articulated by Kimberlé Crenshaw and expanded by Patricia Hill Collins in *Black Feminist Thought*.

31. Ritterhouse, "Etiquette," 23.

32. Cleora Butler, *Cleora's Kitchens*, 39.

33. Parker, *Idella*, 17.

34. Villard, "Negro and the Domestic Problem." 7.

35. Typescript, "A Supplementary Article on Domestic Service Workers by the President of the Domestic Efficiency Association [Mrs. R. Manson Smith [Bertha Whitridge(?) Smith], 4 East Biddle Street, Baltimore," RG 86, Box 20, correspondence regarding Bulletin 39, NARA.

36. Myrdal, *American Dilemma*, 576.

37. Faulkner, *Intruder in the Dust*, 48.

38. Sudie Holton, American Life Histories: Manuscripts from the Federal Writers' Project.

39. Tera Hunter, *To 'Joy My Freedom*, 105.

40. Ritterhouse, *Growing Up Jim Crow*, 14, 25.

41. Ritterhouse, "Etiquette," 21, 25. See also Goldfield, *Black, White, and Southern*, 2.

42. Parker, *Idella*, 19.

43. Parker, *From Reddick to Cross Creek*, 160.

44. Parker, *Idella*, xiii (emphasis in the original). See also ibid., 28.

45. Ritterhouse, *Growing Up Jim Crow*, 14, 25. For a general discussion of employee discipline, see Benson, *Counter Cultures*, 126.

46. Diary of Jennie Akehurst Lines, October 18, October 19, October 20, October 30, 1871 (emphasis in the original), Akehurst-Lines Collection, Box 3, October 17–November 3, 1871, Hargrett Library, University of Georgia, Athens.

47. By this I mean the physical danger to a woman herself, not the pervasive fear from the reign of terror against black males in particular that persisted for more than a hundred years after the Civil War. Freedmen's Bureau reports contain numerous examples of newly freed women suffering beatings from their employers (Sterling, *We Are Your Sisters*, 333–38). Tera Hunter also documented numerous incidents of violence toward domestic workers in Atlanta, one of which ended in the fatal shooting of washerwoman Eliza Jane Ellison (Tera Hunter, *To 'Joy My Freedom*, 31). See also van Zelm, "On the Front Lines of Freedom," 159.

48. Burge, *Diary of Dolly Lunt Burge*, xxxvi.

49. Lumpkin, *Making of a Southerner*, 132.

50. Maud Andrews, "Trials of Housekeeping," *Atlanta Constitution*, December 16, 1888, p. 4. For similar punishments during slavery, see Jacobs, *Incidents in the Life of a Slave Girl*, 12–13.

51. Lumpkin, *Making of a Southerner*, 132.

52. Swann-Wright, *Way Out of No Way*, 79–80.

53. As Dorothy Sue Cobble points out (*Dishing It Out*, 44), white women working as waitresses were also vulnerable to sexual harassment, but African American domestic workers were doubly affected, first by the historical precedents left from slavery and second by the fact that they spent their days in private homes, with no witnesses to their employers' transgressions. For a discussion of sexual abuse of slaves, see Jennings, "'Us Colored Women,'" 60–66.

54. Millward, "More History Than Myth," 161, 165. Much thoughtful theoretical work exists on African American women's bodies. See, for example, Roberts, *Myth of Aunt Jemima*; Spillers, "Mama's Baby, Papa's Maybe"; Wallace-Sanders, *Skin Deep, Spirit Strong*; and Michael D. Harris, *Colored Pictures*, 31–32. For an analysis of sexual violence against African American women during Reconstruction, see Clinton, "Bloody Terrain."

55. Anzaldúa, *Borderlands*, 42.

56. hooks, *Ain't I a Woman*, 36. Some African American men, such as Bishop W. J. Gaines of the African Methodist Episcopal Church, in fact, blamed African American women for their relationships with white men, writing that "colored girls in the South often prefer to be the mothers of white children" (White, *Too Heavy a Load*, 64).

57. "Negro Nurse," "More Slavery at the South," 200; hooks, *Ain't I a Woman*, 52.

58. Sterling, *We Are Your Sisters*, 354.

59. Villard, "Negro and the Domestic Problem," 7.

60. Holtzclaw, *Black Man's Burden*, 154–55.

61. Dollard, *Caste and Class*, 147.

62. Elsa Barkley Brown, "What Has Happened Here," 304.

63. Clark-Lewis, *Living In, Living Out*, 48.

64. "Negro Nurse," "More Slavery at the South," 198. See also Cooper, *Voice from the South*, 111.

65. Gwaltney, *Drylongso*, 146–47.

66. Ibid., 56–57.

67. Smart-Grosvernor, *Thursdays and Every Other Sunday Off*, 60. See also "Negro Nurse," "More Slavery at the South," 197–98.

68. Morgan, "Mammy the Huckster," 97; Tucker, *Telling Memories*, 94–95.

69. Smart-Grosvenor, *Thursdays and Every Other Sunday Off*, 33.

70. "Negro Nurse," "More Slavery at the South," 198. See also DuBois, *Darkwater*, 118.

71. Gwaltney, *Drylongso*, 172. See also Angelou, *I Know Why the Caged Bird Sings*, 5–11.

72. Ritterhouse, *Growing Up Jim Crow*, 27–28.

73. Trudier Harris, *From Mammies to Militants*, 14.

74. Anzaldúa, *Borderlands*, 19.

75. Davidoff, "Gender and the 'Great Divide,'" 18.

76. Henderson, "'Ace of Clubs,'" 69.

77. Titus, "Groaning Tables," 15–16. See also Romero, "Sisterhood and Domestic Service," 332, and Chaplin, "Domestic Service," 104.

78. O'Leary, *From Morning to Night*, 110.

79. Trudier Harris, *From Mammies to Militants*, 15; Lancaster, "Simmering Stew," 76; DuBois, *Darkwater*, 118.

80. Plant Family Reminiscences by "Mrs. Ross (Martha Plant)," 2, Southern Oral History Project, Southern Historical Collection, University of North Carolina at Chapel Hill. Antoinette van Zelm argues that the detached kitchen on a plantation did in fact become space dominated by slaves. Moving the kitchen closer to the house curtailed the ability of those who worked in it to move and speak freely (van Zelm, "On the Front Lines of Freedom," 197–98).

81. Williams-Forson, *Building Houses Out of Chicken Legs*, 77.

82. Charles Spurgeon Johnson, *Patterns of Negro Segregation*, 143.

83. Parker, *Idella*, 83 (emphasis mine).

84. Clark-Lewis, *Living In, Living Out*, 65–66.

85. Watriss, "It's Something Inside You," 139. Interviews with cooks in South Africa under apartheid revealed not being able to eat the food that they had prepared ranked near the top of their list of the worst things about their jobs (Cock, *Maids and Madams*, 53).

86. Parker, *From Reddick to Cross Creek*, 107–8. Dorothy Sue Cobble points out that white women who worked as waitresses were also segregated into eating only in "help kitchens" with dreadful conditions (Cobble, *Dishing It Out*, 40).

87. Quinn, "Transmission of Racial Attitudes," 43. See also Romero, "Sisterhood and Domestic Service," 327.

88. Angelou, *I Know Why the Caged Bird Sings*, 106.

89. Goldfield, *Black, White, and Southern*, 4.

90. Kytle, *Willie Mae*, 205–7. Willie Mae Wright recorded at least two occasions in which she ate with her employers: once after a traumatic event, in which Wright purchased and fixed dinner (137), and once with employers who were not from Atlanta and whose unusual ways first occasioned Wright's suspicion (198). See also Titus, "Dining Room Door," 249.

91. Janeway, *Powers of the Weak*, 9.

92. Fairchilds, *Domestic Enemies*, 103. Early photographs of domestic workers in uniforms are in O'Leary, *From Morning to Night*, dated 1890; and Tucker, *Telling Memories*,

dated 1907. By 1900, wearing livery was common in Washington, D.C., and immigrants from the countryside often found the adjustment to the garb difficult (Clark-Lewis, *Living In, Living Out*, 113). For an explication of Victorian dining, see Williams, *Savory Suppers*. For a southern example of elaborate dining, see *Housekeeping in Alabama*, 235–37.

93. Trudier Harris, *From Mammies to Militants*, 12.

94. Tucker, *Telling Memories*, 175; Clark-Lewis, *Living In, Living Out*, 106, 113–17, 159–60.

95. Parker, *Idella*, 79.

96. O'Leary, *From Morning to Night*, 91.

97. Kousha, "African American Private Household Workers," 222.

98. Watriss, "It's Something Inside You," 79.

99. Dill, "'Making Your Job Good,'" 37.

100. Ibid., 37, 39; Davidoff, "Mastered," 415.

101. Allison Davis, "Socialization," 270; quotation from Goldfield, *Black, White, and Southern*, 2.

102. Watriss, "It's Something Inside You," 77.

103. Powdermaker, *After Freedom*, 119.

104. Clark-Lewis, *Living In, Living Out*, 188.

105. Chafe, Gavins, and Korstad, *Remembering Jim Crow*, 128–29.

106. Thomas, *Secret Eye*, 395, 417.

107. Rawlings, *Cross Creek*, 24.

108. Parker, *Idella*, 61, 64.

109. Parker, *From Reddick to Cross Creek*, 95–96.

110. Millward, "More History Than Myth," 163.

111. Hickey, *Hope and Danger*, 44; Davidoff, "Mastered," 416.

112. Kelley, "'We Are Not What We Seem,'" 89, 91.

113. Thomas, *Secret Eye*, 313.

114. Ibid., 417.

115. Katy Brumby, American Life Histories: Manuscripts from the Federal Writers' Project.

116. Tucker, *Telling Memories*, 175.

117. Ibid., 92.

118. Le Guin, *Home-Concealed Woman*, 204.

119. Diary of Jennie Akehurst Lines, October 29, 1871, Akehurst-Lines Collection, Box 3, October 17–November 3, 1871, Hargrett Library, University of Georgia, Athens.

120. Logan, *Negro in North Carolina*, 89.

121. Knoxville Woman's Building Association, *Knoxville Cook Book*, 254. For deliberate destruction of dishes as revenge, see Angelou, *I Know Why the Caged Bird Sings*, 110–11.

122. Glymph, *Out of the House of Bondage*, 196.

123. Janiewski, *Sisterhood Denied*, 53.

124. Tyree, *Housekeeping in Old Virginia*, 24.

125. Murray, *Proud Shoes*, 159–60.

126. Clark-Lewis, *Living In, Living Out*, 66.

127. E. M. Woods, *The Negro in Etiquette: A Novelty* (St. Louis: Buxton and Skinner, 1899,) 114, quoted in Litwack, *Trouble in Mind*, 171.

128. Tera Hunter, *To 'Joy My Freedom*, 27–28; Tera Hunter, "Domination and Resistance," 346–47. Dorothy Sue Cobble observes that white waitresses in the early twentieth century also maintained a "circular, horizontal movement" among employers, to which they aptly referred as "working the circuit" (Cobble, *Dishing It Out*, 50).

129. Kytle, *Willie Mae*, 138.

130. Ibid., 133.

131. Elwang, "Negroes of Columbia," 27.

132. Long, *Negroes of Clarke County*, 40.

133. Ruth Reed, *Negro Women of Gainesville*, 25; Haynes, "Negroes in Domestic Service," 395.

134. Dill, "'Making Your Job Good,'" 39, 41. See also Glenn, *Unequal Freedom*, 241.

135. Ruth Reed, *Negro Women in Gainesville*, 26.

136. Letter from Helga and Ada Push button [?] to Mrs. Roosevelt, September 20, 1941 (emphasis in the original), RG 86, Box 294, "Domestic Workers Household Employment 1941": File 1941 Anonymous, NARA.

137. Dill, *Across the Boundaries*, 11.

138. Swann-Wright, *Way Out of No Way*, 65.

139. Le Guin, *Home-Concealed Woman*, 203, 210.

140. Watriss, "It's Something Inside You," 79.

141. Tera Hunter, "Domination and Resistance," 347.

142. Kytle, *Willie Mae*, 205–7.

143. Dollard, *Caste and Class*, 301.

144. Bolden, "Forty-two Years a Maid," 148.

145. Parker, *From Reddick to Cross Creek*, 119–20, 130. Rawlings fretted incessantly about Parker's comings and goings. See Tarr, *Private Marjorie*, 98, 121, 125, 139, 167, 171, 175, 178, 198, 221–22, 226, 297, 352, 410, 420.

146. Dollard, *Caste and Class*, 109.

147. Tera Hunter, "Domination and Resistance," 347.

148. Ibid., 347.

149. Grignon, "Commensality and Social Morphology," 29.

150. Helmbold, "Making Choices, Making Do," 309; Cock, *Maids and Madams*, 57.

151. Letter from Club of the Colored Maids, Kannapolis, N.C., to President Roosevelt, November 5, 1941, RG 86, Box 294 "Domestic Workers Household Employment 1941": File 1941 C–D, NARA.

152. Watriss, "It's Something Inside You," 80.

153. Lumpkin, *Making of a Southerner*, 135. See also Fleming, "Servant Problem," 17; and Woofter, *Negroes of Athens*, 62. The return of stolen goods apparently did occur. In Indianola, Mississippi, a cook named Opal borrowed a party dress and three dollars from her employer and then disappeared for several days. John Dollard noted, "Her mistress finally set out to look for her and learned from another Negro that Opal did not intend to come back. Word was sent to her that, if she did not return the dress and the three dollars immediately, she would be arrested for obtaining money under false pretenses. By

the next morning the dress had been secretly returned and hung up in the closet and the three dollars came back with it" (Dollard, *Caste and Class*, 108–9).

154. "Crime of a Negro Cook," *Atlanta Constitution*, June 18, 1899; "Valuable Jewelry Stolen," *Atlanta Constitution*, April 9, 1912; King Diary, January 12, 1867, Hargrett Library, University of Georgia, Athens.

155. Williams-Forson, *Making Houses Out of Chicken Legs*, 26.

156. Rio, "From Feudal Serfs to Independent Contractors," 56–57.

157. Censer, *Reconstruction of White Southern Womanhood*, 74.

158. Claiborne, *Craig Claiborne's Southern Cooking*, 136.

159. Woofter, *Negroes of Athens*, 59, 62.

160. Sanders, *Dori Sanders' Country Cooking*, 3.

161. Waters, *His Eye Is on the Sparrow*, 23.

162. "Negro Problem," 2227 (emphasis in the original). An interview with former slave Katie Sutton indicates that slave cooks fed their children surreptitiously from the slave owner's kitchen:

Yo daddy ploughs de massa's corn,
Yo mammy does the cooking;
She'll give dinner to her hungry chile
When nobody is a lookin.

(former slave Katie Sutton, Evansville, Indiana, interviewed by Luana Creel, n.d., quoted in Weiner, *Mistresses and Slaves*, 119).

163. Woofter, *Negroes of Athens*, 46.

164. Ibid., 59, 61. See also Lumpkin, *Making of a Southerner*, 135.

165. Langhorne, "Domestic Service in the South," 172. See also "Bar the Back Doors," *Atlanta Constitution*, October 3, 1903.

166. *Dallas Morning News*, April 4, 1918.

167. Pringle, *Woman Rice Planter*, 337.

168. "Negro Nurse," "More Slavery at the South," 199.

169. George Rawick, *The American Slave*, vol. 3, pt. 4, p. 2, quoted in Sutherland, *Americans and Their Servants*, 69.

170. Holtzclaw, *Black Man's Burden*, 22–23. See also Chafe, Gavins, and Korstad, *Remembering Jim Crow*, 212.

171. Collins, "Learning from the Outsider Within," S14–S15; quotation from Jessica B. Harris, *Welcome Table*, 31.

172. Davidoff et al., *Family Story*, 170–71. See also Hickey, *Hope and Danger*, 113, and Jones, *Labor of Love*, 127.

173. Collins, *Black Feminist Thought*, 11.

174. Janeway, *Powers of the Weak*, 171, 215.

175. Coser, "Servants," 35. For a sampling of conversations overheard in New York City, revealing domestic workers' knowledge of their employers, see Smart-Grosvenor, *Thursdays and Every Other Sunday Off*, 4. Thavolia Glymph points out that nineteenth-century employers feared gossip by their employees (Glymph, *Out of the House of Bondage*, 8–9, 152–53).

176. Powdermaker, *After Freedom*, 119. Southern memoirist David Cohn, writing in

the late 1940s, observed that white Mississippians had "genial delusions" that "because they live among masses of Negroes, employ Negro cooks, maids, nurses, washerwomen, they intimately understand Negro life" (Cohn, *Where I Was Born and Raised*, 276–77).

177. Powdermaker, *After Freedom*, 119.

178. Kytle, *Willie Mae*, 182, 188.

179. Alma McLain Coleman Brown Diary, January 14, February 13, 1919, Harris Papers, Ms. 734, Box 101, Hargrett Library, University of Georgia, Athens. I have been unable to verify Mary's family name.

180. Kousha, "Best Friends," 155–204.

181. See, for example, Craig Claiborne, *Feast Made for Laughter*, 29, in which he recalls the affections of Blanche, the Claiborne family cook in 1920s Mississippi. See also Le Guin, *Home-Concealed Woman*, 103; Tucker, *Telling Memories*, 53; Kousha, "Best Friends," 205–37; and Wallace-Sanders, *Mammy*, xiv–xvii.

182. For example, in the 1920s, Natchez native Clara Lowenburg wrote that she could not have endured the loss of her mother had it not been for Jinny Shaw, the family's cook, who provided "comforting wisdom" and "loving sympathy" (Ferris, *Matzoh Ball Gumbo*, 103).

183. Romero, "Sisterhood and Domestic Service," 329–30.

184. Kousha, "Best Friends," 156.

185. Parker, *Idella*, 112–13. Parker's and Rawlings's relationship is unusually well documented through Parker's two volumes of autobiography (*Idella* and *From Redding to Cross Creek*) and Rawlings's correspondence with her husband (Tarr, *Private Marjorie*).

186. Kousha, "Best Friends," 180–85.

187. Kytle, *Willie Mae*, 121–22, 125.

188. Ibid., 132.

189. Ibid., 136–37.

190. Litwack, *Trouble in Mind*, 253–54.

191. "Kissed and Hugged Wife of Capt. Hains," *Atlanta Constitution*, May 4, 1909. See also "Mary Yancy's Story," *Dallas Morning News*, April 6, 1894.

192. "Mrs. Graddick Rearrested," *Atlanta Constitution*, March 9, 1900.

193. "Stepmother in Jail," *Atlanta Constitution*, September 3, 1895.

194. Collins, "Learning from the Outsider Within," S16.

195. Coser, "Servants," 32.

196. Romero, "Sisterhood and Domestic Service," 330. For a discussion of "maternalism" between employers and employees, see Rollins, *Between Women*, 173–203.

197. Clipping of "The Housemaid's Boss: A Striking Presentation of a Present-day Problem" by Ava L. Johnson, *Home Economic News* 3, no. 5 (May 1932): 91–92, in RG 86, Box 288, "Domestic Workers Household Employment 1912–1932: File Domestic Workers 1933," NARA.

198. Durr, *Outside the Magic Circle*, 26.

199. Dunlap, "Reform of Rape Law," 354–55.

200. For a discussion of the oppression of African American men's sexuality, see hooks, *We Real Cool*; Carbado, *Black Men on Race*; and Byrd and Guy-Sheftall, *Traps*.

201. Parker, *From Reddick to Cross Creek*, 96.

202. Kytle, *Willie Mae*, 148–50. Idella Parker also feared telling Marjorie Kinnan

Rawlings about her marriage, primarily because she was planning to leave Rawlings's employ (Parker, *From Reddick to Cross Creek*, 139).

203. Interview of "The Lil' Black Girl," 3414–15, Federal Writers' Project Files, Southern Oral History Project, Southern Historical Collection, University of North Carolina at Chapel Hill.

204. "Negro Problem," 2227.

205. Parker, *Idella*, 34–35.

206. Leigh, *Ten Years on a Georgia Plantation*, 166. Mistresses commonly interfered with the rituals of their slaves. For an overview of the literature on white interference with slave weddings, see O'Neil, "Bosses and Broomsticks," 31–33.

207. Ethel Wright Mohamed, oral history interview by Lu Ann Jones, Belzoni, Mississippi, October 23, 1987, An Oral History of Southern Agriculture, Archives Center, National Museum of American History, Smithsonian Institution, Washington, D.C.

208. Katy Brumby, American Life Histories: Manuscripts from the Federal Writers' Project.

209. Romero, "Sisterhood and Domestic Service," 327–28.

210. DuBois, *Darkwater*, 116–17.

211. Hunt, *I Am Annie Mae*, 67–68.

212. Moncure, *Emma Jane's Souvenir Cook Book*, 5.

213. U.S. Census, 1880, New Kent County, Virginia, Black Creek, District 57, p. 3.

214. U.S. Census, 1900, Williamsburg County, Virginia, Williamsburg City, District 123, sheet 9.

215. U.S. Census, 1910, Williamsburg County, Virginia, Williamsburg, District 125, sheet 16.

216. U.S. Census, 1920, Williamsburg County, Virginia, James City, District 165, sheet 20A.

217. U.S. Census, 1930, Williamsburg County, Virginia, Williamsburg Independent City, District 4, sheet 22A.

218. Marion Brown, *Southern Cook Book*, 73.

219. O'Leary, *From Morning to Night*, 7.

220. Tucker, *Telling Memories*, 96.

221. Woofter, *Negroes of Athens*, 59–62.

222. Eva Davis, *Mississippi Mixin's*, 95; Marion Brown, *Southern Cook Book*, 148.

223. Eva Davis, *Court Square Recipes*, 29; *Recipes of the Deep South*, 106–7.

224. Woodson, *Mis-Education of the Negro*, 158–59. See also Joan Marie Johnson, "'Ye Gave Them a Stone,'" 73, and Dill, *Across the Boundaries*, 7, 19.

225. Letter from Miss Ruth Margon to Mrs. Mary Anderson, February 17, 1942, RG 86, Box 295, "Domestic Workers Household Employment 1942–1944": File 1942 M–N, NARA.

226. Clark-Lewis, *Living In, Living Out*, 186–87. Clark-Lewis, "Downstairs, Upstairs," gives Willoughby's name as Cartella Berks.

227. Watriss, "It's Something Inside You," 70.

228. O'Leary, *From Morning to Night*, 124 (emphasis in the original).

229. DuBois, *Darkwater*, 118.

230. Rollins, *Between Women*, 138 (emphasis in the original).

231. "Miss Sallie's Cook," *American Life Histories: Manuscripts from the Federal Writers' Project.*

232. Tucker, *Telling Memories*, 29.

233. Witt, *Black Hunger*, 24.

234. Jo-Ann Morgan identifies the first depiction of the authoritative cook in 1831, in the figure of Aunt Nauntje in James Kirke Paulding's popular novel *The Dutchman's Fireside.* Aunt Nauntje was an "African queen, whose authority by virtue of long and vigorous assertion, was paramount to that of the mistress of the establishment." See Morgan, "Mammy as Huckster," 106.

235. Hellman, *Three*, 549.

236. hooks, *Feminist Theory*, 14.

237. *Pohick Cookery*, 57.

238. Ibid., 5.

239. Benedict, *Road to Dream Acre*, 1–2. See also Durr, *Outside the Magic Circle*, 5, and Boehm, *Making a Way Out of No Way*, 158, 163.

240. *Houston Civic Club Cook Book*, 20.

241. Kuhn, Joye, and West, *Living Atlanta*, 119.

242. Flexner, *Dixie Dishes*, 13; Pollan, "Goodman Family," 11.

243. Tucker, *Telling Memories*, 92.

244. Ethel Wright Mohamed, oral history interview by Lu Ann Jones, Belzoni, Mississippi, October 23, 1987, An Oral History of Southern Agriculture, Archives Center, National Museum of American History, Smithsonian Institution, Washington, D.C.

245. Benedict, *Road to Dream Acre*, 1–2, 4.

246. Moncure, *Emma Jane's Souvenir Cook Book*, 5–6. As Jo-Ann Morgan points out, Aunt Jemima also gave advice, as advertisers sought to increase white women's insecurity and create more desire for their products (Morgan, "Mammy as Huckster," 105).

247. Charles Camp, *American Foodways*, 49.

248. Sudie Holton, American Life Histories: Manuscripts from the Federal Writers' Project. See also Katy Brumby, American Life Histories: Manuscripts from the Federal Writers' Project.

249. Natalie Scott, *Mirations and Miracles*, 38.

250. O'Leary, *From Morning to Night*, 2.

251. Ibid., 53.

252. Witt, *Black Hunger*, 11.

253. *Houston Civic Club Cook Book*, 20.

254. Neuhaus, *Manly Meals*, 49. See also Deck, "'Now Then—Who Said Biscuits?,'" 84, 89.

Chapter Seven

1. Hughes, "Graduation."

2. Logan, *Negro in North Carolina*, 88–89; Neil R. McMillen, *Dark Journey*, 27.

3. O'Leary, *From Morning to Night*, 2–4, 56.

4. Tucker, *Telling Memories*, 204.

5. Chafe, Gavins, and Korstad, *Remembering Jim Crow*, 128–29.

6. Carole Brown, "From the Family Notebook," 298.

7. Woofter, *Negroes of Athens*, 43.

8. Katzman, *Seven Days a Week*, 286, 287.

9. Tera Hunter, "'Women Are Asking for BREAD,'" 64–65.

10. Jones, *Labor of Love*, 134–42.

11. Logan, *Negro in North Carolina*, 93.

12. Maclachlan, "Women's Work," 17, 86; Tera Hunter, "'Women Are Asking for BREAD,'" 74.

13. Lewis, *In Their Own Interests*, 36.

14. Janiewski, *Sisterhood Denied*, 75, 101, 217.

15. Tera Hunter, "'Women Are Asking for BREAD,'" 74.

16. Maclachlan, "Women's Work," 95–96.

17. Emmett J. Scott, "Letters of Negro Migrants," 318. For other examples of cooks seeking to move north see ibid., 315, 316, 317–18, 318–19; and Emmett J. Scott, "More Letters of Negro Migrants," 450.

18. Perkins, "Forgotten Victorians," 133.

19. Hunter, "'Women Are Asking for BREAD,'" 65.

20. Blackwelder, "Women and Leadership," 45. See also Mary V. Robinson, *Domestic Workers*, 4, 5.

21. Enstam, *Women and the Creation of Urban Life*, 80; Dill, *Across the Boundaries*, 19.

22. Blackwelder, *Styling Jim Crow*, 151. Educated African American women could be teachers, nurses, social workers, or librarians. See Shaw, *What A Woman Ought to Be and to Do*; Chirhart, *Torches of Light*; Ramsey, *Reading, Writing, and Segregation*; and Hine, *Black Women in White*.

23. Ladd, "She Walked in Silence," 65, 67.

24. Sudie Holton, American Life Histories: Manuscripts from the Federal Writers' Project. See also Pringle, *Woman Rice Planter*, 340–41, 44.

25. Powdermaker, *After Freedom*, 117–18.

26. Blackwelder, "Women in the Work Force," 346, 348, 349.

27. "War and Post-War Trends in Employment of Negroes," 2.

28. Letter from Club of the Colored Maids, Kannapolis, N.C., to President Roosevelt, November 5, 1941, RG 86, Box 294, "Domestic Workers Household Employment 1941": File 1941 C–D, NARA.

29. Green, "'Where Would the Negro Women Apply,'" 96–97.

30. Ibid., 101–3.

31. Merl E. Reed, "Bell Aircraft," 118, 119, 124.

32. Shockley, *"We, Too, Are Americans,"* 76, 93–95, 155–56.

33. Gilmore and Wilson, "Employment of Negro Women," 319, 321–22.

34. Watriss, "It's Something Inside You," 80.

35. Ibid., 78, 80.

36. Bolden, "Forty-two Years a Maid," 141. I have been unable to discover what a "chute girl" is.

37. Boehm, *Making a Way Out of No Way*, xi; quotation on 204.

38. Blackwelder, *Women of the Depression*, 81.

39. Green, "'Where Would the Negro Women Apply,'" 116, 117.

40. Blackwelder, *Now Hiring*, 145.

41. Wolfbein, "War and Post-War Trends," 2, 3; Wolfbein, "Postwar Trends," 664–65.

42. Bailey and Collins, "Wage Gains," 737.

43. Ibid., 738, 739, 740, 744, 749, 751, 752, 753, 767.

44. Glenn, "Racial Ethnic Women's Labor," 100–101; Terborg-Penn, "Survival Strategies," 141.

45. Anderson and Bowman, "Vanishing Servant," 230.

46. Ibid., 225.

47. Kytle, *Willie Mae*, 205.

48. Gilmore and Wilson, "Employment of Negro Women," 320.

49. Inness, *Secret Ingredients*, 17–19.

50. Jo Ann Robinson, *Montgomery Bus Boycott*, 91–92, 165, 167.

51. Jones, *Labor of Love*, 301–2. MacLean, *Freedom Is Not Enough*, explores the impact of Title VII at length and focuses on its impact on women in chapter 4, "Women Challenge 'Jane Crow.'"

52. U.S. Department of Commerce, Bureau of the Census, *Social and Economic Status*, table 53, p. 74.

53. Michael D. Harris, *Colored Pictures*, 107–24.

54. Farrington, "Faith Ringgold's *Slave Rape* Series," 134, 136.

55. Michael D. Harris, *Colored Pictures*, 117.

56. Ibid., 118.

57. Parker, *Idella*, xi.

Bibliography

Primary Sources

MANUSCRIPT COLLECTIONS

Archives Center, National Museum of American History, Smithsonian Institution,
    Washington, D.C.
  An Oral History of Southern Agriculture
    Mohamed, Ethel Wright. Oral history interview by Lu Ann Jones. Belzoni,
      Mississippi, October 23, 1987
Hargrett Library, University of Georgia, Athens, Georgia
  Akehurst-Lines Collection
  Corra Mae White Harris Papers
  Samuel Porter Jones Papers
  Frances Elizabeth Greer King Diary
Middle Georgia Archives, Washington Memorial Library, Bibb County Library, Macon,
    Georgia
  Jones & Willaford Grocery Account Book, 1893–94
  King Meat Market Ledgers
National Archives and Records Administration, College Park, Maryland
  Record Group 86, Women's Bureau, Office of the Director, General Correspondence
    of the Women's Bureau, 1919–48
Southern Historical Collection, University of North Carolina at Chapel Hill, Chapel
    Hill, North Carolina
  Southern Oral History Project
    Nannie Pharis interviews by Allen Tullos, December 5, 1978, and January 8,
      1979, Burlington, North Carolina. UNC H-39.
  Plant Family Reminiscences by "Mrs. Ross (Martha Plant)"
  Federal Writers' Project Files
    Sarah Howard, Drury Ave., Macon, Georgia, interview by Annie A. Rose,
      Macon, Georgia
    Interview of "The Lil' Black Girl"
The Texas Collection, Baylor University, Waco, Texas
  Logue, Bill. *Oral Memoirs of Bill Logue.*
Woodruff Library, Special Collections, Emory University, Atlanta, Georgia
  Grisham Family Papers

GOVERNMENT PUBLICATIONS

Brown, Jean Collier. *The Negro Woman Worker.* U.S. Department of Labor. Women's
  Bureau. Bulletin of the Women's Bureau, no. 165. Washington, D.C.: Government
  Printing Office, 1938.

DuBois, W. E. B. *The Negroes of Farmville, Virginia: A Social Study*. U.S. Department of Labor. Bulletin of the Department of Labor 3 (January 1898). Washington, D.C.: Government Printing Office, 1898.

Laughlin, Gail. "Domestic Service." In *Report of the Industrial Commission on the Relations and Conditions of Capital and Labor Employed in Manufactures and General Business*. U.S. Industrial Commission. Washington, D.C.: Government Printing Office, 1901.

Robinson, Mary V. *Domestic Workers and Their Employment Relations: A Study Based on the Records of the Domestic Efficiency Association of Baltimore, Maryland*. U.S. Department of Labor, Women's Bureau. Bulletin of the Women's Bureau, no. 39. Washington, D.C.: Government Printing Office, 1924.

U.S. Department of Commerce, Bureau of the Census. Ninth Census of the United States, 1870. Manuscript census.

———. Tenth Census of the United States, 1880. Manuscript census.

———. Twelfth Census of the United States, 1900. Manuscript census.

———. Thirteenth Census of the United States, 1910. Manuscript census.

———. Fourteenth Census of the United States, 1920. Manuscript census.

———. Fifteenth Census of the United States, 1930. Manuscript census.

———. *The Social and Economic Status of the Black Population in the United States: An Historical View, 1790-1978*. Current Population Reports, Special Studies, Series P-23, No. 80.

PUBLISHED WORKS

Angelou, Maya. *Hallelujah! The Welcome Table*. New York: Random House, 2004.

———. *I Know Why the Caged Bird Sings*. New York: Random House, 1970.

Augusta, Ga., Second Presbyterian Church. *Choice Recipes of Georgia Housekeepers by the Ladies of the Second Presbyterian Church, Augusta, Ga*. New York: Trow's Printing and Bookbinding Co., 1880.

Aunt Jemimy's Southern Recipes. New York: Mitteldorfer Straus, [195?].

Baker, Ray Stannard. *Following the Color Line: An Account of Negro Citizenship in the American Democracy*. New York: Doubleday, Page, and Company, 1908.

Barringer, Mrs. [Maria Massey]. *Dixie Cookery; or, How I Managed My Table for Twelve Years. A Practical Cook-Book for Southern Housekeepers*. Boston: Loring, publisher, 1867.

Bass, Rosa Morehead. "Need of Kindergartens." In *Social and Physical Conditions of Negroes in Cities*, 66-68. Atlanta University Publications, no. 2. Atlanta, Ga.: Atlanta University Press, 1897.

Benedict, Jennie C. *The Road to Dream Acre*. Louisville, Ky.: The Standard Printing Co., 1928.

Berry, Riley M. Fletcher. "The Black Mammy Memorial Institute." *Good Housekeeping* (July–December 1922): 562–63.

Bolden, Dorothy. "Forty-two Years a Maid: Starting at Nine in Atlanta." In *Nobody Speaks for Me! Self-Portraits of American Working Class Women*, edited by Nancy Seifer, 138–77. New York: Simon and Schuster, 1976.

Bowen, Cornelia. "A Woman's Work." In *Tuskegee and Its People: Their Ideals and*

Achievements, edited by Booker T. Washington, 211–23. 1905. New York: Negro Universities Press, 1969.

Bowers, Lessie. *Plantation Recipes*. New York: Robert Speller & Sons, 1959.

Breckinridge, Robert J. *From Soup to Nuts*. 3rd ed. *Old Time Recipes that Have Made Kentucky and Louisiana Foods and Liquids Famous. Dinner Service, Celebrations, Toasts And Helpful Hints*. [Lexington, Ky.]: Kentucky Cardinal Dairies, 1936.

Brooks, Robert Preston. *Sanitary Conditions among the Negroes of Athens, Georgia*. Athens: University of Georgia, 1918.

Brown, Carole. "From the Family Notebook." In *The Black Woman: An Anthology*, edited by Toni Cade Bambara, 297–302. New York: Washington Square Press, 2005.

Brown, Charlotte Hawkins. *"Mammy": An Appeal to the Heart of the South*. Boston: Pilgrim Press, 1919.

Brown, Marion. *Marion Brown's Southern Cook Book*. Chapel Hill: University of North Carolina Press, 1968.

———. *The Southern Cook Book*. Chapel Hill: University of North Carolina Press, 1951.

Burge, Dolly Lunt. *The Diary of Dolly Lunt Burge, 1848–1879*. Edited by Christine Jacobson Carter. Athens: University of Georgia Press, 1997.

Burwell, Letitia M. *A Girl's Life in Virginia before the War*. New York: Frederick A. Stokes Co., 1895.

Butler, Cleora. *Cleora's Kitchens: The Memoir of a Cook and Eight Decades of Great American Food*. Tulsa, Okla.: Council Oak Books, 1985.

Butler, Selena Sloan. "Need of Day Nurseries." In *Social and Physical Conditions of Negroes in Cities*, 63–65. Atlanta University Publications, no. 2. Atlanta, Ga.: Atlanta University Press, 1897.

Buttenheim, Frances Ferguson. "A Shared Sensuality." In *At Grandmother's Table: Women Write about Food, Life, and the Enduring Bond between Grandmothers and Granddaughters*, edited by Ellen Perry Berkeley, 76–79. Minneapolis, Minn.: Fairview Press, 2000.

Byerly, Victoria Morris. *Hard Times Cotton Mill Girls: Personal Histories of Womanhood and Poverty in the South*. Ithaca, N.Y.: ILR Press, 1986.

Calvary Church Circle Cook Book. Memphis, Tenn.: Calvary Episcopal Church, 1925.

Central Presbyterian Church, Atlanta, Ga. Ladies' Missionary Society. *The Southern Housekeeper: A Book of Tested Recipes*. Atlanta: Franklin Printing and Publishing Co., 1898.

Chase, Leah. *The Dooky Chase Cookbook*. Gretna, La.: Pelican Publishing Co., 2000.

Chase, Thomas N., ed. *Mortality among Negroes in Cities. Proceedings of the Conference for Investigations of City Problems Held at Atlanta University, May 26–27, 1896*. Atlanta University Publication, no. 1, 2nd ed., abridged, Atlanta, Ga.: Atlanta University Press, 1903.

Claiborne, Craig. *Craig Claiborne's Southern Cooking*. New York: Wings Books, 1987.

———. *A Feast Made for Laughter*. Garden City, N.Y.: Doubleday, 1982.

Clark, Jonell S. *From Fatback to Filet Mignon*. Stone Mountain, Ga.: J. S. Clark, 1998.

Coastal Cookery. St. Simons Island, Ga.: Cassina Garden Club, 1937.

Cohn, David. *Where I Was Born and Raised*. Boston: Houghton Mifflin, 1948.

Cook, Helen A. "The Work of the Woman's League, Washington, D.C." In *Some Efforts*

of American Negroes for Their Own Social Betterment, edited by W. E. B. DuBois,
57–58. Atlanta, Ga.: Atlanta University Press, 1898.

[Cookbook] Compiled by the Woman's Club of South Jacksonville, Jacksonville, Florida.
Jacksonville, Fla.: The Woman's Club, [194?]

Cooper, Anna Julia. "Colored Women as Wage-Earners." *Southern Workman*
(August 28, 1899): 295–98.

———. *A Voice from the South.* Xenia, Ohio: The Aldine Printing House, 1892.

Council, Mildred. *Mama Dip's Kitchen.* Chapel Hill: University of North Carolina Press,
1999.

Cringan, Mrs. John W. *Instruction in Cooking with Selected Receipts. By Mrs. John W.
Cringan, Teacher of Cooking in the Miller Manual Labor School of Albemarle
County, Virginia.* Richmond, Va.: J. L. Hill Printing Co., 1895.

Davis, Allison. "The Socialization of the American Negro Child and Adolescent."
Journal of Negro Education 8 (July 1939): 264–74.

Davis, Eva. *Eva Davis' Court Square Recipes: Southern Cooking at Its Delicious Best.*
Vicksburg, Miss.: Vicksburg and Warren County Historical Society, 1950.

———. *Mississippi Mixin's: A "Gone With the Wind" Cook Book by the Author of Court
House Square Recipes.* Vicksburg, Miss.: N.p., [1960?].

Dickins, Dorothy. "Negro Food Habits in the Yazoo Mississippi Delta." *Journal of Home
Economics* 18 (September 1926): 523–25.

Dickson, Harris. "'Help! Help! Help! The Bogy That Darkens the Sun of Southern
Domesticity." *Delineator* 80 (July 1912): 7, 66–67.

Dollard, John. *Caste and Class in a Southern Town.* New Haven, Conn.: Yale University
Press, 1937.

Dotson, Mary L. "The Story of a Teacher of Cooking." In *Tuskegee and Its People:
Their Ideals and Achievements*, edited by Booker T. Washington, 200–210. 1905.
New York: Negro Universities Press, 1969.

DuBois, W. E. B. *The Negro American Family.* A Social Study made by Atlanta
University Under the patronage of the Trustees of the John F. Slater Fund. Atlanta
University Publications, no. 2. Atlanta, Ga.: Atlanta University Press, 1908.

———, ed. *Darkwater: Voices from within the Veil.* New York: Harcourt, Brace and
Howe, 1920.

———. *Some Efforts of American Negroes for Their Own Social Betterment.* Atlanta,
Ga.: Atlanta University Press, 1898.

Dull, Henrieta Stanley [Mrs. S. R.]. *Southern Cooking.* Atlanta, Ga.: Ruralist Press,
1928.

Durr, Virginia Foster. *Outside the Magic Circle: The Autobiography of Virginia Foster
Durr.* New York: Simon and Schuster, 1987.

Edge, John T. *Fried Chicken: An American Story.* New York: G. P. Putnam's Sons, 2004.

———. *A Gracious Plenty: Recipes and Recollections from the American South.* New
York: G. P. Putnam's Sons, 1999.

———. *Mrs. Wilkes' Boardinghouse Cookbook.* Berkeley, Calif.: Ten Speed Press, 2001.

Edwards, Paul Kenneth. *The Southern Urban Negro as a Consumer.* College Park, Md.:
McGrath Pub. Co., 1932.

Eustis, Célestine, *Cooking in Old Creole Days: La Cuisine Créole à L'usage des Petits Ménages.* New York: R. H. Russell, 1903.

Evans, Mari. *I Am a Black Woman.* New York: Morrow, 1970.

Faulkner, William. *Intruders in the Dust.* New York: Random House, 1948.

———. *The Sound and the Fury.* New York: Random House, 1929.

Fisher, Abby. *What Mrs. Fisher Knows about Old Southern Cooking, Soups, Pickles, Preserves, Etc.* 1881. Bedford, Mass.: Applewood Books, 1995.

Fleming, Walter L. *A Documentary History of Reconstruction: Political, Military, Social, Religious, Educational & Industrial, 1865 to the Present Time.* 1906. Gloucester, Mass.: P. Smith, 1960.

———. "The Servant Problem in a Black Belt Village." *Sewanee Review* 13 (January 1905): 1–17.

Flexner, Marion. *Dixie Dishes.* Boston: Hale, Cushman and Flint, 1941.

Fowler, Damon Lee. *Damon Lee Fowler's New Southern Kitchen: Traditional Flavors for Contemporary Cooks.* New York: Simon and Schuster, 2002.

Fox, Minnie C., comp. *The Blue Grass Cook Book.* New York: Fox, Duffield and Co., 1904.

Gaines, Ernest. *A Lesson before Dying.* New York: Alfred A. Knopf, 1993.

Gibson, Marietta Fauntleroy Hollyd. *Mrs. Charles H. Gibson's Maryland and Virginia Cook Book Containing Numerous Valuable Receipts for Aid in Housekeeping. Prepared and Tested by Mrs. Charles H. Gibson of Ratcliffe Manor, Easton, Talbot County, Maryland.* Baltimore, Md.: John Murphy and Co., 1894.

Gilmore, Harlan, and Logan Wilson. "The Employment of Negro Women as Domestic Servants in New Orleans." *Social Forces* 22 (March 1944): 318–23.

Glover, E. T. *The Warm Springs Receipt-Book.* Richmond, Va.: B. F. Johnson Publishing Co., 1897.

The Guild Cook Book. Compiled by the Guild of St. Thomas Episcopal Church, Abingdon, Virginia. Abingdon, Va.: The Guild of St. Thomas Episcopal Church, 1923.

The Guild Cook Book of Tested Recipes. Compiled by St. Paul's Guild of St. Paul's Episcopal Church, Waco, Texas. Waco, Tex.: St. Paul's Guild, 1901.

Handy Housekeeping: A Manual for Housekeepers and Collection of Thoroughly Tested Recipes Contributed by the Ladies of the Church and Many of their Friends. Charlottesville, Virginia. [Charlottesville, Va.: Woman's Auxiliary Society of the New Baptist Church, 189?].

Harland, Marion [Mary Virginia Terhune]. *Common Sense in the Household: A Manual of Practical Housewifery.* 2nd ed. New York: Charles Scribner's Sons, 1884.

———. *Marion Harland's Autobiography: The Story of a Long Life.* New York: Harper and Brothers, 1910.

Harris, Eugene. "The Physical Condition of the Race: Whether Dependent upon Social Conditions or Environment." In *Social and Physical Conditions of Negroes in Cities,* 20–28. Atlanta University Publications, no. 2. Atlanta, Ga.: Atlanta University Press, 1897.

Haviland, Laura S. *A Woman's Life-Work.* 1889. New York: Arno Press, 1969.

Haynes, Elizabeth Ross. "Negroes in Domestic Service in the United States." *Journal of Negro History* 8 (1923): 384–442.

Hellman, Lillian. *Three: An Unfinished Woman, Pentimento, Scoundrel Time*. Boston: Little, Brown and Co., 1979.

Hervey, Antoinette B. "The Saints in My Kitchen." *Outlook* 100 (February 17, 1912): 367–71.

Holtzclaw, William Henry. *The Black Man's Burden*. 1915. New York: Negro Universities Press, 1970.

Hooker, Richard J., ed. *A Colonial Plantation Cookbook: The Receipt Book of Harriott Pinckney Horry, 1770*. Columbia: University of South Carolina Press, 1984.

Household Manual and Practical Cook Book: Embracing Many Hundreds of Valuable Recipes . . . with Numerous Miscellaneous Suggestions, Invaluable to Housekeepers by the Ladies of St. Paul's Guild, Waco, Texas. Waco, Tex.: St. Paul's Episcopal Church, St. Paul's Guild, 1888.

Housekeeping in Alabama. Anniston, Ala: G. H. Norwood, 1893.

Houston Civic Club Cook Book. [Houston, Tex.]: Mrs. V. Z. Crawford, 1906.

Howard, Mrs. B. C. [Jane Grant Gilmore Howard]. *Fifty Years in a Maryland Kitchen*. 1873. Revised by Florence Brobeck. New York: M. Barrows and Company, 1944.

Hughes, Langston. "Graduation." In *The Collected Poems of Langston Hughes*, edited by Arnold Rampersad, 315. New York: Vintage Classics, 1994.

Hunt, Annie Mae. *I Am Annie Mae: An Extraordinary Woman in Her Own Words*. Collected and edited by Ruthe Winegarten. Austin, Tex.: Rosegarden Press, 1983.

Hunter, Ethel Farmer. *Secrets of Southern Cooking*. Chicago: Ziff-Davis Company, 1948.

Hurst, Fannie. *Imitation of Life*. New York: Harper and Brothers, 1933.

Jacobs, Harriet A. *Incidents in the Life of a Slave Girl Written by Herself*. 1861. Edited with an introduction by Jean Fagan Yellin. Cambridge, Mass.: Harvard University Press, 1987.

Johnson, Charles Spurgeon. *Patterns of Negro Segregation*. New York: Harper and Brothers, 1943.

Jordan, Vernon E. *Vernon Can Read! A Memoir*. New York: Public Affairs, 2001.

Knoxville Woman's Building Association. *Knoxville Cook Book*. Knoxville, Tenn.: Bean, Warters & Co., 1901.

Kuhn, Clifford M., Harlon E. Joye, and E. Bernard West. *Living Atlanta: An Oral History of the City, 1914–1948*. Athens: University of Georgia Press, 1990.

Kytle, Elizabeth. *Willie Mae*. 1958. Athens: University of Georgia Press, 1993.

Ladd, Florence. "She Walked in Silence." In *At Grandmother's Table: Women Write about Food, Life, and the Enduring Bond between Grandmothers and Granddaughters*, edited by Ellen Perry Berkeley, 65–69. Minneapolis, Minn.: Fairview Press, 2000.

Langhorne, Orra. "Domestic Service in the South." *Journal of Social Science* 39 (November 1901): 169–75.

Lawrenceburg's Treasury of Personal Recipes Compiled by the Woman's Club of Lawrenceburg, Kentucky. [Kansas City, Mo.: Bev-Ron Pub. Co., 1961].

Lee, Harper. *To Kill a Mockingbird*. Philadelphia, Pa.: Lippincott, 1960.

Le Guin, Magnolia Wynn. *A Home-Concealed Woman: The Diaries of Magnolia Wynn Le Guin, 1901–1913*. Edited by Charles A. Le Guin. Athens: University of Georgia Press, 1990.

Leigh, Frances Butler. *Ten Years on a Georgia Plantation since the War*. London: Richard Bentley and Son, 1883.

The Lone Star Cook Book. Published by the Ladies' [*sic*] of the Dallas Free Kindergarten and Training School, Dallas, Texas. Dallas, Tex.: Samuel Jones Co., 1901.

Long, Frances Taylor. *The Negroes of Clarke County, Georgia, During the Great War*. Phelps-Stokes Fellowship Studies, no. 5. Bulletin of the University of Georgia 19 (September 1919).

Lumpkin, Katharine DuPre. *The Making of a Southerner*. 1946. Athens: University of Georgia Press, 1981.

Lustig, Lillie S., S. Claire Sondheim, and Sarah Rensel, comps. and eds. *The Southern Cook Book of Fine Old Recipes*. Reading, Pa.: Culinary Arts Press, 1935.

Lynch, John Roy. *Reminiscences of an Active Life: The Autobiography of John Roy Lynch*. Edited and with an introduction by John Hope Franklin. Chicago: University of Chicago Press, 1970.

McCullers, Carson. *The Member of the Wedding*. Boston: Houghton Mifflin, 1946.

McCulloch-Williams, Martha. *Dishes and Beverages of the Old South*. 1913. Knoxville: University of Tennessee Press, 1988.

McKinney, Emma and William McKinney. *Aunt Caroline's Dixieland Recipes*. Chicago: Land and Lee, 1922.

McPhail, Mrs. Clement Carrington. *F.F.V. Receipt Book*. Richmond, Va.: West, Johnston and Co., 1894.

Mitchell, S. Weir. Introduction to *Cooking in Old Creole Days: La Cuisine Créole à L'usage des Petits Ménages*, by Célestine Eustis, xiii–xiv. New York: R. H. Russell, 1903.

Moncure, Blanche Elbert. *Emma Jane's Souvenir Cook Book [and Some Old Virginia Recipes; Collected by Blanche Elbert Moncure]*. Williamsburg, Va.: [Moncure?], 1937.

Moody, Anne. *Coming of Age in Mississippi: An Autobiography*. New York: Dell Publishing, 1968.

Murray, Pauli. *Proud Shoes: The Story of an American Family*. New York: Harper and Row, 1956.

Myrdal, Gunnar. *An American Dilemma: The Negro Problem and Modern Democracy*. 1944. Edison, N.J.: Transaction Publishers, 1996.

Neal, Bill. *Biscuits, Spoonbread, and Sweet Potato Pie*. New York: Alfred A. Knopf, 1996.

"Negro Nurse." "More Slavery at the South." *The Independent* 72 (1912): 196–200.

"The Negro Problem: How It Appears to a Southern White Woman." *The Independent* 54 (1902): 2224–28.

Norris Economy Cook Book: Compiled by Norris Women's Fellowship. Norris, Tenn.: Norris Women's Fellowship, 1951.

Parker, Idella. *Idella: Marjorie Rawlings' "Perfect Maid."* Gainesville: University Press of Florida, 1992.

Parker, Idella, with Bud and Liz Crussell. *Idella Parker: From Reddick to Cross Creek*. Gainesville: University Press of Florida, 1999.

Patterson, Betty Benton. *Mammy Lou's Cook Book*. New York: Robert M. McBride and Co., 1931.

Penn, I. Garland. "The Educational Progress of the Afro-American Race." In *The College of Life; or, Practical Self-Educator: A Manual of Self-improvement for the Colored Race Forming an Educational Emancipator and a Guide to Success*, edited by Henry Davenport Northrop, 81–85. 1895. Miami, Fla.: Mnemosyne Publishing, Inc., 1969.

Perry, Minnie L. "The Carrie Steele Orphanage of Atlanta, Ga." In *Some Efforts of American Negroes for Their Own Social Betterment*, edited by W. E. B. DuBois, 60–61. Atlanta, Ga.: Atlanta University Press, 1898.

Pohick Cookery: Old Southern Recipes. Lorton, Va.: Pohick Episcopal Church, n.d.

Porter, Mrs. M. E. *Mrs. Porter's New Southern Cookery Book and Companion for Frugal and Economical Housekeepers; Containing Carefully Prepared and Practically Tested Recipes for All Kinds of Plain and Fancy Cooking*. 1871. New York: Arno Press, 1973.

Powdermaker, Hortense. *After Freedom: A Cultural Study in the Deep South*. New York: Viking Press, 1939.

Pringle, Elizabeth Waites Allston. *A Woman Rice Planter*. New York: Macmillan Co., 1914.

Rankin, Jane Lee, and Eugene Callender. *Cookin' Up a Storm: The Life and Recipes of Annie Johnson*. South Fallsburg, N.Y.: Grace Publishers, 1998.

Ravenel, Harriott Horry. *Eliza Pinckney*. New York: Charles Scribner's Sons, 1896.

Rawlings, Marjorie Kinnan. *Cross Creek*. New York: Charles Scribner's Sons, 1942.

———. *Cross Creek Cookery*. New York: Charles Scribner's Sons, 1942.

Recipes of the Deep South, Quota Club of Macon, Georgia. Macon, Ga.: Quota Club, 1948.

Redwine, W. A. *Brief History of the Negro in Five Counties*. Chronicles of Smith County 11, no. 2 (1972): 13–68. (Orig. pub. 1901.)

Reed, Ruth. *The Negro Women of Gainesville, Georgia*. Bulletin of the University of Georgia 22 (December 1921).

Rushin, Kate. *The Black Back-ups*. Ithaca, N.Y.: Firebrand Books, 1993.

Sanders, Dori. *Dori Sanders' Country Cooking: Recipes and Stories from the Family Farm Stand*. Chapel Hill, N.C.: Algonquin Books, 1995.

Scott, Emmett J. "Letters of Negro Migrants of 1916–1918." *Journal of Negro History* 4 (July 1919): 290–340.

———. "More Letters of Negro Migrants of 1916–1918." *Journal of Negro History* 4 (October 1919): 412–65.

Scott, Natalie. *Mirations and Miracles of Mandy: Some Favorite Louisiana Recipes*. New Orleans, La.: R. H. True, 1929.

Selected Southern Recipes: Compiled by the Colonial Villa and Dedicated to Cosmovilla. Orange, N.J.: Chronicle Pub. Co., 1909.

Sholes' Directory of the City of Macon, July 1st, 1878. Macon, Ga.: A. E. Sholes, 1878.

Smalls, Alexander. *Grace the Table: Stories and Recipes from My Southern Revival*. New York: HarperCollins, 1997.

Smart-Grosvenor, Vertamae. *Thursdays and Every Other Sunday Off: A Domestic Rap*. New York: Doubleday, 1972.

Smedes, Susan Dabney. *Memorials of a Southern Planter*. Baltimore, Md.: Cushings and Bailey, 1887.

Smith, Joseph E. "Care of Neglected Children." In *Social and Physical Conditions of Negroes in Cities*, 41–43. Atlanta University Publications, no. 2. Atlanta, Ga.: Atlanta University Press, 1897.

Smith, Mary Stuart Harrison. *Virginia Cookery-Book, Comp. by Mary Stuart Smith*. New York: Harper, 1885.

Smitherman, Mrs. James E. [Ina Scott Thompson]. *The Louisiana Plantation Cook Book*. Shreveport, La.: Journal Printing Co., 1930.

Stone, Birdie K. [Mrs. Albert A.], comp. *The Roanoke Cook Book: Favorite Recipes by Some of Roanoke's Good Housekeepers*. Roanoke, Va.: Woman's Civic Betterment Club, 1907.

Stoney, Louisa Cheves Smythe (Mrs. Samuel G). *The Carolina Rice Cook Book*. Charleston, S.C.: The Carolina Rice Kitchen Association, 1901.

Studio, Charleston, S.C. *Charleston Recipes*. Charleston, S.C.: Walker, Evans, and Cogswell Co., 1928.

Tarr, Rodger L., ed. *The Private Marjorie: The Love Letters of Marjorie Kinnan Rawlings to Norton S. Baskin*. Gainesville: University Press of Florida, 2004.

Thomas, Ella Gertrude Clanton. *The Secret Eye: The Journal of Ella Gertrude Clanton Thomas, 1848-1889*. Edited by Virginia Ingraham Burr. Chapel Hill: University of North Carolina Press, 1990.

Timlin, Octa Lee. *Sandwiches, Salads and Desserts. By Octa Lee Stephen Timlin*. [Galveston, Tex.: Octa Lee Timlin, ca. 1929].

Towles, Louis Palmer, ed. *A World Turned Upside Down: The Palmers of South Santee, 1818-1881*. Columbia: University of South Carolina Press, 1996.

Tucker, Susan. *Telling Memories Among Southern Women: Domestic Workers and Their Employers in the Segregated South*. Baton Rouge: Louisiana State University Press, 1988.

Tyree, Marion Cabell, ed. *Housekeeping in Old Virginia: Containing Contributions from Two Hundred and Fifty Ladies in Virginia and Her Sister States*. New York: G. W. Carleton & Co., 1877.

Vaughn, Kate Brew. *Culinary Echoes from Dixie*. Cincinnati, Ohio: The McDonald Press, 1914.

Villard, Oswald Garrison. "The Negro and the Domestic Problem." *Alexander's Magazine* 1 (November 15, 1905): 5–11.

Villas, James, with Martha Pearl Villas. *My Mother's Southern Kitchen: Recipes and Reminiscences*. New York: Macmillan, 1994.

Walker, Alice. *In Search of Our Mothers' Gardens*. San Diego, Calif.: Harcourt Brace Jovanovich, 1983.

———. *Living by the Word: Selected Writings, 1973-1987*. San Diego, Calif.: Harcourt Brace Jovanovich, 1984.

"War and Post-War Trends in Employment of Negroes." *Monthly Labor Review* 60 (January 1945): 1–5.

Warren, Mildred Evans. *The Art of Southern Cooking*. Garden City, N.Y.: Doubleday & Company, 1969.

Washington, Mrs. Booker T. [Margaret Murray]. "What Girls Are Taught, and How."
    In *Tuskegee and Its People: Their Ideals and Achievements*, edited by Booker T.
    Washington, 68–86. 1905. New York: Negro Universities Press, 1969.

Washington, Queenie Woods, ed. *Sewanee Cook Book: A Collection of Autographed
    Receipts from Southern Homes and Plantations*. Nashville, Tenn.: Baird-Ward, 1926.

Waters, Ethel. *His Eye Is on the Sparrow: An Autobiography*. New York: Doubleday,
    1951.

Watriss, Wendy. "It's Something Inside You." *Southern Exposure* 4 (1977): 76–81.

Weatherford, W. D. *Negro Life in the South: Present Conditions and Needs*. New York:
    Young Men's Christian Association Press, 1910.

Welty, Eudora. "The Little Store." *In Mississippi Writers: Reflections of Childhood and
    Youth. Vol. 2; Nonfiction*. Edited by Dorothy Abbott, 639–46. Jackson: University
    Press of Mississippi, 1986.

———. *The Ponder Heart*. New York: Harcourt Brace & World, 1953.

Wilson, Mrs. Henry Lumpkin. *Tested Recipe Cook Book*. Atlanta, Ga.: The Foote and
    Davies Company, 1895.

Wolfbein, Seymour L. "Postwar Trends in Negro Employment." *Monthly Labor Review*
    65 (1947): 663–65.

———. "War and Post-War Trends in Employment of Negroes." *Monthly Labor Review*
    60 (1945): 1–5.

Woodson, Carter G. *The Mis-Education of the Negro*. 1933. Chicago: African
    American Images, 2000.

———. "The Negro Washerwoman: A Vanishing Figure." *Journal of Negro History* 15
    (July 1930): 269–77.

Woofter, T. J., Jr. *The Negroes of Athens, Georgia*. Phelps-Stokes Fellowship Studies,
    no. 1. Bulletin of the University of Georgia 14 (December 1913).

Wright, Richard. *Black Boy: A Record of Childhood and Youth*. New York: Harper and
    Brothers, 1945.

Young Men's Christian Association, Petersburg, Va., Ladies' Auxiliary. *The Old Virginia
    Cook Book of 600 Tested and Proved Recipes Furnished by Noted Virginia
    Housewives, Few, If Any, Having Ever Before Appeared in Print*. [Petersburg, Va.:
    Fenn & Owen, 1894?].

Zimmer, Anne Carter. *The Robert E. Lee Family Cooking and Housekeeping Book*.
    Chapel Hill: University of North Carolina Press, 1997.

INTERNET SOURCES

American Life Histories: Manuscripts from the Federal Writers' Project, 1936–1940.
    ⟨http://memory.loc.gov/ammem/wpaintro/wpahome.html⟩. January 10, 2008.
        "Bea, the Wash Woman" [Sarah Hill]
        Berry, Fannie
        Brumby, Katy
        Holton, Sudie
        "Miss Sallie's Cook" [Annie Squire]
        "Ole an' Broke" [Mandy Long Roberson]

Robinson, Charlie and Lucinda

Sellers, Henrietta Elizabeth

Public Broadcasting System. "American Experience/Eleanor Roosevelt/FBI Files—
Eleanor Clubs."

⟨http://www.pbs.org/wgbh/amex/eleanor/sfeature/fbi_ec_03.html⟩. December 27,
2008.

NEWSPAPERS

Atlanta Constitution	*Tyler [Texas] Journal*
Dallas Morning News	*Tyler [Texas] Morning Telegraph*
Tyler [Texas] Daily Courier	*Tyler [Texas] National Index*
Tyler [Texas] Daily Courier Times	*Tyler [Texas] Semi-Weekly Courier-Times*
Tyler [Texas] Evening Democrat-Reporter	

Secondary Sources

BOOKS

Abarca, Meredith E. *Voices in the Kitchen: Views of Food and the World from Working-Class Mexican and Mexican American Women.* College Station: Texas A&M University Press, 2006.

Anderson, James. *The Education of Blacks in the South, 1860–1935.* Chapel Hill: University of North Carolina Press, 1988.

Anzaldúa, Gloria. *Borderlands/La Frontera: The New Mestiza.* 3rd ed. San Francisco, Calif.: Aunt Lute Books, 2007.

Bay, Mia. *The White Image in the Black Mind: African-American Ideas about White People, 1830–1925.* New York: Oxford University Press, 2000.

Beasley, Ellen. *Alleys and Back Buildings of Galveston: An Architectural and Social History.* College Station: Texas A&M University Press, 2007.

Benson, Susan Porter. *Counter Cultures: Saleswomen, Managers, and Customers in American Department Stores, 1890–1940.* Urbana: University of Illinois Press, 1986.

Bentley, Amy. *Eating for Victory: Food Rationing and the Politics of Domesticity.* Urbana: University of Illinois Press, 1998.

Bercaw, Nancy. *Gendered Freedoms: Race, Rights, and the Politics of Household in the Delta, 1861–1875.* Gainesville: University Press of Florida, 2003.

Berry, Daina Ramey. *"Swing the Sickle for the Harvest Is Ripe": Gender and Slavery in Antebellum Georgia.* Urbana: University of Illinois Press, 2007.

Birnbaum, Michele. *Race, Work, and Desire in American Literature, 1860–1930.* Cambridge: Cambridge University Press, 2003.

Blackwelder, Julia Kirk. *Now Hiring: The Feminization of Work in the United States, 1900–1995.* College Station: Texas A&M University Press, 1997.

———. *Styling Jim Crow: African American Beauty Training during Segregation.* College Station: Texas A&M University Press, 2003.

———. *Women of the Depression: Caste and Culture in San Antonio, 1929–1939.* College Station: Texas A&M University Press, 1984.

Boehm, Lisa Krissoff. *Making a Way Out of No Way: African American Women and the Second Great Migration*. Jackson: University Press of Mississippi, 2009.

Borchert, James. *Alley Life in Washington: Family, Community, Religion, and Folklife in the City, 1850–1970*. Urbana: University of Illinois Press, 1980.

Bower, Anne, ed. *Recipes for Reading: Community Cookbooks, Stories, Histories*. Amherst: University of Massachusetts Press, 1997.

Braudel, Fernand. *The Structures of Everyday Life: The Limits of the Possible*. London: Collins, 1981.

Brundage, W. Fitzhugh. *The Southern Past: A Clash of Race and Memory*. Cambridge, Mass.: Belknap Press of Harvard, 2005.

Byrd, Rudolph P., and Beverly Guy-Sheftall, eds. *Traps: African American Men on Gender and Sexuality*. Bloomington: Indiana University Press, 2001.

Camp, Charles. *American Foodways: What, When, Why and How We Eat in America*. Little Rock, Ark.: August House, 1989.

Camp, Stephanie M. H. *Closer to Freedom: Enslaved Women and Everyday Resistance in the Plantation South*. Chapel Hill: University of North Carolina Press, 2004.

Carbado, Devon. *Black Men on Race, Gender, and Sexuality: A Critical Reader*. New York: New York University Press, 1999.

Censer, Jane Turner. *The Reconstruction of White Southern Womanhood, 1865–1895*. Baton Rouge: Louisiana State University Press, 2003.

Chafe, William H., Raymond Gavins, and Robert Korstad, eds. *Remembering Jim Crow: African Americans Tell about Life in the Segregated South*. New York: New Press, 2001.

Chang, Grace. *Disposable Domestics: Immigrant Women Workers in the Global Economy*. Cambridge, Mass.: South End Press, 2000.

Chirhart, Ann Short. *Torches of Light: Georgia Teachers and the Coming of the Modern South*. Athens: University of Georgia Press, 2005.

Clark-Lewis, Elizabeth. *Living In, Living Out: African American Domestics in Washington, D.C., 1910–1940*. Washington, D.C.: Smithsonian Institution Press, 1994.

Clinton, Catherine. *Tara Revisited: Women, War and the Plantation Legend*. New York: Abbeville Press, 1995.

Cobble, Dorothy Sue. *Dishing It Out: Waitresses and Their Unions in the Twentieth Century*. Urbana: University of Illinois Press, 1991.

Cock, Jacklyn. *Maids and Madams: Domestic Workers under Apartheid*. London: Women's Press, 1989.

Collins, Patricia Hill. *Black Feminist Thought: Knowledge, Consciousness, and the Politics of Empowerment*. Boston: Unwin Hyman, 1990.

Cowan, Ruth Schwartz. *More Work for Mother: The Ironies of Household Technology from the Open Hearth to the Microwave*. New York: Basic Books, 1983.

Davidoff, Leonore. *Worlds Between: Historical Perspectives on Gender and Class*. New York: Routledge, 1995.

Davidoff, Leonore, Megan Doolittle, Janet Fink, and Katherine Holden. *The Family Story: Blood, Contract and Intimacy, 1830–1960*. London and New York: Longman, 1999.

De Silva, Cara, ed. *In Memory's Kitchen: A Legacy from the Women of Terezín.* Translated by Bianca Steiner Brown. Northvale, N.J.: Jason Aronson, Inc., 1996.

Dill, Bonnie Thornton. *Across the Boundaries of Race and Class: An Exploration of Work and Family Among Black Female Domestic Servants.* New York: Garland Publishing, 1994.

Diner, Hasia. *Erin's Daughters in America: Irish Immigrant Women in the Nineteenth Century.* Baltimore, Md.: Johns Hopkins University Press, 1983.

Douglas, Mary. *The World of Goods.* New York: Basic Books, 1979.

Dudden, Faye E. *Serving Women: Household Service in Nineteenth-Century America.* Hanover, N.H.: Wesleyan University Press, 1983.

Egerton, John. *Southern Food: At Home, on the Road, in History.* New York: Alfred A. Knopf, 1987.

Enstam, Elizabeth York. *Women and the Creation of Urban Life: Dallas, Texas, 1843–1920.* College Station: Texas A&M University Press, 1998.

Fairchilds, Cissie. *Domestic Enemies: Servants and Their Masters in Old Regime France.* Baltimore, Md.: Johns Hopkins University Press, 1984.

Ferris, Marcie Cohen. *Matzoh Ball Gumbo: Culinary Tales of the Jewish South.* Chapel Hill: University of North Carolina Press, 2005.

Flandrin, Jean-Louis, and Massimo Montanari, eds. *Food: A Culinary History from Antiquity to the Present.* New York: Columbia University Press, 1999.

Fox-Genovese, Elizabeth. *Within the Plantation Household: Black and White Women of the Old South.* Chapel Hill: University of North Carolina Press, 1988.

Gabaccia, Donna R. *We Are What We Eat: Ethnic Food and the Making of Americans.* Cambridge, Mass.: Harvard University Press, 1998.

Genovese, Eugene D. *Roll, Jordan, Roll: The World the Slaves Made.* New York: Pantheon Books, 1972.

Glenn, Evelyn Nakano. *Unequal Freedom: How Race and Gender Shaped American Citizenship and Labor.* Cambridge, Mass.: Harvard University Press, 2002.

Glymph, Thavolia. *Out of the House of Bondage: The Transformation of the Plantation Household.* New York: Cambridge University Press, 2008.

Goings, Kenneth. *Mammy and Uncle Mose: Black Collectibles and American Stereotyping.* Bloomington: Indiana University Press, 1994.

Goldfield, David R. *Black, White, and Southern: Race Relations and Southern Culture, 1940 to the Present.* Baton Rouge: Louisiana State University Press, 1990.

Graham, Sandra Lauderdale. *House and Street: The Domestic World of Servants and Masters in Nineteenth-Century Rio de Janeiro.* Austin: University of Texas Press, 1992.

Greene, Christina. *Our Separate Ways: Women and the Black Freedom Movement in Durham, North Carolina.* Chapel Hill: University of North Carolina Press, 2005.

Gutman, Herbert G. *The Black Family in Slavery and Freedom, 1750–1925.* New York: Alfred A. Knopf, 1976.

Gwaltney, John Langston. *Drylongso: A Self-Portrait of Black America.* New York: Vintage Books, 1981.

Hale, Grace Elizabeth. *Making Whiteness: The Culture of Segregation in the South, 1890–1940.* New York: Vintage Books, 1998.

Harley, Sharon, and Rosalyn Terborg-Penn, eds. *The Afro-American Woman: Struggles and Images*. Port Washington, N.Y.: Kennikat Press, 1978.

Harris, Jessica B. *The Africa Cookbook*. Simon and Schuster, 1998.

———. *Iron Pots and Wooden Spoons: Africa's Gifts to New World Cooking*. New York: Atheneum Books, 1989.

———. *The Welcome Table: African-American Heritage Cooking*. New York: Simon and Schuster, 1995.

Harris, Michael D. *Colored Pictures: Race and Visual Representation*. Chapel Hill: University of North Carolina Press, 2003.

Harris, Trudier. *From Mammies to Militants: Domestics in Black American Literature*. Philadelphia, Pa.: Temple University Press, 1982.

Hecht, J. Jean. *The Domestic Servant Class in Eighteenth-Century England*. London: Routledge and Paul, 1956.

Heldke, Lisa. *Exotic Appetites: Ruminations of a Food Adventurer*. New York: Routledge, 2003.

Hess, Karen. *The South Carolina Rice Kitchen: The African Connection*. Columbia: University of South Carolina Press, 1992.

Hickey, Georgina. *Hope and Danger in the New South City: Working-class Women and Urban Development in Atlanta, 1890–1940*. Athens: University of Georgia Press, 2003.

Higginbotham, Evelyn Brooks. *Righteous Discontent: The Women's Movement in the Black Baptist Church, 1880–1920*. Cambridge, Mass.: Harvard University Press, 1993.

Hill, Bridget. *Servants: English Domestics in the Eighteenth Century*. New York: Oxford University Press, 1996.

Hine, Darlene Clark. *Black Women in White: Racial Conflict and Cooperation in the Nursing Profession, 1890–1950*. Bloomington: Indiana University Press, 1989.

Hirsch, Jerrold. *Portrait of America: A Cultural History of the Federal Writers' Project*. Chapel Hill: University of North Carolina Press, 2003.

Hoffschwelle, Mary. *The Rosenwald Schools of the American South*. Gainesville: University Press of Florida, 2006.

Holt, Sharon Ann. *Making Freedom Pay: North Carolina Freedpeople Working for Themselves, 1865–1900*. Athens: University of Georgia Press, 2000.

Hondagneu-Sotelo, Pierrette. *Doméstica: Immigrant Workers Cleaning and Caring in the Shadows of Affluence*. Berkeley: University of California Press, 2001.

hooks, bell. *Ain't I a Woman: Black Women and Feminism*. Boston: South End Press, 1981.

———. *Feminist Theory: From Margin to Center*. Boston: South End Press, 1984.

———. *Yearning: Race, Gender, and Cultural Politics*. Boston: South End Press, 1990.

———. *We Real Cool: Black Men and Masculinity*. New York: Routledge, 2003.

Horn, Pamela. *The Rise and Fall of the Victorian Servant*. Stroud, UK: Sutton, 2004.

Horowitz, Roger. *Putting Meat on the Table: Taste, Technology, Transformation*. Baltimore, Md.: Johns Hopkins University Press, 2006.

Hunter, Tera. *To 'Joy My Freedom: Southern Black Women's Lives and Labors after the Civil War*. Cambridge, Mass.: Harvard University Press, 1997.

Inness, Sherrie A. *Secret Ingredients: Race, Gender, and Class at the Dinner Table*. New York: Palgrave Macmillan, 2006.

Janeway, Elizabeth. *Powers of the Weak*. New York: Alfred A. Knopf, 1980.

Janiewski, Dolores. *Sisterhood Denied: Race, Gender, and Class in a New South Community*. Philadelphia, Pa.: Temple University Press, 1985.

Jones, Jacqueline. *Labor of Love, Labor of Sorrow: Black Women, Work and the Family from Slavery to the Present*. New York: Basic Books, 1985.

Katzman, David M. *Seven Days a Week: Women and Domestic Service in Industrializing America*. New York: Oxford University Press, 1978.

Katznelson, Ira. *When Affirmative Action Was White: An Untold History of Racial Inequality in Twentieth-Century America*. New York: W. W. Norton, 2005.

Kirby, Jack Temple. *Mockingbird Song: Ecological Landscapes of the South*. Chapel Hill: University of North Carolina Press, 2006.

Kyriakoudes, Louis M. *The Social Origins of the Urban South: Race, Gender, and Migration in Nashville and Middle Tennessee, 1890–1930*. Chapel Hill: University of North Carolina Press, 2003.

Leavitt, Sarah H. *From Catharine Beecher to Martha Stewart: A Cultural History of Domestic Advice*. Chapel Hill: University of North Carolina Press, 2002.

Lewis, Earl. *In Their Own Interests: Race, Class, and Power in Twentieth-Century Norfolk, Virginia*. Berkeley: University of California Press, 1991.

Litwack, Leon F. *Trouble in Mind: Black Southerners in the Age of Jim Crow*. New York: Alfred A. Knopf, 1999.

Logan, Frenise A. *The Negro in North Carolina, 1786–1894*. Chapel Hill: University of North Carolina Press, 1964.

MacLean, Nancy. *Freedom Is Not Enough: The Opening of the American Workplace*. Cambridge, Mass.: Harvard University Press, 2006.

Manring, M. M. *Slave in a Box: The Strange Career of Aunt Jemima*. Charlottesville: University of Virginia Press, 1998.

Maza, Sarah. *Servants and Masters in Eighteenth Century France: The Uses of Loyalty*. Princeton, N.J.: Princeton University Press, 1983.

McBride, Theresa Marie. *The Domestic Revolution: The Modernization of Household Service in England and France, 1820–1920*. New York: Holmes & Meier, 1976.

McElya, Micki. *Clinging to Mammy: The Faithful Slave in Twentieth-Century America*. Cambridge, Mass.: Harvard University Press, 2007.

McMillen, Neil R. *Dark Journey: Black Mississippians in the Age of Jim Crow*. Urbana: University of Illinois Press, 1989.

Megginson, W. J. *African American Life in South Carolina's Upper Piedmont*. Columbia: University of South Carolina Press, 2006.

Meyerowitz, Joanne J. *Women Adrift: Independent Wage Earners in Chicago, 1880–1930*. Chicago: University of Chicago Press, 1988.

Minnick, Lisa Cohen. *Dialect and Dichotomy: Literary Representations of African American Speech*. Tuscaloosa: University of Alabama Press, 2004.

Neuhaus, Jessamyn. *Manly Meals and Mom's Home Cooking: Cookbooks and Gender in Modern America*. Baltimore, Md.: Johns Hopkins University Press, 2003.

Neverdon-Morton, Cynthia. *Afro-American Women of the South and the Advancement of the Race, 1895–1925*. Knoxville: University of Tennessee Press, 1991.

O'Donovan, Susan Eva. *Becoming Free in the Cotton South*. Cambridge, Mass.: Harvard University Press, 2007.

Odum, Howard W. *Race and Rumors of Race: Challenge to American Crisis*. Chapel Hill: University of North Carolina Press, 1943.

O'Leary, Elizabeth L. *From Morning to Night: Domestic Service in Maymont House and the Gilded Age South*. Charlottesville: University of Virginia Press, 2003.

Opie, Frederick Douglass. *Hog and Hominy: Soul Food from Africa to America*. New York: Columbia University Press, 2008.

Ownby, Ted. *American Dreams in Mississippi: Consumers, Poverty, and Culture, 1830–1998*. Chapel Hill: University of North Carolina Press, 1999.

Palmer, Phyllis. *Domesticity and Dirt: Housewives and Domestic Servants in the United States, 1920–1945*. Philadelphia, Pa.: Temple University Press, 1989.

Pilcher, Jeffrey M. *Que Vivan los Tamales! Food and the Making of Mexican Identity*. Albuquerque: University of New Mexico Press, 1998.

Rachleff, Peter. *Black Labor in the South: Richmond, Virginia, 1865–1890*. Philadelphia, Pa.: Temple University Press, 1984.

Ramsey, Sonya. *Reading, Writing, and Segregation: A Century of Black Women Teachers in Nashville*. Urbana: University of Illinois Press, 2008.

Raper, Arthur F. *The Tragedy of Lynching*. Chapel Hill: University of North Carolina Press, 1933.

Ritterhouse, Jennifer. *Growing Up Jim Crow: How Black and White Southern Children Learned Race*. Chapel Hill: University of North Carolina Press, 2006.

Roberts, Diane. *The Myth of Aunt Jemima: Representations of Race and Region*. New York: Routledge, 1994.

Robinson, Jo Ann. *The Montgomery Bus Boycott and the Women Who Started It: The Memoir of Jo Ann Gibson Robinson*. Knoxville: University of Tennessee Press, 1987.

Rollins, Judith. *Between Women: Domestics and Their Employers*. Philadelphia, Pa.: Temple University Press, 1985.

Romines, Ann. *The Home Plot: Women, Writing and Domestic Ritual*. Amherst: University of Massachusetts Press, 1992.

Salmon, Lucy Maynard. *Domestic Service*. 1897. New York: Arno Press, 1972.

Schwalm, Leslie A. *A Hard Fight for We: Women's Transition from Slavery to Freedom in South Carolina*. Urbana: University of Illinois Press, 1997.

Shaw, Stephanie J. *What a Woman Ought to Be and to Do: Black Professional Women Workers during the Jim Crow Era*. Chicago: University of Chicago Press, 1996.

Shockley, Megan Taylor. *"We, Too, Are Americans": African American Women in Detroit and Richmond, 1940–1954*. Urbana: University of Illinois Press, 2004.

Short, Frances. *Kitchen Secrets: The Meaning of Cooking in Everyday Life*. New York: Berg, 2006.

Smith, Andrew F., ed. *The Oxford Encyclopedia of Food and Drink in America*. New York: Oxford University Press, 2004.

Sokolov, Raymond. *With the Grain*. New York: Alfred A. Knopf, 1996.

Solinger, Rickie. *Wake Up Little Susie: Single Pregnancy and Race before Roe v. Wade.* New York: Routledge, 1992.

Spivey, Diane M. *The Peppers, Cracklings, and Knots of Wool Cookbook: The Global Migration of African Cuisine.* New York: State University of New York Press, 2000.

Spruill, Julia Cherry. *Women's Life and Work in the Southern Colonies.* 1938. New York: W. W. Norton and Company, 1972.

Stansell, Christine. *City of Women: Sex and Class in New York, 1789–1860.* New York: Alfred A. Knopf, 1986.

Sterling, Dorothy, ed. *We Are Your Sisters: Black Women in the Nineteenth Century.* New York: W. W. Norton, 1984.

The Story of a Pantry Shelf, An Outline History of Grocery Specialties. New York: Butterick Publishing Company, 1925.

Strasser, Susan. *Never Done: A History of American Housework.* New York: Pantheon Books, 1982.

Sutherland, Daniel E. *Americans and Their Servants: Domestic Service in the United States from 1800 to 1920.* Baton Rouge: Louisiana State University Press, 1981.

Swann-Wright, Dianne. *A Way Out of No Way: Claiming Family and Freedom in the New South.* Charlottesville: University of Virginia Press, 2002.

Symons, Michael. *A History of Cooks and Cooking.* Urbana: University of Illinois Press, 2004.

Tannahill, Reay. *Food in History.* New York: Crown Publishers, 1988.

Theophano, Janet. *Eat My Words: Reading Women's Lives through the Cookbooks They Wrote.* New York: Palgrave, 2002.

Tilly, Louise A., and Joan W. Scott. *Women, Work, and Family.* 1989. New York: Routledge, 1989.

Toussaint-Samat, Maguellonne. *History of Food.* Translated by Anthea Bell. Malden, Mass.: Blackwell Publishers, 1992.

Turner, Patricia A. *Ceramic Uncles and Celluloid Mammies: Black Images and Their Influence on Culture.* Charlottesville: University of Virginia Press, 1994.

Visser, Margaret. *The Rituals of Dinner: The Origins, Evolution, Eccentricities and Meaning of Table Manners.* New York: HarperCollins, 1991.

Wallace-Sanders, Kimberly, ed. *Mammy: A Century of Race, Gender, and Southern Memory.* Ann Arbor: University of Michigan Press, 2008.

———. *Skin Deep, Spirit Strong: The Black Female Body in American Culture.* Ann Arbor: University of Michigan Press, 2002.

Weiner, Marli F. *Mistresses and Slaves: Plantation Women in South Carolina, 1830–80.* Urbana: University of Illinois Press, 1998.

White, Deborah Gray. *Too Heavy a Load: Black Women in Defense of Themselves, 1894–1940.* New York: W. W. Norton, 1999.

Williams, Susan. *Savory Suppers and Fashionable Feasts: Dining in Victorian America.* Knoxville: University of Tennessee Press, 1996.

Williams-Forson, Psyche A. *Building Houses Out of Chicken Legs: Black Women, Food, and Power.* Chapel Hill: University of North Carolina Press, 2006.

Witt, Doris. *Black Hunger: Food and the Politics of U.S. Identity.* New York: Oxford University Press, 1999.

Wolcott, Victoria W. *Remaking Respectability: African American Women in Interwar Detroit*. Chapel Hill: University of North Carolina Press, 2001.

Yuhl, Stephanie E. *A Golden Haze of Memory: The Making of Historic Charleston*. Chapel Hill: University of North Carolina Press, 2005.

ARTICLES AND ESSAYS

Alexander, Leslie. "The Challenge of Race: Rethinking the Position of Black Women in the Field of Women's History." *Journal of Women's History* 16 (2004): 50–60.

Anderson, C. Arnold, and Mary Jean Bowman. "The Vanishing Servant and the Contemporary Status System of the American South." *American Journal of Sociology* 59 (1953): 215–30.

Anderson, Mary. "The Plight of Negro Domestic Labor." *Journal of Negro Education* 5 (1936): 66–72.

Bailey, Martha J., and William J. Collins. "The Wage Gains of African-American Women in the 1940s." *Journal of Economic History* 66 (2006): 737–77.

Bardenstein, Carol. "Transmissions Interrupted: Reconfiguring Food, Memory, and Gender in the Cookbook-Memoirs of Middle Eastern Exiles." *Signs* 28 (2002): 353–87.

Barnett, Evelyn Brooks. "Nannie Helen Burroughs and the Education of Black Women." In *The Afro-American Woman: Struggles and Images*, edited by Sharon Harley and Rosalyn Terborg-Penn, 97–108. Port Washington, N.Y.: Kennikat Press, 1978.

Bay, Mia. "From the 'Ladies Car' to the 'Colored Car': Black Female Travelers in the Segregated South." Lecture given at the University of Texas at Arlington, Arlington, Texas, March 13, 2008.

Blackwelder, Julia Kirk. "Women and Leadership: A Century of Change in the South." In *The American South in the Twentieth Century*, edited by Craig S. Pascoe, Karen Trahan Leathem, and Andy Ambrose, 39–55. Athens: University of Georgia Press, 2005.

———. "Women in the Work Force: Atlanta, New Orleans, and San Antonio, 1930–1940." *Journal of Urban History* 4 (1978): 331–58.

Blassingame, John W. "Using the Testimony of Ex-Slaves: Approaches and Problems." *Journal of Southern History* 41 (1975): 473–92.

Blaszcyk, Regina Lee. "Cinderella Stories: The Glass of Fashion and the Gendered Marketplace." In *His and Hers: Gender, Consumption, and Technology*, edited by Roger Horowitz and Arwen Mohun, 139–64. Charlottesville: University of Virginia Press, 1998.

Boris, Eileen. "Cleaning and Caring for the Welfare State." Paper presented at the Fourteenth Berkshire Conference on the History of Women, Minneapolis, Minnesota, June 2008.

Brewer, Rose M. "Theorizing Race, Class and Gender: The New Scholarship of Black Feminist Intellectuals and Black Women's Labor." In *Theorizing Black Feminisms: The Visionary Pragmatism of Black Women*, edited by Stanlie M. James and Abena P. Busia, 13–30. New York: Routledge, 1993.

Broom, L., and J. H. Smith. "Bridging Occupations." *British Journal of Sociology* 14 (1963): 321–34.

Brown, Elsa Barkley. "'What Has Happened Here': The Politics of Difference in Women's History and Feminist Politics." *Feminist Studies* 18 (1992): 295–312.

Chaplin, David. "Domestic Service and Industrialization." *Comparative Studies in Sociology* 1 (1978): 97–127.

Clark-Lewis, Elizabeth. "Downstairs, Upstairs in DC: How White Folk Looked to Those Who Served Them." *Washington Post*, November 27, 1984.

———. "'This Work Had a End': African-American Domestic Workers in Washington, D.C., 1910–1940." In *"To Toil the Livelong Day": America's Women at Work, 1780–1980*, edited by Carol Groneman and Mary Beth Norton, 196–212. Ithaca, N.Y.: Cornell University Press, 1987.

Clinton, Catherine. "Bloody Terrain: Freedwomen, Sexuality, and Violence during Reconstruction." In *Half Sisters of History: Southern Women and the American Past*, edited by Catherine Clinton, 136–63. Durham, N.C.: Duke University Press, 1994.

Cole, Stephanie. "'Neither Matron nor Maid': Race, Gender, Class and Marriage in Jim Crow Texas." Paper in author's possession.

———. "A White Woman, of Middle Age, Would Be Preferred: Children's Nurses in the Old South." In *Neither Lady nor Slave: Working Women of the Old South*, edited by Susanna Delfino and Michele Gillespie, 76–101. Chapel Hill: University of North Carolina Press, 2002.

Collins, Patricia Hill. "Gender, Black Feminism, and Black Political Economy." *Annals of the American Academy of Political Science* 486 (2000): 41–53.

———. "Learning from the Outsider Within: The Sociological Significance of Black Feminist Thought." *Social Problems* 33 (1986): S14–S32.

Coser, Lewis A. "Servants: The Obsolescence of an Occupational Role." *Social Forces* 52 (1973): 31–40.

Cowan, Ruth Schwartz. "Two Washes in the Morning and a Bridge Party at Night: The American Housewife between the Wars." *Women's Studies* 3 (1976): 47–71.

Cox, Karen L. "From Aunt Jemima to Scarlett O'Hara: Images of Southern Women in Popular Culture, 1890s–1940s." Paper presented at the Eighth Southern Conference on Women's History, Columbia, South Carolina, 2009, in author's possession.

Davidoff, Leonore. "Gender and the 'Great Divide': Public and Private in British Gender History." *Journal of Women's History* 15 (2003): 11–27.

———. "Mastered for Life: Servant and Wife in Victorian and Edwardian England." *Journal of Social History* 7 (1974): 406–28.

Deck, Alice A. "'Now Then—Who Said Biscuits?' The Black Woman Cook as Fetish in American Advertising, 1905–1953." In *Kitchen Culture in America: Popular Representations of Food, Gender, and Race*, edited by Sherrie A. Ennis, 70–93. Philadelphia, Pa.: University of Pennsylvania Press, 2001.

di Leonardo, Micaela. "Women's Work, Work Culture, and Consciousness." *Feminist Studies* 11 (1985): 489–96.

Dill, Bonnie Thornton. "'Making Your Job Good Yourself': Domestic Service and the Construction of Personal Dignity." In *Women and the Politics of Empowerment*, edited by Ann Bookman and Sandra Morgen, 33–52. Philadelphia, Pa.: Temple University Press, 1988.

Dowdy, G. Wayne. "The White Rose Mammy: Racial Culture and Politics in World War II Memphis." *Journal of Negro History* 85 (2000): 308–14.

Dubert, Isidro. "Modernity without Modernization: The Evolution of Domestic Service in North-West Spain, 1752–1900." *Gender & History* 18 (2006): 199–210.

Dunlap, Leslie K. "The Reform of Rape Law and the Problem of White Men: Age-of-Consent Campaigns in the South, 1885–1910." In *Sex, Love, Race: Crossing Boundaries in North American History*, edited by Martha Hodes, 352–72. New York: New York University Press, 1999.

Enstad, Nan. "Fashioning Political Identities: Cultural Studies and the Historical Construction of Political Subjects." *American Quarterly* 50 (1998): 745–82.

Fairchilds, Cissie. "Master and Servants in Eighteenth Century Toulouse." *Journal of Social History* 12 (1979): 368–93.

Farrington, Lisa E. "Faith Ringgold's *Slave Rape* Series." In *Skin Deep, Spirit Strong: The Black Female Body in American Culture*, edited by Kimberly Wallace-Sanders, 128–52. Ann Arbor: University of Michigan Press, 2002.

Faust, Drew, Hendrik Hartog, David A. Hollinger, Akira Iriye, Patricia Nelson Limerick, Nell Irvin Painter, David Roediger, Mary Ryan, and Alan Taylor. "Interchange: The Practice of History." *Journal of American History* 90 (2003): 576–611.

Fienberg, Lorne. "Charles W. Chesnutt and Uncle Julius: Black Storytellers at the Crossroads." *Studies in American Fiction* 15 (1987): 161–73.

Flandrin, Jean-Louis, and Massimo Montanari. Introduction to the original edition of *Food: A Culinary History from Antiquity to the Present*, edited by Jean-Louis Flandrin and Massimo Montanari, 1–9. New York: Columbia University Press, 1999.

Fowler, Damon L. "Historical Commentary." In *Mrs. Hill's Southern Practical Cookery and Receipt Book*, xiii–xliv. Columbia: University of South Carolina Press, 1995.

Furstenberg, Frank F., Jr., Theodore Hershberg, and John Modell. "The Origins of the Female-Headed Black Family: The Impact of the Urban Experience." *Journal of Interdisciplinary History* 6 (Autumn 1975): 211–33.

George, Rosemary Marangoly. "Recycling: Long Routes to and from Domestic Fixes." In *Burning Down the House: Recycling Domesticity*, edited by Rosemary Marangoly George, 1–20. Boulder, Colo.: Westview Press, 1998.

Glenn, Evelyn Nakano. "The Dialectics of Wage Work: Japanese-American Women and Domestic Service, 1905–1940." *Feminist Studies* 6 (1980): 432–71.

———. "Racial Ethnic Women's Labor: The Intersection of Race, Gender and Class Oppression." *Review of Radical Political Economics* 17 (1983): 86–108.

Goldman, Anne. "'I Yam What I Yam': Cooking, Culture, and Colonialism." In *De/Colonizing the Subject: The Politics of Gender in Women's Autobiography*, edited by Sidonie Smith and Julia Watson, 169–95. Minneapolis: University of Minnesota Press, 1992.

Green, Laurie B. "'Where Would the Negro Women Apply for Work?': Gender, Race, and Labor in Wartime Memphis." *Labor: Studies in Working-Class History of the Americas*, 3 (2006): 95–117.

Grignon, Claude. "Commensality and Social Morphology: An Essay of Typology." In

Food, Drink and Identity: Cooking, Eating and Drinking in Europe since the Middle Ages, edited by Peter Scholliers, 23–33. Oxford: Berg, 2001.

Grossman, Atina. "Trauma, Memory, and Revenge: Gendered Interactions between Jews and Germans in Postwar Occupied Germany." Paper presented at the American Historical Association Annual Meeting, Chicago, Illinois, January 2003.

Grubb, Alan. "House and Home in the Victorian South: The Cookbook as Guide." In *In Joy and in Sorrow: Women, Family, and Marriage in the Victorian South*, edited by Carol Bleser, 154–75. New York: Oxford University Press, 1991.

Haber, Barbara. "Cooking to Survive: The Careers of Alice Foote MacDougall and Cleora Butler." In *From Betty Crocker to Feminist Food Studies: Critical Perspectives on Women and Food*, edited by Arlene Voski Avakian and Barbara Haber, 120–42. Amherst: University of Massachusetts Press, 2005.

Hall, Robert L. "Africa and the American South: Culinary Connections." *Southern Quarterly* 44 (Winter 2007): 19–52.

———. "Food Crops, Medicinal Plants, and the Atlantic Slave Trade." In *African American Foodways: Explorations of History and Culture*, edited by Anne L. Bower, 17–44. Urbana: University of Illinois Press, 2007.

Harley, Sharon. "For the Good of Family and Race: Gender, Work, and Domestic Roles in the Black Community, 1880–1930." *Signs* 15 (1990): 336–49.

———. "Nannie Helen Burroughs: 'The Black Goddess of Liberty.'" *Journal of Negro History* 81 (1996): 62–71.

———. "When Your Work Is Not Who You Are: The Development of a Working-Class Consciousness among Afro-American Women." In *Gender, Class, Race and Reform in the Progressive Era*, edited by Noralee Frankel and Nancy S. Dye, 42–55. Lexington, Ky.: University Press of America, 1991.

Haug, Kate. "Myth and Matriarchy: An Analysis of the Mammy Stereotype." In *Dirt and Domesticity: Constructions of the Feminine*, 38–57. New York: Whitney Museum of American Art, 1992.

Heldke, Lisa M. "Foodmaking as a Thoughtful Practice." In *Cooking, Eating, Thinking: Transformative Philosophies of Food*, edited by Deane W. Heldke and Lisa M. Heldke, 203–29. Bloomington: Indiana University Press, 1992.

Hess, Karen. "What We Know about Mrs. Abby Fisher and Her Cooking." Afterword to *What Mrs. Fisher Knows about Old Southern Cooking, Soups, Pickles, Preserves, Etc.*, by Abby Fisher, 75–94. Bedford, Mass.: Applewood Books, 1995.

Hine, Darlene Clark. "Black Women's History, White Women's History: The Juncture of Race and Class." *Journal of Women's History* 4 (1992): 125–33.

Hunter, Tera W. "Domination and Resistance: The Politics of Wage Household Labor in New South Atlanta." In *"We Specialize in the Wholly Impossible": A Reader in Black Women's History*, edited by Darlene Clark Hine, Wilma King, and Linda Reed, 343–57. Brooklyn, N.Y.: Carlson Publishing, 1995.

———. "'The Women Are Asking for BREAD, Why Give them STONE?': Women, Work, and Protests in Atlanta and Norfolk during World War I." In *Labor in the Modern South*, edited by Glenn T. Eskew, 62–82. Athens: University of Georgia Press, 2001.

Jennings, Thelma. "'Us Colored Women Had to Go through a Plenty': Sexual Exploitation of African American Slave Women." *Journal of Women's History* 1 (Winter 1990): 45–75.

Johnson, Joan Marie. "'Ye Gave Them a Stone': African American Women's Clubs, the Frederick Douglass Home, and the Black Mammy Monument." *Journal of Women's History* 17 (2005): 62–86.

Judson, Sarah Mercer. "'Leisure Is a Foe to 'Any Man': The Pleasures and Dangers of Leisure in Atlanta during World War I." *Journal of Women's History* 15 (2003): 92–116.

Kaplan, Elaine Bell. "'I Don't Do No Windows': Competition between the Domestic Worker and the Housewife." In *Competition: A Feminist Taboo?*, edited by Valerie Miner and Helen E. Longino, 92–105. New York: Feminist Press at the City University of New York, 1987.

Kelley, Robin D. G. "'We Are Not What We Seem': Rethinking Black Working-Class Opposition in the Jim Crow South." *Journal of American History* 80 (1993): 75–112.

Kousha, Mahnaz. "African American Private Household Workers and 'Control' of the Labor Process in Domestic Service." *Sociological Focus* 27 (1994): 211–26.

Lewis, Earl. "To Turn as on a Pivot: Writing African Americans into a History of Overlapping Diasporas." *American Historical Review* 100 (1995): 765–87.

Linsley, Judith W. "Main House, Carriage House: African-American Domestic Employees at the McFaddin-Ward House in Beaumont, Texas, 1900–1950." *Southwestern Historical Quarterly* 103 (July 1999): 17–52.

Lubar, Steven. "Men/Women/Production/Consumption." In *His and Hers: Gender, Consumption, and Technology*, edited by Roger Horowitz and Arwen Mohun, 7–37. Charlottesville: University of Virginia Press, 1998.

McCluskey, Audrey Thomas. "'We Specialize in the Wholly Impossible': Black Women School Founders and Their Mission." *Signs* 22 (1997): 403–26.

McIntosh, William Alex, and Mary Zey. "Women as Gatekeepers of Food Consumption: A Sociological Critique." *Food and Foodways* 3 (1989): 317–32.

McMillen, Sally. "Mothers' Sacred Duty: Breast-feeding Patterns among Middle- and Upper-Class Women in the Antebellum South." *Journal of Southern History* 51 (1985): 333–56.

Millward, Jessica. "More History Than Myth: African American Women's History since the Publication of *Ar'n't I a Woman?*." *Journal of Women's History* 19 (2007): 161–67.

Morgan, Jo-Ann. "Mammy the Huckster: Selling the Old South for the New Century." *American Art* 9 (1995): 86–109.

Munro, George E. "Food in Catherinian St. Petersburg." In *Food in Russian History and Culture*, edited by Musya Glants and Joyce Tomre, 31–48. Bloomington: Indiana University Press, 1997.

Nadasen, Premilla. "'Maids' Honor Day': Domestic Workers and the Struggle for Dignity and Representation." Paper presented at the Fourteenth Berkshire Conference on the History of Women, Minneapolis, Minnesota, June 2008.

O'Neil, Patrick W. "Bosses and Broomsticks: Ritual and Authority in Antebellum Slave Weddings." *Journal of Southern History* 75 (2009): 29–48.

Palmer, Phyllis. "Household Work and Domestic Labor: Racial and Technological

Change." In *My Troubles Are Going to Have Trouble with Me: Everyday Trials and Triumphs of Women Workers*, edited by Karen Brodkin Sacks and Dorothy Remy, 80–91. New Brunswick, N.J.: Rutgers University Press, 1984.

Parkhurst, Jessie. "The Role of the Black Mammy in the Plantation Household." *Journal of Negro History* 23 (1938): 359–69.

Patton, June. "Moonlight and Magnolias in Southern Education: The Black Mammy Memorial Institute." *Journal of Negro History* 65 (1980): 149–55.

Perkins, Elizabeth A. "The Forgotten Victorians: Louisville's Domestic Servants, 1880–1920." *Register of the Kentucky Historical Society* 85 (1987): 111–37.

Pollan, Howard. "The Goodman Family." *Chronicles of Smith County* 5 (1966): 1–15.

Procida, Mary. "Feeding the Imperial Appetite: Imperial Knowledge and Anglo-Indian Domesticity." *Journal of Women's History* 15 (2003): 123–49.

Quinn, Olive Westbrooke. "The Transmission of Racial Attitudes among White Southerners." *Social Forces* 33 (1954): 41–47.

Reddy, Chandan C. "Home, Houses, Nonidentity: Paris Is Burning." In *Burning Down the House: Recycling Domesticity*, edited by Rosemary Marangoly George, 355–79. Boulder, Colo.: Westview Press, 1998.

Reed, Merl E. "Bell Aircraft Comes South: The Struggle by Atlanta Blacks for Jobs during World War II." In *Labor in the Modern South*, edited by Glenn T. Eskew, 102–34. Athens: University of Georgia Press, 2001.

Revel, Jean-François. "Culture and Cuisine." In *Cooking, Eating, Thinking: Transformative Philosophies of Food*, edited by Deane W. Curtin and Lisa M. Heldke, 145–52, 244–50. 1982. Bloomington: Indiana University Press, 1992.

Riggs, Marlon. "Unleash the Queen." In *Black Popular Culture*, edited by Michele Wallace and Gina Dent, 99–105. Seattle, Wash.: Bay Press, 1992.

Ritterhouse, Jennifer. "The Etiquette of Race Relations in the Jim Crow South." In *Manners and Southern History*, edited by Ted Ownby, 20–44. Jackson: University Press of Mississippi, 2007.

Rodrigue, Jessie M. "The Black Community and the Birth Control Movement." In *Gendered Domains: Rethinking Public and Private in Women's History*, edited by Dorothy O. Helly and Susan M. Reverby, 244–60. Ithaca, N.Y.: Cornell University Press, 1992.

Romero, Mary. "Not Just Like One of the Family: Chicana Domestics Establishing Professional Relationships with Employers." *Feminist Issues* 10 (1990): 33–41.

———. "Sisterhood and Domestic Service: Race, Class and Gender in the Mistress-Maid Relationship." *Humanity and Society* 12 (1989): 318–46.

Rouse, Jacqueline Anne. "Out of the Shadow of Tuskegee: Margaret Murray Washington, Social Activism, and Race Vindication." *Journal of Negro History* 81 (1996): 31–46.

Schreck, Kimberly. "Her Will against Theirs: Eda Hickam and the Ambiguity of Freedom in Postbellum Missouri." In *Beyond Image and Convention: Explorations in Southern Women's History*, edited by Janet L. Coryell, Martha H. Swain, Sandra G. Treadway, and Elizabeth H. Turner, 99–118. Columbia: University of Missouri Press, 1998.

Schwalm, Leslie A. "'Sweet Dreams of Freedom': Freedwomen's Reconstruction of Life and Labor in Lowcountry South Carolina." *Journal of Women's History* 9 (Spring 1997): 9–38.

Sharpless, Rebecca. "'She Ought to Taken Those Cakes': Market Relationships between Town and Farm Women." Paper given at the Sixth Southern Conference on Women's History, Athens, Georgia, June 2003.

Simon, Bryant. "Fearing Eleanor: Racial Anxieties and Wartime Rumors in the American South, 1940–1945." In *Labor in the Modern South*, edited by Glenn T. Eskew, 83–101. Athens: University of Georgia Press, 2001.

Smith, Doris. "In Search of Our Mothers' Cookbooks: Gathering African-American Culinary Traditions." *Iris: A Journal about Women* 26 (1991): 22–27.

Somerville, Siobhan. "Domestic Renovations: The Marriage Plot, the Lodging House, and Lesbian Desire in Pauline Hopkins's *Contending Forces*." In *Burning Down the House: Recycling Domesticity*, edited by Rosemary Marangoly George, 232–56. Boulder, Colo.: Westview Press, 1998.

Spillers, Hortense. "Mama's Baby, Papa's Maybe: An American Grammar Book." *Diacritics* 17, no. 2 (1987): 65–81.

Stanonis, Anthony J. "Just Like Mammy Used to Make: Foodways in the Jim Crow South." In *Dixie Emporium: Tourism, Foodways, and Consumer Culture in the American South*, edited by Anthony J. Stanonis, 208–33. Athens: University of Georgia Press, 2008.

Sutherland, Daniel. "A Special Kind of Problem: The Response of Household Slaves and Their Masters to Freedom." *Southern Studies* 20 (1981): 151–66.

Terborg-Penn, Rosalyn. "Survival Strategies among Afro-American Women Workers: A Continuing Process." In *Women, Work and Protest: A Century of U.S. Women's Labor History*, edited by Ruth Milkman, 139–55. New York: Routledge and Kegan Paul, 1985.

Tilly, Louise A. "Comments on the Yans-McLaughlin and Davidoff Papers." *Journal of Social History* 7 (1974): 452–59.

Titus, Mary. "The Dining Room Door Swings Both Ways: Food, Race, and Domestic Space in the Nineteenth-Century South." In *Haunted Bodies: Gender and Southern Texts*, edited by Anne Goodwyn Jones and Susan V. Donaldson, 243–56. Charlottesville: University Press of Virginia, 1997.

———. "'Groaning Tables' and 'Spit in the Kettles': Food and Race in the Nineteenth-Century South." *Southern Quarterly* 30 (1992): 13–21.

Tyler, Pamela. "'Blood on Your Hands': White Southerners' Criticism of Eleanor Roosevelt during World War II." In *Before "Brown," Civil Rights and White Backlash in the Modern South*, edited by Glenn Feldman, 96–115. Tuscaloosa: University of Alabama Press, 2004.

Wilkins, John W. "Dr. Thomas Hunt Hall's Life in Jamestown, 1854–1879." *Chronicles of Smith County* 21 (1982): 15–29.

Wing-Leonard, Deborah. "Figs, Flappers, and Fignolias: Working Women of the 1920s Texas Gulf Coast." *Sound Historian* 11 (2008): 49–67.

Wolcott, Victoria W. "'Bible, Bath, and Broom': Nannie Helen Burroughs's National Training School and African American Racial Uplift." *Journal of Women's History* 9 (Spring 1997): 89–110.

Wynter, Sylvia. "Sambos and Minstrels." *Social Text* 1 (1979): 149–56.

Yentsch, Anne. "Excavating the South's African American Food History." In *African American Foodways: Explorations of History and Culture*, edited by Anne L. Bower, 59–98. Urbana: University of Illinois Press, 2007.

INTERNET SOURCES

ACH Food Companies. "Durkee Famous Sauce." ⟨http://www.spiceadvice.com/dev/durkee-homeuse/spices-famous-sauce.php⟩. August 2, 2007.

Boston Historical Society and Museum. "Sweet History: Dorchester and the Chocolate Factory." ⟨http://www.bostonhistory.org/bakerschocolate/bioco_wbaker.htm⟩. March 14, 2007.

Lea & Perrins. "About Lea & Perrins." ⟨http://leaperrins.com/about-lea-perrins.aspx⟩. February 10, 2008.

McIlhenny Company. "History of McIlhenny Company and Tabasco." ⟨http://www.tabasco.com/tabasco_history/mcilhenny.cfm#targ⟩. December 27, 2008.

Piggly Wiggly LLC. "Where It Began." ⟨http://www.pigglywiggly.com/cgi-bin/customize?aboutus.html⟩. May 15, 2007.

Texas State Historical Association Handbook of Texas Online. "Light Crust Doughboys." ⟨http://www.tshaonline.org/handbook/online/articles/LL/xgl1.html⟩. January 11, 2008.

University of Alabama University Libraries. "David Walker Lupton African American Cookbook Collection." ⟨http://www.lib.ua.edu/lupton/luptonlist.htm⟩. October 17, 2009.

Wallace-Sanders, Kimberly. "Southern Memory, Southern Monuments, and the Subversive Black Mammy." ⟨http://www.southernspaces.org/contents/2009/wallace-sanders/1a.htm⟩. July 1, 2009.

DISSERTATIONS AND THESES

Burley, Laurita Mack. "Reconceptualizing Profession: African American Women and Dietetics at Tuskegee Institute, 1936–1954." Ph.D. diss., Georgia State University, 2005.

Cole, Stephanie. "Servants and Slaves: Domestic Service in the Border Cities, 1800–1850." Ph.D. diss., University of Florida, 1994.

Elwang, William Wilson. "The Negroes of Columbia, Missouri." M.A. thesis, University of Missouri, 1904.

Helmbold, Lois Rita. "Making Choices, Making Do: Black and White Working-Class Women's Lives and Work during the Great Depression." Ph.D. diss., Stanford University, 1983.

Henderson, Ashley S. "'The Ace of Clubs': A Social and Architectural History of the Draughon-Moore House, Texarkana, Texas, 1885–1985." M.A. thesis, Baylor University, 2008.

Hunter, Lee A. "The Myth of the Mammy in Nineteenth-Century Southern Women's Fiction." Ph.D. diss., Georgia State University, 1998.

Jackson, Esther Cooper. "The Negro Woman Domestic Worker in Relation to Trade Unionism." M.A. thesis, Fisk University, 1940.

Johnson, Elondust Patrick. "Performance, Cultural Identity, and Feminist Practice in the Oral History of an African American Domestic Worker." Ph.D. diss., Louisiana State University, 1996.

Kousha, Mahnaz. "Best Friends: Power Relations among Black Domestics and White Mistresses." Ph.D. diss., University of Kentucky, 1990.

Lancaster, Sonya J. "The Simmering Stew: Race and Gender in Southern Kitchens." Ph.D. diss., University of Kansas, 1997.

Maclachlan, Gretchen Ehrmann. "Women's Work: Atlanta's Industrialization and Urbanization, 1879–1929." Ph.D. diss., Emory University, 1992.

Morsman, Amy Feely. "The Big House after Slavery: Virginia's Plantation Elite and Their Postbellum Domestic Experiment." Ph.D. diss., University of Virginia, 2004.

Rio, Cecilia M. "From Feudal Serfs to Independent Contractors: Class and African American Women's Paid Domestic Labor, 1863–1980." Ph.D. diss., University of Massachusetts–Amherst, 2001.

Tippett, Robin Christine. "The Economic Activities of Women in McLennan County, Texas, 1850–1880." M.A. thesis, Texas Christian University, 2006.

van Zelm, Antoinette Gray. "On the Front Lines of Freedom: Black and White Women Shape Emancipation in Virginia, 1861–1890." Ph.D. diss., College of William and Mary, 1998.

Index

Black Mammy Memorial Monument, xvi

Blanche, 232 (n. 181)

Boardinghouses: cooks' work in, 33, 34; as living facilities for cooks, 95–96, 112

Bolden, Dorothy, 152, 178

Bolden, Ethel Beulah Woodson, 22–23, 24, 107

Bowen, Cornelia, 27

Bowers, Lessie, xx

Branch, Martha, 131

Brazil: slavery in, 221 (n. 5); domestic work in, 222 (n. 30)

Bread: cornbread, 40–41; biscuits, 41–42; yeast bread, 42–45, 204 (n. 48)

Breckinridge, Robert J., xxvii

Bridget, 55

Broadles, Nellie, 111

Brookfield, Mrs. John W., 167–68

Brown, Alma McLain Coleman, 211 (n. 3)

Brown, Carole, 174

Brown, Elsa Barkley, 139

Brown, Hallie Q., xvi

Brown, Jean Collier, 85

Brown, Marion, 52

Brown, Mildred, 70

Brumby, Katy, 162; housing, 97, 99; leisure, 105; religion, 107; family, 112–13; aging, 127, 128; grumpiness, 148; wages, 186

Burge, Dolly, 137

Burleigh plantation, Mississippi, 3–4

Burroughs, Nannie Helen, 27, 201 (n. 94)

Butler, Cleora Thomas, 25–26, 197 (n. 1); beginning as a cook, xi; wages, xv–xvi, 185; autobiography, xix; sharing recipes, xxi–xxii; culinary training, 29; meals prepared by, 29, 53; recipes by, 59, 60; and hats and hat making, 104–5; and leisure, 106; fear of racial violence, 133

Butler, Priscilla, 68

Cally, 46

Cameron, Anne Ruffin, 149

Cameron family, 131

Campbell, Leigh, 36–37

Cannon, Katie Geneva, 20

Caroline, 16, 38, 136, 149

Carrie, 41

Carrington, Maria Louisa, 110

Chappel, Lou, 112

Charleston, South Carolina, 97

Charlotte, North Carolina, 196 (n. 38)

Chase, Carolyn, 140

Chase, Leah, 25

Chickens. See Meat

Child bearing and rearing, 119–26, 222 (n. 65); gynecological difficulties, 120; child care, 121–26; impact of work day length on, 124–25. See also Abortion; Birth control; Kindergartens; Orphanages

Children as domestic workers, 21, 22–23

Chloe (cook for Pringle family): travel by, 17; recipes by, 50, 53, 54, 60; and hats, 10; fear of being accused of theft, 156

Chloe (New Orleans): recipes by, 48, 53, 55, 56, 60

Christian, Emma Jane, xxvii–xxviii; food acquisition, 36, 53; bread baking, 42; desserts, 47, 48; vegetable preparation, 58; relationship with Moncure family, 163–64; as cooking teacher, 169

Christy, George, 190 (n. 14)

Church attendance, 70–71, 107

Civil rights movement, 152, 180

Claflin University, 26

Claiborne, Kathleen, 155

Clara, xxiv

Clarissy ("Aunt Clarissy"), 40

Clark, Jonell, 97–98, 99, 102, 123, 124–25

Clarke County, Georgia, 185

Cleanup after meals, 63

Clement, Mrs. H. A., 89, 107, 186

Cleo: recipes by, xxiii, xxvii, 55, 56

Clothing, 103–5

Club of the Colored Maids, 153, 177

Clyburn, Elizabeth, 68, 97, 186

Coleman, Annette, 102

Collins, Elizabeth, 13

Graves, Anna, 178
Gray, Emmie, 71
Great Depression, 176, 213 (n. 48)
Great Migration, xvii–xviii, 175
Green, Fannie, 8
Green, Nancy, xv
Green, Zelda, 174
Greensboro, North Carolina, 186
Gregory, Sam, 138
Grisham, Georgia, 13
Gruber, Nell, 19–20

Hampton, Virginia, 186
Hannah (Georgia), 122
Hannah (South Carolina), 5
Harris, Corra, 158, 211 (n. 3)
Harris, Joel Chandler, 190 (n. 14)
Harris, Samuel F., 28
Hattie, xv
Hawkins, Nannie, 186
Health conditions of African Americans, 98–99. *See also* Child bearing and rearing
Hefley, Winnie, 121–22, 166–67
Hellman, Lillian, 167
Hickman, Eda, 71–72
Hill, Sarah, 20, 125
Hiring practices, 11–14
Hoge, Agnes, 55
Holmes, Mattie, 61
Holton, Sudie, 135, 170, 176
Holtzclaw, William Henry, 28, 75–76, 156–57
Home demonstration cooking training, 29–30
hooks, bell, 93, 167
Hours of work: lack of standardization of, 65–66; and length of workday, 66–69; impact of employers' entertaining on, 68–69; and working on Sunday, 70–71
Houser, Mary, 114
Houser, Pete, 114
Housing: "living in," 89, 90–93; "living out," 89–90, 93–98; rental property, 97; public housing, 97–98; and housework

for own families, 99. *See also* Boarding-houses
Houston, Texas, 186
Howard, Florence, 15, 29, 73
Howard, Mary, 17, 116
Howard, Sarah, 15, 73, 122
Huff, L. G., 34, 66, 68, 69; chores at home, 99; wages, 186
Hughes, Dora, 96
Hulda, 59
Hunt, Annie Mae, 63; hiring, 14; supplemental income, 80; clothing, 104; and birth control, 119; child care, 123; affection for employer, 163; wages, 186
Hupes, Roxanna, 65, 186
Hutchins, Julia, 127

Ice, availability of, 203 (n. 27)
Imitation of Life (Hurst), 190 (n. 14)
India, domestic workers in, 193 (n. 63)
Indianola, Mississippi, 93, 101
Inez, 22
Intersectionality, 226 (n. 30)
Iredell County, North Carolina, 175
Irish domestic workers, 109, 220 (n. 1)
Island Grove, Florida, racial violence in, 133–34

Jackson, Mississippi, housing conditions in, 97
Jacobs, Harriet, 191 (n. 22)
Jellies and preserves, 60–61
Jenkins, Agnes, 26
Jenkins, Sallie, 166
Johnson, Nancy, 149
Jones, Esther, 166
Jones, Janie, 96
Jordan, Mary Belle, 7–8; clothing, 104; church attendance, 107
Jude ("Mam Jude"), xxvii; cornbread, 40; griddlecakes, 42; rice pudding, 46; puff pastry, 47; fish *en papillote*, 55; boiled crab creole, 56; cornbread dressing, 56; fig preserves, 60
Juliette, 22

transportation in, 94–95; decline in domestic workers in, 174; impact of World War II on, 177–78; wages in, 185; proportion of domestic workers to population of, 196 (n. 48); single women in, 221 (n. 16)

Richmond [Virginia] Working Woman's Home, 125

Ringgold, Faith, 180

Rituals. *See* Funerals; Weddings

Roberson, Mandy Long, 115

Robinson, Charlie, 96–97, 102

Robinson, Lucinda, 96–97, 100, 102; wages, 186

Rosa, 36–37

Rosenwald schools, 30

Ross, Claudia, 44

Ross, Martha Plant, 14, 142

Rudy, Nora, 185

Rushin, Kate, xvi–xvii, 109

Rutherford, Katherine, 66, 105

Saar, Betye, 180–81

Salads, 59–60

Sally, 70

San Antonio, Texas, 95, 177, 186, 222 (n. 43)

Sanders, Dori, 54

Sanders, Harriet, 127–28

Sarah ("Aunt Sarah"), 72

Sarah (mother of Zipporah), 140–41

Sassafras, Cypress & Indigo (Shange), xxi

Sauces and condiments, 60

Scott, Natalie, xxvi

Scott, Pattie, 116

Seabrook, Katie, 53, 56

Seafood. *See* Fish and seafood

Segregation: in grocery stores, 37; in employers' households, 91, 141–45, 228 (nn. 80, 86); in housing, 93–94; in shopping, 104–5; of personal relationships, 134–35

Sellers, Henrietta Elizabeth, 25, 106

Sexual abuse by employers. *See* Relationships between employees and employers: sexual abuse

Shaw, Jinny, 232 (n. 182)

Shays, Ruth, 86

Shelman, Cornelia, 115, 148

Shopping. *See* Food: acquisition of

Simms, William Gilmore, 190 (n. 14)

Sims, Altha, 177

Sims, Anna, 114

Sims, Coatney, 114

Slaves. *See* Enslaved women

Smart-Grosvenor, Vertamae, 141

Smith, Anna, 68, 86

Smith, Audrey, 76

Smith, Bertha Whitridge, 134

Smith, Celeste, 54

Smith, Olive, 39

Smith, Rosa, 63

Smith, Rosie Lee, 200 (n. 78)

Smyer, Garland A., 83

Social Security, domestic workers' exclusion from, 86

Solomon, Maidie P., 112

Sophie ("Aunt Sophie"), 41, 164, 165

Sound and the Fury, The (Faulkner), 190 (n. 14)

Soups, 56

South Africa, domestic work in, 203 (n. 23); 218 (n. 64); 228 (n. 85)

Spelman College, 29

Spices and flavorings, 45–46

Squire, Annie, 107, 166

Stafford, Jane, 12

Stanford, Sallie Bell, 112

Staples, Daniel, 154–55

Stereotypes of cooks, xiii–xvii, 19, 66, 190 (nn. 14, 15). *See also* Aunt Jemima; Mammy

Stone, Marie, 91

Stoves. *See* Cooking: technology in

Stuffing. *See* Dressing

Sue ("Aunt Sue"), 42

Sug ("Aunt Sug"), 46

Sunday, working on. *See* Hours of work